ADDING SPACE
WITHOUT ADDING ON

HERB HUGHES

CREATIVE HOMEOWNER PRESS®

A DIVISION OF FEDERAL MARKETING CORPORATION,
24 PARK WAY, UPPER SADDLE RIVER, NEW JERSEY 07458

Manufactured in United States of America

Current Printing (last digit)
10 9 8

Editorial Director: Shirley M. Horowitz
Editor: Marilyn M. Auer
Art Director: Leone Lewensohn
Designer: Paul Sochacki
Additional Drawings: Norman Nuding

Cover photograph: Georgia Pacific
Corporation, 133 Peachtree St., N.E.,
P.O. Box 105605, Atlanta, GA 30348.

We wish to extend our thanks to the many de-
signers, companies, and other contributors who
allowed us to use their materials and gave us
advice. Their names, addresses, and individual
identifications of their contributions can be
found on page 159.

LC: 81-67295
ISBN: 0-932944-60-4 (paper)
ISBN: 0-932944-61-2 (hardcover)

CREATIVE HOMEOWNER PRESS®
BOOK SERIES
A DIVISION OF FEDERAL
MARKETING CORPORATION
24 PARK WAY,
UPPER SADDLE RIVER, NJ 07458

ADDING SPACE
WITHOUT ADDING ON

FOREWORD

Many homeowners complain that while they like their present homes, there just is not enough room. This book addresses the problem by helping the homeowner find and use space he did not realize existed. The changes suggested can be accomplished economically because they are, for the most part, interior changes that are within the scope of the skills of most homeowners. This book can make it possible to take the home you like and convert it into the home you will love.

PROJECTS

CONTENTS

7
BUILDING
STAIRWAYS

Types of stairways and how to plan a new flight. How to construct new stairways and a loft access ladder. Choosing a new stair location, and appropriate stair design.   *Pg. 80*

8
CLOSETS
& STORAGE

Planning and designing efficient and convenient storage; adding closets, kitchen cupboards, and storage niches. Making use of space between studs and under stairs.   *Pg. 86*

9
BASEMENT
CONVERSIONS

Preparing your basement for conversion; adding an exterior door or window; finishing interior walls and ceilings; designing for best use. Waterproofing methods interior/exterior.   *Pg. 99*

10
ATTIC
CONVERSIONS

Determining potential space in your attic; framing partitions, knee walls; building a gable or small shed dormer; finishing the interior; ventilating area. Planning possible uses and layout. *Pg. 124*

11
GOING UP
INSTEAD OF OUT

Opening a room by creating a vaulted ceiling; building decorative beams; building lofts either overlooking or within a room. Adding a second floor over a garage, necessary reframing.   *Pg. 142*

APPENDICES

This room was created by removing a wall, adding ceiling beams and new wood flooring to maintain a sense of the original period of the home.

1
REDESIGNING
VERSUS ADDING ON

Many young couples who have bought a first home find themselves almost overwhelmed by the square footage. Often, in fact, there are entire extra rooms unused and without furniture. Unfortunately, this abundance of space has a way of dwindling very quickly. As the family grows, the home appears to shrink simultaneously. The rooms that were so large when they were empty soon become cluttered and difficult to walk through as they are transformed into children's bedrooms, home offices, hobby centers, or playrooms. Even without children, a home seems to shrink in a very short period of time.

RECOGNIZING CRAMPED QUARTERS
The first sign that your home is becoming too cramped is a sudden lack of storage space. The old joke about the closet that opens with an avalanche of bowling balls and ironing boards is true in many homes. You may begin to notice that your children always seem to be playing under your feet; or, no matter how hard you try to keep the house picked up, it always looks cluttered. The realization comes that the house is simply not big enough. If you like the home and neighborhood, you will not want to move. The obvious solution, then, is a home addition. However, many home

Clerestory windows give light without filling wall space in this kitchen. Open island and slanted ceiling increase the sense of spaciousness.

additions cost much more than a re-evaluation and re-layout of the existing house.

THE PROBLEMS WITH ADDING ON

The best solution to any problem is often not the most obvious one. An approach

A dramatic vaulted ceiling and stone walls are suited to the open area of this room. The smaller, low ceiling nook looks better paneled.

that cannot be seen easily, but uses a little ingenuity, may turn out to be the most efficient and simplest answer to the problem. This is commonly the case with the cramped quarters.

Cost Per Square Foot

The first obstacle to adding on, and usually the largest, is the extremely high cost of construction and of interest rates for home improvement loans. It is no secret that the construction industry has been besieged by inflation in recent years. Unfortunately for the do-it-yourselfer, the cost of building materials has skyrocketed in the last decade. It is common for a homeowner to plan a 600-square-foot addition only to find that he has a 400-square-foot pocketbook.

Heating and Cooling Costs

There is a cost to adding on that many homeowners do not comprehend until the work has been completed. Any addition increases the space that has to be heated or cooled; consequently, there is an increase in monthly utility bills. Recently, the cost of fuel has risen faster than any other aspect of the economy, and this is expected to continue. The expense of any addition will continue even when the home improvement loan has been paid in full.

Floor Plan Efficiency

Many additions result in an inefficient layout. Homes are normally designed as closed systems and are not planned with future expansion in mind. Most city and suburban lots are subject to regulations governing where and what you can build on your lot. These rules further restrict the possibilities of an addition. Many times, the only place an addition can be added legally is at the rear of the house, and this is not always the ideal spot. If you need more space because of the already inefficient layout of your home, then an addition in an awkward spot may only compound the problem instead of solving it.

AN ALTERNATE APPROACH

Just as family needs change over a period of time, so do lifestyles. As a result, an efficient home of yesterday often contains bottlenecks for today. Even new homes are designed more to meet certain economies than to provide maximum efficiency. This is not, however, a shortcoming of the construction industry. Each family has individual needs, and to meet these needs most efficiently, a home would have to be designed around the family that will live there. In our society, we try to meet the basic housing needs of as many people as

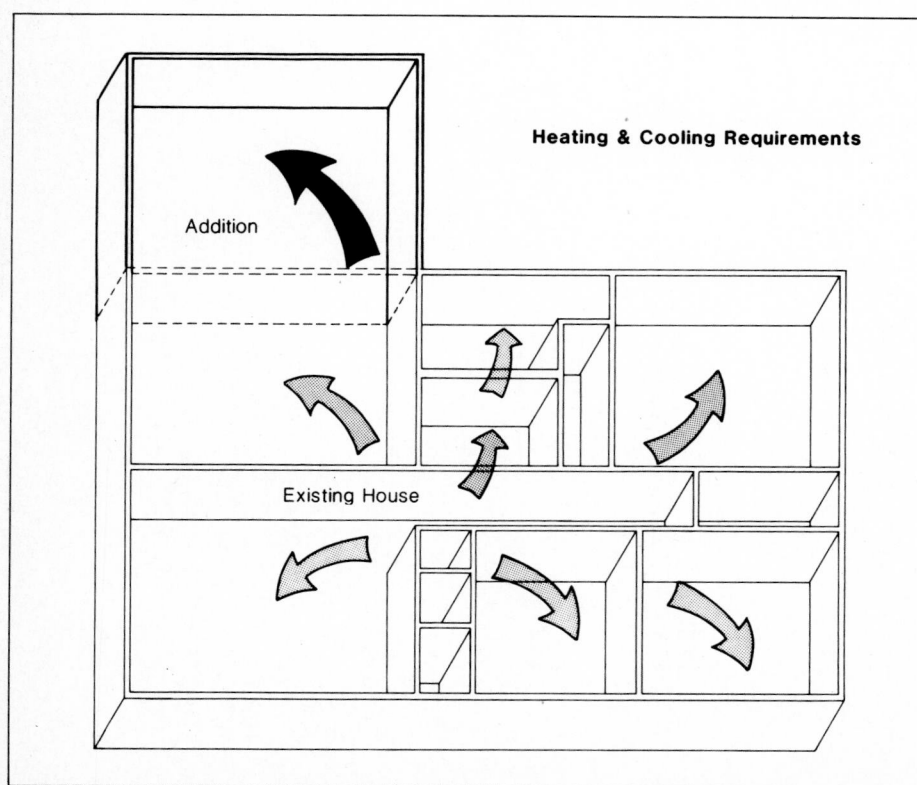

An addition will place a greater load on your heating and cooling system. Even if your unit will handle the load, the increased expense may be greater than you can afford.

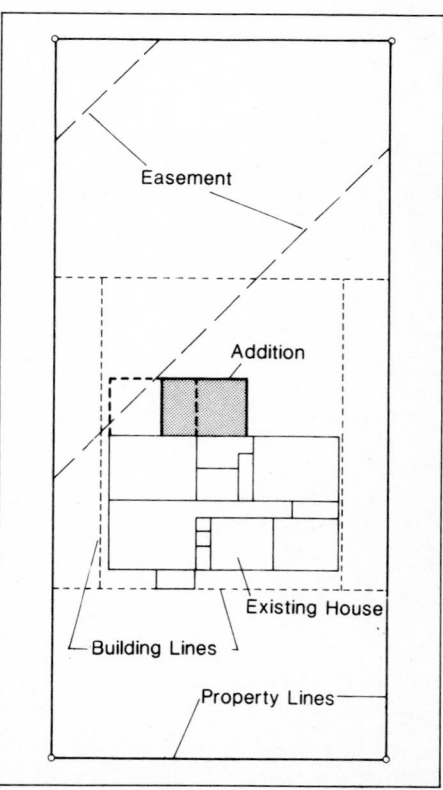

Easements and building lines may lead to awkward placement of an addition.

possible, and it is economically and logistically impossible to design each house around a different family. Even if it were possible to do this, Americans move from one place to another too often for the designs to remain effective.

Effect on the Yard Space

An addition will require that part of your yard be displaced and that much of the landscaping be destroyed during construction, requiring replacement when the job is done. Exterior finish materials will be required on the addition to match the home as it is. If the house is more than a few years old it may be very difficult to make the match close. It also may be hard to tie in the addition smoothly with the existing house.

THE ADVANTAGES OF REDESIGN

You cannot create additional space in your present home, but you certainly can and should make the most efficient use of the space you have before you resort to an addition. By taking a closer look at your home and your living patterns you may be able to get the extra space you need with a few simple changes, instead of an addition. By removing or adding a wall or two, changing a door location, adding some clever storage arrangements, changing a room's classification, and/or installing

An addition to the back of this home will mean removal of plantings that are well developed and attractive. This will be expensive.

The addition of a pool and deck has occupied all the usable backyard space in this lot.

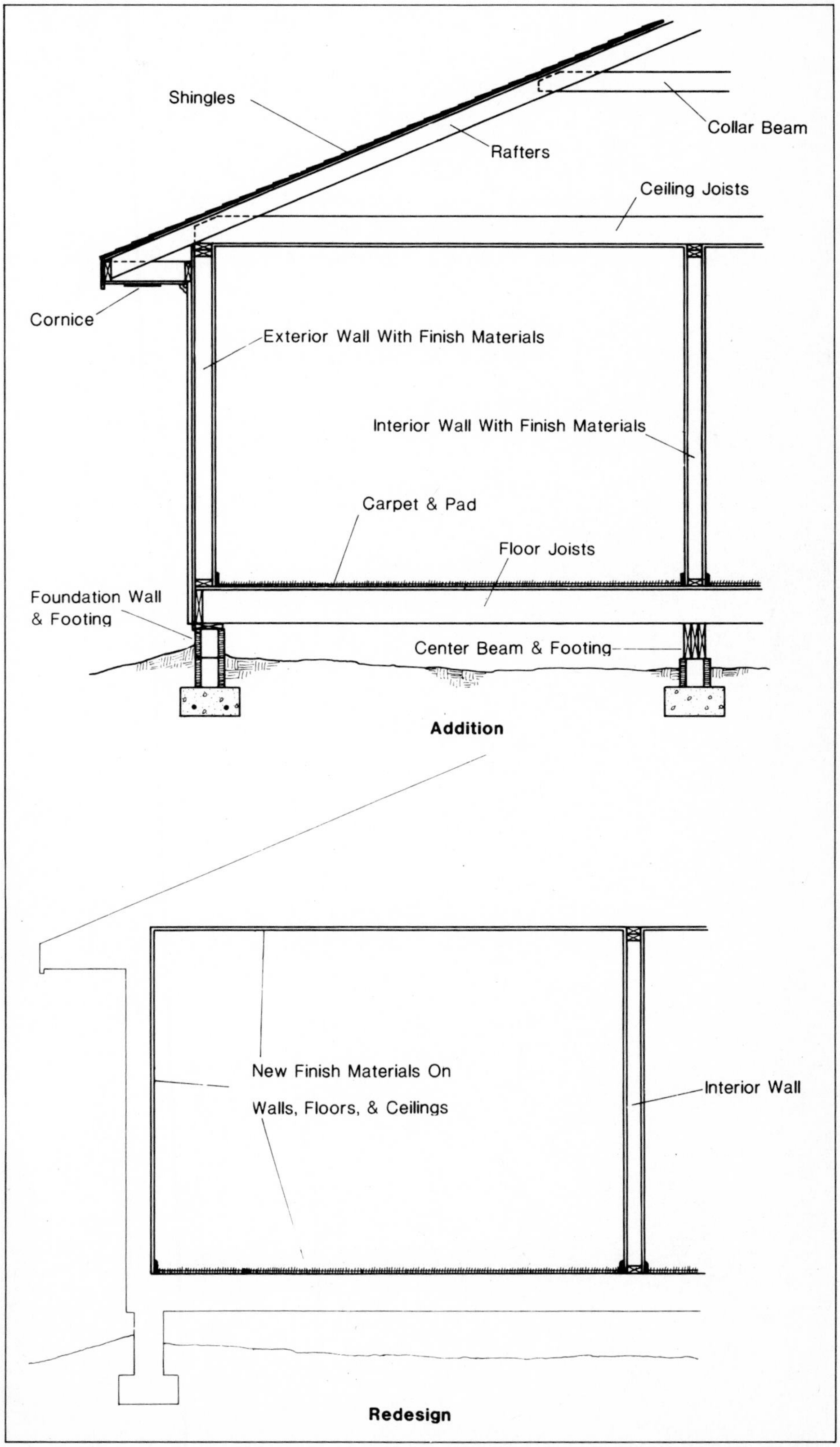

double-use areas, your home can become comfortable, efficient, and spacious.

Cost Estimate

It does not take long to realize that a few changes to your home will cost substantially less than an addition. If you do most of the work yourself, then the only major cost will be the finish materials for floors, walls, and ceilings. In fact, by redesigning you can afford to use better materials than you may have been able to afford with an

Shingles

Collar Beam

Rafters

Ceiling Joists

Cornice

Exterior Wall With Finish Materials

Interior Wall With Finish Materials

Carpet & Pad

Floor Joists

Foundation Wall & Footing

Center Beam & Footing

Addition

New Finish Materials On

Walls, Floors, & Ceilings

Interior Wall

Redesign

The cost of new materials will be strikingly different between redesign and additions. A room may be redesigned by only moving a wall and installing new wall, ceiling and floor materials.

addition, since you will have less money tied up in structural materials. The much lower cost of the work will allow you greatly to reduce the amount of a home improvement loan. You even may be able to meet the costs with savings and avoid high interest rates altogether.

Solving Problem Areas

Almost every homeowner complains of particular ''problem areas'' in the home. Just adding a room will not change these. For instance, if a front bedroom lacks sufficient closet space, an addition at the rear of the house will not provide more closets in that bedroom. You can add a bedroom with ample closet space, but the rear loca-

tion may be the wrong place for a bedroom. You may also end up with a wasted room at the front of the house. A more sensible approach would be to rework the walls in the bedroom and provide the needed closet space.

THE DISADVANTAGES OF REDESIGN

While redesigning your home is the most sensible approach to gaining usable space, it is not without its pitfalls.

Living With Construction

Trying to carry on normal living routines around construction is difficult at best, even with an addition that does not inter-

fere with the functioning of the rest of the house. Redesign, depending on the extent of the work to be done, can be much more than just annoying. You may, in fact, need to leave the home for a few days during the heaviest part of the construction. There are, however, several ways in which the burden of living with construction can be lessened. These are:

1. Prepare your family (and yourself) for the disruption you will suffer. Explain it fully beforehand, and enlist their patience and support.
2. Remove curtains, plants, and furniture in work areas and cover them in any area where the dust of construction may be heavy.
3. Set specific timetables for construction and make every effort to keep the work on schedule. If you are doing much of the work yourself, be realistic about what you can handle and how quickly you can get the work done. Recogniz-

This loft space has many uses. The loft overlooks the living room and is above the kitchen.

The same carriage house has a small balcony that provides a view and gardening space.

This home is gaining a new room by enclosing a porch above a walkout basement area.

This modern, efficient kitchen is the result of a redesign of the space. The original kitchen area now contains a separate wet bar and a new powder room, more storage and a planning desk.

ing beforehand that you will be in chaos for a month is easier to accept than two to three weeks of construction mess after you had promised your family that the work could be done in five days.

4. Keep children and neighbors away from the construction area. This will help avoid law suits and will keep work from being disrupted.

5. Clean up the work area every day. This will not only help prevent possible injuries, but a job always goes more smoothly and quickly in clean surroundings.

6. If you will have to leave your home for a period of time, plan it far in advance. Make arrangements for a place to stay; estimate the dates as accurately as possible.

Limited Potential

Although redesigning your home is an effective method of gaining more space at a minimum of cost, it may not be enough. Your need for extra space may be too great, or your home may already be well designed for your family's needs. Still, the high cost of an addition can be avoided. Redesign first to get the maximum use of your present living area. Then, consider expanding into some already enclosed or partially enclosed space before you resort to a completely new addition.

ALTERNATIVE: EXPANDING UP OR DOWN

Many remodelers overlook areas that can be used for expansion to greatly reduce the cost of construction. These include the attic, basement, garage/carport, enclosed porches, and additions over a garage. Since the basic structural components are already in place, the materials required to turn them into usable living area is substantially less than it would be for an addition.

There are, however, structural and other considerations which can limit or prohibit the use of these areas. Each possible expansion area is covered in separate chapters later in the book to help. Read these chapters carefully and study your home thoroughly before finalizing any plans.

CHECKLIST: REDESIGN VS. ADDING ON

When trying to decide whether to redesign existing space or to add living space, there are factors that should be considered.

The illusion for more space can be created by a vaulted ceiling, coordinated wall finishes and natural light from windows and skylights.

A Study of Your Home

Does it fit your needs well, or is there a great deal of wasted space? After deter-mining your family's living pattern as out-lined in Chapter 2, you will recognize whether your home is well utilized or not.

An attic in a large home can be converted into an entire apartment. This spacious area was finished off and new space created by adding a loft.

A bright dining area was created in this space, a former breezeway. The open side was enclosed with a bay window wall and the old exterior siding left in place.

Consider Your Family Status

If your family is young and growing, it is possible that redesign alone will not fill all your needs. However, note that young children spend a great deal of time outside and, consequently, do not require much space. As a general rule, however, the older a child gets the more living area he or she needs. Always plan with future needs in mind. On the other hand, if your children are reaching the age at which they are beginning to leave home, redesign may well make your home everything you ever wanted, without adding to the square footage.

Estimate Construction Cost

One of the more difficult points to evalu-ate is whether or not you can afford an addition. It is easy to plan a home or an addition that will meet all your needs, but in view of the construction and energy costs today, a redesign may be the wisest and, possibly, the only economical an-swer to developing more living space.

Evaluate Construction Ease

Another point to consider, though perhaps much less important than the matter of actual cost, is the relative ease of construc-tion alternatives. Can your redesign be accomplished without having to live in chaos or in a motel for 4 or 5 weeks? You may be able to ease the inconvenience by doing the work in stages. Can you add on just where you need to add on? A drasti-cally sloping lot may prohibit a needed addition.

Look At Your Neighborhood

One complication that is often overlooked when planning additions is the fact that you may be "overbuilding" for your neighborhood. If you add substantially to your home, and it is located in a neighbor-hood of smaller houses, the chances of getting your money back when you sell it may be slim. In part, the value of your home is established by the value of your neighbors' homes.

Check Zoning/Building Restrictions

Since almost all neighborhoods have re-strictions controlling where you can build on your lot, you must check thoroughly before you begin planning to add on. Many areas have minimum front, rear, and side set-back requirements. There could also be utility easements across your property that will drastically limit the area in which you may build. It is possible for these restrictions to so severely curtail what you can do that an addition is almost beyond consideration. Of course, none of these would be a problem when redesigning your home; no work is required on the exterior.

MAKING A DECISION

Before you decide what to do, finish reading this book to become fully aware of all your options. By determining your living patterns, as shown in Chapter 2, you will be able to see how much redesign will help. Remaining chapters will show you what areas can be converted into usable living space. Once you understand the various approaches you can take, it will be much easier to decide just how to go about gaining more living space.

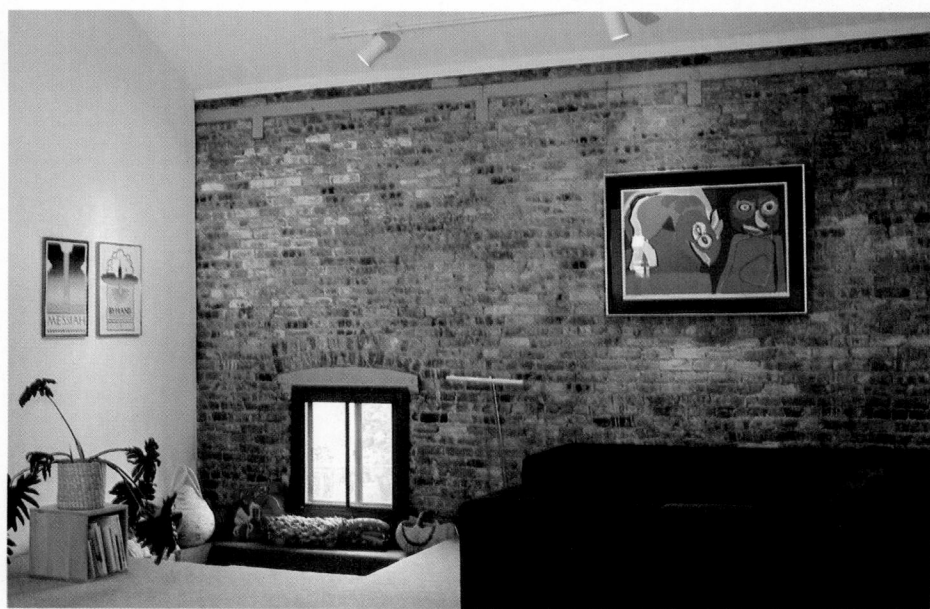

This carriage house was turned into a townhouse without making any exterior changes in the building. The original brick walls are a major decorative feature of the new interior. The kitchen and loft above were created by new construction. The result is a modern, efficient living unit.

Storage space was created in this bedroom by taking advantage of the wall space and placing the bed on top of specially built storage drawers.

This wet bar was built as part of a kitchen remodeling. It is open to a Great Room but accessible from the kitchen.

A small modification to an outside wall allowed the installation of this set of windows to add light and space to the room.

A planning desk and a complete storage wall was added to this house when the oversize kitchen was redesigned into more useful areas.

2
REDESIGNING
YOUR HOME

Although you probably have a good idea of how your home is used and how you would like to change it, the best and most efficient plan can be designed only after careful study.

IDENTIFYING YOUR LIVING PATTERN

It is possible that all the extra space you need actually exists in your present home. However, you may not recognize this unless you establish a visual reference of how your home is used. Sketching your family's living pattern on paper will enable you to see how easily rooms and areas of rooms are used and how the traffic flows through the house. This first step is essential in developing a sound plan, and could reveal some surprising information.

Making A Sketch Floor Plan

The first thing you will need to do is draw a sketch floor plan of your home. Make a rough sketch. Measure the length and width of each room and write the dimen-

sions on the sketch. Draw in the approximate locations of all built-in features such as plumbing fixtures, kitchen and bath cabinets, and other permanently positioned units. Work from this sketch to draw your floor plan. You do not need an architectural quality floor plan. Single lines may be used for walls and free-hand marks are sufficient for built-ins. The drawings, however, should show reasonably accurate dimensions. Use a scale of 1/4 inch equals one foot actual size. This scale creates a good working size on the floor plan. If you are completely unused to this type of work, sketching the floor plan may take more than one attempt. The extra time it takes to produce the floor plan will pay future dividends by getting your project off to an accurate start.

If you are fortunate enough to have or have access to a set of plans from which your home was constructed, your work will be much easier. Simply lay a sheet of transparent tracing paper over the original plans and sketch the basic layout of the

home. Trace the walls and other major physical features, but do not sketch in all the details. A simple, single-line sketch will be the easiest to work from when establishing living patterns for redesigning. Be sure to include any changes in the home made since the original construction if they are not shown on the prints. Write the room names on the sketch floor plan; no other lettering is necessary.

If you feel you need a more accurate drawing, you may draw one to scale; you will need a T-square, a triangle and a drafting board. Align the T-square with the top of the board and tape a piece of paper even with the lower edge of the T-square. Move the T-square to the center of the page and draw a very light, horizontal guideline across the paper. Rest a triangle on the T-square and draw a vertical line through the approximate center in the other direction. Use these lines to establish the other measurements.

After you have measured the actual length of your home. Mark the distance on

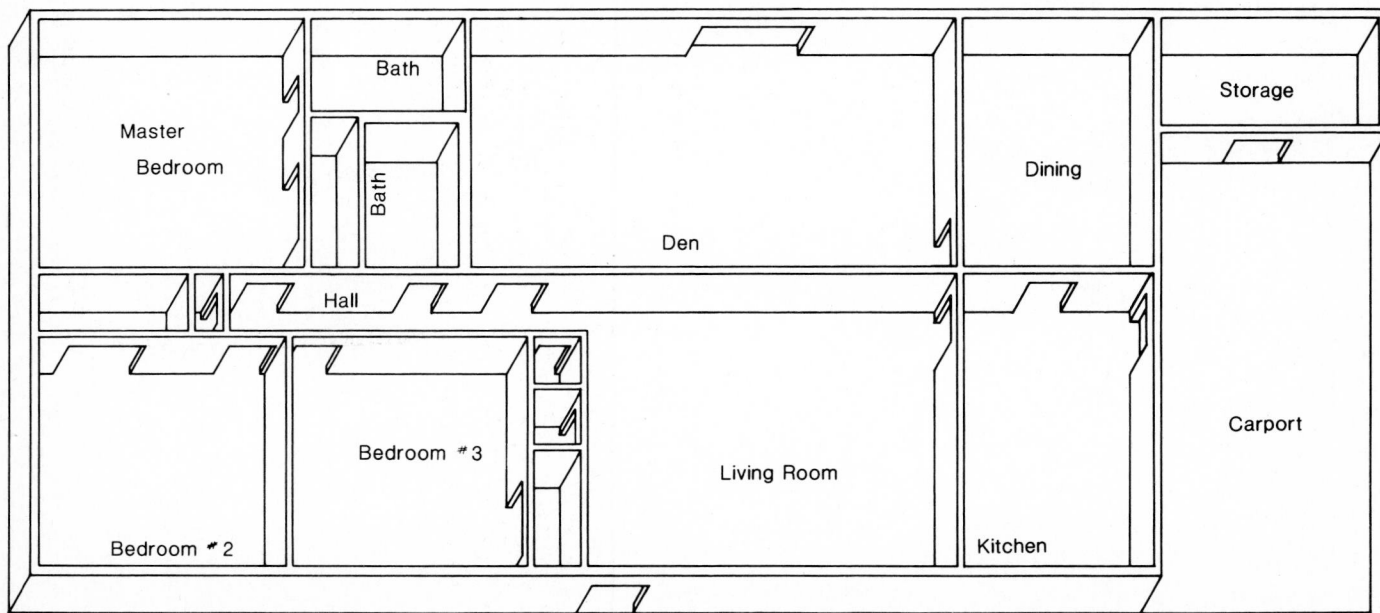

This drawing is based on a simple floor plan but has the walls drawn in perspective for better view of door and window placement.

the horizontal line, one-half to the right and one-half to the left of the center. Repeat for the width along the vertical line. Using the T-square for the horizontal lines and the triangle supported on the T-square for the vertical lines, extend the lines to the full size of the house. Make adjustments for any jogs or extensions beyond the basic outline of the house. This will give you a scale drawing of the outside of the house. Locate the door and windows along the walls. To accurately judge the placement of the interior walls, measure from the edge of a window to nearest interior perpendicular wall, transfer the measurement to the drawing, and extend the line for the interior wall.

Living Patterns

Once you have made your floor plan, overlay it with a sheet of tracing paper. Since you will be making a number of sketches, you may want to invest in a roll of durable, "rag" tracing paper. This paper is available from any business that sells drafting supplies. Mark the corners of the floor plan so that it will be easy to maintain the orientation of the drawing each time you refer to it.

Indicating your living patterns. Using a colored pencil, mark the pattern of your activities on an average weekday onto the overlay. Indicate your movements with a line and make a circle at any spot where

you lay, sit, or stand for a period of time. This process may take a little time, but it is important that you fully document all your movements. Freehand lines are all that is necessary for the sketch to serve its purpose.

Once you have completed marking the weekday patterns, repeat the process for a typical weekend. This is necessary, since some areas of the home may get little use during the week, but may be a favorite spot for weekend relaxation.

Tracing the family living patterns. Repeat the process again for each member of the family. Since well traveled areas, such as halls, will become almost solid with colored marks, the family's patterns will only need to be marked where they differ from yours.

An experienced home designer will go through a similar process, both consciously and unconsciously, in his head. If you don't have the training and experience to recognize a living pattern easily, as most people do not, the outlined process is recommended strongly, even though it may take an hour or more.

Underworked and Overworked Rooms

With the family living pattern established on paper, it will be easy to see which areas are underused and which areas are overused. Look at the distribution of color

throughout the house, and the uses will be obvious.

A room that is rarely used will be mostly uncolored, or the color will represent only the traffic flow through that room to get to another room. This room can be "reclaimed" for other, more useful purposes. It may be reclassified as a different type of room, or combined with other rooms and spaces to make a new, larger room. Such a room may also be subdivided for storage, closet, bath, or other small rooms. In fact, a portion of an under utilized room may be used for a smaller room, while the remainder is combined with another room to expand that space.

Rooms that show heavily colored areas may be overworked for their size. If you have such a room, you probably already know that it is cramped and should be enlarged. This can often be accomplished by taking space from an adjacent room that is less heavily used. A room with both colored and uncolored areas also may be too large for the way it is used. Perhaps you should reclassify this room for another, more extensive function. You may wish to take a portion of the room for a closet or storage, or combine space with an adjacent room to reduce the size of the original room so it more closely fits actual use. This will take planning and should involve the whole family so all possible uses are considered.

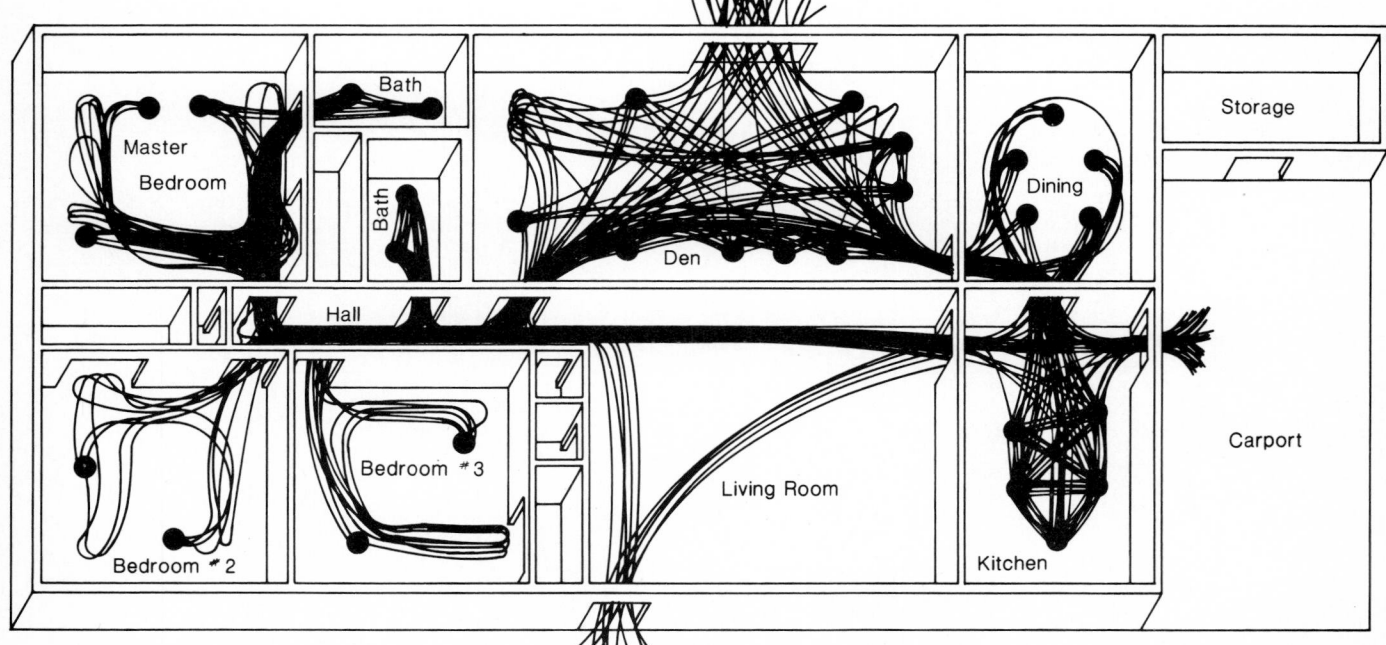

Existing Living Pattern

This is an example of a family living pattern. Certain areas in this home are obviously under used. There is room for change.

Unused Rooms

Most of the homes built around the middle of the century, and a few of the homes still being built today, tend to be ''boxy''. This results in a number of small rooms, each having a separate function. This pattern does not fit today's casual lifestyles very well. These designs usually will result in some rooms being overworked while others are rarely, if ever, used. Such a house, however, with a clever rearranging of walls, can be made comfortable for a modern family. The ''boxy'' house can be broken up and the unused rooms turned into usable living space by removing or moving walls.

Frequently, if you have a rarely used room it is the formal living room. Although many people are reluctant to eliminate a formal living room, it is impractical to maintain one if the only times you enter it are to entertain visitors or to clean it. At today's construction and energy prices, strong consideration should be given to converting the formal living room into useful living space. Many new homes, in fact, no longer have a formal living room. Instead, the trend is to combine the den and living room into a large great room that better suits the casual entertaining and

Furniture may designate a special use area. This office could exist in a formal living room.

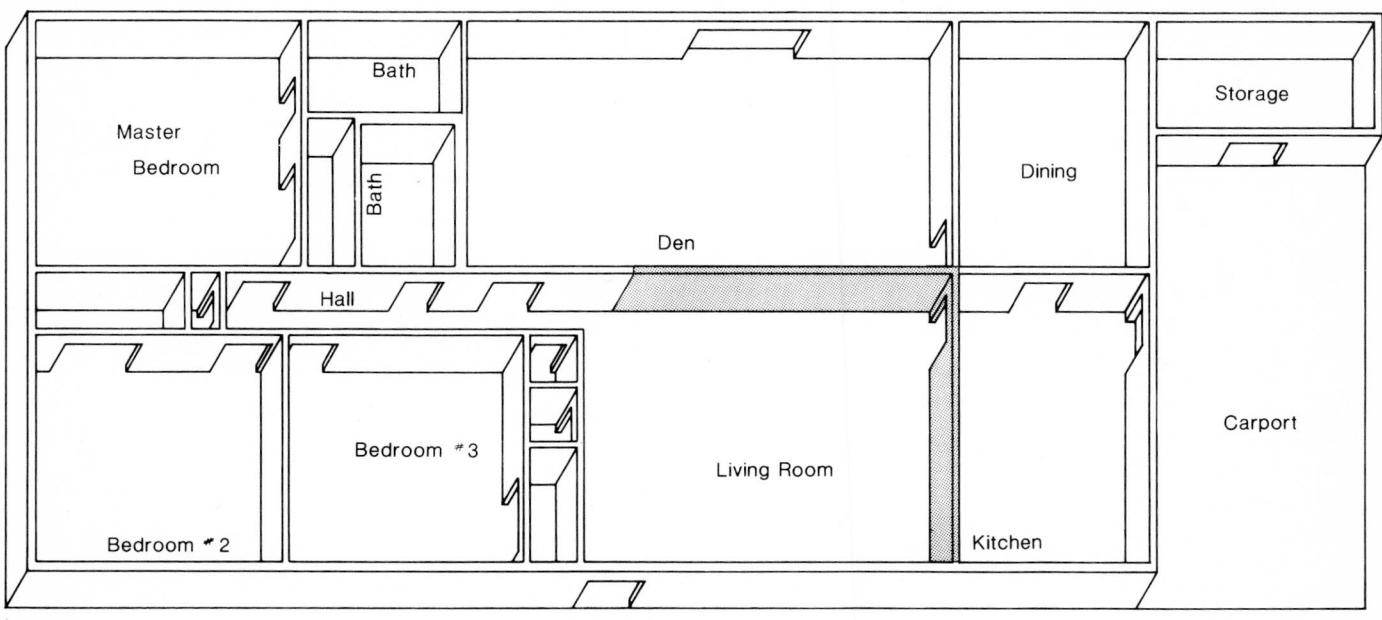

Existing Floor Plan

Part of the plan for changing this home is removal of these walls to create a new open area as a family center.

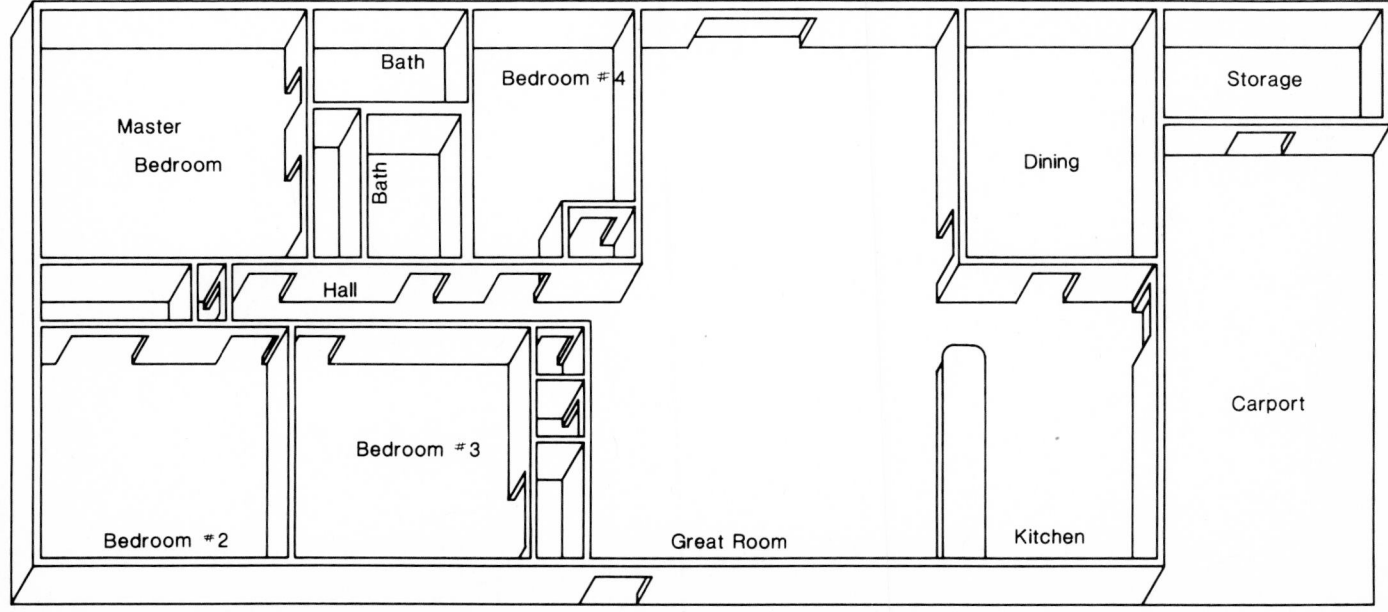

The open area is now a Great Room that is better adapted to the less formal life of the family. A formal dining room remains for entertaining.

A prefabricated fireplace added to a room can create a new focus and increase room use.

easy lifestyles of today. Open kitchens are often linked to family rooms, with cabinet dividers to separate the kitchen area.

Traffic Flow

Another factor that will be easy to see with the colored paths is the general traffic pattern through the house. If the solid color traffic areas are unnecessarily round-about or extremely long, you may consider rear-

ranging the walls and/or doors to straighten and shorten the paths. This will help make your home more convenient and comfortable. It may be that a simple door and/or wall change can eliminate a traffic bottleneck and solve all your problems.

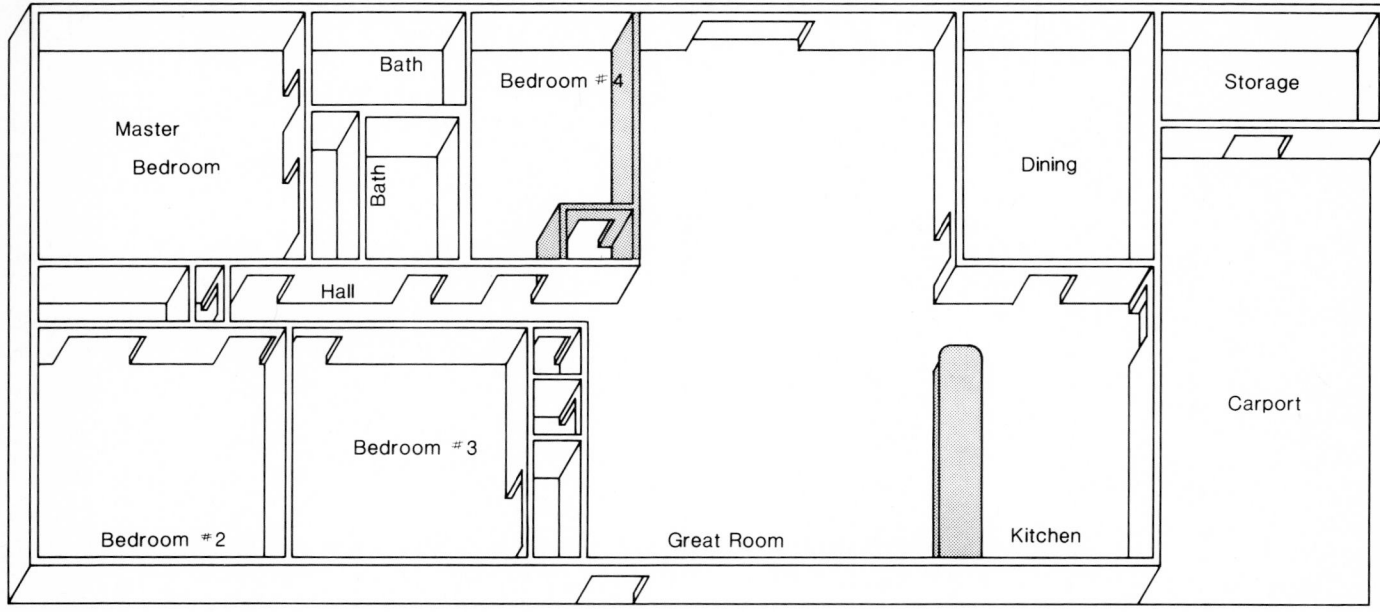

Redesigned Floor Plan

The additions needed to complete the redesign include a low divider/counter between the Great room and the kitchen and new bedroom walls.

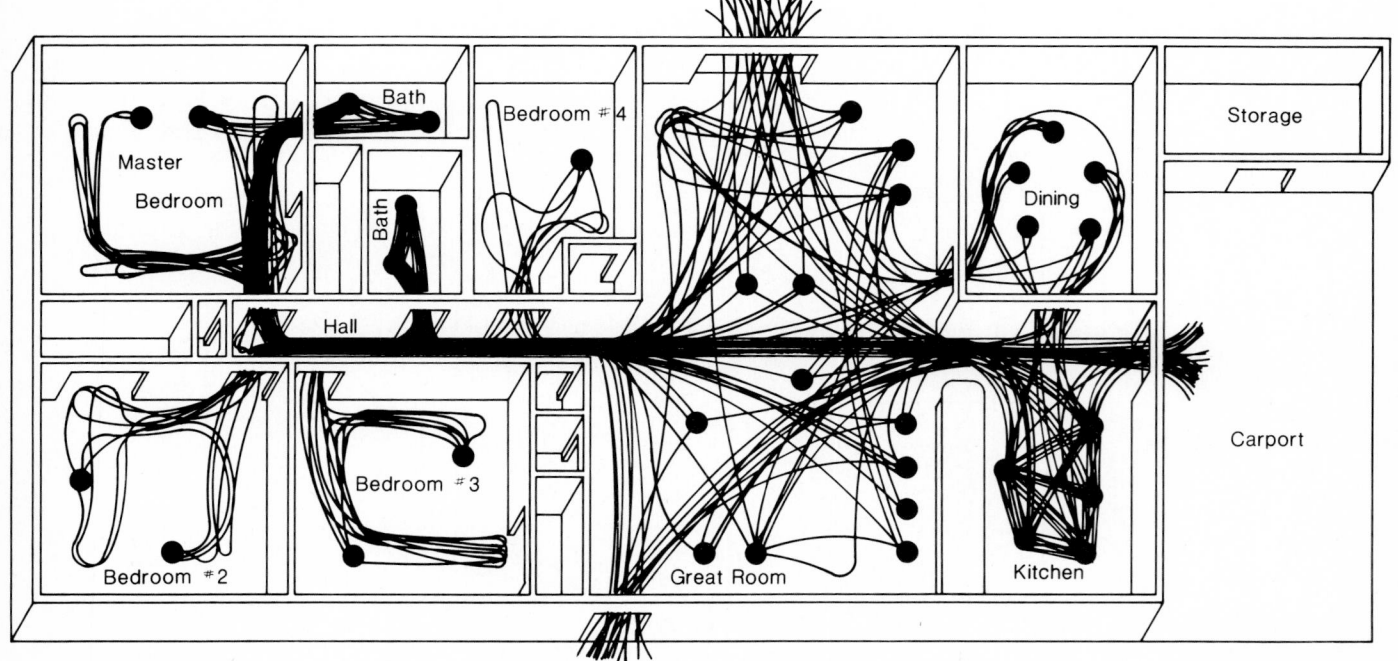

Redesigned Living Pattern

The new living pattern shows better utilization of the space in the home without creating a new bottleneck for the traffic flow.

3
ROOM RELATIONSHIPS
& RECLASSIFICATION

Before your home can be designed to suit you and your family's needs, there are a number of general considerations that should be discussed. There are also some ways in which the new work can be simplified, keeping construction time and cost as low as possible.

ALTERNATIVE USES OF ROOMS
Although changing interior walls can help solve your space problems, too much wall rearrangement can defeat the original purpose of redesign — getting more space at less cost. First, take a long look at how each room is presently used. Then consider alternate uses for each room.

Unchangeable Rooms
Some rooms have no logical alternative use.

Baths. Because of the plumbing in bathroom walls, baths will almost always remain baths, unless they are very large and can be subdivided. If very large, a bath could possibly be converted to a kitchen if that change fits the overall plan. The plumbing connections would be easily convertible for such an alteration.

Kitchens. While a kitchen, in all likelihood, will need to remain a kitchen, the nearby areas of the house — living room, den, dining room, or family room — can often be reclassified or opened up to the kitchen area. This would involve wall and door changes.

Bedrooms. These usually need to remain bedrooms. However, a spare bedroom may be reclassified for a variety of uses: office, studio, even a dining area if the room is situated properly and a conveniently located door can be added. Of course, if the spare bedroom is adjacent to the living or family room in the house (or can be made so by shifting bedroom usage), the space can be opened up and made a part of another area. Although most bedrooms will need to remain bedrooms, a second use often can be introduced.

Load-bearing walls. Existing walls should not be removed indiscriminately. Although most interior walls are only room dividers, and can be removed without any worry, some may be "bearing", or load-carrying, walls. These cannot be removed without installing a beam to carry the load. If you are unsure about which walls are bearing walls, consult an expert before you begin tearing out a wall. Chapter 4 (Adding and Removing Walls) offers a full discussion of bearing walls.

Room Orientation
The relationship of your rooms to the path of the sun can have a strong influence on your heating and air conditioning bills, as well as interior illumination. Of course, your home is already built and the rooms have to remain where they are. However, when you are reclassifying rooms, give some consideration to the following guidelines.

Kitchen. A kitchen on the east or southeast receives the brightness and warmth of the morning sun and avoids the afternoon heat from the west. This is im-

While baths are seldom adaptable to other uses, a sunny bath is a good place for plants.

Opening a wall can give you an eating area in or near your kitchen and add general light.

A pantry or a back entry/porch usually contains enough room for a kitchen eating area.

A small family will find this area a comfortable, as well as attractive, dining room.

portant in a room that is warmer than the rest of the house during meal preparation. In cold climates, the second-best location

Sunny rooms are often popular for family social activities. They look warm and pleasant.

Bedrooms need to be cheerful, but the most important quality is quiet and seclusion.

would be on the south or southwest. However, in warmer climates a northeast position would be a good choice.

Dining room or area. The dining room should face east, south or southeast and be close to the kitchen. This location should provide natural light from the sun. West is a reasonable second choice, especially when summer daylight savings time provides dinnertime sunsets.

Bathroom. Since privacy is the prime consideration, bathroom orientation is not as significant as its being located near existing water and drain lines. A moderately high fence is one way to gain privacy. In order to keep costs down, the bathroom should be adjacent to — directly above, or back-to-back with — the plumbing for the kitchen or another bath.

Great/Family/Recreation Room. With the possible exception of north, the family room can be oriented in any direction. South or west locations are more desirable because natural light will be provided in the afternoon. However, consideration should be given to energy conservation measures for all south- and west-facing rooms. You should plan to provide aids to cooling such as an extended roof overhang and carefully placed deciduous trees and plants.

Living room. Again, south and west are the best locations for this type of room. However, if your living room is only rarely and formally used (as many are now) east, or even north, can be considered, if necessary.

Bedroom. Since the bedroom usually is occupied in the morning, east and south-

east locations are preferred. The morning sun will help warm the cool of night. The second choice of location would be south and then northeast.

Storage/utility rooms and garage/carports. For the cooler climates, placing these facilities on the north side provides a buffer between the prevailing winds and the living areas of the house. In warmer climates, where summer heat is more of a problem than the winter cold, the reverse positioning would be best. However, laundry centers that create their own heat always would be better placed on the north, northeast, or northwest.

Using and Controlling the Natural Light

There are ways to make use of the sun's energy without making drastic changes to your home. The installation of a skylight or clerestory windows, for instance, will not only brighten a room, but should warm the room in winter. If the skylight can be opened, it will help keep the home cooler in summer by allowing the hot air to rise out through the skylight while drawing cooler air in through the windows.

A long roof overhang or carefully located deciduous trees will help keep the summer sun from shining through the windows, lessening heat gain. During the winter, the lower angle of the winter sun will shine through the bare branches and

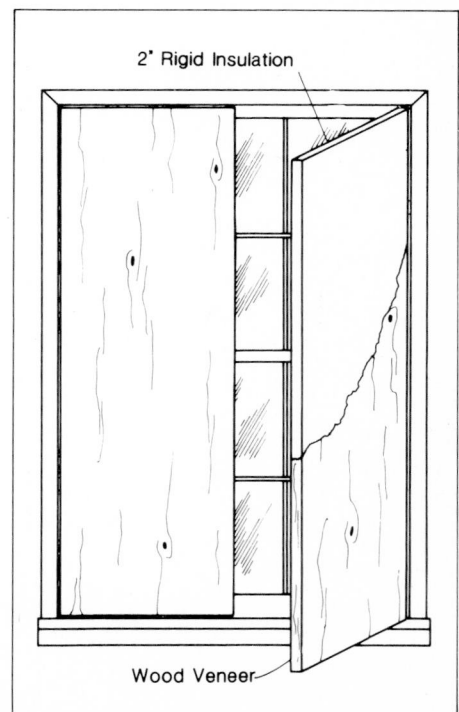

2" Rigid Insulation

Wood Veneer

Install insulated shutters on windows that receive the force of cold, winter wind.

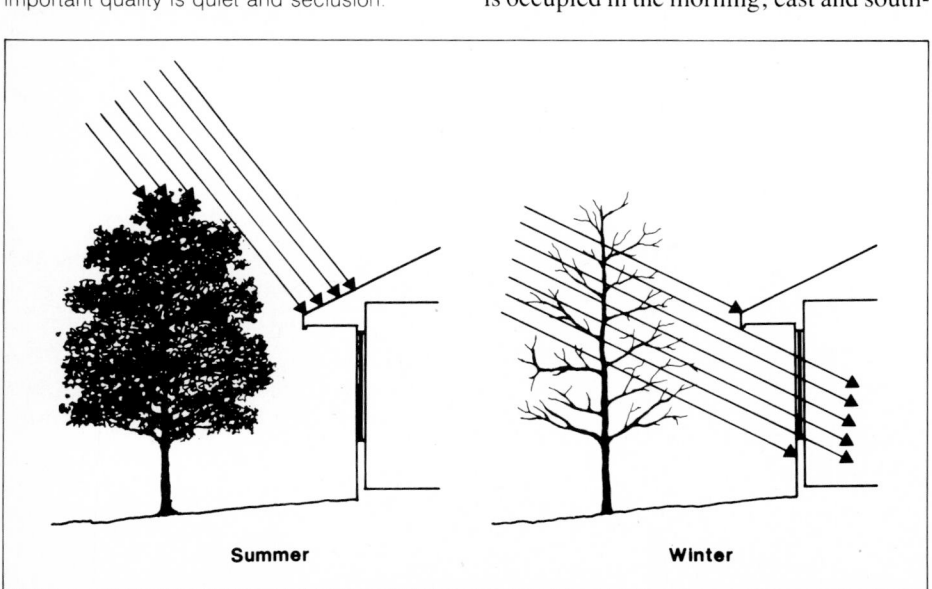

Summer   **Winter**

Light and heat from the sun can be controlled to achieve comfortable temperatures. Plan overhang proportion and tree plantings so that there is summer shade and winter sun in your rooms.

under the overhang to warm the house. Wood covers, with 2-inch rigid insulation inside, can be constructed as shades for windows and skylights to help keep the home cooler in summer by blocking the hot sun, and warmer on cool nights by keeping the heat inside.

MAKING YOUR ROOMS WORK TOGETHER

A home should not be viewed as a series of unrelated rooms tacked together but should be seen as subdivisions that enhance the whole. Rooms should be arranged to suit your family members' individual lifestyles, but the uses should be kept within a general framework of good planning practices.

Relative Positions

Access to the kitchen. The dining room should, whenever possible, adjoin the kitchen. The family room, great room, or den should provide easy access to both the kitchen and dining room. It should have access to the outside. Since much of today's warm-season living and entertaining is done on a patio or deck, there should also be easy access from the kitchen to the patio or deck. This is especially true if your family loves to cook and/or eat outdoors. It is desirable to be able to supervise the daytime area and the family entrance into the house from the kitchen.

Living/dining rooms. If you still want a formal living room, select a location near the front door and somewhat removed from the more casual areas of the house. If this use must be combined with that of another room, the dining room is the logical combination since a formal dining area is less often used than most other rooms.

Privacy needs. Bedrooms and baths require privacy. In no case should anyone have to go through a bedroom to get to any

other room. Baths should be located so that they are not visible from the daytime

activity areas of the house but be reasonably accessible from all areas.

Both formal and informal dining areas are near this kitchen. This is a good arrangement.

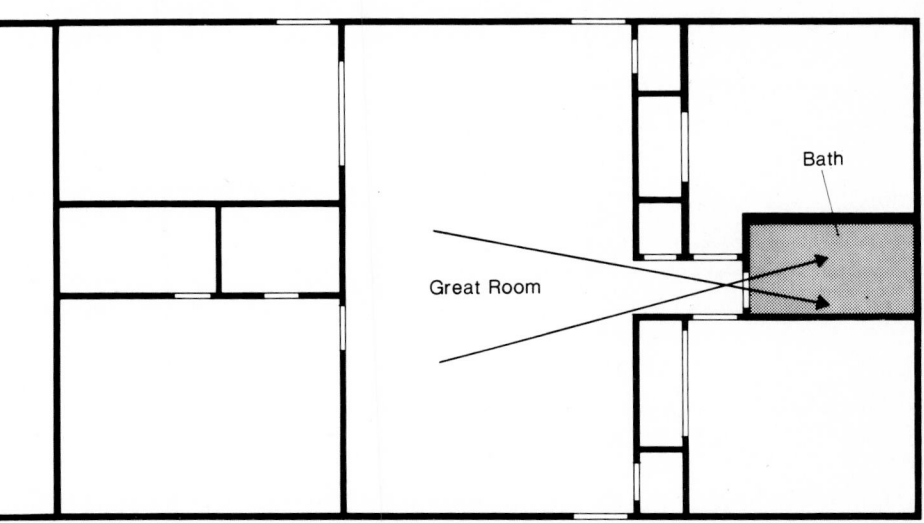

Undesirable

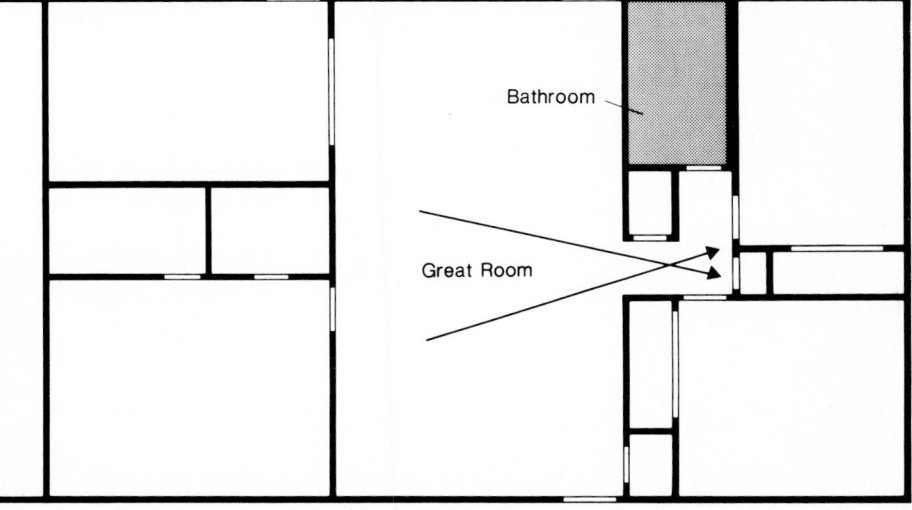

Desirable

Plan of this living/dining room is spacious and allows light to spill from area to area.

Always plan the layout of your rooms and halls so that entrances to bedrooms and baths are shielded from direct view from areas where you will entertain visitors or hold family gatherings.

Bedrooms may be clustered for privacy. Privacy can be increased by using closets, storage rooms, and baths as buffers between the bedrooms and other areas of the home, reducing the transmission of sound from living areas to private areas. You can, however, separate the master bedroom or a guest bedroom from the remaining bedrooms if you prefer. A master bedroom can be located on the opposite side of the house, or on a different floor from the other bedrooms. Be careful to preserve privacy when separating bedrooms. This becomes more difficult when the bedrooms are not clustered. Separation of the bedrooms may require the installation of a sound insulating wall to insure privacy. (See Chapter 4)

Changing Entrances

Changing exterior doorways can be expensive. It is best to work with the locations as they are. However, if a change will greatly enhance the new interior design, one can be made. Usually an exterior door change will mean that you create an additional entrance to the house. If you change entrance locations or close up an entrance, be careful that no room is farther than 50 feet from an outside emergency exit. The distance should be much less for a bedroom occupied by a handicapped or elderly person. In this case, it is preferable to build a door to the outside directly into the bedroom.

A family entrance (rear or side) will be improved by enclosing a small "mud room" to help keep the rest of the house clean, especially in regions that receive considerable rainfall. The mud room may include a sink and/or small shower stall, and it should be close to or contain the washer and dryer. The finish materials in the mud room should be durable and easy to clean.

EXPANDING INTO OTHER AREAS

If your plans include expansion into an attic or basement, there are several factors to consider.

Attic and Basement Uses

You should not attempt to use the attic or basement for a high traffic room such as a family or great room. These areas are too far away from the kitchen, dining room, and other related areas of the house to be easily accessible. On the other hand, the attic or basement, equipped with a small refrigerator or compact kitchen, may function well as a recreation room. The separation helps keep the noise of games away from the other living areas of the house.

Other uses for attic or basement space include children's bedrooms, a master bedroom suite, an office, a studio, an

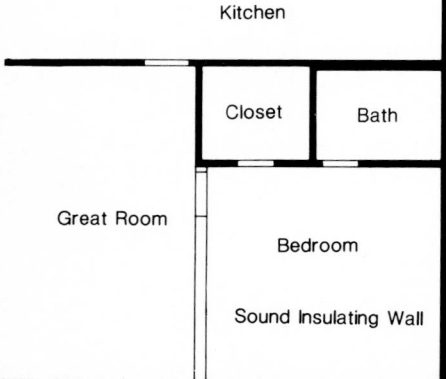

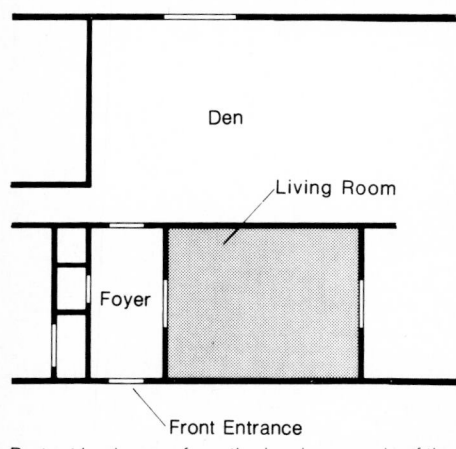

Protect bedrooms from the louder sounds of the more active living areas. Use closets, foyers and sound insulation to baffle noise.

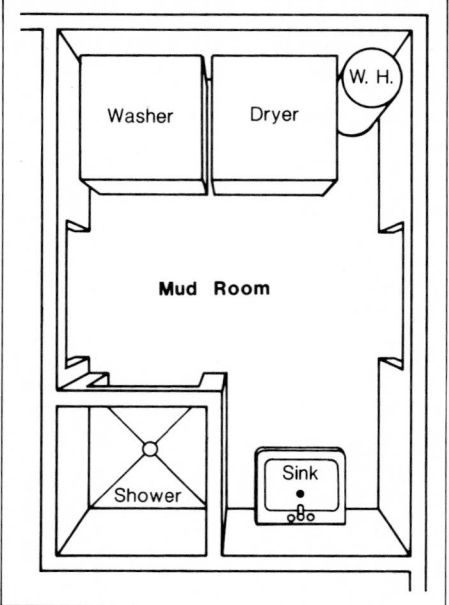

A back porch mud room/laundry is nice for an active family or if someone gardens.

Basement space is often left idle because the area is thought to be dark and/or damp. When the problems are studied and solved, expansion possibilities are nearly unlimited.

adult retreat, or a TV room. (See Chapter 9, "Basement Conversion", and Chapter 10, "Attic Conversions", for more details.) Be sure a new attic bath is placed directly over an existing bath or the kitchen so that plumbing hookups can be made easily. Be careful in designing a bath, or any type of plumbing, in the basement. You may not be able to make the plumbing hookups necessary without substantial expense. (See Chapter 5, "Adding New Plumbing and Wiring/Bathrooms".)

Lofts and Vaulted Ceilings

You can sometimes find space you need by opening up attic areas to rooms on lower floors. A study/office, a library, a hobby room or stereo center may be placed in a loft overlooking an existing room. Vaulting the ceiling of a family room and creating a loft in the adjacent attic space would mean that an adult could supervise children at place and still have a separate work area.

To double the use of floor space in a bedroom, build a sleeping loft and use the area below for desk space. A large bedroom subdivided into two rooms may be too small for standard furniture, and a sleeping loft/desk-dresser may solve the space problem.

Carports, Garages and Porches

These areas are logical places for expansion. However, they require more specialized construction and are more difficult to convert than interior space. Existing roof and beams must be supported while frame walls are constructed. Application of exterior finish materials is within the skills of a do-it-yourselfer, but look at the more economical redesign of interior spaces before looking outside.

ROOM SIZES

The following table shows the minimum acceptable size of various rooms as set forth by the Department of Housing and Urban Development. For your planning, however, it should be noted that these government standards are bare minimum. An additional column, with a more desirable minimum, is also provided. You

ROOM SIZES

Room	DHUD Minimum	Preferred Minimum
Living Room	11x16	12x18
Family Room /Den	10½x10½	12x16
Great Room	—	14x20
Kitchen*	—	—
Master Bedroom	—	12x16
Other Bedrooms	8x10	11x14
Baths (Full)	5x7	5x9

*The size of the kitchen will vary greatly with the type of cabinet and appliance layout.

may wish to make your rooms much larger than these minimums, depending on your needs and lifestyle and the space available.

SUGGESTIONS FOR DOUBLE-USE AREAS

A good way to maximize the use of space in a cramped home is to provide areas that can be used for dual purposes. Quite often this will work well when an active use is combined with a passive use. Although there is no absolute distinction between the two, an active use generally involves much more human movement than a passive use. Examples of active uses are hobby/craft centers, art studios, and home offices. Passive uses can include sleeping, conversation, and reading. Some uses, such as watching TV or enjoying a stereo, could be considered active or passive, depending on how much this activity will interfere with parallel activities. A painter or needlepointer may be able to work where a stereo is on, another person might be too distracted.

Another way to plan double-use of areas is to take advantage of the fact that many areas of the home are only used during certain times. A bedroom, for instance, is used predominantly at night for sleeping. This allows it to be converted to other, more active purposes in the daytime. The dining room is used for its intended purpose only at mealtimes, leaving it available for other uses during most of the day or night. But a double-use area cannot be successful if the design is makeshift. The dual uses must be carefully planned for, as discussed below.

Uses That Combine Well

Art Studio (painting and sculpture). There are three very important factors to keep in mind when finding an area for an art studio. First, good lighting, both natural and artificial, is essential. Second, all surface finish materials should be durable and easy to clean, especially floors. Third, paints, other chemicals, breakable materials, and sharp tools must have a safe, lockable storage area that cannot be opened or reached by small children.

Bedrooms usually are not the best site for an art studio. While a bedroom is a common choice for double-use area, it often has a carpet or other type of floor finish that is susceptible to damage. If you must use a bedroom for an art studio, provide a

If ventilation is adequate to expel noxious and toxic fumes of artist's materials and if you can provide good lighting and work surfaces, a basement is an excellent studio area.

drop cloth, such as a sheet of canvas, for the floor when you invest in the other artist's equipment.

When it is properly prepared, a dining room is a good choice for an art studio because there is usually good natural light. Another suitable location is an unfinished attic that can be turned into an art studio. At a minimum you will have to provide a simple plywood floor, coated with sealer, and skylights or other natural lighting. Ventilation is another requirement. Unfortunately, in areas of weather extremes you will have to put in considerable work and expense to insulate, finish, and install heating and/or air conditioning.

Photographic studio. The photographer needs available electrical service, artificial lighting, and light-tight covers for windows and doors in order to attain total darkness in the daytime. Lockable storage also should be provided for photographic chemicals and equipment. Though not an absolute essential, a sink is desirable and makes work much easier.

It is difficult to provide this type of use in conjunction with another use. The most logical place for a darkroom is in a storage room, if there is enough space. Since a storage room does not have heavy daily traffic, there is less chance of disturbance. A storeroom provides plenty of area to store photo equipment when not in use. Another possible location is in an unfinished attic or basement, but this is a less desirable place because temperature changes affect both chemicals and film life. Specific temperatures are required for safe processing of film.

In a home with more than one bathroom, a photographer may take over the "spare" bath for a darkroom. This will work only if there is a light fixture that will accept a safelight and a flat surface near an outlet for an enlarger. While a piece of plywood may be laid across the bathtub to hold the developing trays, it is advisable that this surface be more permanent.

The chemicals used in photo processing and printing will not harm porcelain; however, these chemicals may stain vinyl and plastic. Therefore, it is necessary to protect surfaces that may receive splashes or spills when prints are transferred from tray to tray.

If you have a bath with convenient storage or room for a fold-down work surface, and this is not the only bath, a darkroom/bathroom combination is logical.

Sewing Center. A convenient storage area, an electrical outlet, and adequate lighting are the important requirements for a sewing center. A sewing area can be placed in many areas of the home: the master bedroom, the dining or even the family room, if sewing is done mainly during the day and the family room is used mostly in the evening and on weekends. A storage cabinet that allows the sewing machine and work to be easily accessible, but hidden quickly, is suggested.

Home office/study. The home office/study has approximately the same requirements as the sewing center. It can be placed in any of several rooms. However, the family room is usually a poor choice because the office or study is often needed in the evening when the family room is busy and noisy. The dining room also may not be the best choice if it is close to a room that is noisy in the evening. If your office is in a room in which you entertain, you may want to provide a hideaway-style desk that closes over the work surface.

Hobby/craft center. The requirements for the hobby/craft center will vary depending on the particular type of activity, but basically the ingredients needed are storage, electrical outlets, and good lighting. The best location usually is a bedroom. Often, the hobbyist will work in the evening when the family room is in use. Be aware that some hobbies and crafts may involve rough wear of finish materials in a room, so provide any necessary floor covering and use durable wall materials in the work area. Some hobby activities, such as jewelry making or pottery are simply too awkward, noisy or

Some hobby activities can be carried on without intruding on the main function of a room.

A stereo center can be installed in a small space in a closet, cupboard or cabinet. This system is neatly stored in protective drawers that pull out for access and use.

messy for a double-use area. Hobbies obviously unsuitable for ordinary rooms should be pursued in the basement, attic, or carport/garage.

Stereo/music center. The requirements for this use will vary widely. For example: an elaborate stereo system will require several electrical outlets; a budding violinist needs little more than a small space and normal room lighting to practice. For the musically oriented family, the great room may be ideal for musical uses. More commonly, however, the best place for a music room is a bedroom. Consider installing sound insulation in the walls between the music room and other rooms, and between floors in a two story home.

Garden center. Since plants can brighten any room, the indoor gardener is at liberty to work almost anywhere there is an easily cleaned surface. The only requirement is that the room receive the proper amount of natural light for the types of plants being grown. A potting shelf and a small sink located in a mud room will simplify transplanting and propagation activities.

SETTING UP A DOUBLE-USE WORK AREA

There are three keys to insuring the success of a double-use area. Storage must be immediately at hand so that the additional activity is hidden when the room is being used for its primary purpose. The ideal method is to construct a closet that can neatly hide everything behind attractive doors. A shallow closet or cabinet can be designed with a fold-down work top, drawers, storage compartments, and whatever else is necessary for the particular activity. Careful planning of the storage area is necessary to get the most storage from the least space. Carefully think through the processes involved in the second use, measure the items to be stored, and design your storage area so everything will fit neatly.

Most activities will require convenient electrical outlets, at desk-top level and/or standard level, and all require proper lighting. An activity that needs natural light will need to be placed accordingly. Artificial lighting can be provided inconspicuously by installing recessed spots in the ceiling above the activity area and by providing fluorescent fixtures at the proper level in the storage/work area. Fluorescent fixtures work well for active uses because they are cool, put out more light than incandescents of the same rating, and use less electricity.

DESIGNING FOR THE ELDERLY AND HANDICAPPED

If there is an elderly or handicapped person in the home, you will want to observe the following standards to make life easier and safer for everyone. The material included here is for elderly and wheelchair restricted persons. For more detailed information on specific problems, and for information on handicaps other than wheelchair restriction, contact the Department of Housing and Urban Development. You may also be able to get guidance from the Veteran's Administration, the Visiting Nurse Association, or your health department.

Wheelchair Dimensions

When considering the problems of designing for a wheelchair user, you should understand that there are two basic types of chairs, usually referred to as large chairs and small chairs. The small chairs are more commonly used today because of the ease of maneuverability.

Small chairs. The most commonly found wheelchair is the self-propelled model with drive wheels at either the front or the back. For the person operating largely on his or her own, the model with the drive wheel at the rear is most easily controlled. The center of gravity allows the user to navigate steps and curbs, but it does require considerable upper body strength. If the chair is often propelled by an attendent, the rear location of the drive wheel is also preferred.

The chair with the drive wheels in front is easier for a weaker person to use because it has a shorter turning radius, requires less strength to propel, and is less resistant to friction from the flooring surface than a rear-wheel driven chair.

Large chairs. Large wheelchairs are designed to be pushed and are meant to provide maximum comfort for those who are not able to propel a chair themselves. They require considerably more room.

Turning Radii

Small chairs that are propelled by their rear wheels require a circular space 5 feet-4 inches in diameter for a 360° turn. Front-propelled wheelchairs require somewhat less space in which to turn.

90 degree turns from straight-line travel. Small chairs need a minimum of 3 feet in which to turn into a 32-inch space. Large chairs require a full 5 feet of width in which to turn into a 32-inch space.

90 degree turns through doors or openings. There must be no obstacles within 3 feet of a doorway 32-inches wide in order for a small chair to make the turn and move through the door. The larger the

SEATED ADULT REACH

Reach	Distance	Notes
Vertical	54 to 78 inches	The average is 60 inches
Horizontal (I)	28½ to 33½ inches	One arm extended
Horizontal (II)	54 to 71 inches	Both arms extended from sides
Diagonal	48 inches above floor	One arm extended toward shelf or wall

WHEELCHAIR DIMENSIONS

Adult Wheelchair	Dimension	Notes
Length	42 to 44 inches	Unoccupied; footrests attached.
Length	Add 4 to 6 inches	With adult occupant
Width	22½ to 26½ inches	Unoccupied
Width	Add 4 to 6 inches	Allows for elbows and hands
Seat height	19½ inches	Average above-floor height
Seat depth	16 inches	Front-to-back measurement
Arm height	29½ inches	Average above-floor height
Over-all height	36 inches	Average above-floor height to top of backrest
Turning radius (I)	60 x 60 inches	Makes for tight full-circle turns
Turning radius (II)	63 x 63 inches	Preferred amount of turning space

These measurements are the result of extensive scientific study and should be used as a guide when planning and finishing areas to be used by a handicapped individual.

opening, however, the closer an obstacle may be to the door and still allow the chair a clear passage.

A large chair must have at least 4 feet-3 inches of unobstructed space to make a turn into a doorway.

Doors and Ramps

Both exterior and interior doors should be designed so that persons in wheelchairs do

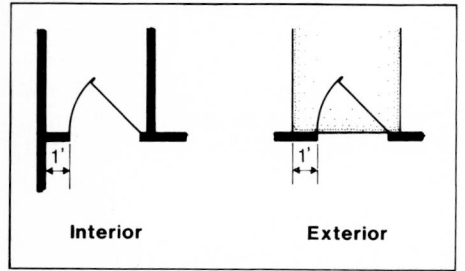

Interior   **Exterior**

Provide one foot of space on the handle side of a door for the ease of a wheelchair user.

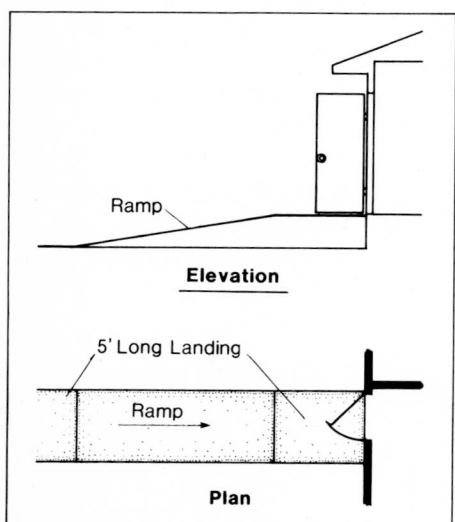

Elevation

Plan

A 5 foot landing at the top of a ramp provides minimum maneuvering room for a wheelchair.

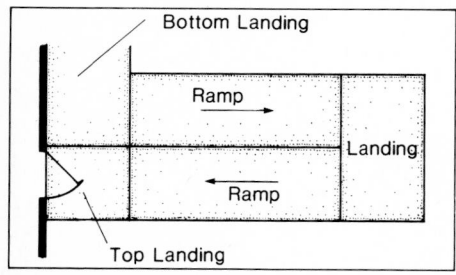

Provide several landings and short ramps if a change in elevation is extensive.

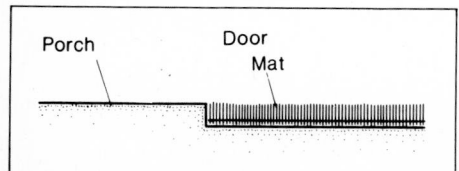

Door mats and thresholds must be level with floors for ease of access and smooth transit.

not have to back up to open the door. Provide at least one foot of clear space at the open edge of the door to allow the wheelchair user room to pull the door open. This will allow the wheelchair user to move to the side of the door and then to open it without backing up.

Ramps. Where steps are required for normal usage, a ramp should be provided for persons in wheelchairs. Ideally, a ramp should be at least 42 inches wide and should have a slope no more than one inch of rise per one foot of length. The top of a ramp should have a minimum 5-foot level space in front of a door or other opening. A ramp may be constructed of poured concrete or of framed lumber with a finished floor. Installation of flooring is discussed in Chapter 5. Wood framing outside the house should be of pressure treated lumber with concrete footings sunk in the ground.

Minimum requirements for doors and ramps. In addition to a 5-foot clear space in front of doors with a minimum opening of 32 inches, ramps should have a slope of no more than 8.33%. A level landing should be provided for every six feet of grade change, and there should be a curb on either side of the ramp to protect the user from rolling off. There must also be railings and illumination to at least 5 footcandles on all ramps and doors.

There can be no change of grade at thresholds. At entrances, door mats and grates with snow or sand traps can be hazardous for a person in a wheelchair. Install door mats so that they are recessed slightly below the surface of the landing. Grates

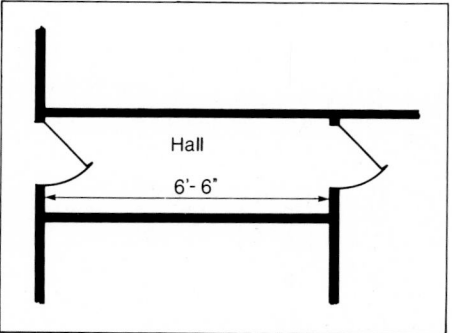

Wheelchair users need a minimum of 6 feet 6 inches between facing doors in a hallway.

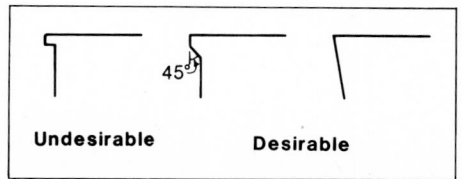

Undesirable   Desirable

Stair nosings must be smooth or gently angled or a handicapped person may trip on the edge.

should have openings no larger than ⅜ inch by ⅜ inch.

Any double door units must have at least one leaf that provides the minimum opening of 32 inches. Two consecutive doors should be no closer than 6 feet-6 inches with a continuous, level floor on either side of each door.

Horizontal throw-bars are more appropriate than knobs, latches or vertical handles. It is recommended that the doors open under 5 to 8 pounds of pressure.

Stairs. If there are elderly persons, or persons wearing leg braces, in your home, avoid squared nosing on stairs. Install risers that have a slant. Two types of recommended stair nosings are shown. If stairs are a problem, consider installation of an electrically operated elevator chair that mounts into the staircase wall to carry handicapped or disabled persons up and down.

Baths

When remodeling or adapting a bathroom for the elderly or handicapped individual, the two most important considerations are access and safety. There must be free access through the door and a full turning area in the bath. In addition, careful consideration must be given to providing the user with a safe and easy-to-use facility. No one should experience frustration or fear of bathroom hazards.

Access. In addition to a doorway that is at least 32 inches wide, the bathroom must have a clear area of at least 54 inches by 54 inches in which to turn a wheelchair. The threshold should be flush so that the chair may pass through the door easily. Because of the problem of the amount of space a hinged door takes up, it may be advisable to install a folding door or to install wall-mounted track and create a sliding door.

If the wheelchair user is able to stand briefly, it may be possible to put a smaller,

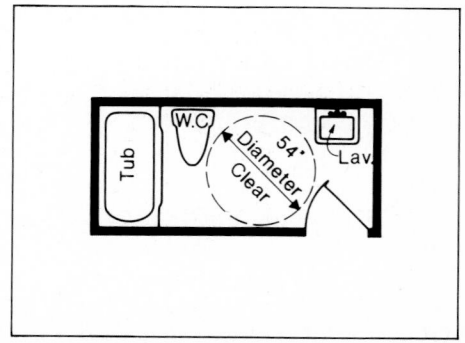

Bathrooms must provide a clear 54 inch turning circle for full maneuvering of a wheelchair.

rolling chair — such as a stenographer's chair — in the bathroom and have the wheelchair user shift to that whenever he or she uses the facilities.

Floor covering. Although the floor surface should be one that allows the wheelchair to move easily, under no circumstance should the floor be slippery. A resilient sheet vinyl or a thin, dense, indoor-outdoor carpet provides the best surface for the floor.

Safety. It is vital to provide strong, well anchored grab bars in the bathroom. Do not use towel bars because they are too light-weight. Purchase the best possible grab bars and place them next to the toilet, the lavatory, and in the tub or shower enclosure. If the room is large, you may need additional grab bars near the doorway.

The bars must be installed with heavy bolts, firmly anchored in the studs. You may have to open walls to find the studs.

Sinks and lavatories. There are several different sinks manufactured for the wheelchair user. These models have shallow lavatory bowls that permit the person in the wheelchair to move up to the bowl without striking his or her knees. The unit should be small and narrow enough so that the faucets can be reached without difficulty. The ideal height is 34 inches above the floor.

Because it is next to impossible for a seated person to reach a wall-mounted, recessed medicine cabinet, it is advisable to provide countertop space on one or both sides of the sink. Storage may be provided with open shelves or swing-out bins.

Faucets and handles. Small, decorative knobs may be difficult for the handicapped or disabled to use. It is better to provide single handled levers or flat, wrist-blade faucet handles. The faucet itself may be a standard unit or a gooseneck style, depending on which is appropriate to the needs of the user.

Stall showers. A conventional stall shower is not designed for a disabled person; however, there are several units that have been designed especially for access on a wheelchair or other rolling chair. These units have wider doors and uniquely designed thresholds that allow the chair to roll into the shower but prevent water from flowing out. These shower units come in complete, molded fiberglass stalls or as terrazzo shower pans.

The complete units have built-in shelves; the shower pan units may be installed in custom designed stalls. Both are large enough to accommodate a rolling shower chair.

Bathtubs. The standard bathtub presents an almost insurmountable problem to a disabled person. The surface is usually slippery and the sides too low to provide good handholds. However, there are tubs with non-skid finishes, tubs with molded seats, tubs with integral grab bars, and tub chairs and benches that allow a person with limited strength and dexterity to move from a wheelchair to the side of the tub and into the tub. The hand-held shower head allows a person to sit on a stool or tub chair, and direct the shower spray as needed.

Toilets. There are a number of toilets available for the handicapped. The most common need is for a higher seat. Several manufacturers offer higher-than-normal toilets that provide a seat at 18 inches above-the-floor. One toilet may be installed in a corner and another comes with grab bars as part of the seat unit. A standard, wall-hung toilet is another good choice for a bath for the disabled or handicapped. This unit will not obstruct the wheelchair and may be installed at any convenient level.

HOW HIGH, HOW WIDE
REACH DIMENSIONS FOR THE DISABLED

Use these dimensions as guides to making a new or existing bathroom accessible, comfortable, convenient.

Doorways   30 to 32 inches wide; 36 inches is ideal

Doorknobs   36 inches above floor level

Horizontal handrails and grab bars for wheelchair users   29 to 32 inches above floor for adults.

Horizontal handrails and grab bars for ambulatory adults   34 to 40 inches above floor level.

Window sills   not less than 28 inches nor more than 36 inches above floor level.

Light switches   30 to 36 inches above floor.

Lavatory vanities and countertops   32 inches (average) between top of surface and floor level. Clear opening between bottom edge of the counter or vanity top and floor must be 30 inches to accommodate wheelchair arms. If the person is an ambulatory adult, vanities and countertops that are from 34 to 36 inches high will be appreciated.

Lavatory vanities and countertops width   (front to back) of 18 inches for most adults; 20 inches for those with a long reach.

Toilets   18 inches from floor level to top of rim for most adults, especially the ambulatory elderly.

Bathtubs   if the disability seems to call for a low tub, the 14 inch high receptor tubs mentioned in the section on Small Spaces and Powder Rooms would be adequate. Tubs with higher sides, however, may be needed for leverage or simply to instill feelings of safety. In such cases, the conventional bathtub will probably be advantageous.

Shower stalls   at least 36 by 36 inches; 54 by 54 inches is better.

Towel bars for wheelchair users   29 to 32 inches above floor for adults.

Towel bars for ambulatory adults   34 to 40 inches above floor for adults.

Hanging rods, hooks for clothing for wheelchair users   no higher than 48 inches above floor level for adults.

Mirror, shelves, medicine cabinets for wheelchair users   should be centered quite low; from 30 inches to no higher than 40 inches above floor level.

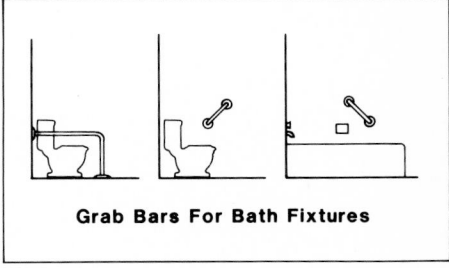

Grab Bars For Bath Fixtures

Grab bars must be positioned and secured well to provide assistance to the handicapped.

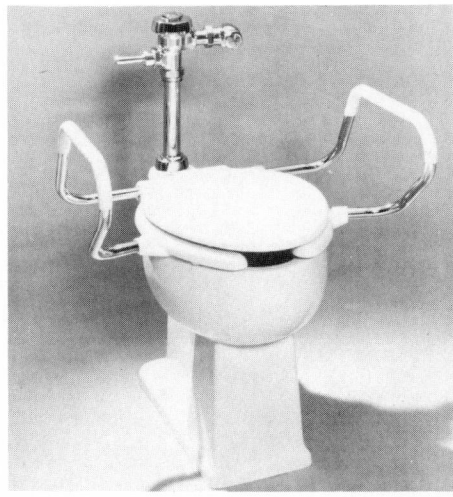

This toilet has a higher seat than normal as well as integral grab bars to aid the user.

REDESIGNING YOUR LIVING SPACE

While referring to your drawings of living patterns, make a list of all unused areas and rooms, and all overworked areas. Note any traffic patterns that are not as short and direct as they could be. Then compile another list of the things you would like but do not have in your home now — such as extra closet space, an additional bedroom, a fireplace, or whatever you find it lacks.

Sketching the Designs

Overlay your original sketch floor plan with a clean sheet of tracing paper. Be sure to mark the corners of the floor plan on the new sheet so that you can easily orient the overlay later.

Make a number of redesign sketches and orient them over the floor plan to compare different ideas. Refer to your lists, then sketch out ideas for changing walls and doors to better meet your needs. While designing is fun, it requires careful thought and analysis.

Your Final Design

Once you have exploited all your design possibilities, making as many sketches as you have ideas, compare your designs. Select the one, or more probably the combination of ideas, that appears to most nearly fill your needs. Then make a redesigned floor plan by sketching the part of the original floor plan that will remain and the new elements onto a single sheet. This new floor plan should be the basis for remodeling your home. First, however, it should be tested to see how well it accomplishes what it is supposed to.

The New Living Pattern

Overlay the redesigned floor plan with a clean sheet of tracing paper, marking the house corners onto the sheet, and draw out your family living pattern as discussed in Chapter 2. Since you have not had experience living in the redesigned home, drawing the living pattern will not be as straightforward as it was before. It will take some careful consideration and some calculated guesses. However, as best you can, adapt your living pattern to the new design.

Now compare the new living pattern with the original. If you have planned carefully, the new lines will show a more even distribution of color throughout the

rooms and straighter and shorter traffic patterns. If you find that there are still problems of room usage and traffic flow, take another look at your new design and reconsider the possible solutions. At worst, the problems should have been narrowed down. If the new living pattern shows an over-abundance of color

throughout, redesign may simply not be enough to meet your space needs. You should then consider expanding into other enclosed space, as detailed in later chapters, before you decide on an addition.

If, however, you are satisfied with your design, you are ready to get started on the changes. How-to information follows.

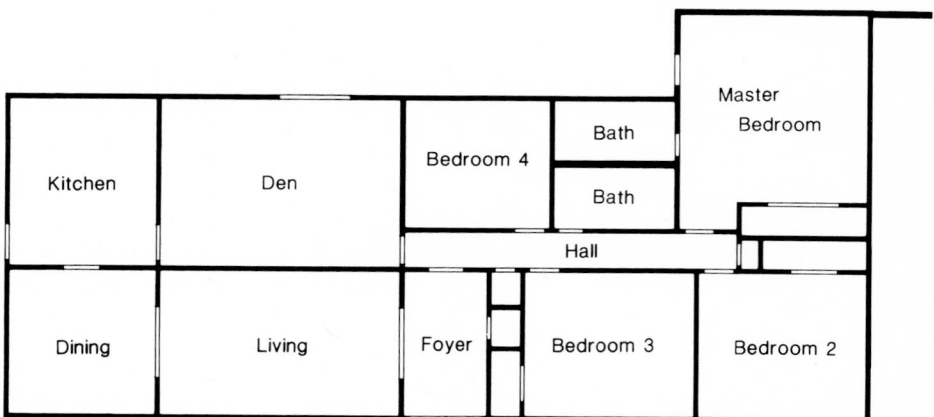

Existing Floor Plan

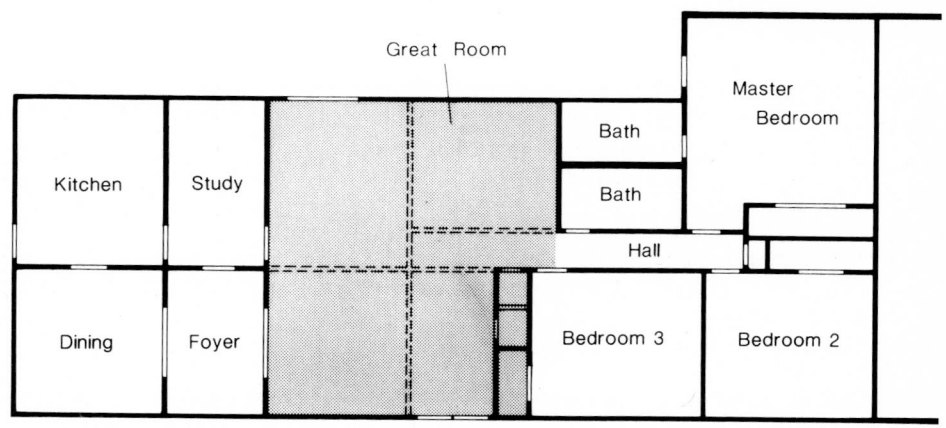

First Redesign

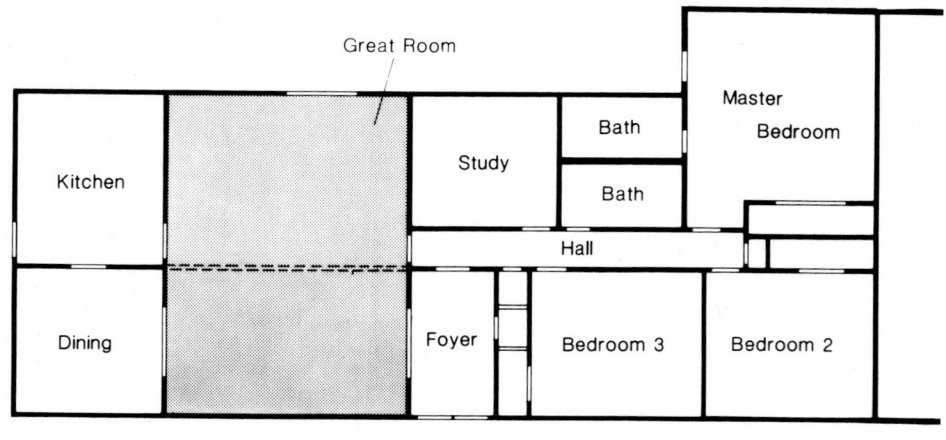

Second Redesign

What seems an ideal arrangement may improve if you give more thought to your plan. Here, second thoughts reassigned room use and made fewer structural changes for easier remodeling.

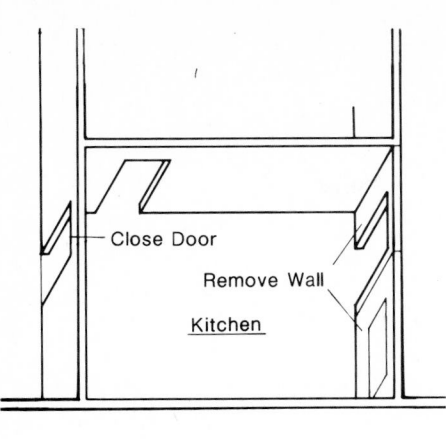

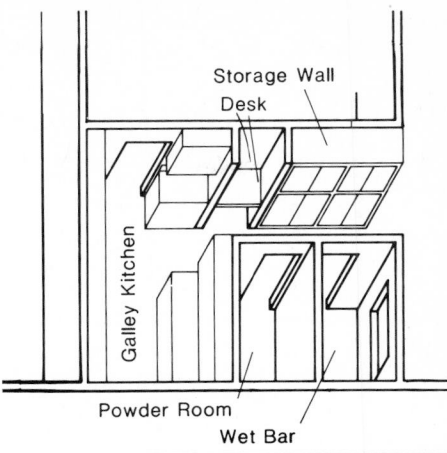

Before   **After**

One small area, an open kitchen, was transformed into four spaces. The galley kitchen now uses less than half the original space and is arranged for maximum efficiency. A hall passage provides space for a full storage wall and built-in planning desk. The rest of the area is divided between a powder room and a complete wet bar with pass-through access to the newly created Great Room.

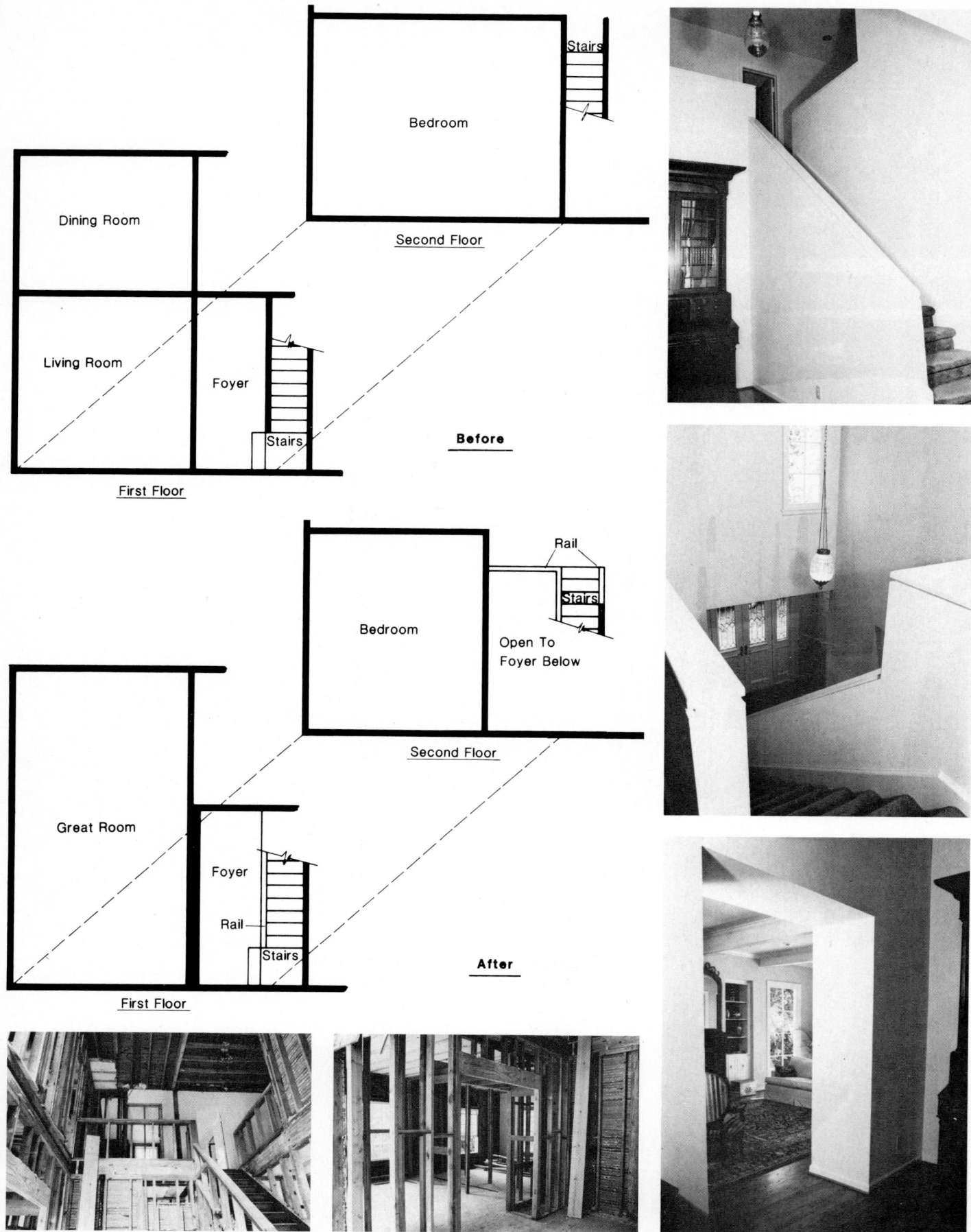

The living and dining rooms in this house were made into one Great Room by removing the dividing wall. The foyer was opened with a vaulted ceiling that took a small amount of space from a second floor bedroom. A window now opens into the upper level of the foyer. The staircase was also reframed and refinished. The clean lines of the walls allow the period accents of the lamp and windows to be the center of attention.

4
REMOVING & ADDING INTERIOR WALLS

The difficulty of taking out a wall or putting up a new wall will depend upon the type of wall (exterior, interior bearing, or interior partition), the type of construction (stud frame or masonry), the type of surface material (gypsumboard, plaster, or paneling), and the location of the wall in the house. Most such work can be done by the do-it-yourselfer with relatively few tools. This chapter will deal only with interior walls. Chapter 9 (Basement Conversions) will include a discussion of making changes in exterior (foundation) walls.

Before beginning, you will have to get approval from your building department. All work must be up to code standards.

TYPICAL WALL CONSTRUCTION
Materials

Framing. By far the most common wall construction is the wood-framed wall. This consists of a 2x4 (often pressure-treated) bottom plate, a double 2x4 top plate, and 2x4 studs at 16 inches on center. Sometimes a wall may have framing 24 inches on center; in very old homes the spacing may vary. The framing lumber may be any of a large variety of wood species, in grades that meet local code specifications in effect at time of building.

Surface materials. For most post World War II homes, the surface is gypsumboard. This material also may be

Substantial changes to walls will completely change the look of a home. This residence, a small urban, late Victorian building, has been modernized by removing and moving walls to allow more window light to reach interior space. The fireplace and chimney were left exposed.

called wallboard, drywall, plasterboard, or carry the trade name Sheetrock. Prefinished paneling is commonly used also. Prior to the Fifties, interior walls usually were covered with plaster over wood or metal lath. Paneling was used occasionally in older homes, but since prefinished panels were not available, it was normally finished after installation. Although plaster is still used today, it is not common in homes. The use of plaster has given way to the easier-to-install and less-expensive gypsumboard.

Brick or block. Depending upon the location of the home, the type of home, and the age of the home, it also is possible that some interior walls are of brick or concrete block. These may or may not be surfaced with other materials, such as plaster or paneling.

Bearing or Load-Carrying Walls

Although most interior walls are little more than room dividers and can be removed without structural worries, some may be load-carrying or "bearing" walls. Usually a bearing wall will run the length of the house and sit roughly in the center. However, the loading-carrying walls may also jog, and the function may not be readily apparent. The bearing wall helps cut down the span of the ceiling joists, allowing use of shorter lengths of lumber. Depending upon the size of your house, or the type of soil under it, you may have more than one interior bearing wall, or you may have none at all.

Often, this can be determined by looking at the construction plans for your home, if they are available. You may also be able to tell by looking in the attic. An interior wall that is perpendicular to the ceiling joists and directly beneath where the joists are joined (either by lapped joints or butt joints) is a bearing wall. Interior walls running parallel to the joists are not bearing walls. Homes framed with roof trusses normally have no interior bearing walls. If you are unsure about the location of load-carrying walls, or if there has been a considerable amount of settling, have an expert (such as a homebuilder or city building inspector) look at your home. An experienced builder should be able to tell you, in just minutes, what walls, if any, are bearing walls.

If it is necessary for the success of your redesign, a portion of the bearing wall can be removed. However, you will have to install a beam to support the ceiling before the wall is removed. This beam will carry the load horizontally and transfer it to the portions of the bearing wall that are to remain. The load is then sent vertically to the foundation.

There are two ways in which the beam can be installed. If you are putting the beam in the attic, it can be placed first, followed by removal of the wall. It is best to have the new beam and fastening system designed by an architect or engineer, who will tell you exactly what is needed and how to make the installation in your particular home. Attic beams, hidden from view, are often harder to install than exposed beams.

If you want the beam to be exposed, a two-step process is required. Temporary

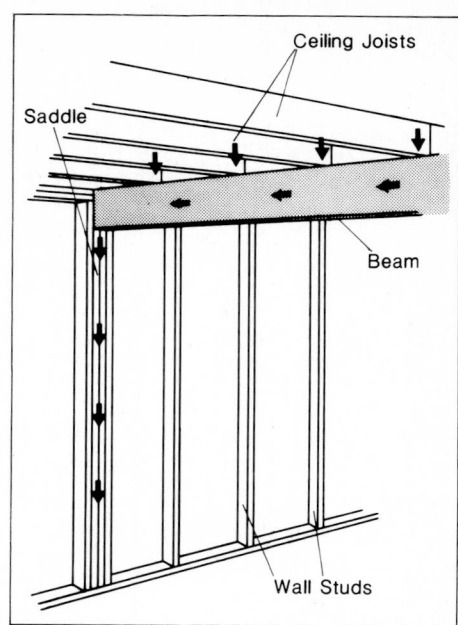

If you remove a load-bearing wall, a beam that fits into saddle studs may be substituted.

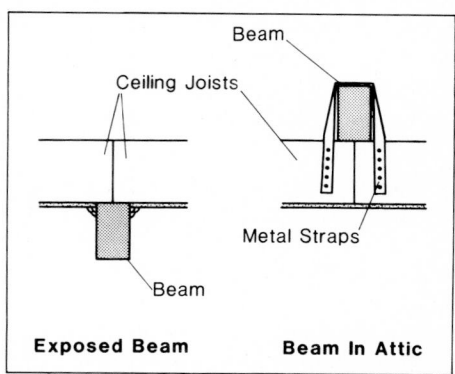

Beams may be placed above or below the ceiling but they must reach into the bearing walls.

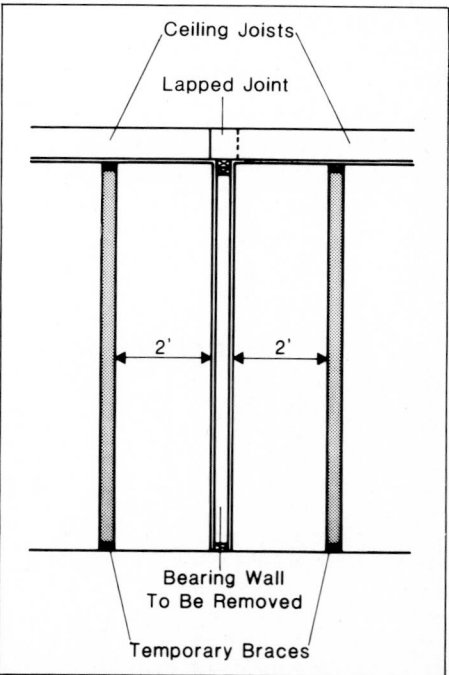

Before removing a bearing wall, you must brace the ceiling with 2x4, or heavier, stock.

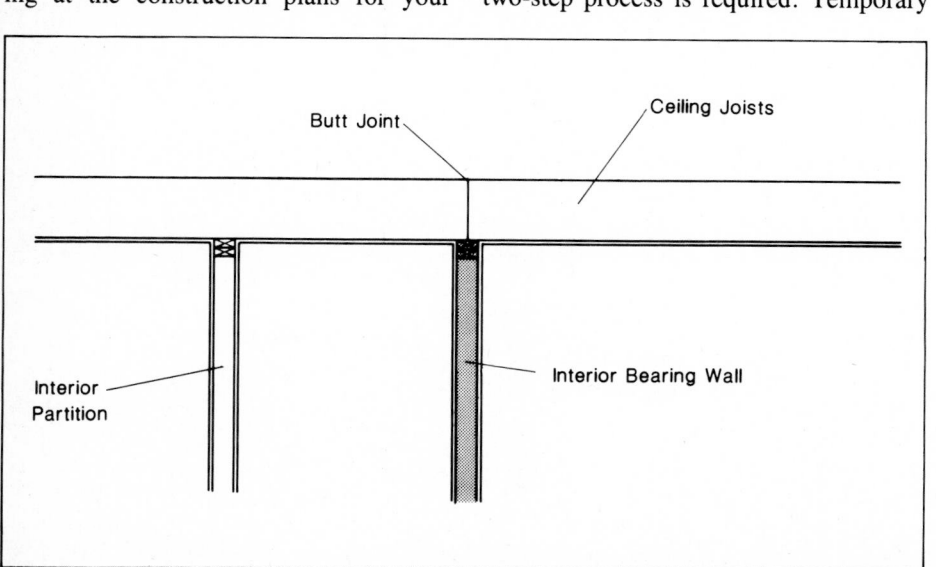

An interior partition fits beneath the ceiling joists and does not carry any weight to the foundation. An interior load-bearing wall actually supports the weight of the joists if the house is so large that joists must butt in the middle to provide a span from one side to the other.

vertical supports must be positioned on each side of the wall that is to be removed. The wall then can be taken out and, finally, the new beam set in place. Installation of a beam can be a more difficult, strenuous and tedious project than other work and, unless you are confident you can handle it, consider subcontracting this portion of the work. Even if you are planning to do the rest of the job yourself, you may find having this job done by a professional is more economical of time and money. If you prefer to do the work yourself, be careful not to leave the ceiling unsupported at any time.

A bearing wall has been removed. The location is visible in both the ceiling and floor between braces that support overlap joints of joists.

The required support beam is matched by false beams that give the room period style.

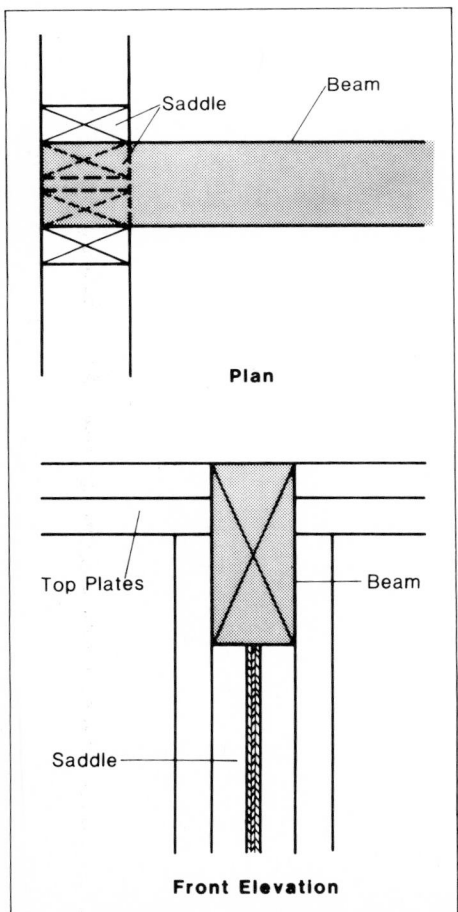

One type of saddle fits a beam at right angle to a wall. It uses four studs and a spacer.

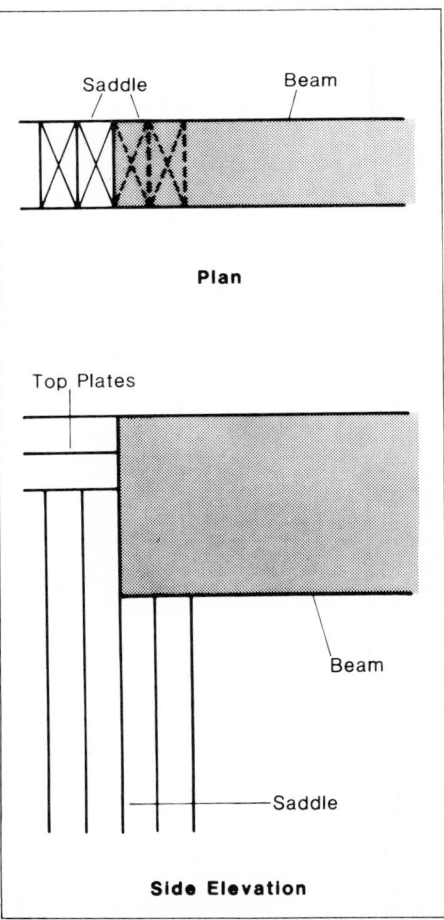

To fit beam parallel to a wall, saddle is two studs nailed to double studs and top plates.

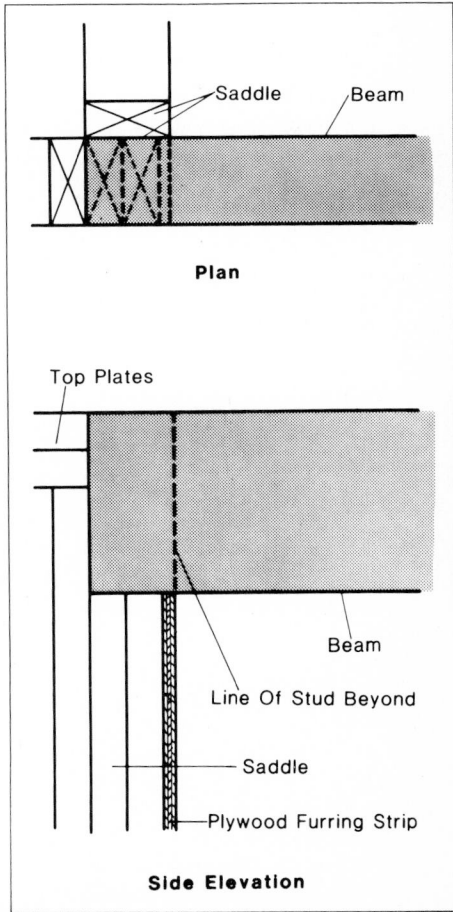

A beam at a wall L sits on two studs. A furring strip makes the two wall faces even.

Types of Beams

Basically, there are three types of beams that can be used to replace support of load-carrying walls. These are the solid wood beam, laminated beam, and the steel beam.

It is worth repeating that computing the size and design of the beam to fit your circumstances is a complicated procedure and should be done by an expert. Retain an architect or structural engineer to make the computations for you. He will be able to tell you what size you will need in each type of beam and which type is the most economical for your purposes.

Solid wood beams. The solid wood beam is attractive when exposed, but it will also work well if hidden in the attic. This is significant, because as the length of bearing wall to be removed becomes longer, the size of the beam needed to provide equal support becomes increasingly larger. However, solid beams in a very large size can be extremely expensive. For this reason, the laminated wood beam may be a better choice for this use.

Laminated wood beams. There are two types of laminated beams: solid and truss types. The solid beam is made by joining several pieces of lumber and gluing the layers under pressure. This creates a stronger unit than a solid piece of the same size. For instance, a laminated beam consisting of eight 2x4s is roughly equivalent to a 6x12 solid beam in strength, but can cost much less. As the size of the beam required increases in width, height, or length, so do the cost differences. The

solid laminated beam may be installed in the attic, but the more common use is as an exposed beam because of the attractive appearance of the finished wood.

Laminated truss beam. The truss type laminated beam is constructed of a combination of plywood and lumber glue-nailed together in a rectangular truss shape. This type of beam is economical. It is usually installed in the attic because of the need to trim it out if it is exposed.

Steel beam. For very long spans, carrying a particularly heavy load, the most economical beam to use is of steel. A steel beam can be adapted easily for use in the attic, but can also be exposed by trimming out with lumber.

HOW TO REMOVE A WALL

The following instructions are for non-load-bearing walls.

Electrical and Plumbing

Before you begin removing any wall, disconnect electrical wiring and plumbing pipes in the wall. **Do not take chances!** There is always a possibility of a shock, of a fire or of water damage to the home when removing a wall. Even if you have shut off the circuit to the plugs in the wall you are removing, there is a possibility still that there is a live wire in the wall cavity. Shut off power at your circuit box. There also could be a plumbing pipe in the wall even if there are no plumbing fixtures immediately adjacent to it. Determine the path of your plumbing risers from your basement. Drive a long, thin nail through

the subflooring from the basement to give you a guide marker if you are not sure which wall they pass through. Plumbing and electrical are discussed in depth later in this book.

If you are not completely familiar with the wiring and plumbing in your home, shut the electricity and water completely off when you begin removing the wall surface. If you need light or power tools, leave on one circuit in a completely different area of the house and run a heavy-duty extension cord to your working area for a lamp or your tools. Once the wall surface has been removed, all electrical conduit and plumbing lines will be visible and can be rerouted or removed, as necessary. Have an expert take care of this part of the work if you are not experienced at it. Planning for these changes is discussed in the chapter on plumbing and on wiring.

Removing A Masonry Wall

Depending on the age of the mortar, a brick or concrete block wall can be quite easy or very difficult to remove. If the mortar is old enough, it may crumble, making it easy to remove bricks intact. You can use a gentle hammer stroke to clean the excess mortar from the bricks. You may want to re-use them or, since used bricks bring a premium price, sell them.

Check in the attic to be sure the wall does not extend into an upper story. If it does not, remove a brick or block on the top row with a hammer and masonry chisel. The first brick or block will be the

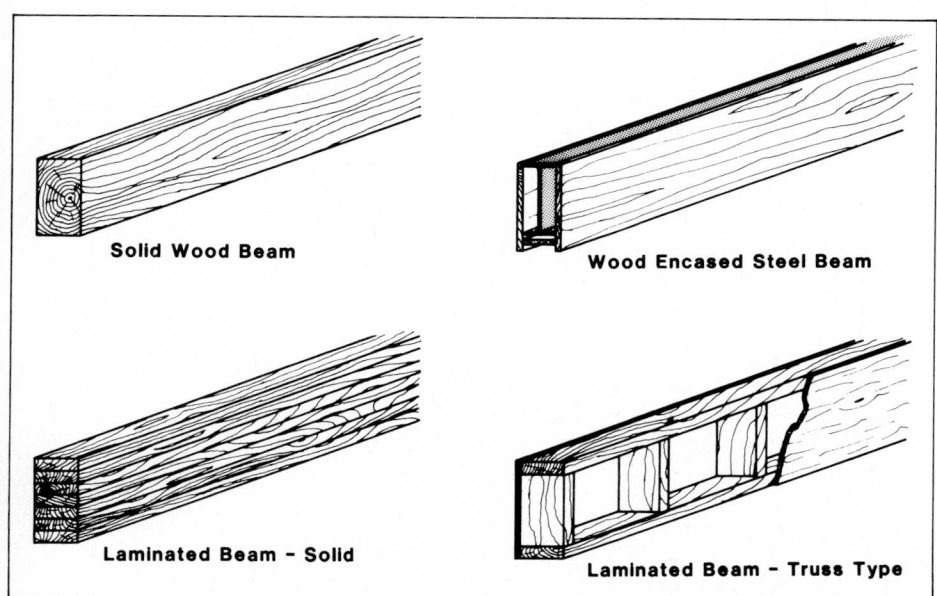

Solid Wood Beam

Wood Encased Steel Beam

Laminated Beam - Solid

Laminated Beam - Truss Type

The solid wood beam is very attractive, but the two laminated styles and the steel beam are less expensive and, size for size, stronger than the solid wood beam.

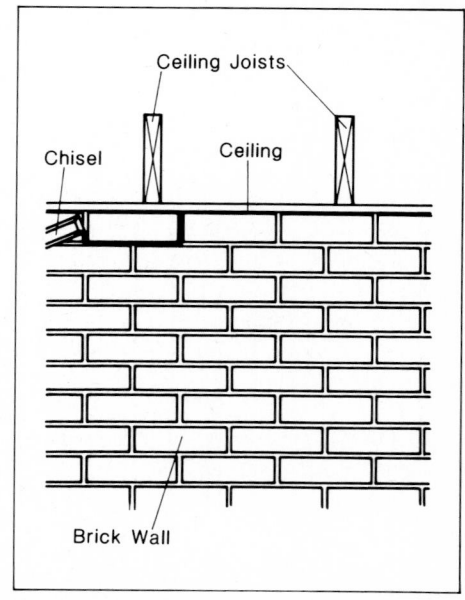

Ceiling Joists

Chisel

Ceiling

Brick Wall

To remove a masonry wall, chisel mortar from a unit at the top of the wall and work down.

hardest to remove. Once you have removed one, there will be more room to chip the mortar from the remaining units. Then remove the rest of the bricks or blocks in that row and work across the succeeding courses in the same fashion until you have removed the entire wall.

Safety Precautions

Since this is dusty work, you should wear a breathing mask. Cover or remove all furniture in the room. ALWAYS wear goggles to protect your eyes. Even experienced workers have lost an eye performing just such a job.

Never try to remove a first-floor brick wall if a section of the wall continuing on the second floor is to remain. Although it is possible to provide proper temporary and permanent support for such a wall, usually the cost will be prohibitive. It is

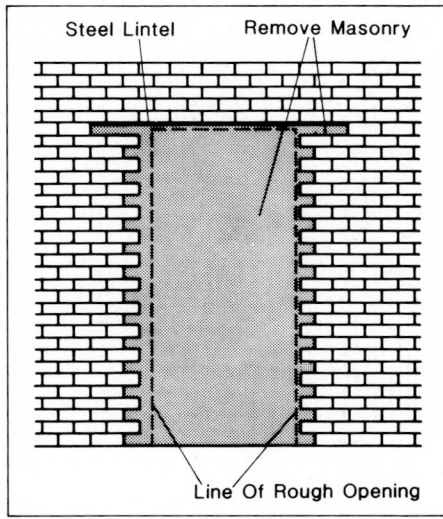

To create a door, work from the top of the opening. Install a steel lintel to support brick.

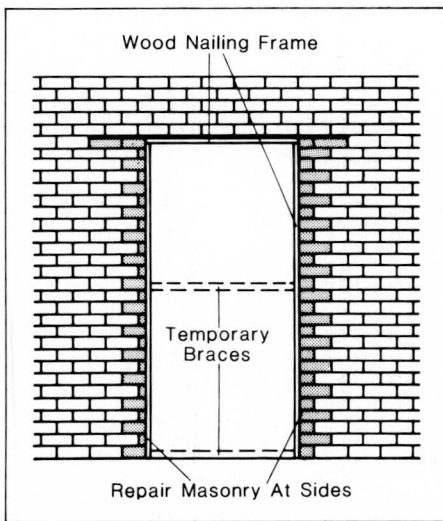

Repair masonry and frame in rough opening. Use temporary braces until new masonry is set.

more reasonable to design around the situation. If you remove a portion of a brick wall for a door or passageway, install a steel lintel in the wall by mortaring it above the opening before you begin removing the brick completely.

Frame Walls

Normally, a stud-framed wall will be much easier to remove than a masonry wall. The degree of difficulty in removing the wall will vary depending upon the surface material.

Plaster or plasterboard walls. Whether plaster or gypsumboard, the surface must be removed from the wall. Use a hammer to do this. Work carefully at the wall corners, near the edges of the wall surface that will remain, in order to keep later patch work at a minimum. Never bang away with a sledge hammer. This could cause structural damage to framing in floors and ceilings and adjacent walls.

Cutting a doorway opening. If you are removing only a portion of a wall, such as for a door, measure and mark the area to be removed. Gently pry off the baseboard. Remove the wall surface so that each side aligns with the middle of a stud. To remove gypsumboard, cut along marked lines with a utility knife and straightedge. Then remove the inside material. For plaster, determine the thickness of the plaster and set a circular saw equipped with a masonry blade at that

depth to cut through the plaster. You may also use a hammer and chisel. When removing plaster, especially if it is old, work carefully to avoid cracking areas that are not to be removed. Once the plaster has been removed pry off the wood lath with a hammer.

Creating a mid-height wall. If you want to remove the top half of a wall, first mark and cut the surface material. Cut through studs with a reciprocating saw or crosscut saw. Cap studs with a 2x4 (or whatever lumber is needed) to serve as a nailing surface for wallboard. Disconnect the studs where they meet the top plate (as given below).

Paneled walls. If the walls are paneled, work carefully and try to remove the panels intact. If they are older, solid wood panels, they can be refinished (removing paint if necessary) and reused or sold.

Remove any trim or molding. To avoid damaging the paneling, place a thin piece of plywood between your hammer or crowbar and the paneled wall to pry off the trim. To remove the paneling, pry a little at a time all along one edge. Do not try to pry one nail up completely before moving to the next. Work on each nail a little at a time until you have freed an edge. Then work on the next set of nails. You may need a long crowbar to reach the middle portion of a wide panel.

Removing wall framing. The stud wall can easily be disassembled and taken

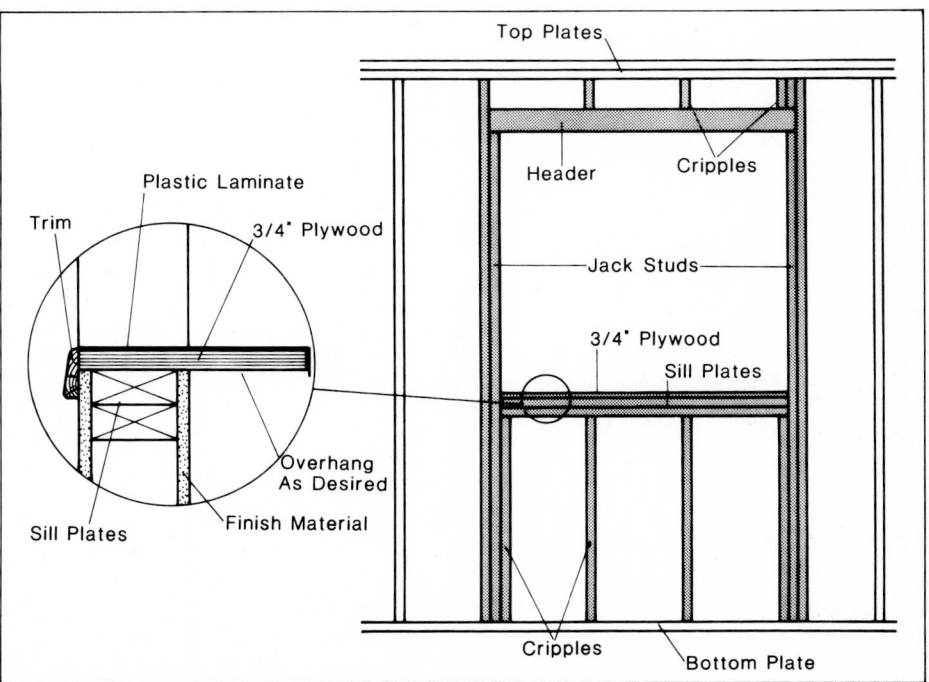

An opening for a pass-through is framed exactly like a window. An overhanging shelf may be added and the walls finished to match the walls of the adjoining rooms.

down once the surface material is removed. There is a special tool, a nail claw, designed to lift out large nails without severely damaging the framing lumber. Get one to save time and effort. If you cannot find one, use two regular hammers as shown in the photograph. Sharpen the claws of the hammer from time to time with a file to keep an edge that will slip under the nail head.

Remove the framing one piece at a time, beginning with the studs. Pull the toe nails out at the top and bottom and ''wiggle'' the stud out from the remaining framing. Do not hit the stud hard; this could cause damage. If the stud does not come out easily, tap it lightly with a hammer, alternately at the top and bottom. Do not strike the stud in the middle. Continue until all the studs are removed. Be careful, however, because when the studs are out, the top plates might fall down. To prevent this, leave a stud at each end to support the top plate, which should not have been nailed to the ceiling joists. Pull any nails out of the top plates and remove it. Then take out the two end studs. Finally, remove the nails or pins holding the bottom plate down and lift it out of place.

You may be able to reuse the wood. Some older homes were framed with hardwood, and you should be able to find a market for this valuable material if you do not do any fine woodworking yourself.

ADDING NEW WALLS

Adding a simple partition to a home is not difficult and can be handled easily by the do-it-yourselfer. There are some drawbacks, however, to adding partitions. Each new wall creates new corners. Corners restrict traffic flow, furniture arrangement, usable space, and visibility. Indiscriminate addition of new walls can make a home boxy and cramped.

Suggested Wall Placements

There are times, of course, when a new wall is needed. For instance, consider an older home with a large 16-foot x 20-foot country kitchen. If you need the existing dining room as a study/studio but still require a formal dining room for entertaining, the old kitchen could be divided to provide an 11-foot x 16-foot kitchen, a 9-foot x 13-foot dining room, and a hallway as shown. The resulting kitchen can be more efficient and more attractive.

Sometimes it will be necessary to subdivide three rooms into two larger rooms. In this case, two walls will be removed and a new one added. Whatever the arrangement you choose, be sure your reason for adding a new wall is a good one.

Creating a New Space

To discuss building a new wall, we will use the example kitchen above. This project will cover all the factors you will need to know. The information can be adapted to build one straight wall or a more complicated job of building several new walls.

Preparing the room. Unless the floor has a very hard covering, remove the existing flooring material. If it is carpet or cushioned vinyl, it may be re-used in another area or discarded depending on your plans. A hard floor, such as wood or vinyl asbestos, can be left in place. If you have an older home with linoleum floors, plan to work over it instead of trying to remove it. True linoleum was put down in several layers and is very difficult to get up. Once the walls are in place, a smooth underlayment can be put over the linoleum as a base for the new finish flooring material.

Measuring the spaces. Locate the position of one new wall by measuring from an existing, parallel wall. Measure and mark two or more points for the new wall and snap a chalkline between the marks. Measure out 3½ inches from the chalkline (the width of a 2x4) and mark another line. Repeat the process for the other new wall. Then, at the ''T'' intersections, where the new walls meet the existing walls, pinpoint locations of the existing studs. You will have to take out any existing stud that is within 1½ inches on either side of the lines marking the position of the new wall. Protective eye wear should be used whenever sawing or nailing.

Snap chalkline to locate your wall. Remeasure. It is easier to move a mark than a wall.

Sharpened, claws on lower hammer dig into wood and slide under the nailhead to pry it up.

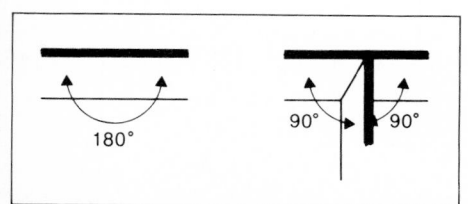

Be sure your new walls are carefully placed and built absolutely square with good corners.

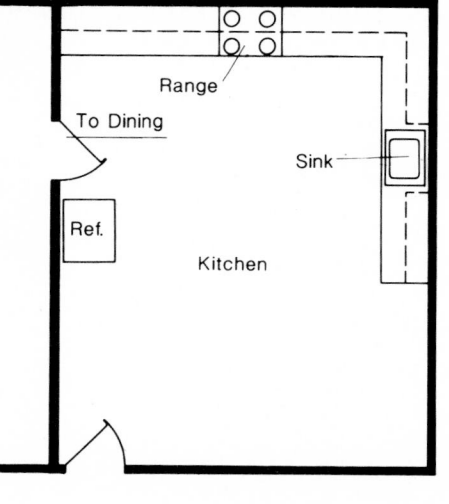

Before

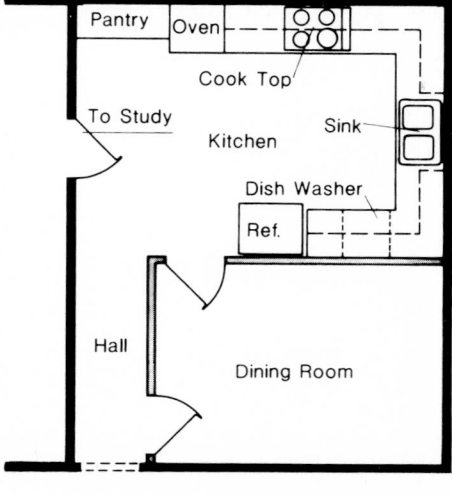

After

A more efficient kitchen and an entirely new dining room were created from this kitchen space by adding two walls and revising the layout of the kitchen.

Removing wall surface. In all cases, remove the existing wall surface back to the center of the stud nearest to each side of the new wall. Remove the surface from floor to ceiling. Use a utility knife and a straightedge to cut through gypsumboard. To remove plaster, follow directions given previously. You may also remove plaster with a hammer and chisel, but be careful not to crack the plaster beyond the area you intend to remove. For paneling, carefully remove the sheet or planks where the new wall intersects. The paneling can be cut and reused.

Constructing new framing. Cut to size and nail 2x4 bottom plates into the floor between the chalklines. Use 12d common nails to attach the bottom plate to a wood-framed foundation and concrete nails if you have a slab foundation. Toenail the new bottom plate to the existing bottom plate at wall intersections. Toenail the two bottom plates together where the new wall makes an "L".

Construct a "T" for each intersection with an existing wall and an "L" for each new wall corner. Note that the part of the "T" that goes into the new wall is 1½

inches longer than the part that goes into the existing wall. This is because a single top plate will suffice for the new partition, whereas the existing wall will normally have two. If your house is older it may be framed with lumber that is 1¾ inches thick instead of 1½ inches. If this is the case, the stud in the "T" that goes into the new wall should be 2 inches longer to allow for the difference between the doubled original plate (3½ inches total thickness) and the 1½ inch thickness of the new wall top plate.

Toenail the completed "T's" and

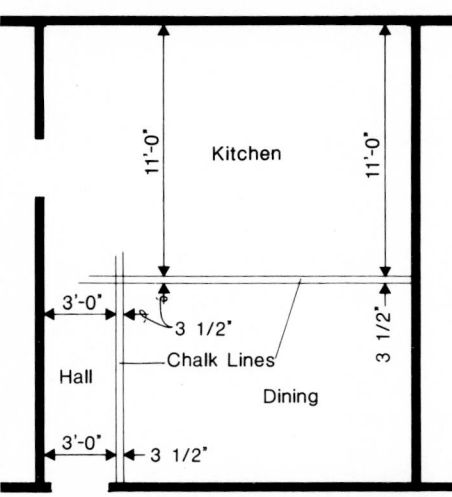

Chalklines mark locations of bottom plates. Marks are spaced to the width of the lumber.

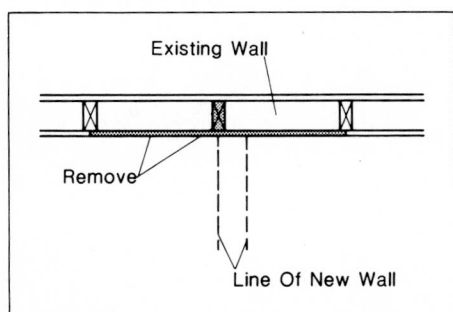

Remove wall surface to the center of studs on either side of joint of new wall and old.

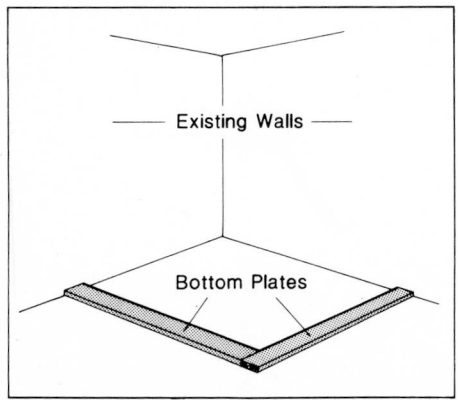

Set bottom plates in position, check location and measurements before nailing to the floor.

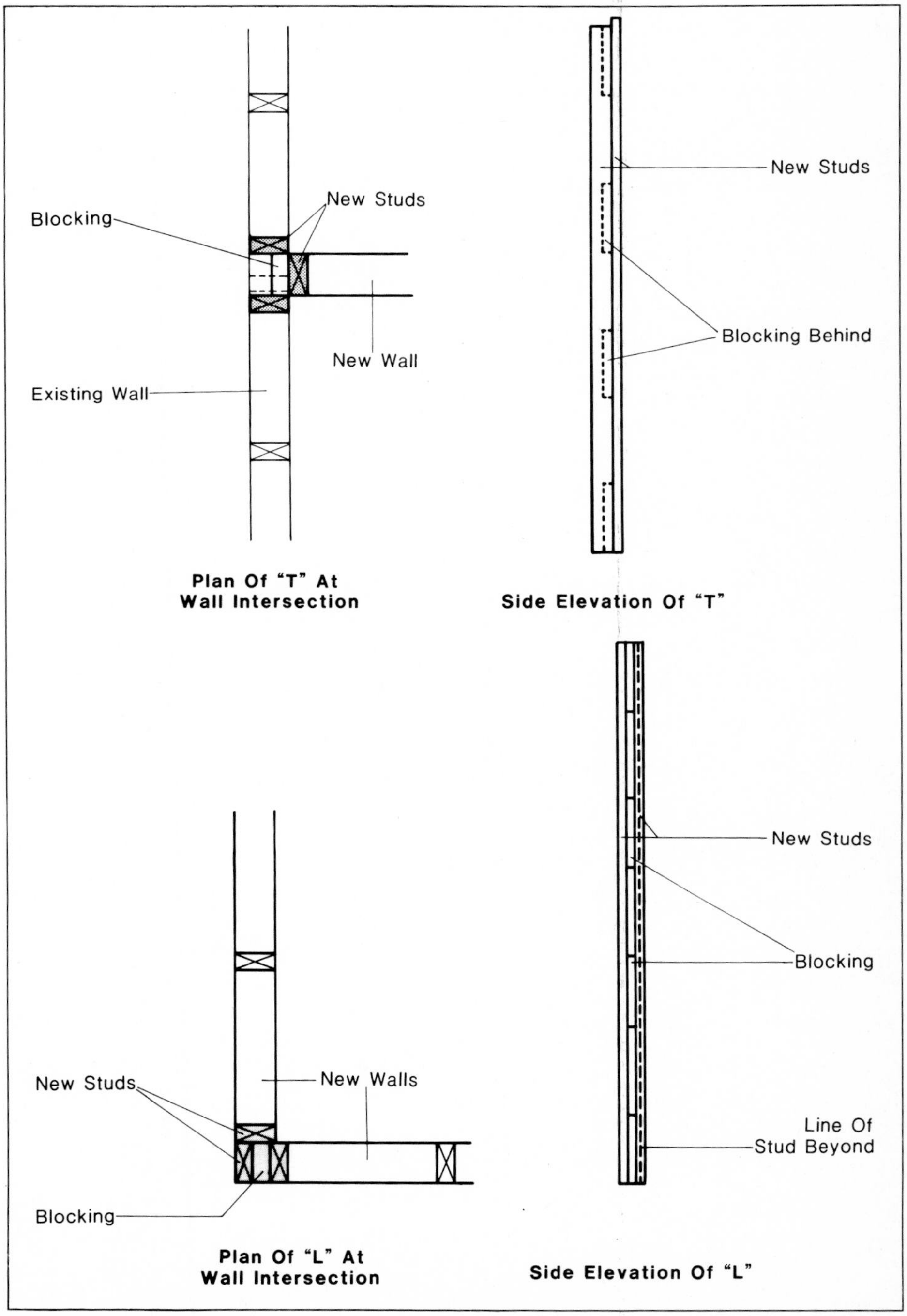

Plan Of "T" At Wall Intersection

Side Elevation Of "T"

Plan Of "L" At Wall Intersection

Side Elevation Of "L"

Intersection with an existing wall uses a T that joins the new wall with the old. An L is required at corners of new walls to give stability to the corner.

"L's" into place with 10d common nails, level, and brace temporarily as shown. Cut and place the top plates. One wall will be perpendicular to the ceiling joists, for which the top plate can be nailed directly up into each joist. The other wall will be parallel to the joists, requiring that blocking be placed in the attic between the two joists so the top plate can be nailed into the blocking. Toenail the top plates securely to the "T" and "L" pieces.

Starting from the "T" intersection, measure 16 inches along the bottom and top plates. Use a carpenter's square to draw a line perpendicular to the length of the plate. Mark an "X" on the side of the line nearest the existing wall. Continue to mark every 16 inches, using the square as a guide, until you reach the "L". Then locate any doors in the new walls and mark them on the bottom plate.

Cut the studs to size and secure them by toenailing top and bottom, leaving an open space for the door. Usually, precut studs will not fit in such remodeling jobs because you are using only one top plate or because your ceiling may not be standard height. Each 2x4 stud will have to be cut to size.

Framing door openings. The chart below gives sizes for rough openings of various door sizes. Determine the door size you are using; place a stud between the top and bottom plates on each side of the door, creating an opening three inches wider than the rough opening. Saw through and remove the bottom plate between these studs. Cut two 2x4 jack studs as long as the rough opening for the height of the door including the thickness of the bottom plate you just removed. Nail these into place against the previously installed new studs. Cut and nail into place the 2x4 double header and complete the door framing by adding the short pieces (cripples) from the headers to the top plate.

DIMENSIONS FOR NEW DOORS

Door size*	Width of rough opening	Height of rough opening
2068	2'3½"	6'11½"
2468	2'7½"	6'11½"
2668	2'9½"	6'11½"
2868	2'11½"	6'11½"
3068	3'3½"	6'11½"

*These numbers represent the width and height of the door. For instance, a 2668 door is 2 feet 6 inches wide and 6 feet 8 inches high. (A standard residential door is 6 feet 8 inches high.)

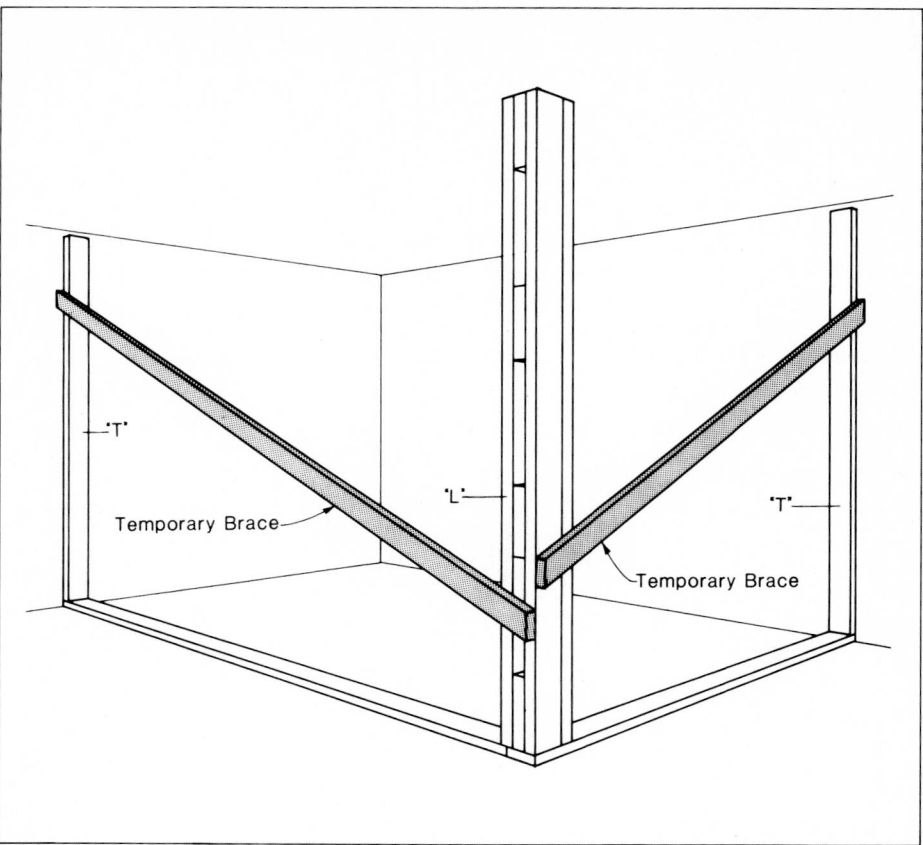

T and L sections are toenailed to the bottom plate. They do not reach the ceiling so that a top plate may be added. Temporary braces are required to hold the T and L sections vertical. Check level and plumb carefully and reset if necessary before adding the top plates.

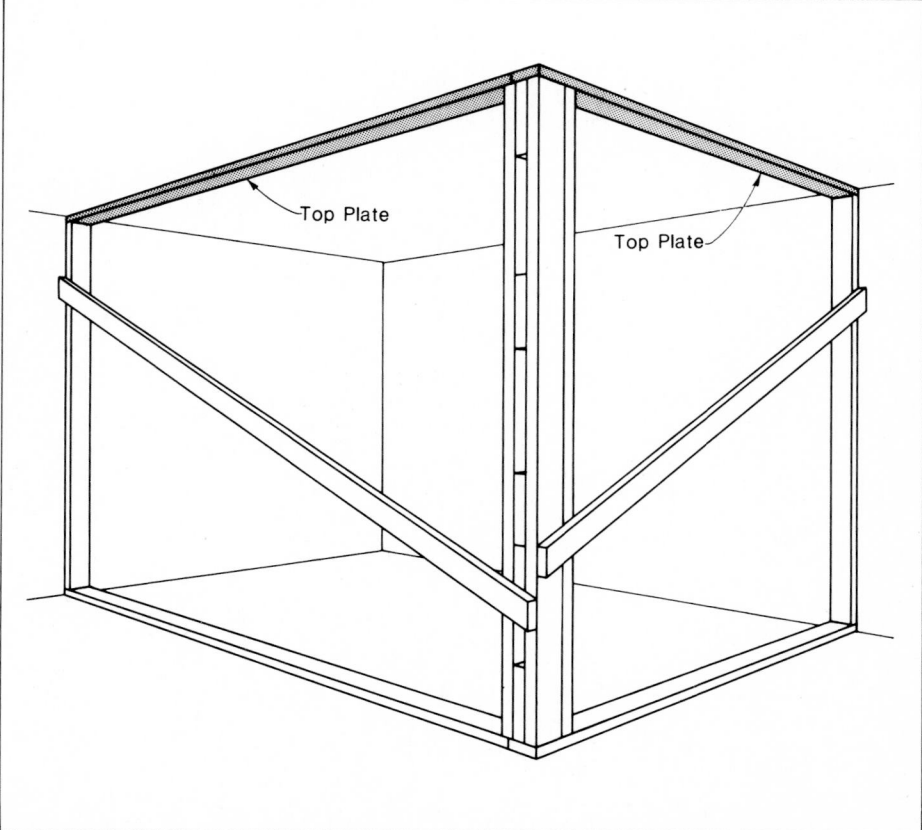

Top plates each overlap part of the L corner section. Top plates are nailed into the ceiling joists and toenailed into the T and L sections. You will have to locate ceiling joists. If the wall is not under a joist, you will have to provide a nailing surface.

Cripples are spaced to match normal stud centerings.

When the framing is complete, install any electrical or plumbing work prior to putting up the wall surface. The installation of wall surfaces and other finish materials is discussed in Chapter 6.

DOOR CHANGES
Removing a Door
First, remove the door itself from the hinges. Then pry off the trim around the door jamb and finally remove the jamb itself, including any shims used to plumb the door. Nail a 2x4 bottom plate into place, securing to the foundation and toenailing into the existing bottom plate at either end. Then add a 2x4 at the top, nailed to the header and through the adjacent studs. Next, nail in place 2x4 studs to each side and one in the center. For a very large opening you may need more than one inside 2x4. Place studs on 16 inch centers. Finish the wall by applying the wall surface as described in Chapter 6. Careful finish work must be done and a prime coat applied before covering the area. New wall paint will help avoid a "patched" look.

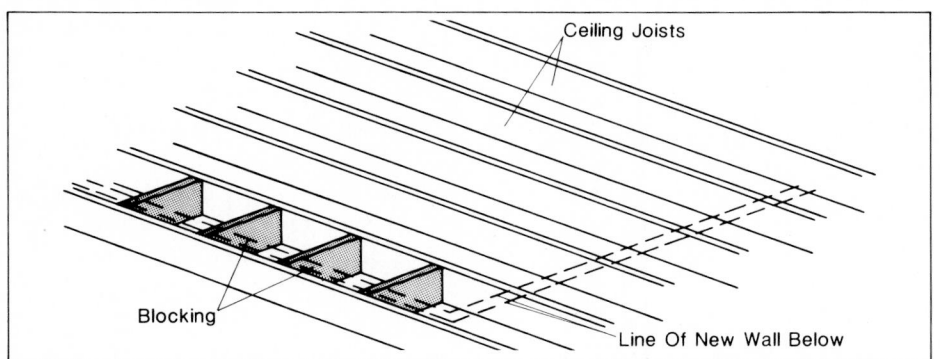

If one of the top plates is located between ceiling joists, install blocking to nail into.

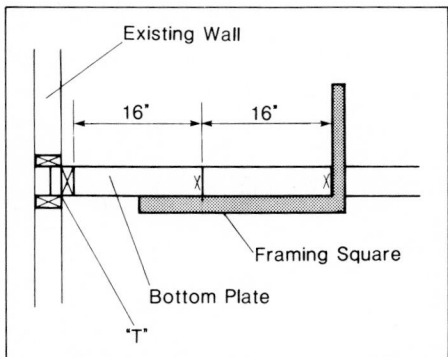

Locate studs as 16 inches on center from outside face of the T stud and mark the plate.

When location has been set, toenail studs into the plates with 10d or 12d common nails.

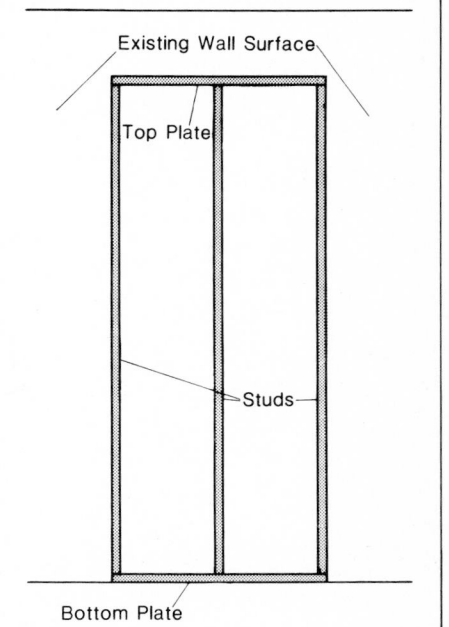

To remove a door, fill in opening with new framing, remove trim and cover with wallboard.

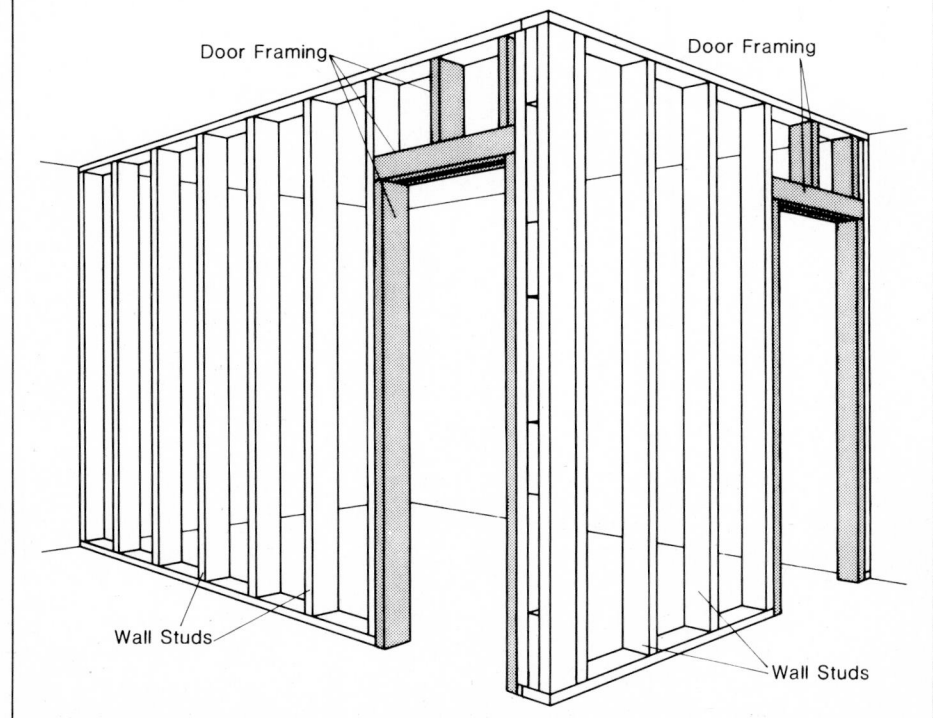

Doors are framed with doubled headers and cripple studs; section of bottom plate is sawed out.

Opening is now filled with new framing. New wall surface will be nailed to furring strips.

Here, one window has been framed shut and a door is being reframed to become a window.

Adding a Door

Remove a four-foot width of wall surface, floor to ceiling, to a stud on each side of the area where the door is to be placed. The sides of the four foot width should fall on the center of an existing stud. Remove the wall surface neatly, as previously described in this chapter. Be sure all electrical and plumbing work in the wall is disconnected before you begin working.

Remove the existing framing as required and frame the rough opening of the door as detailed above. Reroute any electrical and/or plumbing over the door or beneath the floor framing, as required. Place a sheet of gypsumboard or paneling to match the existing wall surface when refinishing the wall (see Chapter 6) at the points where the surface material was removed. You now have the whole wall including the rough opening that was created, covered by the sheets. Now punch a hole in the sheet in the approximate center of the rough opening. Use a keyhole saw. Then cut over to the side stud of the rough opening and cut out the wallboard over the opening. Finish the wall surface. Install the new door following the manufacturer's directions, using shims to assure a plumb installation.

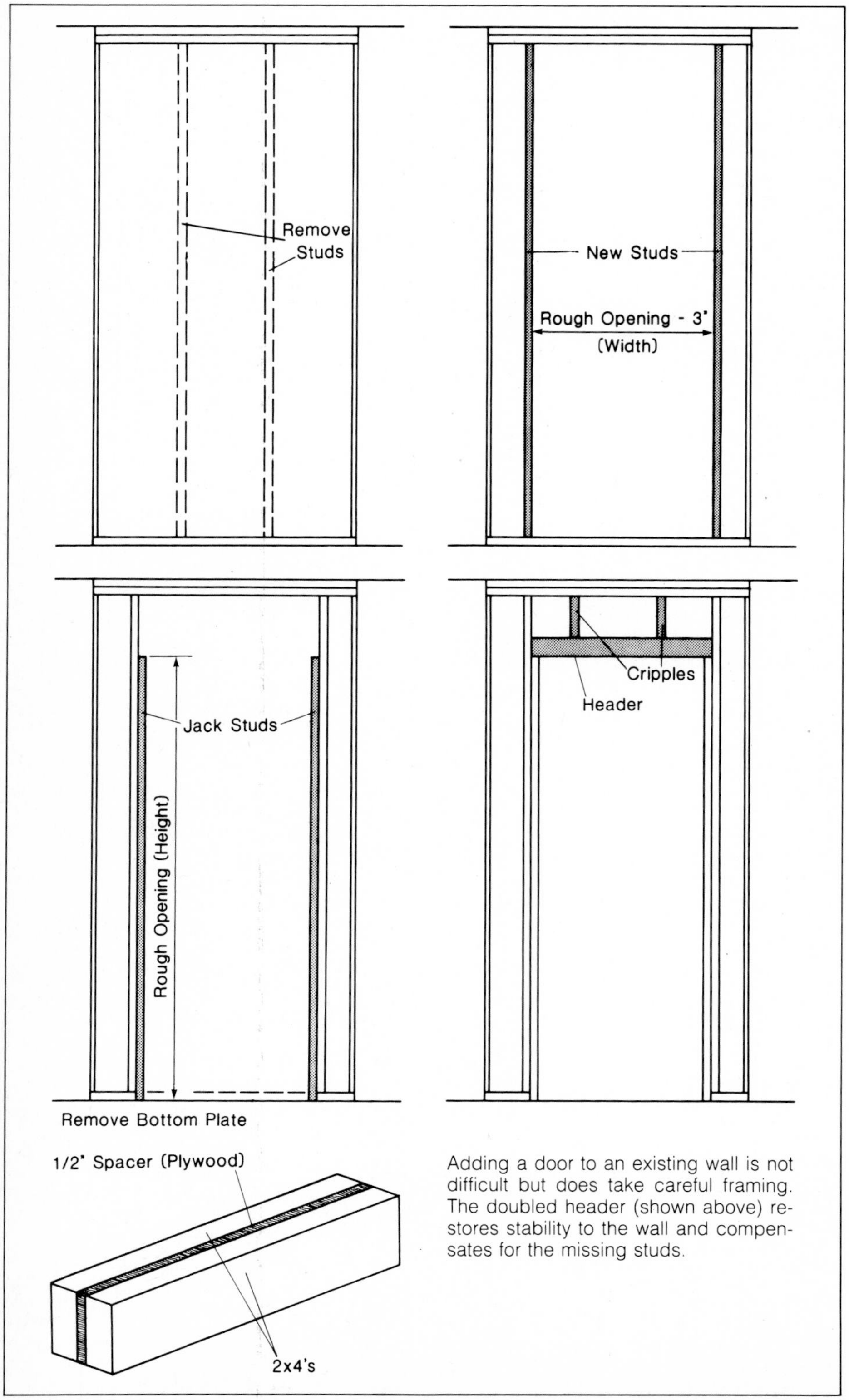

SOUND-INSULATING WALLS

Special wall construction is required to achieve highly effective sound insulation. Simply placing insulation in a standard wall usually will not be sufficient. Generally, a heavy wall transmits less sound than a thin one. A double brick wall with an air space, a sand-filled block wall, or a reinforced concrete wall is very effective against sound transmission as long as all pores are sealed with heavy paint. These walls are highly impractical as interior partitions in most homes because of cost and weight. There are, however, several

Remove Studs

New Studs

Rough Opening - 3' (Width)

Cripples

Header

Jack Studs

Rough Opening (Height)

Remove Bottom Plate

1/2" Spacer (Plywood)

2x4's

Adding a door to an existing wall is not difficult but does take careful framing. The doubled header (shown above) restores stability to the wall and compensates for the missing studs.

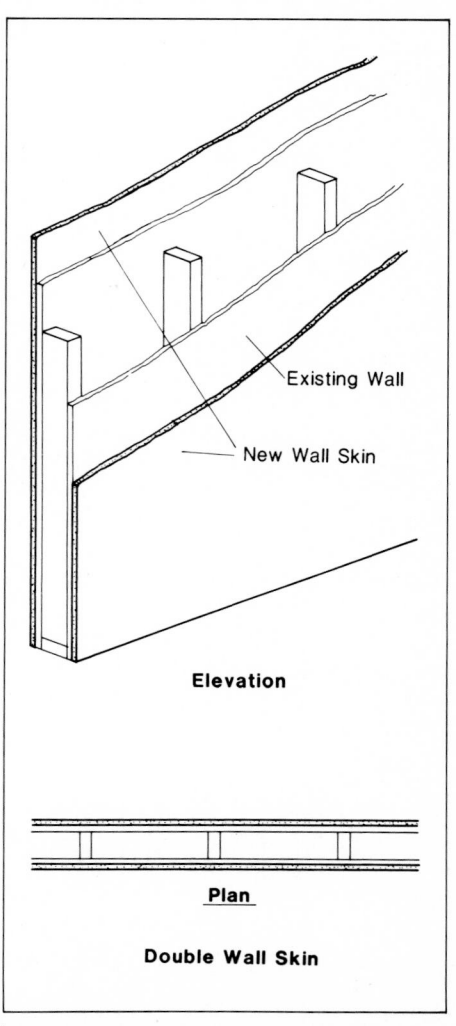

Elevation

Plan

Double Wall Skin

Simple method of sound insulating existing walls is to add another layer to each side.

methods of constructing a stud wall that will work well in providing good sound insulation.

Double Wall Skin

One of the simplest ways to provide sound insulation, though slightly less effective than a new wall, is adding a second skin to one or both wall surfaces. This is suitable for either gypsumboard or plaster construction. This method can be used on existing walls, but both layers on each side should be taped and filled to eliminate openings.

Spring-Mounted Wall Skin

One of the best methods of insulating against sound is to mount wall skins to the studs with specially designed spring clips. These clips are available in several types, and all clips absorb the vibrational energy of sound. It is easy and inexpensive to install new walls with any of the types of clips. Use a face-mounted clip on existing walls. These attach directly over the exist-

ing wall skin; you then mount the new wall skin onto the spring clips. All seams must be well sealed when using clips. Clips may be used on one or both sides of a wall. If no fasteners come with the clips, attach clips with 4d box nails.

Staggered Studs

The staggered stud wall is actually two stud walls with a single wall skin on each. Studs are staggered for a minimum separation of two inches between the walls. Al-

though effective against sound, there is a higher cost because twice as many studs are required. The staggered-stud method is used for new walls and is difficult to adapt to an existing wall.

Double Wall

A close relative of the staggered-stud wall, the double wall adds a single-face partition to increase the sound insulation effectiveness of an existing wall. New studs are installed two inches from the ex-

A sound room built into a basement space was designed to hold all equipment desired.

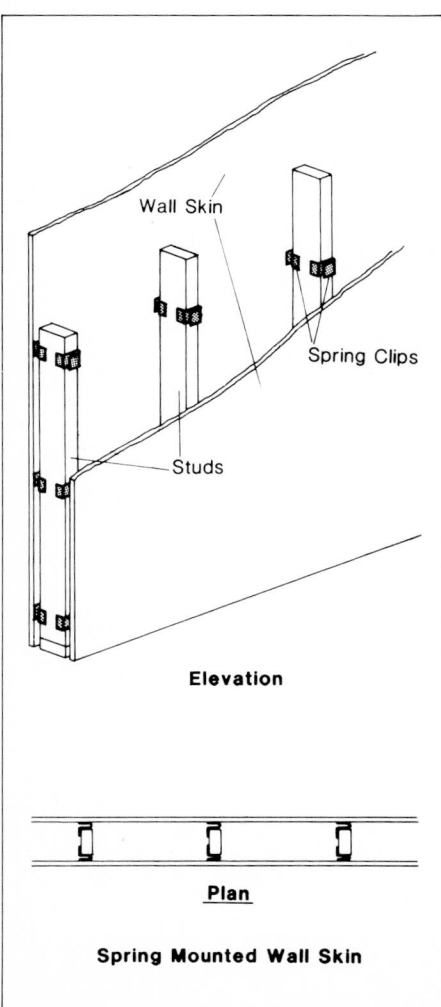

Spring Mounted Wall Skin

New stud walls can be covered with spring-mounted wallboard to absorb sound.

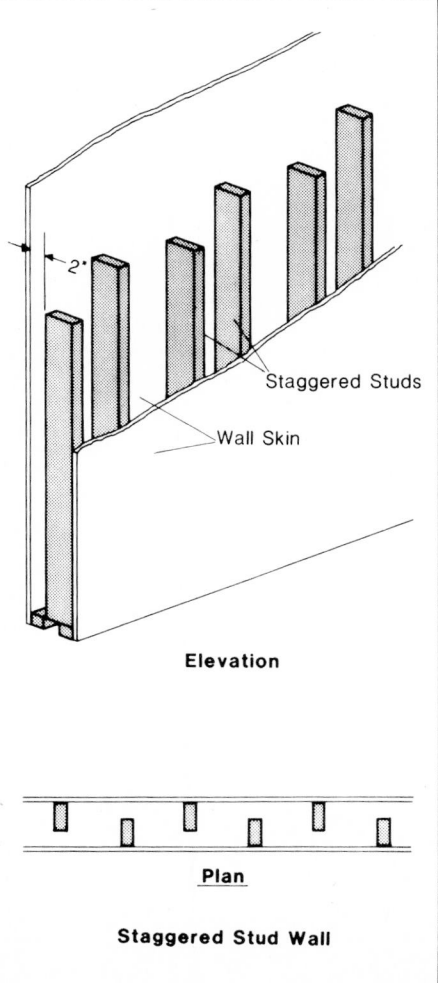

Staggered Stud Wall

Staggered studs create a thick wall. If more insulation is needed, weave it between studs.

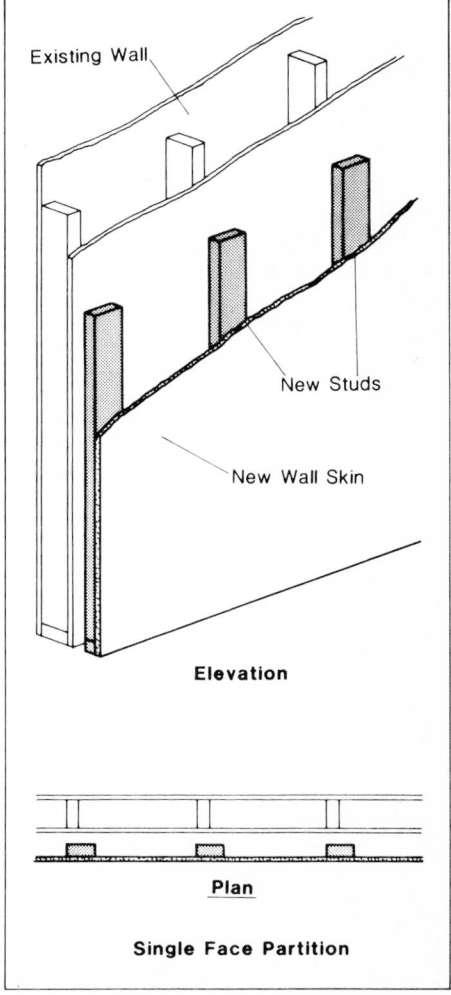

Single Face Partition

Another system requires installing a flat stud wall spaced away from original wall.

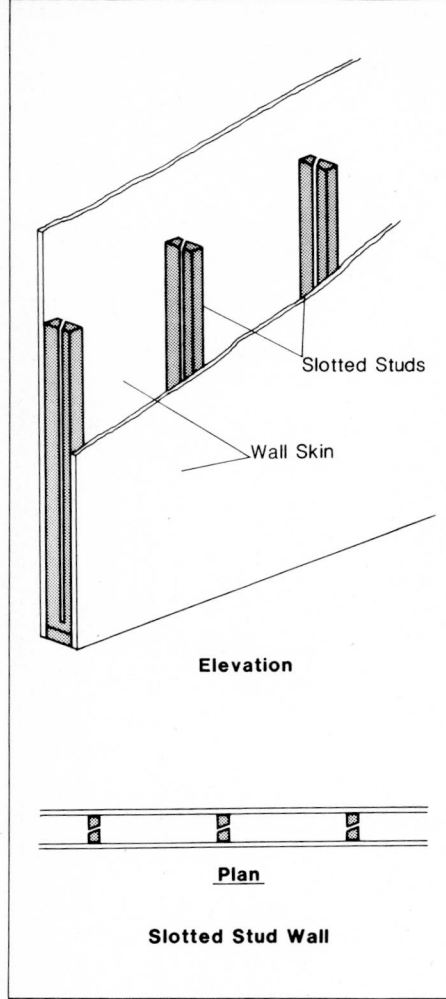

Elevation

Plan

Slotted Stud Wall

Cutting slots down the studs will also increase the sound insulating qualities.

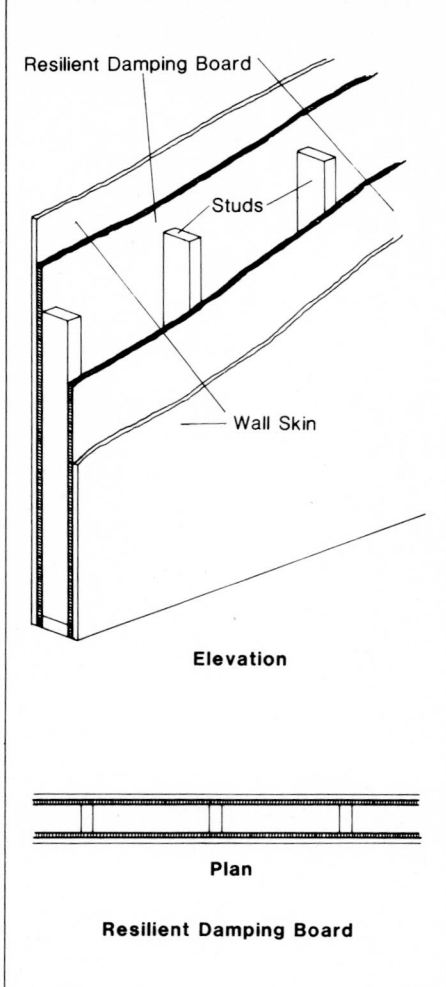

Elevation

Plan

Resilient Damping Board

Cover new walls or walls stripped to the studs with resilient damping board and wallboard.

EFFECTIVENESS OF SOUND INSULATION

Type of sound insulation*		Percent reduction in sound transmission over standard wall construction
Double wall skin	One side	9
	Two sides	15
Spring mounted wall skin	One side	18
	Two sides	30
Staggered studs		27
Double wall		30
Split or slotted studs		22
Resilient damping board		30
Sound absorbing blanket		15

*This chart shows the effectiveness of each method of sound insulation in relation to a standard stud wall. To determine the total effectiveness of a combination of methods (such as a staggered-stud wall with double-skin on one side and an acoustical-blanket included) add the largest percentage of improvement to one-half the remaining percentages.

isting wall and at right angles to existing studs. A single wall skin is then attached to the new studs. Although this is a very effective method for stopping sound transmission through an existing wall, its added width can cut down on room size perceptibly.

Building with Split or Slotted Studs

This is a sensible sound insulating wall where money and space are strong considerations. The wall studs are split at an angle with a ripsaw to within an inch of either end. This technique is used for new walls, and it would be inadvisable to attempt this in an existing wall.

Using Resilient Damping Board

This board is a product specially constructed to insulate against sound transmission. The resilient damping board goes underneath the wall skin and is highly effective if properly applied in strict accordance with the manufacturer's recommended procedures. On new walls the board may be applied directly to the studs. On existing walls it is attached to the existing wall skin. Then a new wall skin is applied.

Installing a Sound-Absorbing Blanket

A sound-absorbing blanket, like thermal insulation, can increase the effectiveness of a wall that is not rigidly constructed. A blanket can be installed in spring-mounted, staggered-stud, double-wall or slotted-stud walls. In other walls there would be little or no increased efficiency.

Sealing Openings

Any holes, cracks, or openings can drastically reduce the value of sound insulating walls. Doors in a sound-insulating wall should be either solid core or of a special acoustical style. Use sealing strips with spring-contacting metal weather stripping around all edges. Rubber gaskets are only fair; felt sealing strips are poor protection against the transmission of sound.

5
ADDING PLUMBING & WIRING/BATHROOMS

With few exceptions, the bathroom of the past was complicated and expensive to build, and unimaginative. In recent years all this has changed. Today, plumbing fixtures come in an array of colors, a variety of styles and an assortment of sizes never previously known. Fixtures and accessories, as well as pipe, are available in new materials that are less expensive, lighter, and easier to install. Instead of having to hire an expensive contractor, today's do-it-yourselfer plumber is free to create a unique design even for a small bath. He also is able, with a little instruction, to do most or all of the installation work himself.

ADDING A NEW BATH

An expanding family often needs a bathroom more than any other space. Even two people may find that a second bath will ease morning schedule conflicts. A new bathroom need not remain a dream. A second bathroom can be added at a minimum of cost and difficulty.

Locating the New Bath

Probably the most important consideration for the new bath is the location. The location not only should be convenient for use, but it also should be located so that plumbing hookups are easy and inexpensive. A new bath that is far from any existing plumbing may require considerable cutting and patching of the walls, and costly work on stack and supply pipes, especially if your home rests on a concrete slab foundation.

If the new bath is to be upstairs in a two-story home, you have a little more freedom in deciding the location. A bathroom can be placed adjacent to existing upstairs plumbing (if there is any) or directly above a room on the first floor that contains plumbing. For an attic expansion, place the new bath above existing plumbing;

there usually is no existing plumbing in the attic. The new wall that will contain the plumbing should be directly above the existing wall with plumbing.

With these location limitation factors in mind, look at the family's living pattern (see Chapter 2). Determine the preferred location for the bath from the standpoint of

An extra bathroom is usually one of the items on the list of home improvements that everyone wants. An extra bath can be installed in a very small space and add needed convenience.

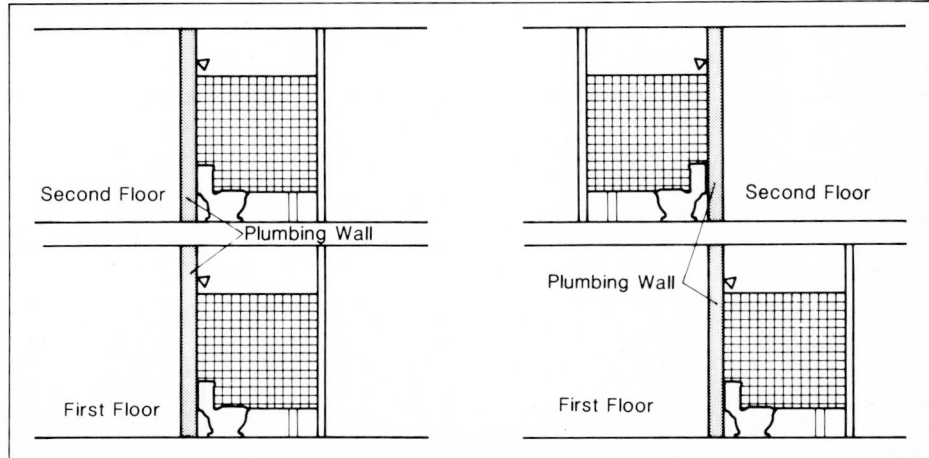

It is relatively easy to add a second floor bathroom if you place it directly over or immediately adjacent to the existing first floor bath. Either system is acceptable construction.

use; then decide where it can be installed most easily. The ease of installation is governed by nearness to existing plumbing and availability of usable space. The new bath should be adjacent to an existing bath, the kitchen, or other plumbing. It should also be located in a space that can be spared from another room or can be made available by changing other areas of the home. You may find that a good compromise is the only solution, since the ideal location does not present itself often.

Space requirements. The minimum space you will need for a full bath is 5x7 feet. You may want to make the new bath larger, or you may only want to add a powder room (½ bath), which requires less space. A full range of bath designs follows later in the chapter to help you in designing a location for and the shape of the new bath.

Basement restrictions. Exercise caution when adding a new bath beneath the main floor, such as in a basement. If you already have plumbing in the basement, place the bath adjacent to this. If there is no basement plumbing, it may be because the area is too low to drain into the sewer, which works on a gravity flow. In that case a bath can be added, but a pump will be required to drain the bath facilities into the higher sewer. There is a toilet designed for basements below the level of the main sewer line. This toilet forces wastes, under pressure, up to the drain level. The fixture uses very little water and is efficient; however, it is quite costly, several hundred dollars. Before making up your mind about basement installations, compare costs of having your sewer line changed, using a pressure lift toilet and making major changes in the lines to the first or second floors. Whether or not you are willing to go to this extra expense (plus the periodic maintenance common with such systems) depends on how much you need a bath in the basement.

Adding and Supporting Pipe

If you will be bringing supply pipes and drains into a new area, you may find that your local code requires some of the work be done by a licensed plumber. Check your codes before going very far in your plans. In any case, plumbing pipes will go into place more quickly and easily if you plan for the installation properly.

Wall space requirements. Any wall in which water supply and drain/vent pipes are to be run usually must be thicker than a standard partition wall, with 2x6 studs. This extra depth allows space for the cast-iron or plastic drain pipe, which has a 3-inch diameter. It also provides ample room for support blocking for the pipe and for air chambers to prevent water hammer problems.

Pipe support. Any time a pipe must change direction or travel a long horizontal distance, it must be supported. Long runs may be held with wood blocking, 2x4s nailed to studs or joists, or metal straps.

Support at a turn should be placed before the rise so the pipe can move along the horizontal run as it expands and contracts with temperature changes.

Cuts in studs or joists. If you must cut notches in studs or joists to allow a new run of pipe to pass through a wall or floor, the notches must be covered with metal plates attached to the studs or joists with wood screws.

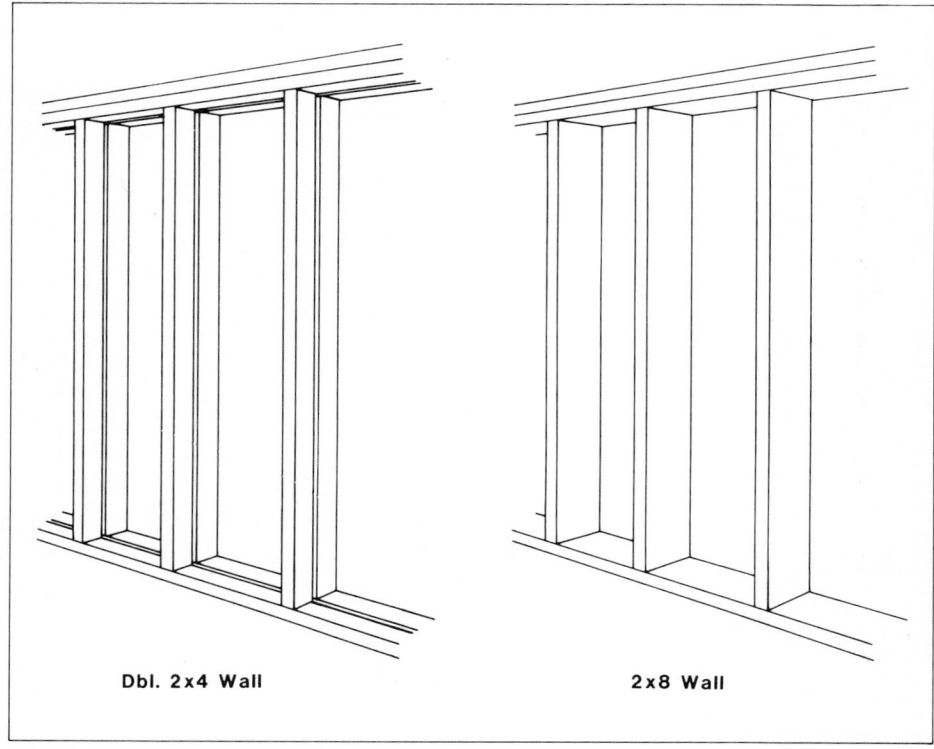

Dbl. 2x4 Wall   **2x8 Wall**

The wall that contains the plumbing must be more spacious than a regular stud wall. Use 2x8s or doubled 2x4 studs to provide needed thickness for the plumbing pipes.

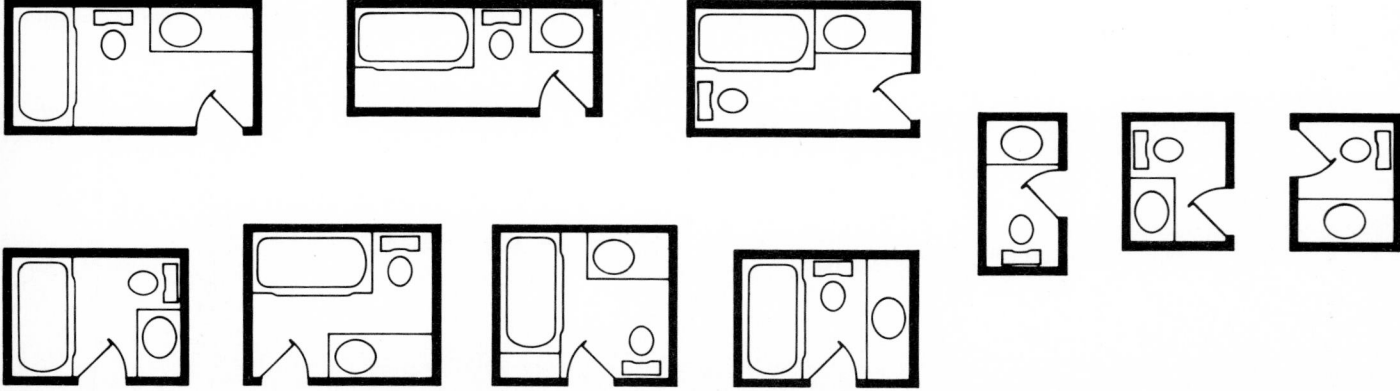

Bathroom or powder room fixtures may be arranged in a variety of ways. Fixtures come in several sizes to fit available space.

DWV pipe problems. Drain/Waste/Vent pipe usually requires considerable support. The base of the closet bend and the drain from the toilet to the main drain, always need blocking support to keep the line from shifting. The connection between the toilet and the drain is sealed only by a wax or putty ring. If the closet bend is not well supported, it could pull away and break the putty seal. This would create a monstrous leak and a monumental inconvenience.

Planning the Pipe Route

While hot and cold water supply lines may be run through almost any wall, soil pipe — usually cast iron or copper — is three, four or more inches in diameter. It is more difficult to install this pipe and it will not fit into an ordinary stud wall.

Whenever you add or reroute pipe for an efficient path to where you plan to put in new fixtures, draw up a plan and check the space in the walls before you begin disassembling or installing the pipe. Draw the plan to scale, either ¼ or ½ inch equal to one foot, on graph paper. Indicate the existing supply lines; make several copies of this drawing. Now draw in alternative routings, rearrangements, and branchings. Preplanning means that you will get through the project without finding your measurements do not allow for the existing pipe, or the space needed for air chambers. Keep new hot and cold water supply pipes at least 6 inches apart.

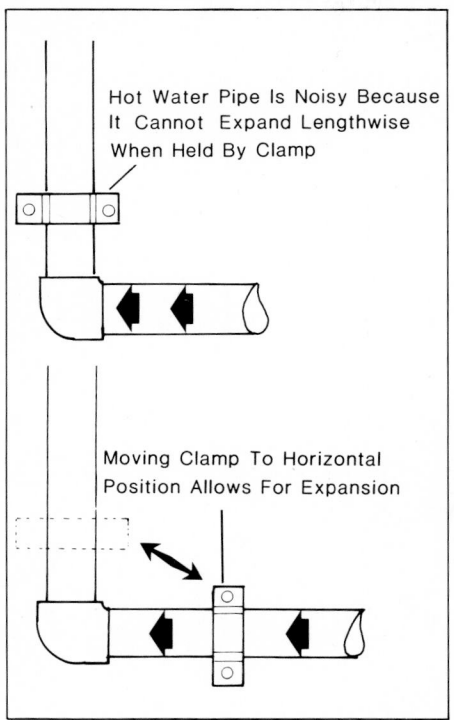

Hot water pipe supports should be located so pipe can move as it expands.

Wherever possible at least two fixtures should be placed against the same wall to make pipe and drain line installation as short and simple as possible to save time and money.

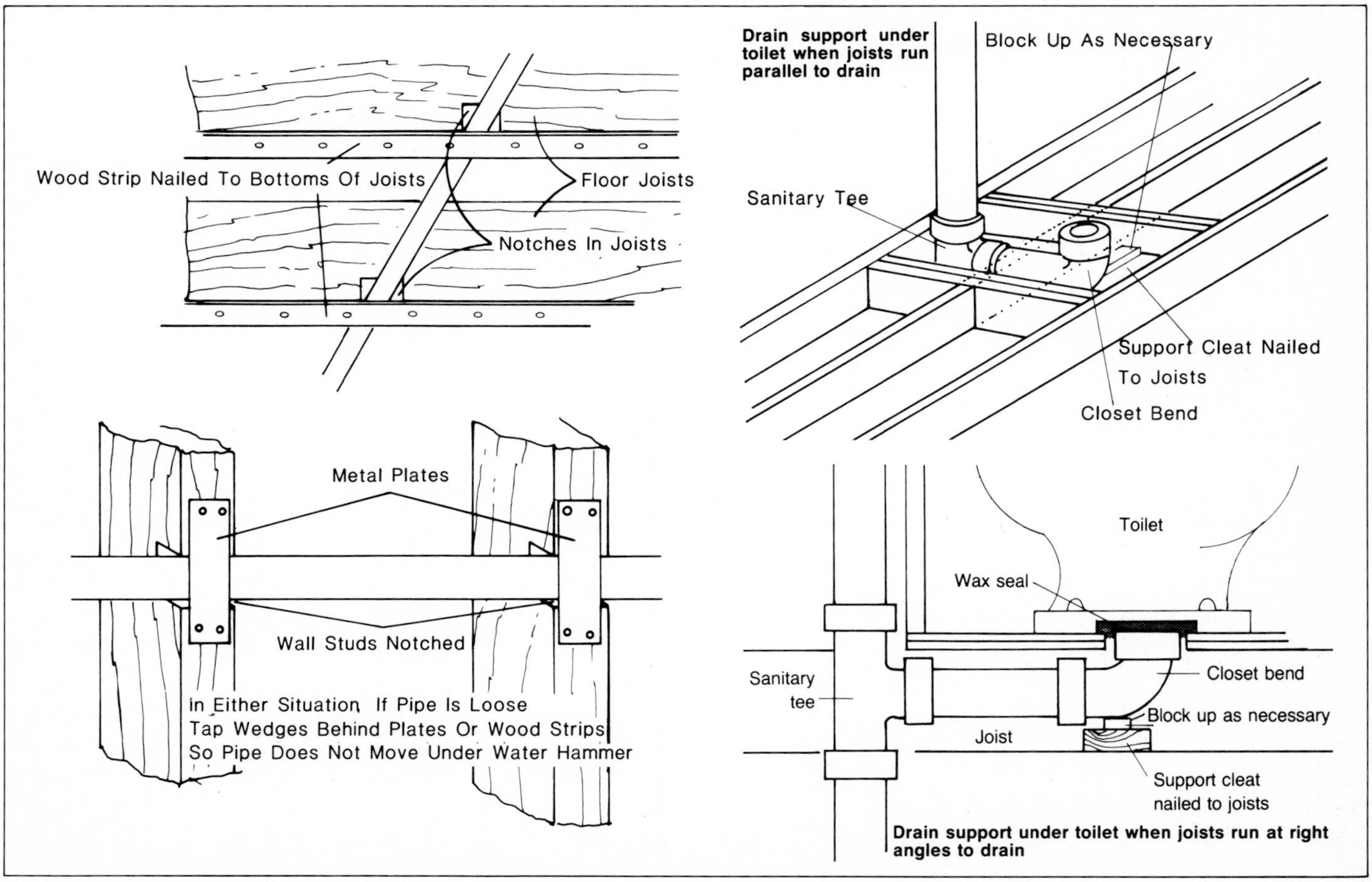

All supply pipes and drains must have adequate support to prevent leaks that can occur if pipes shift when water passes through pipe run.

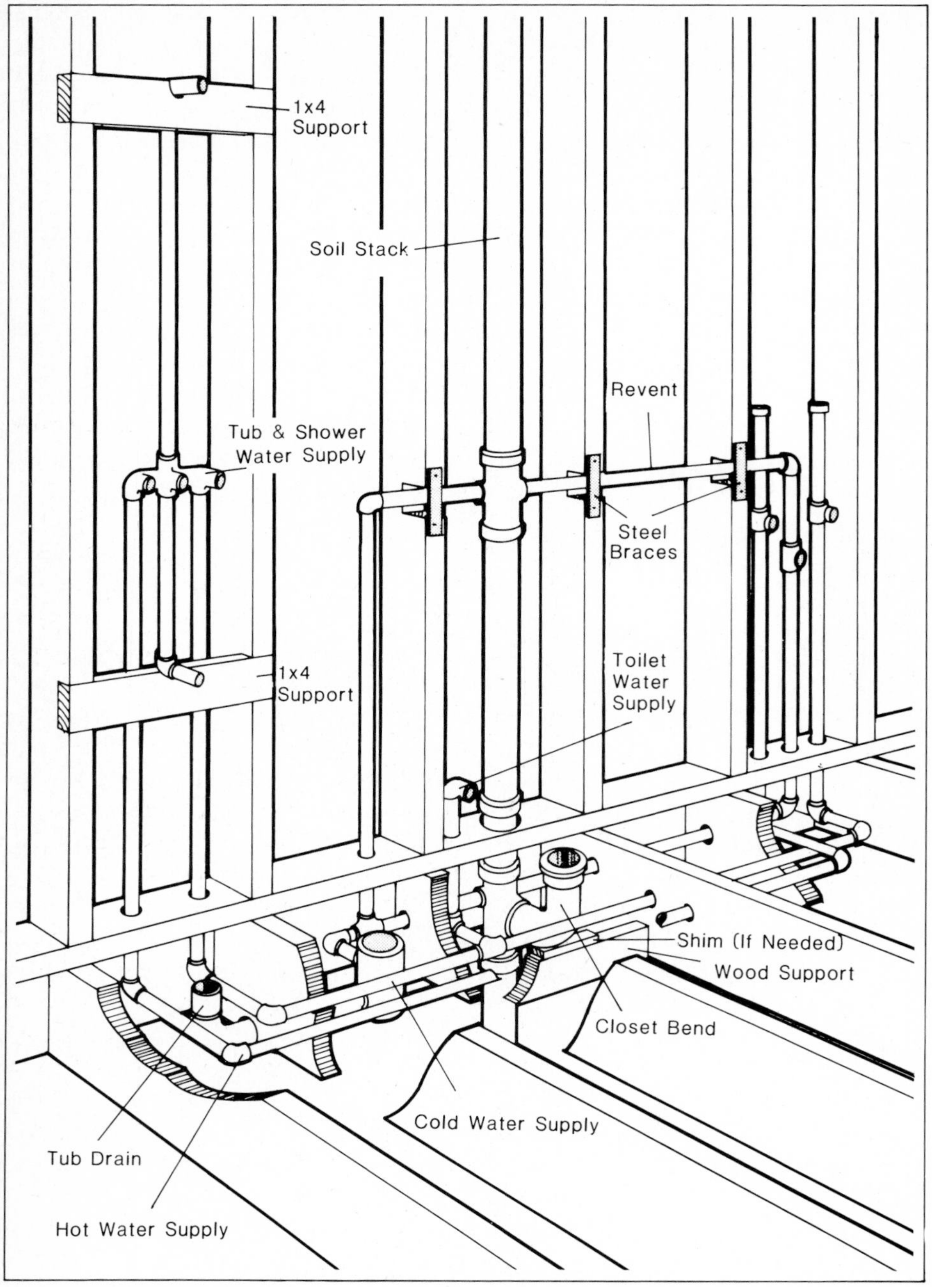

Soil Stack

1x4 Support

Tub & Shower Water Supply

1x4 Support

Revent

Steel Braces

Toilet Water Supply

Tub Drain

Hot Water Supply

Shim (If Needed)

Wood Support

Closet Bend

Cold Water Supply

While a bathtub is an awkward fixture and difficult to relocate, the pipes are easier to move than those for the toilet because of the size of and the support needed for the toilet drain.

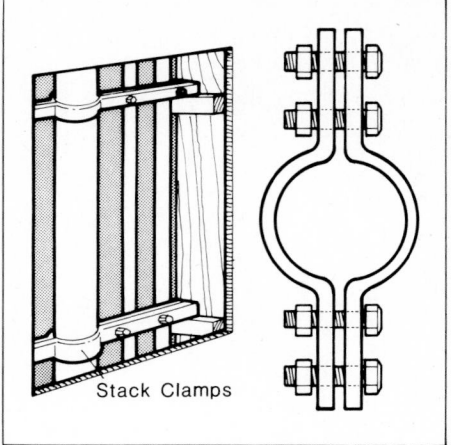

Stack Clamps

The soil stack is usually made of cast iron. Stack clamps are needed to provide proper support.

When the plumbing is exposed, you can start to make the new connections.

Making Connections to the Stack

Purchase two "stack clamps." Stack clamps are perforated steel straps bolted together at the ends. Nail 2x2 or 2x4 blocks to the studs for stack clamp support. In addition, you will need rubber sleeves and 4 regular (not "stack") clamps. These clamps are used to hold the heavy cast iron (or copper) main drain line in position. If you do not clamp the stack, it can settle and tear the flashing on the roof and cause a leak.

Rent a cutter for cast-iron drain pipe; for copper or plastic stack pipes, use a hacksaw. The fitting will be a hubless Tee or Tee-Y that joins to the stack with rubber collars and stainless steel clamps. A Tee has a right angle projection; the Tee-Y has the projection at an angle. The Tee-Y allows a smoother flow of liquid. If you install fixtures back-to-back, you want to use a cross.

Installing the Fitting

Nail in the support cleats; make sure they are level. Nail the stack clamps to the cleats so that one will be above and the other below the cutting lines. Mark the location for the fitting onto the stack.

Turn off the water supply before cutting the pipe. Cut along the marked lines. Slip the rubber sleeves over the cut ends, positioning them just above and below the pipe opening. Insert the Tee or Tee-Y fittings. Slide the rubber sleeves so that both joints are covered by the sleeves. Place two metal clamps over each sleeve and tighten.

To install a cross where there was a Tee-Y, disconnect the old fitting, then

The main drain runs directly from the bathroom wall to the basement. The vent goes through the roof. A Tee runs below the floor to connect the toilet to the drain. The vanity and tub drains connect to the main drain. Vents for all lines join the main vents which is the extension of the drain. Adding a toilet fixture will require a new connection to the main drain and will be 3 or 4 inches in diameter. If you move the toilet, the old main drain will have to be extended to the new fixture. Drains from the bathtub and vanity basin can be connected to the new main drain below the toilet, rather than running connections back to the original drain.

EXTENDING THE EXISTING PIPES
Finding Existing Pipes

Look for a projecting vent on your roof. This establishes the location of the vertical drain-vent stack, the largest pipe in your house. It is 4 inches or larger and is usually cast iron. The run is nearly vertical. Use this as a starting point to find other pipes and fixtures.

Although hot and cold supply lines usually run near the drain stack, they may jog in surprising directions. You may have to drill test holes to determine the exact locations of the pipes. When you have found the pipes, you may use a keyhole saw or heavy utility knife to cut an opening.

make the cuts 3 inches above and 3 inches below the location of the old Tee-Y. Slide the sleeve collars and clamps for the connection onto the cut ends, insert the fitting and clamp in place. Leave the support clamps in place. The fitting should be angled at about 45 degrees so that the pipe from the fitting is close to the wall.

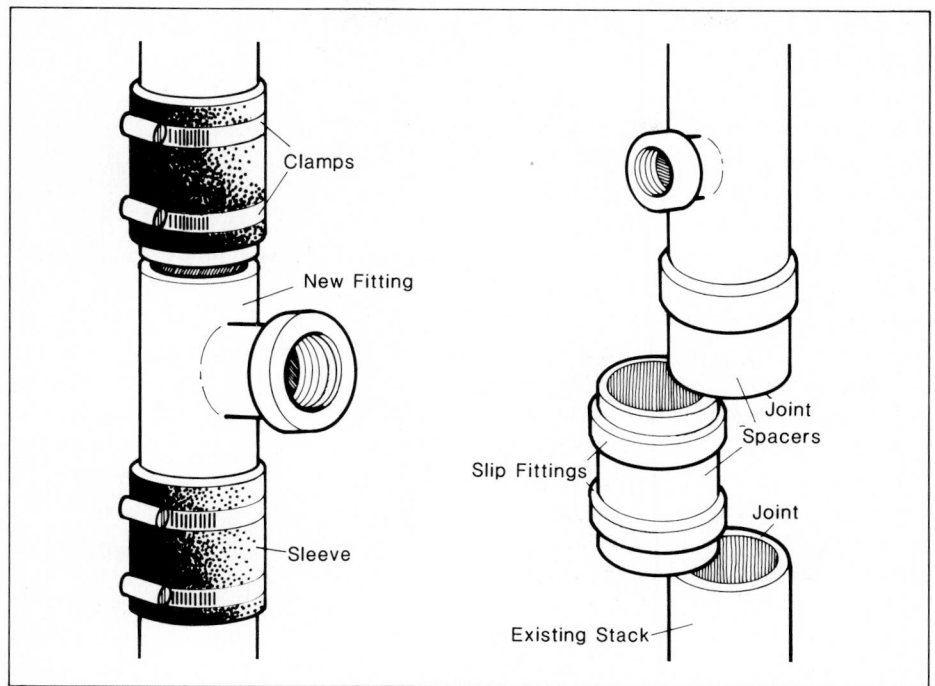

You may add a connection to an existing stack by cutting out a section and inserting a Tee or Tee-Y section and sealing the joints with rubber sleeves and clamps.

Cutting the Copper or Plastic Pipes

For a copper or plastic stack, the lower cut is usually 8 inches below the inlet center of the pipe.

Venting and reventing. The new toilet drain will have to be vented through the roof. Drains from the tub and vanity require "reventing," attaching to drain vent with smaller pipe. Venting and reventing allow atmospheric pressure to enter the drain and prevent a partial vacuum that could cause slow drainage, or cause a backup of one drain into another. Vents and revents are required by all building codes for sanitary reasons. Do not make a drain installation without proper venting and reventing.

Connections to Hot and Cold Water Pipes

The water must be shut off before you start. If you must cut the pipes, drain water from the pipes before making a cut.

Adding Tee fittings. First, turn off the water supply. The connections for new hot and cold water pipe are made with Tee fittings. If the lines are copper, sweat-solder the Tees into the lines after cutting out an

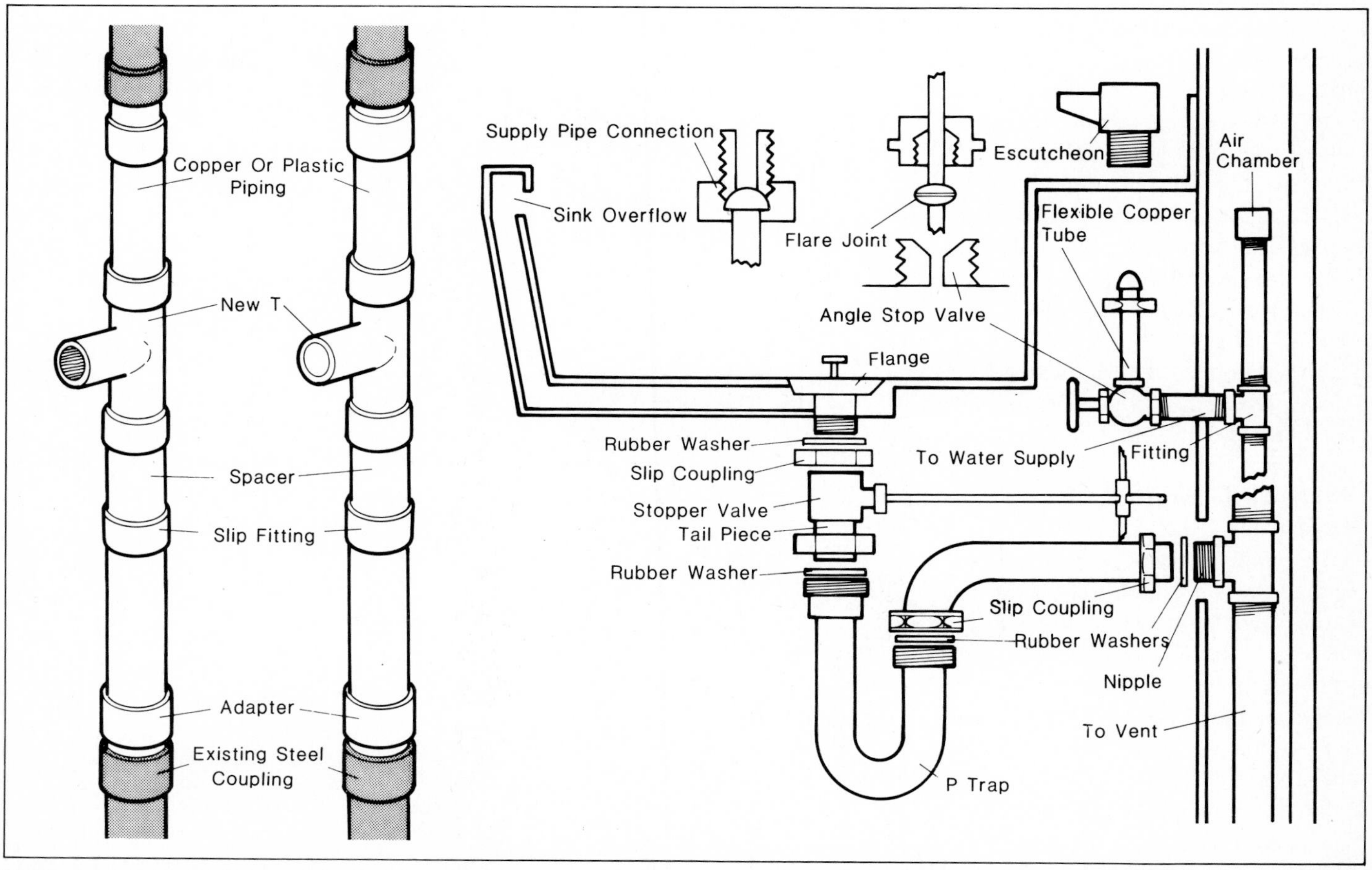

There are several possible ways to make new connections to existing plumbing. Some pipe is compatible with others; some pipe is not. Learn about the pipe before purchasing any supply or drain pipe for additional plumbing for a new bath or powder room. Be sure to allow for installation of air chambers at the top of each run of supply pipe to prevent water hammer damage to pipes.

8-inch section. Spring the lines to one side while you insert the fittings. A more practical method is to use polybutylene fittings with compression nuts at each end. Seal the fitting onto the upper riser first. These fittings will seal on copper, plastic or steel pipe. Snug up the compression nuts at each end of the fitting with a wrench. Do not overtighten. Leave the wall open for a couple days. When there is pressure in the supply lines, you can see any minor leaks. A slight, gentle snugging up on the nuts each day will stop any leaks.

You can use various adapters with the compression Tees to connect to rigid copper tubing, more practical than flexible polybutylene pipe. You also can joint Tees to rigid PVC or a PVC rigid pipe where the connections are solvent-welded.

Existing steel or brass hot and cold water pipes. Turn off the water supply. Cut the riser with a pipe cutter or hacksaw. Take out pipe section. Because the pipe section can be quite long, you may need more than one wall opening. Use two wrenches if unscrewing the fittings at the joints.

Add adapters to each steel coupling. Install plastic or copper pipe on the upper adapter. Then cement or solder in the new pipe. Add another length of pipe to the lower adapter, but cut it so that it reaches 3 inches below the bottom of the Tee. Last, cut a spacer to fit into the 3-inch gap. Install it with slip fittings. The Tee should be placed at a 45 degree angle to the wall.

Back-to-back fixtures. For copper or plastic pipe, you can install new Tees on the risers either above or below any existing Tees. For brass or steel, place the new Tees at right angles from the wall, either above or below the old Tees.

INSTALLING NEW PIPES
Abandon the old pipes and install new copper tubing or plastic pipe, if your local building codes permit it. Start at the main shutoff valve that is on the house side of the meter.

Start at the shutoff valve and use a reducing bell (coupling) to increase the pipe at least one size larger than the existing pipe. That is, if the present pipe is ¾ inch, replace it with a 1 inch pipe. Run 1 inch pipe throughout the house until it is close to a fixture, then reduce down to the usually required ⅜ or ¼ inch lines that run to the faucets. What the larger pipe does is

provide a larger volume of water in the house to maintain pressure.

As a word of caution, if the line from the meter to the street main is badly plugged it will have to be replaced.

Closing the Wall
After you have made your connections to the basin, nail cleats on either side of the opening against the studs. Nail plasterboard to the cleats. For a neat application, install the plasterboard before you make your connections to the basin. Cut round openings for the pipes. Just as for soil pipes, leave the wall open a couple of days (to make sure there are no leaks) before you close up the wall. You can seal off the short lines to pressure-test them by using valves with compression nuts.

When you are sure there are no leaks, you shut off the water, remove the valves, apply the wallboard, and finish the rest of the piping work. Once the wall has been closed, cut off the pipe extensions to the proper length so that a 90 or 45 degree elbow can be attached. It will direct the water line close to, and parallel to, the wall.

Projections through a wall. It will be necessary to run a short length of pipe through the wall surface from the Tees in the supply lines. Mark the replacement

plasterboard and drill ¾ to 1 inch holes for ½ inch pipe or tubing. Use a wood bit or hole saw. Install a chrome-plated escutcheon to hide ragged hole edges. Slide it on before making the connections or, if you forget to make the connections first, use a clamp-on escutcheon.

Pipework for the Toilet
You can install a toilet easily if the new bathroom is to be on the first floor and there is a basement under it. If code allows run the drain to the main stack in the basement. Build a temporary support for the two required stack clamps. If the fitting provides complete support to the soil pipe, the temporary support can be removed after the Tee or Tee-Y has been installed. If there is any doubt, the support should be made permanent. You may wish to have a professional plumber cut the vent and install this fitting for you.

Adding a Second Vanity Basin
Rather than a completely new bathroom, you might be thinking in terms of improving your existing bathroom. If what you want is a double facility in the bathroom, one easy solution is addition of a second vanity basin.

Extension within an existing bathroom. You can make all connections out-

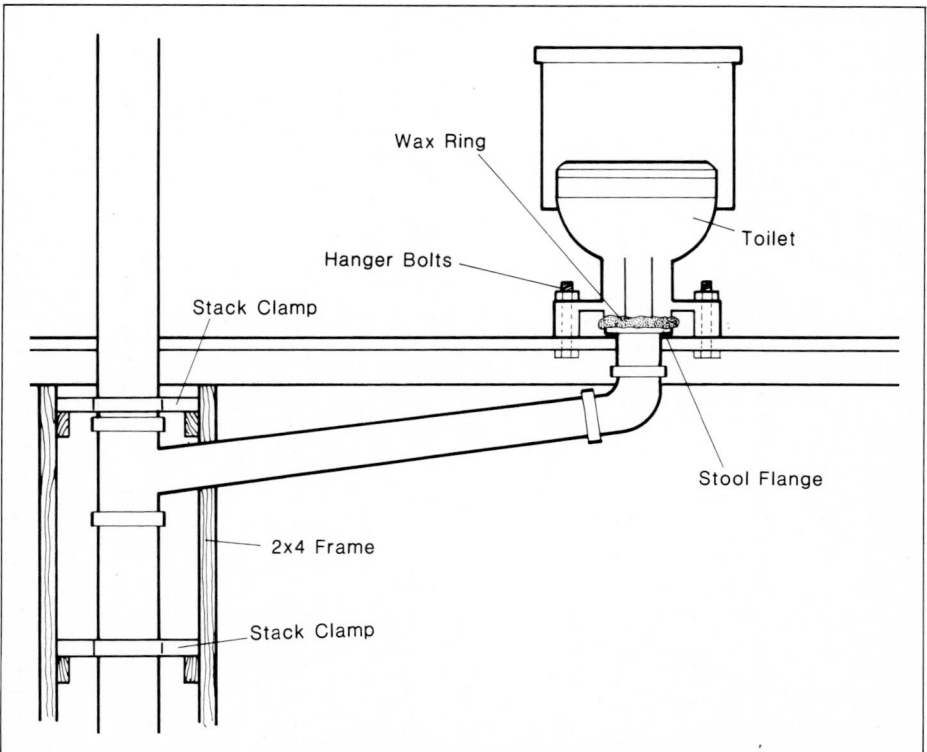

A wax ring fills any gap between the base of the stool and the opening of the drain. The main drain/vent stack is held in position by stack clamps. This is important when the weight of a long run of drain from the toilet would tend to pull the drain out of line.

side the wall for this project and not have to open the wall.

To provide water to the new vanity, cut the existing supply lines under the present vanity and install Tee fittings. Do the same for the drain line. Remove the existing trap with slip joint fittings and replace it with a Tee fitting to which the drain from the new vanity will be attached. The drain for the second vanity must start higher than the existing one, so there is a definite downward slope from the new vanity basin to the existing one. If there is no slope to the drain you will have later problems with a clogged drain. Without the angled drain, the long drain line from the new basin will fill with water, sediment and soap scum that will plug the line.

Extension to an adjacent room. If you want a new vanity basin on the wall opposite an existing bathroom but not aligned with it, the work involved requires opening the wall and extending the supply and drain lines along the wall. However, the exposed pipes are not attractive. Some homeowners paint them bright colors and consider them a sort of "graphic." For those homeowners who would rather hide the pipes there are several options.

Hiding exposed pipes for an extended pipe installation. Build an extended vanity cabinet to conceal the pipes and to give more counter space and storage beneath. Storage shelves can be assembled over the pipes. Another option is to build out the wall to just above the highest pipe and to close it in. There will be a shelf several inches wide and the pipes will be out of sight. Cover the built-out wall with hardboard or plywood attached with screws. This allows access to the pipes if repairs are necessary.

There are many attractive ways to conceal plumbing pipes and unfinished surfaces of fixtures. Plan and design both the practical and decorative features.

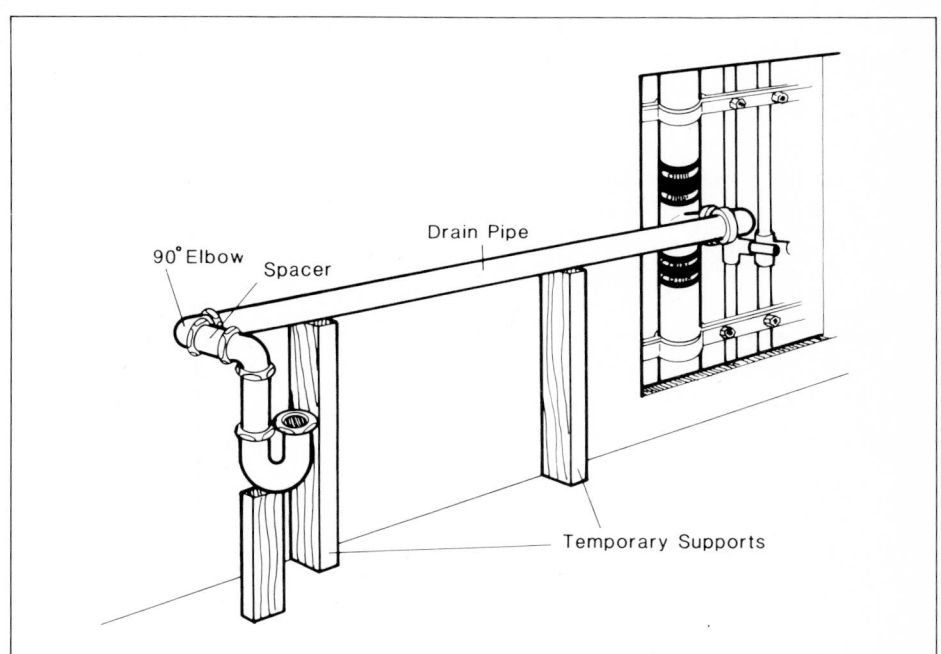

It is easier to run a new pipe outside a wall than inside. Blocking provides support.

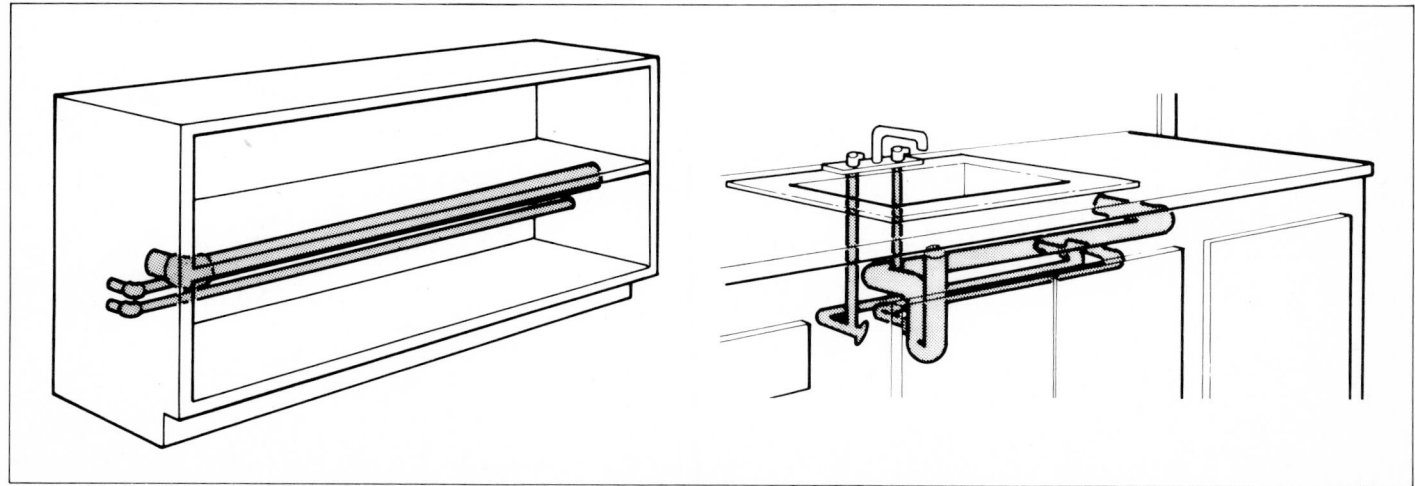

Cabinets and shelving can be built to hide outside-the-wall plumbing pipes while providing excellent storage areas that leave pipes accessible.

Providing Openings in Fixtures for Pipes

Pipes for the vanity. Place the new cabinet in position and drill pilot holes down through the bottom shelf of the cabinet and through the floor. Bore holes for the hot and cold water supply lines and for the drain line.

Before enlarging the holes, check the basement or crawl space to be sure the pilot holes are not located where the path of the pipe will be obstructed. If a pilot hole hits a floor joist, then move the cabinet a few inches. Relocate the hole or holes in the bottom shelf of the vanity as needed. Then drill holes to a size to accept the pipes. Move the cabinet and redrill the holes to provide clearance for the pipes you will use. When the cabinet is replaced in position, run the pipes up through the floor and the cabinet shelf.

Pipes for toilet installation. The supply line to a toilet is exposed and routed through the floor or the wall. Routing the line through the floor is easier. The hole for the pipe is located once the toilet is temporarily positioned. If the tank connection and the hole in the floor are a bit out of line, copper or plastic piping can be bent to accommodate any misalignment. Steel pipes will be more difficult to fit, and the usual solution is to drill an oversize hole in the floor to allow movement of the pipe. Plug or caulk around the pipe after it is in place. Fit an escutcheon plate around the pipe at the floor juncture, to cover the connection neatly.

PROVIDING ADDITIONAL ELECTRICAL SERVICE

Although BX cable and conduit are much lighter than plumbing pipe, long runs of cable or conduit require support to keep them in place and prevent slippage.

Codes may require all electrical hookups be done by a licensed electrician, but you may save considerable time and money by conferring with your electrician and by providing all needed pathway support yourself — such as boxes, blocking, metal clamps, notched studs, and plate protection for notches.

Although you can install the cable or conduit in the walls, you should have the connections made by an electrician unless you have had prior experience in this area. Electricity can be very dangerous; if you have any questions or doubts about codes, installation techniques, or equipment, do not attempt the electrical work yourself.

Running Electrical Cable

Never attempt to do any electrical work while the electrical power is on. Cut off the main power switch before beginning to work. We are assuming here that you will be extending wiring in the house. Evaluate your existing usage to find out if a new circuit is needed. In some cases, you may have a circuit available. Again, we suggest that you let an electrician handle the actual hookups (unless you have had previous electrical experience). You still will be able to save money by carrying out the repetitive work of stringing cable, cutting openings or mounting boxes.

BX. This is cable enclosed in a flexible metal casing. The hot black and neutral white wires are paper-wrapped; the ground wire is green. BX flexes and turns around corners easily. It is used in dry indoor locations and protects wires from nails used in carpentry or decorating projects.

Conduit. In many areas cable must be enclosed in galvanized steel pipe called thin-walled conduit. In many areas, conduit is required when more than 3 feet of BX cable is exposed in a basement. Run insulated single-conductor wires — black, white and green — through the pipes. Do not try to run plastic or BX cable through conduit. Conduit can hold a number of cables. It comes in a variety of diameters and in 10-foot lengths.

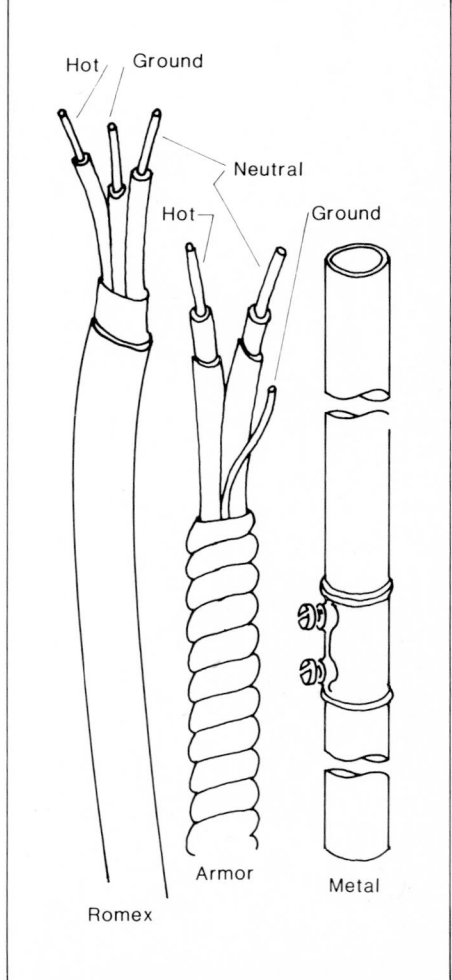

Most communities require either conduit or armor cable for modern electrical wiring.

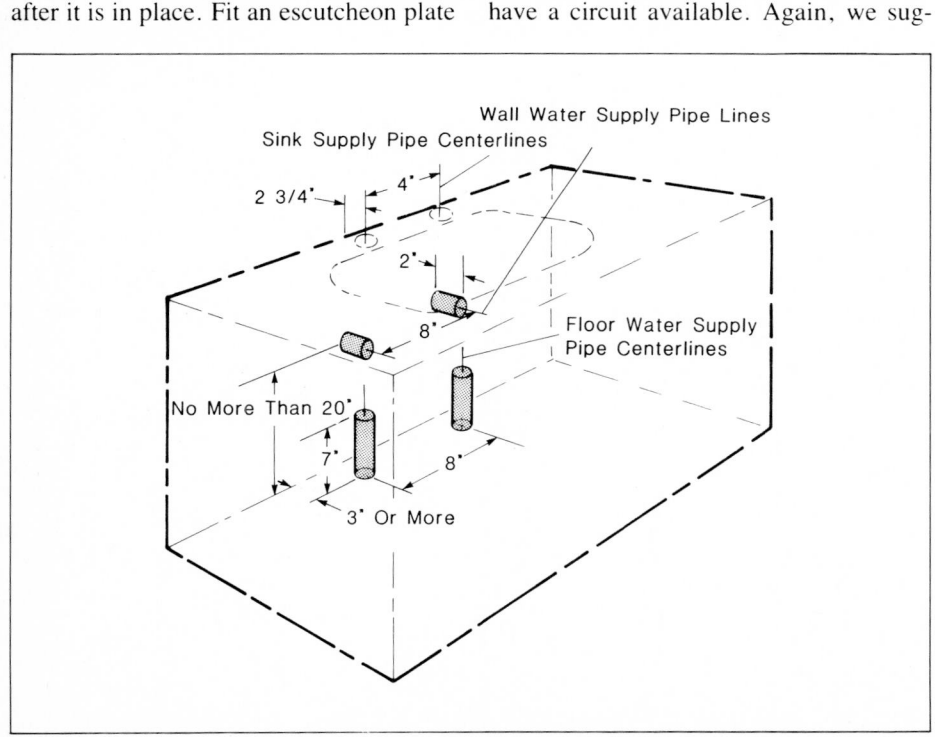

Supply pipes may come up through the floor or out of the wall. Whichever choice is best for you, measure carefully for accurate and trouble-free installation.

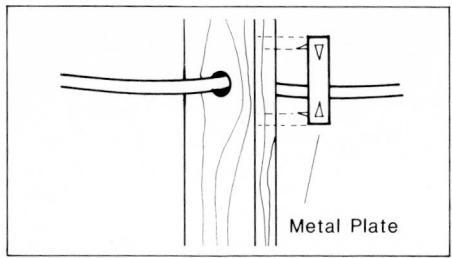

If you must run cable through a 2x4, you must install a protective face plate on the stud.

Anchoring and Supporting BX

When the cable must run perpendicular to wall studs, ceiling or floor joists, drill ⅝-inch holes through the members. When the cable runs parallel to framing attach it with metal clamps available at electrical supply houses or with electricians' staples. Tap the staples around the cable lightly and do not puncture or press into the cable. Staples are used as the fastest way to secure cable, but the best way is to use clamps.

The ⅝-inch holes in framing members may be drilled with a power or a hand drill. Cables are supported by the members themselves. Clamped or stapled cable should be supported at least every 4 feet. There must be a clamp no more than one foot away from convenience outlets or switch boxes.

Precautions when drilling through 2x4s. When you drill through small members, such as 2x4s, the National Electric Code requires that you add a metal plate cover to the front edge (the edge that faces the finish material). This prevents you, or anyone else from hitting the wire with the nail when finish materials are installed over the members. The metal plates are available at electrical supply houses. They have self-contained spikes so they can be hammered directly to the studs or other small members. The code states that the plates must be used wherever holes drilled for cable are less than 2 inches from the finished surface.

Using furring strips for perpendicular alignment. If you are unable to drill framing members to string cable perpendicular to the members because insulation or finish materials are in the way, you can nail a furring strip, typically a 1x3, perpendicular to the members and attach the cable to that. However, furring strips cannot be covered with materials such as sheetrock or paneling. If you are going to put a new wall surface up, you must reroute the cable so it will not interfere.

How to Use Conduit

You may be required by the code to use conduit. Your code will specify the kind of conduit you must use, usually electro-metallic tubing (EMT), or Type AC armored cable. Both kinds of conduit are installed in about the same manner as BX. Run conduit through framing members if the direction is perpendicular to the framing; hang it with clamps or staples if parallel. Clamps or staples should be no more than 4½ feet apart. Space a support one foot from all boxes. Have the electrical subcontractor install a run of conduit to show you how it attaches to the boxes.

You may run conduit perpendicular to framing. Notch the framing so that the conduit will be flush with the face of the members. Then cover the conduit and notch with a metal plate, as for BX.

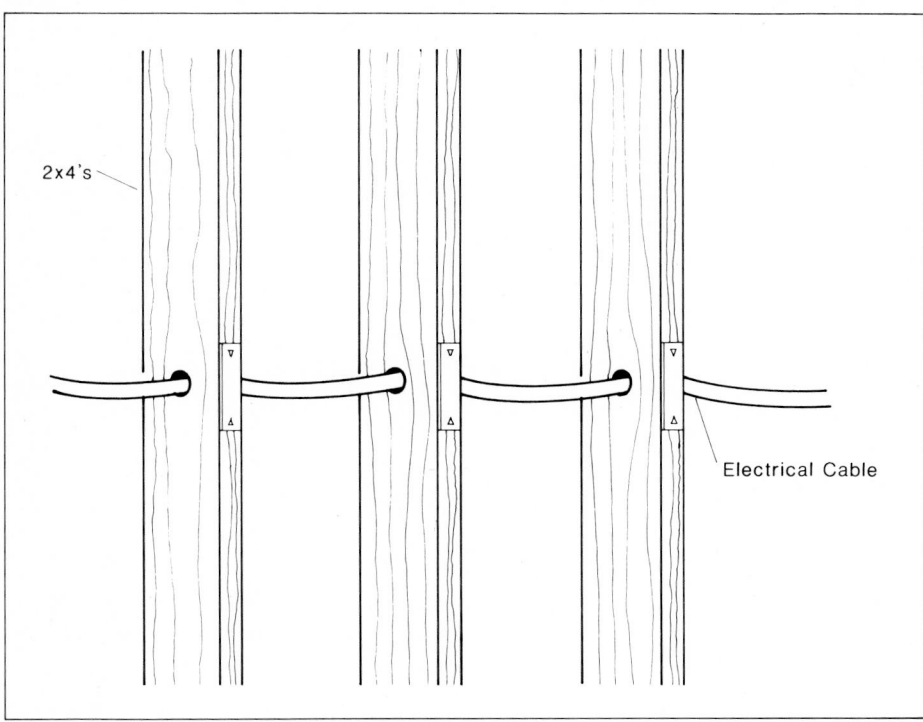

Use a plate on each stud through which cable passes. Plates will prevent anyone from driving a nail into the cable when installing drywall or doing any later carpentry work.

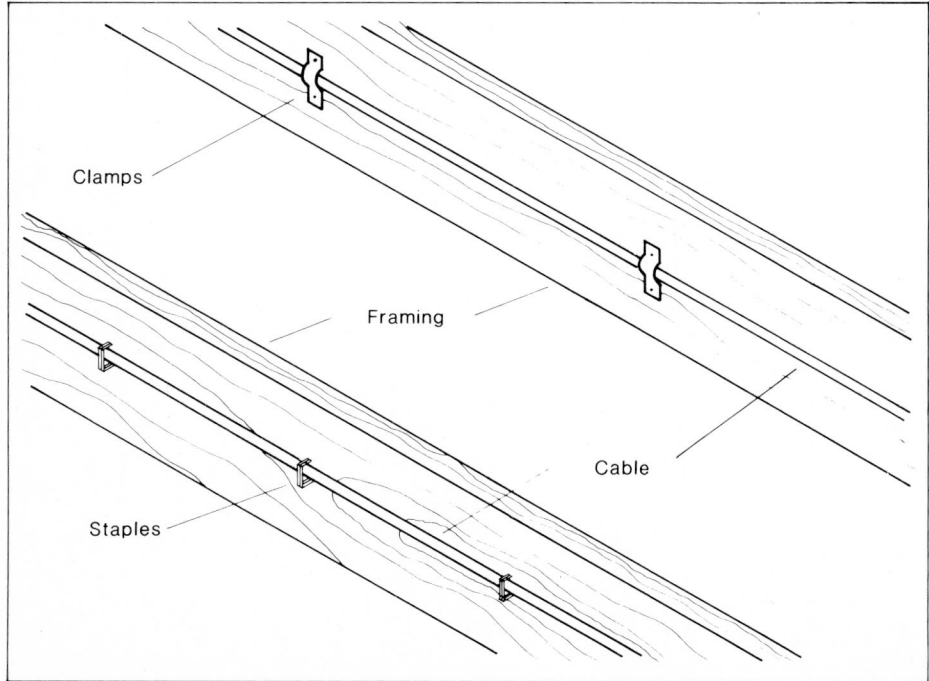

Cable that runs along the side of a joist may be held in place with clamps or staples. Clamps are more durable, but they are also more difficult to install in tight places.

Bending conduit. Have the contractor show you how to bend conduit if a cover must be turned. Bending conduit requires the use of a hickey conduit bender. The hickey conduit bender is a simple tool shaped roughly like a "T". The top and the leg of the T are curved and have a clamp attachment. The leg of the T (handle) is about 30 inches long. The procedure is a fairly simple one:

(1) attach the conduit through the clamp attachment;

(2) put the conduit on the ground or floor;

(3) with your foot on the conduit, push the handle down, bending the conduit.

Stringing the Wiring Through the Conduit

The next step is to put the wiring in the conduit. Your wiring must conform to the local codes. The wires must be color-coded in the standard colors: green or bare for ground wire, black, and white (and red for four-wire circuits). Always use a ground wire. Ask the electrician to check your wire before you run it through the conduits. For short runs (several feet), you can simply push the wire through.

"Fishing" the wire. You will have to "fish" the wire through longer runs using some wire stiff enough to push through the conduit by itself. Then hook the more limber circuit wires to the fish wire and pull the circuit wires to the box. Watch the electrical subcontractor "fish" one run of conduit; you can then do the remainder of the work. Fishing technique requires common sense and patience. To get through old walls, drill a hole to string the cables or conduit and wiring. This work may be done best by an electrical contractor. Always have the system inspected.

Mounting the Boxes

Your electrical plan should pinpoint the locations of all the metal boxes for outlets and switches. Then you can run the cable or conduit to them.

The boxes are designed to mount by nailing directly to the framing or by attaching with metal framing devices. The devices may be part of the box itself or may clamp to the box. The devices give latitude in the placement of the box. You may need a light switch closer to a door jamb than the wood framing allows. The metal device would permit you to put the box closer to the jamb. Electrical supply houses carry these devices. If you have had no experience with electrical work, have the electrical contractor show you how to mount the boxes — or have him mount the boxes so you can string the cable to them.

BATHROOM DESIGN
New Materials and Accessories

Bathtubs. The tub no longer has to be the porcelain coated, cast-iron standard rectangle that takes four strong men to set in place. Today's fiberglass tubs, which no longer flex to the touch as earlier models did, are available in circular, oval, square, angled, deep Roman style, as well as the standard rectangle. Many styles are available in apronless models that are easily adaptable to a sunken or raised installation, greatly reducing the former expense of luxury arrangement. The standard rectangle is now deeper than the older cast-iron or steel models by one or two inches.

Some fiberglass fixtures, however, have the finish sprayed on in a "gel coat". These surfaces are more easily damaged than those of fixtures that have the color and surface integrally molded in. Be careful when selecting fixtures for your new

Running cable to a ceiling fixture requires the use of fish tape to pull the wires through the wall. Two access holes are needed and will have to be repaired when the work is complete.

This prefabricated tub enclosure includes a set of grab bars and a small storage area.

bath. A few extra dollars spent initially may be saved down the road in reductions in maintenance and replacement.

Bathtub and shower enclosures. The bathtub recess, a popular type of construction, also is available in prefabricated units. These commonly are made of fiberglass, but there is also a new marble-like material that is easy to work with. The finishes of some of the newer materials, which are virtually identical to marble in appearance, go all the way through so that scratches or cigarette burns can be sanded away with very fine sandpaper. These new tub enclosures and prefabricated shower stalls are much easier to install and can be handled by the less-experienced do-it-yourselfer, following the manufacturer's instructions.

Enclosures come in two basic forms. One is the integral enclosure where tub and walls are one piece. If this type is used in a new bath, it must be placed in the room before the framing is complete; otherwise, you may have to remove some studs to get it in. Before buying a unit like this, be sure there is an entrance to your home of sufficient size to allow you to get it in. The other form of enclosure contains a separate tub and four panels for the walls. This type can be easily used in new or old baths, since the sections can be carried through a door as narrow as 24 inches.

The same materials are available for shower stalls. They may be purchased as an integral unit, or as panels. They come in several different types of materials. The new materials usually are easy to cut and fit, and resist damage better than older materials. Shown is one attractive but inexpensive way to build a new bath with shower stall panels.

Toilets. The water closet is also available in a variety of new styles. These include: elongated bowls, corner models for small spaces, styles for the elderly and/or handicapped, which are equipped with grab bars, are higher or have raised seats, wall hung models that allow installation at any required height, and styles with low

A luxurious bathroom is a matter of providing the basic necessities in an attractive setting. This tub is a whirlpool model that gives both a bath and a massage.

This tub enclosure provides a small storage shelf between the showerhead and the faucets.

A simple tub enclosure has soap dishes and shelves accessible to both tub or shower user.

A low-profile, water saving toilet is economical and fits below a vanity shelf extension.

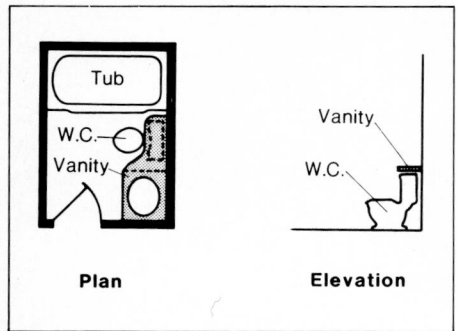

The vanity extension provides a practical shelf and still allows tank access.

A lavatory bowl with a dramatic design may be the focus of your new powder room.

A vanity top with an integral lavatory is an attractive feature in a bath/dressing area.

tanks that allow you to extend a vanity top over the tank and increase the counter space in a small bath. There are various models that use very little water for flushing, as well as different flushing actions.

Lavatories. The revolution in lavatories has also added to the homeowner's design freedom. The freestanding lavatory is returning to popularity and is ideal for the cramped bathroom because it requires a minimum of space. These newer styles not only are space saving, but also are very attractive. Vanity bowls are available in almost every imaginable color and style, as well as in several types of materials. You may also purchase and easily install vanity tops with integral bowls. These come in either fiberglass or the new marble-like materials.

Because of the wide variety of styles, colors, and materials available, visit a plumbing fixture dealer before you design your new bath. Consider all the options available to you — and how they will work in the space that is available — before you make your decisions.

Individualizing the Bathroom

Different design features, such as a partitioned water closet, indoor gardens, or connecting walk-in closets, may be included in your designs.

There are several ways that even a small bath can be given an open, larger feeling and a touch of elegance without going to a great deal of expense. First, if the length and width are limited, consider going up.

Height. A vaulted ceiling can add a new dimension to a small bath, giving it interest and a feeling of roominess. The existing ceiling can be removed. The walls extended to the rafters and a new ceiling material attached to the rafters. Insulation is needed in the extended walls and above the new ceiling. The ceiling joists, if properly tied to adjacent walls,

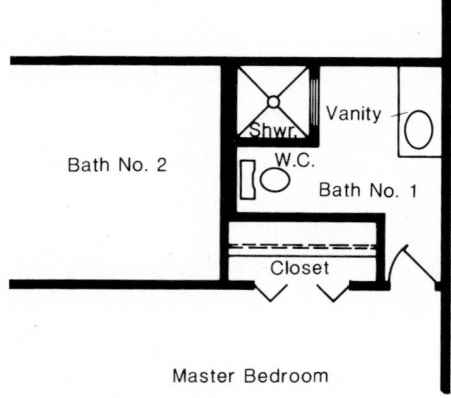

Before

An adequate, but slightly cramped, bath just off the master bedroom is common in new homes.

After

A slight change takes little from the bedroom but provides a larger bath and closet.

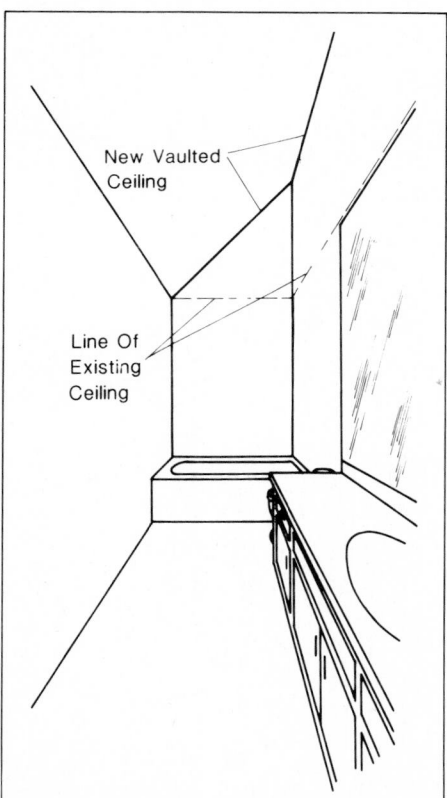

A small bath can be enlarged visually by opening the ceiling to the attic rafters.

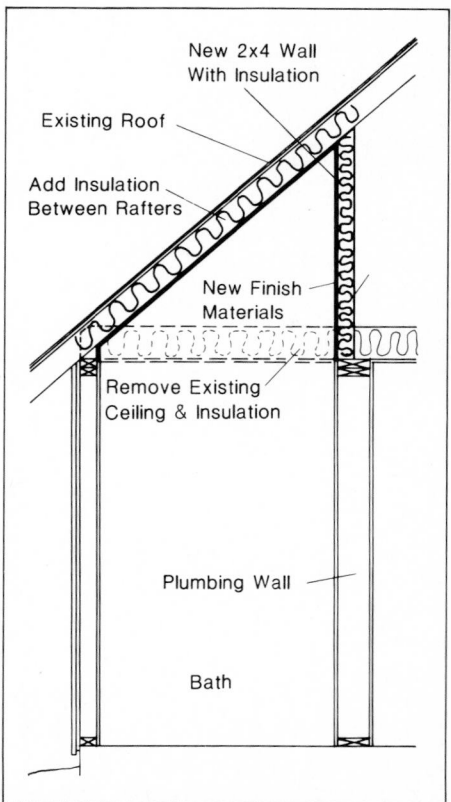

New insulation must be added to the roof and the new wall to control possible condensation.

can be removed under the vaulted ceiling; or they can be left in position and stained or painted for additional effect. If your roof is built with prefabricated trusses, some new framing (including heavier rafters) will be required around and over the bath before any portion of the truss system can be removed (see Chapter 10). However, you do not have to remove the trusses.

Remove the ceiling surface and trim out the trusses with new lumber and molding. Since the trusses remain intact, there is no chance of structural damage.

Light. Another way to give the small bath a feeling of spaciousness is to let in a lot of natural light. This can be done in several ways. Skylights are available in a variety of styles and sizes and can be added to a vaulted ceiling or to a standard ceiling by constructing a light well from the roof to the lower floor (see Chapter

A new, European bath uses a skylight rather than a dormer window to provide light. The ceiling is steeply angled, but there is plenty of headroom, so a dormer is not needed.

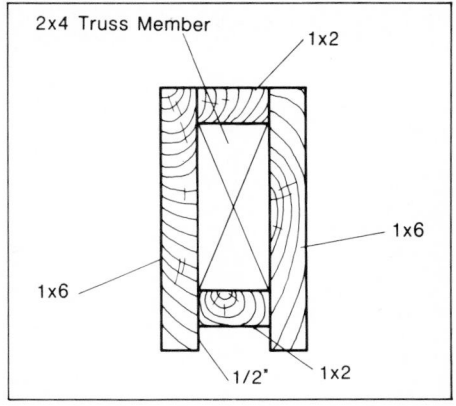

A truss or other joist that cannot be removed can be faced with attractive finish lumber.

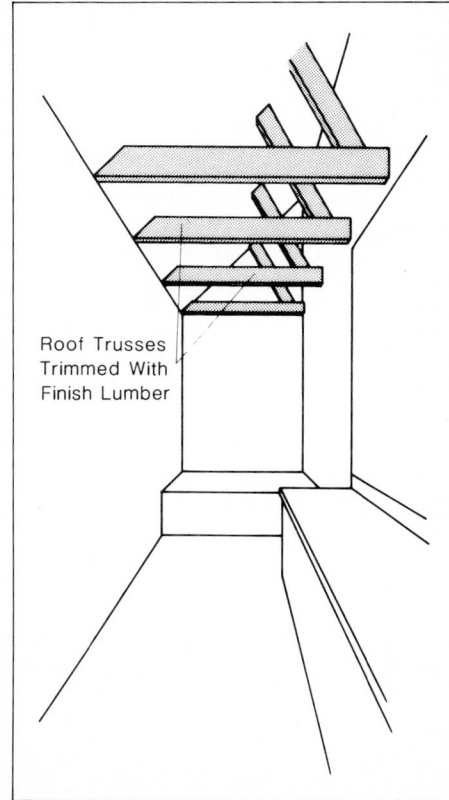

Framed trusses become the decorating focal point of this bath with a newly opened ceiling.

If your attic roof is relatively flat, you can install a skylight that is designed to angle toward the sun. This design will bring more light into your room space below.

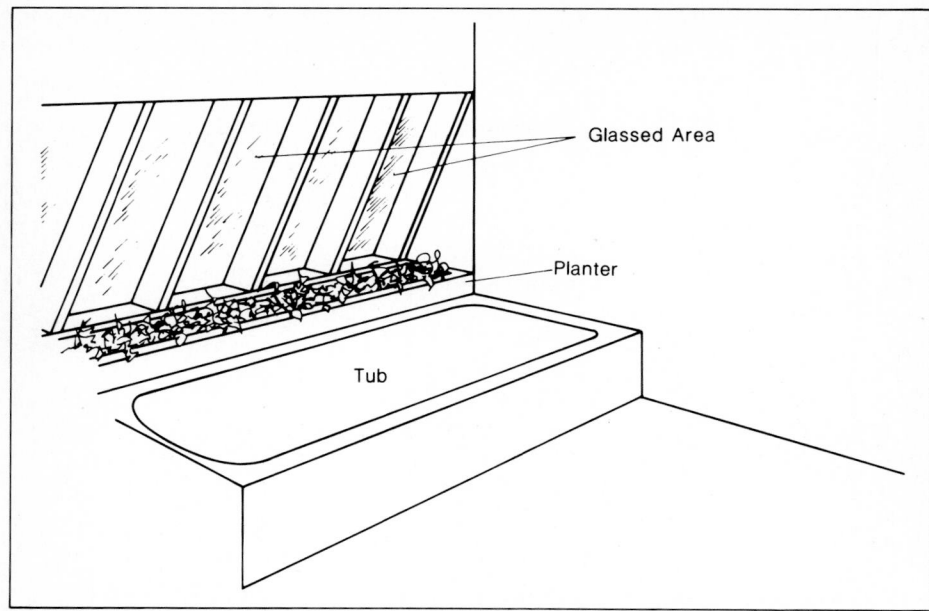

A greenhouse window over the tub will provide excellent light in a bath as well as provide a place for plants. If privacy is a problem, use frosted glass in the windows.

Regular windows and a skylight combine to provide light and ventilation for the bath.

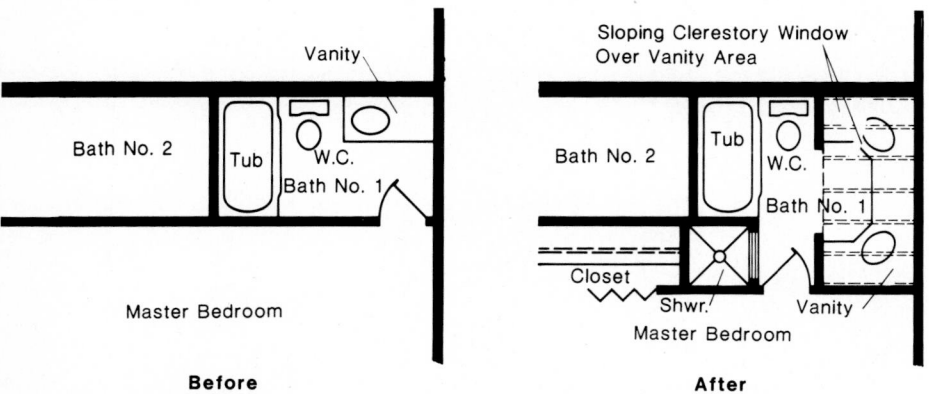

A few changes in tne walls made substantial changes to this master bedroom suite. A new closet, a shower and a second sink in a new vanity were added. Clerestories provide light and privacy.

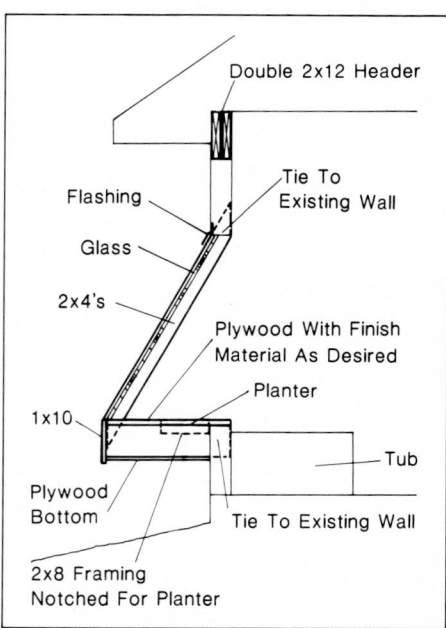

Greenhouse window reaches to the line of the overhang. Framing ties into existing wall.

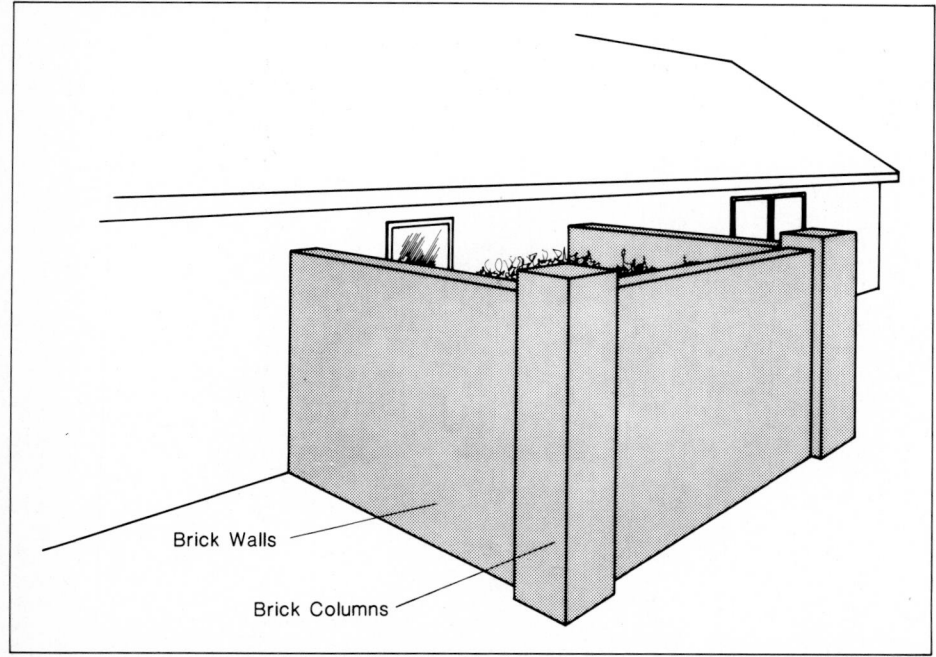

A solid brick wall around a bathroom provides privacy while allowing an expanse of clear glass and providing a private sunbathing area for the family.

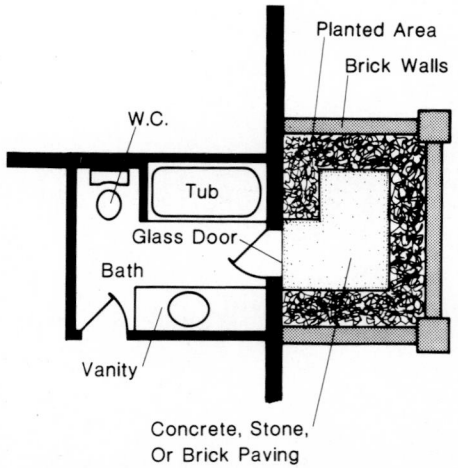

A small window may be replaced with a glass door for access to private patio.

11). Clerestory windows can also add an abundance of natural light, but the roof construction of your home may make this solution difficult to realize. A skylight may be an easier and less expensive choice. One other way to bring natural light into the bath is to install a floor to ceiling window. You may use smoked or clear glass or a combination of the two, with a protective wall as needed for privacy.

A partial greenhouse in the bath not only brings in more natural light, but also helps enhance the feeling of spaciousness. A greenhouse window can be placed at the tub, or in another area of the bathroom, such as opposite the vanity. Of course, it will need to be placed in an outside wall. If privacy is then a problem, use frosted glass or build a privacy wall or fence.

Reflections. Of course, the time-honored approach of using mirrors to enlarge a small space still works. Liberal use

A small bath is enlarged, at least visually, when one or more walls are covered by mirrors.

of mirrors will make a small bath look and feel roomier. You do not have to stop the mirror at the ends of the vanity; wrap it around a corner if you have the wall space. The wall opposite the vanity is another good place for large mirrors, especially floor-to-ceiling mirrors. Some luxury baths even include mirrored ceilings to help open up the look of the room.

Mirror tile. One of the easiest ways to cover a large expanse of wall space is with mirror tile. These tiles usually come in 12-by 12-inch units, which makes handling relatively simple.

Installing mirror tile. You will need a clean, smooth surface in order to attach mirror tiles securely. If you are applying tile to an old wall, wash and rinse the surface thoroughly. Patch and seal cracks and holes. If you are applying the tile to new wallboard, first cover the surface with a good quality sealer.

The tiles are attached to the wall with small, adhesive mounting squares that come with the tiles. Peel off the protective backing on one side of the squares and mount on the back corners of the tiles.

To position properly on the wall, snap a chalkline to establish the vertical center of the area you wish to cover with the tile. Mark the horizontal with a straightedge using a level as a guide. Position the first four tiles at the junction of the two lines. To attach, remove the protective paper from the back of the mounting squares, align the tile, and press into place.

Cutting mirror tile. If you must cut tiles to fit at corners, scribe a line with a glass cutter, using a carpenter's square to ensure a straight line, and snap over the edge of a raised surface. While an experienced glasscutter does this easily and

safely, you should probably wear gloves to protect your hands when cutting the glass. If you must fit a tile around a light fixture, switch, or outlet box, you will have to cut the tile into several sections vertically and then cut one section into three pieces to create one piece that will fit above the opening and one that will fit below. If you must fit around doors and windows, you will also have to cut the tile into several pieces to achieve a perfect fit.

Plate glass mirrors. Large mirrors of heavy plate glass may achieve the effect you desire without covering an entire wall. Wall mirrors and full-length mirrors designed to be hung on doors are generally available in large stores featuring plate glass. A high quality, float-glass mirror about four feet square would create a strong impact in a small bath.

Hanging a wall mirror. A mirror designed to be wall hung is usually equipped at the time of purchase with hanging rings that are permanently attached by brackets welded to the backing frame. Depending upon your situation and location, you may attach a heavy, stranded picture wire to the rings and attach heavy-duty picture hooks to studs in the bathroom or dressing room wall. The rings, however, are usually placed to match standard stud centering. A more secure installation is achieved by carefully measuring so that the mirror will be level and driving 3 inch wood screws into the studs so the heads project just enough to catch the mirror rings. The mirror will lie flat against the wall.

Full length mirrors. These mirrors are usually designed to be hung on the back of a door. They usually are hung with special, decorative mounting screws that are driven through holes drilled in the corners

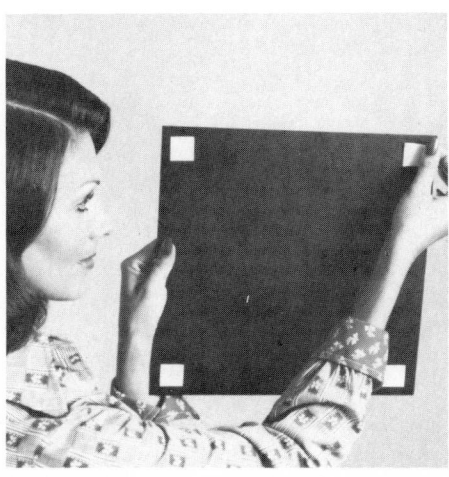

Apply adhesive tabs to the back of each mirror tile. Set near each corner.

Carefully set each tile in position. Align first tiles with chalklines snapped on wall.

A carpenter's square is a good straightedge when scribing a mark to cut tile.

of the mirror itself or with mounting brackets that hold the mirror in place. If you wish to install a full length mirror on a wall, you must attach it to studs. Door mounting is covered in Chapter 8 on Closets.

Patios. Another way to enlarge the appearance of the small bath is to build a small garden and/or sunbathing area on the outside of the house adjacent to the bathroom. A privacy fence must be constructed around the area so that it is accessible only from the bathroom. The access could be a sliding or other glass door at the tub, shower, stall, or other part of the bath. This concept is not extremely expensive or difficult to build, and it adds a whole new dimension to the bathroom. The door and windows bring in considerable natural light and make the space an integral part of the outdoors. The garden/sunbathing area can work for your bath, and many other designs can be made to suit your individual tastes and situation.

Construction

Construction of the new walls for the bathroom will be similar to that explained in Chapter 4. But if the new bath does not directly abut an existing plumbing wall, you will have to construct one wall that will be a plumbing wall large enough to accommodate the large plumbing stack that vents up through the roof. The new plumbing wall can be constructed using 2x6 or 2x8 framing lumber, or it may be a double 2x4 wall. Plumbing should go into the walls when the framing is complete, before the finish material is installed.

If you want to do your own plumbing work, including the piping and setting of fixtures, check all code restrictions and regulations. Study plumbing directions provided with the installation sheets for your fixtures. There are plumbing supply stores that specialize in providing help and guidance to the do-it-yourselfer plumber. Draw up plans, measure carefully and take your time. Install pipe properly with good support and proper positioning and air chambers. For more detailed information see *Modern Plumbing for Old and New Houses* 2nd edition.

Wall surfaces for the bathroom can be applied as discussed in Chapter 6, except that you must use a water-resistant gypsumboard. There is ceramic tile in large, pregrouted sheets that are easy for the do-it-yourselfer to install. Tile is applied directly over the water-resistant gypsumboard; follow the manufacturer's recommendations.

THE EXISTING BATH

If you want to expand an existing bath — in actual size or only in appearance — or simply update the design, the ideas presented for a new bath will, for the most part, work equally well. There are, however, several other matters to consider when working on an existing bath.

First, there are the existing conditions to deal with. To actually make the bath larger you will have to remove old walls and create new walls. This, of course, will require a sacrifice of space from adjoining rooms. You may need to make adjustments in other areas to get the space you need. It may be a little expensive to change locations of existing plumbing fixtures unless you are doing the plumbing work yourself. It is a good idea to keep the water closet in the same place and design around it, but this is not mandatory if the present location does not fit well with your plans.

The least expensive way to open up an existing bath is with the methods mentioned before — creating a vaulted ceiling, skylight, or extensive use of mirrors — and leaving the plumbing fixtures in the same locations. Original fixtures can be replaced with new fixtures, and new wall treatments can be used easily but moving the fixtures to different locations can be expensive, especially if your home is on a

Storage can be added to a bath by adding a vanity cabinet. Another possibility is adding a shelf just above head level.

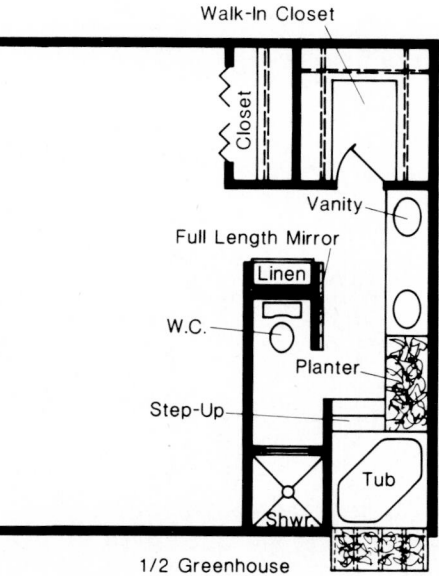

A large bathroom space allows great freedom of design and variety in planning.

Compartmenting the bath allows considerable privacy even with a greenhouse window.

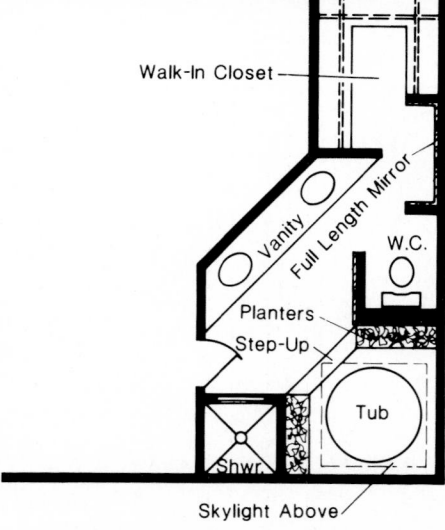

An oblique wall may allow better use of space than the usual right angle wall.

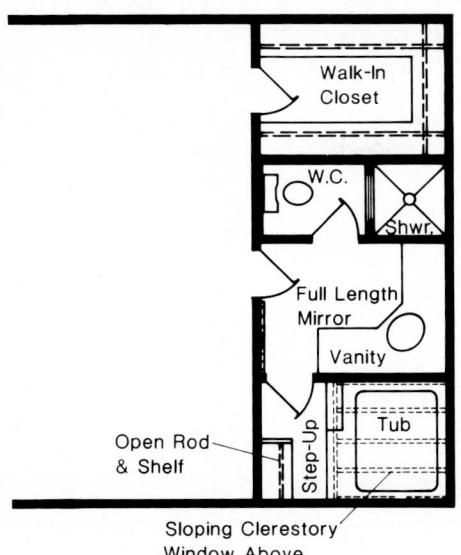

Compact arrangements using clerestory windows that take no wall space can be successful.

A stall shower is a practical solution when bathing facilities are needed in small areas.

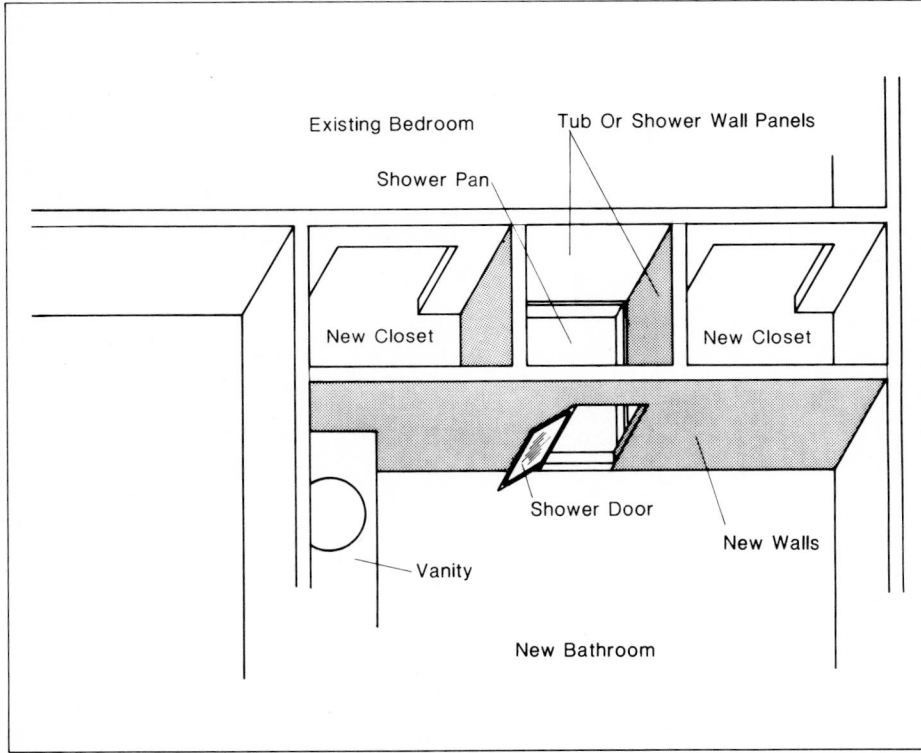

The unit shown in photograph above can be added by borrowing a little space from an adjoining room and using the rest of the "borrowed" space for closets.

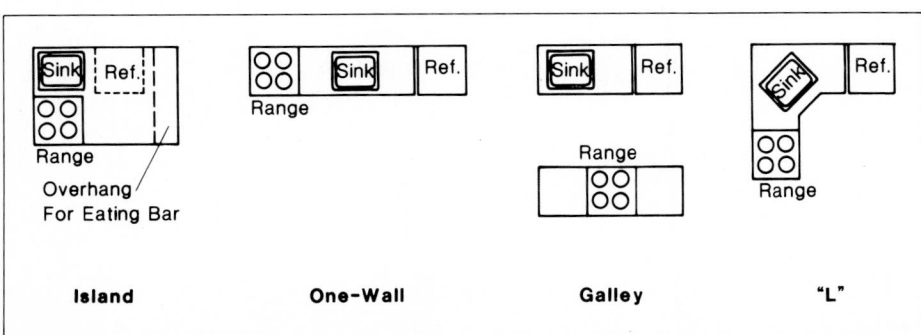

Compact kitchens can be designed in ways to fit into specific small areas. While any of these would be inadequate for a main kitchen, all would be good for one person or snack preparation.

concrete slab foundation. It is possible to design around an existing bath and to make it more luxurious at a minimum of cost. Use these ideas and adapt them to your individual situations.

KITCHENETTES

There are a number of reasons for wanting to add an extra, small kitchen, or "kitchenette" to your home. It can be that an elderly, handicapped, or other person in the household desires a degree of privacy. You may want a kitchenette in a recreation room, upstairs, in an attic expansion, or in a basement expansion. Whatever your reason for adding a kitchenette, the factors regulating its location are the same as for a new bath. It must be convenient for use and adjacent to or directly over existing plumbing for easy, inexpensive plumbing hookups. However, since the plumbing in the kitchenette is restricted to a sink — and possibly a dishwasher and/or icemaker refrigerator — the location is not quite as restricted as for a bath. The drains for these items go out through the wall instead of the floor and may run some distance through a wall, by gravity flow, before joining the main drain. Of course, the longer the distance, especially in existing walls, the more difficult and expensive the work.

A compact kitchenette can be designed in several ways, but the most popular is the one-wall kitchen. There are many designs possible.

A visit to an appliance store will also reveal a variety of compact appliances that allow you to build a small kitchenette. There are designs that combine more than one appliance in a single unit. The limited cabinets in the kitchenette should be arranged for efficiency. The discussion of space-saving cabinetry in Chapter 8 also applies to the kitchenette.

MISCELLANEOUS PLUMBING

Other plumbing features you may consider adding include a clothes washer connections and a closet, a deep sink in the utility room, or a wet bar. In each case, as it is with other new plumbing, location adjacent to or directly above existing plumbing lines will save considerable money and effort. There are various ways to add features that are plumbing-based improvements. If your use study shows that you may take some space from a room, you may use the space to add plumbing.

A good-size wet bar that is open to both the kitchen and the entertaining area provides excellent storage and eases many problems of service during parties.

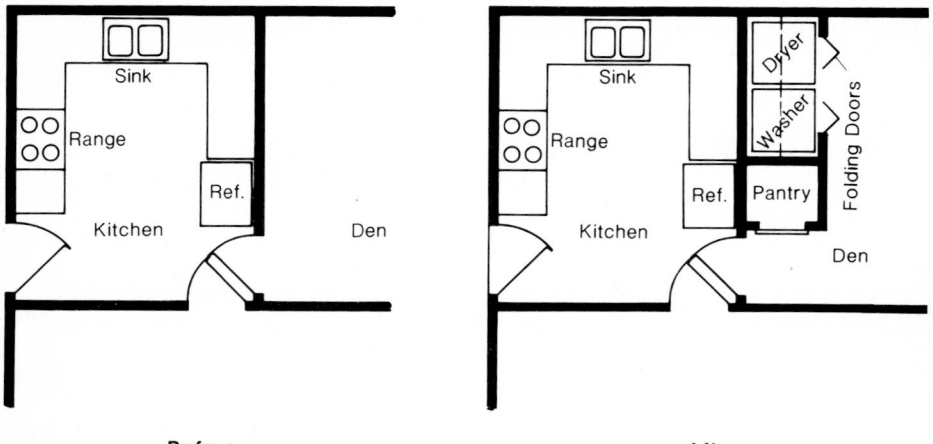

Before   **After**

When plumbing is accessible in a nearby room, any plumbing related fixtures may be added to adjacent rooms. This den lost a few feet when the household gained a first-floor laundry room.

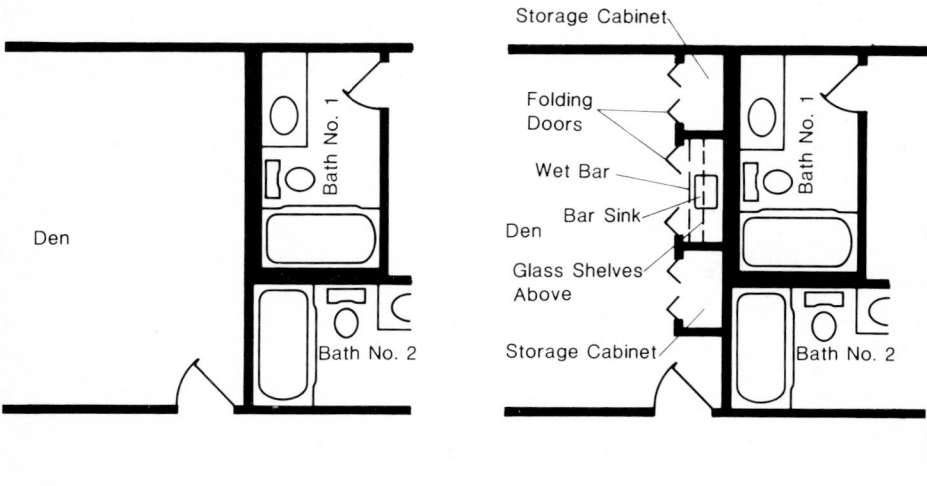

Before   **After**

Tapping into bathroom plumbing allowed this homeowner to put a wet bar into the den. Very little space was used, and considerable storage space was added.

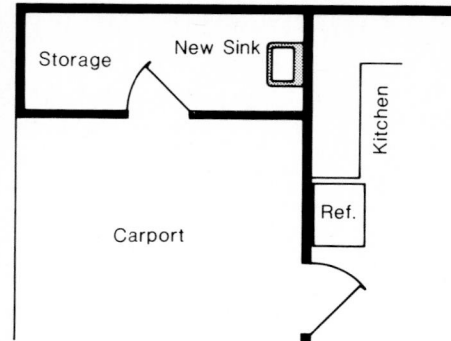

A sink in a garage area is practical in a temperate climate or a well insulated storage area.

This kitchenette is unobtrusive in a small living/dining area because of careful design.

For large families with teenagers, adding a lavatory in a bedroom may solve many problems.

6

INSTALLING INTERIOR FINISHING MATERIALS

When the old walls have been removed and the new walls framed-in, you may install any needed extensions of plumbing and electrical work. (See Chapter 5.) Then you are ready to add the finish materials. Even if you have not made any wall changes, you may still want to install new finish materials to give the rooms a fresh look. Most contemporary finish materials for floors, walls, and ceilings can be installed easily by the do-it-yourselfer with simple tools; many dealers will provide installation instructions. Do-it-yourself finishing work can save a lot of money; however, there are a few difficult tasks that usually should be left to a professional. This chapter will deal with installation of all commonly used finish materials and will point out those that present installation problems.

COVERING THE WALLS

A new wall is most commonly finished with the same material as on the existing adjacent walls, but you may want to vary the decor by covering the new wall with paneling, wallpaper, or gypsumboard that contrasts with the existing walls. Or you may decide to change the surface of all the walls in the room and use paneling throughout.

Gypsumboard

Even if the original walls are plaster, you may want to use gypsumboard on the new walls for ease of construction and economy. Properly applied, there will be no apparent difference between the gypsumboard and the plaster surfaces. When the walls have been painted or papered, they will be identical in finish texture.

Sizes. Wallboard thicknesses range from ¼ inch to ⅝ inch and the board comes in three types: regular, fire resistant, and water resistant. Gypsumboard comes in sheets four feet wide. The most

The materials you choose for the walls, ceiling and floors of your room must be as carefully chosen and coordinated with and complementary to all of your furnishings.

common size is 4 feet by 8 feet, but lengths range from 6 to 14 feet. However, a full range of sizes may not be available in your area; check to see which sizes are available before designing the layout pattern of the sheets. Use ½-inch or ⅝-inch-thick sheets when applying directly to studs and ¼-inch or ⅜-inch-thick sheets when applying to an existing wall surface.

Nailing plan. Carefully plan out the job before you begin to apply the gypsumboard. First, learn what size sheets are available in your area and draw a layout and nailing plan on paper. A good plan will save cutting, material waste, and give you the fewest number of seams. For a standard eight-foot ceiling, install panels horizontally, installing the upper panel first. This will keep the seams to a minimum and put them at a good working level.

Installation procedures. If you plan to put gypsumboard on your ceiling, it should be applied there first. Then lay the top row of panels for a horizontal installation on the wall and, finally nail the bottom row. If your ceiling is higher than the standard 8 feet, use longer sheets applied vertically, if these sheets are available; or install standard sheets horizontally. Leave the additional space in the middle and cut sheets to fit between the top and bottom sheets, so all seams will be at a comfortable working height.

Precautions. Whenever cutting or sanding gypsumboard, use a respirator or dust mask.

Cutting and nailing. To cut gypsumboard, score the face paper with a sharp bladed utility knife guided by a metal straight edge. Snap the core of the board over a solid, continuous edge with a quick motion; then cut the back paper. Measure and mark all telephone or electrical wall outlets and switches onto the face of the board. Cut along the lines and then diagonally from the corners; knock out the pieces with a hammer.

Use gypsumboard nails to apply the sheets. Nail into studs or if your wall is not even, add furring strips to studs and then nail to the furring strips. Nail in far enough so the surface of the board is dimpled but so the paper is not broken. Nails should be 5 to 7 inches apart on ceilings and 6 to 8 inches apart on walls. The nails should be between ½- and ⅜-inch from the edge of the boards. When nailing the lower sheets into place, use a lever, to hold the sheet firmly, but not forcefully, against the upper sheet. After the sheets are nailed in place, use a saw to cut out door and other large openings.

Installing outside corner bead. Apply metal bead to outside corners for strength. The bead strip should be nailed through the gypsumboard and into the framing underneath. Use a drywall knife to apply a 6-inch wide coat of joint compound on each side of the bead. Apply a second coat, about 9 inches wide, after the first is dry.

Taping inside corners. Crease regular gypsumboard tape lengthwise in the center before applying it to inside corners. Apply a coat of joint compound to either side of the joint; apply the tape while the compound is still wet. When the compound is dry, apply another coat, about 6

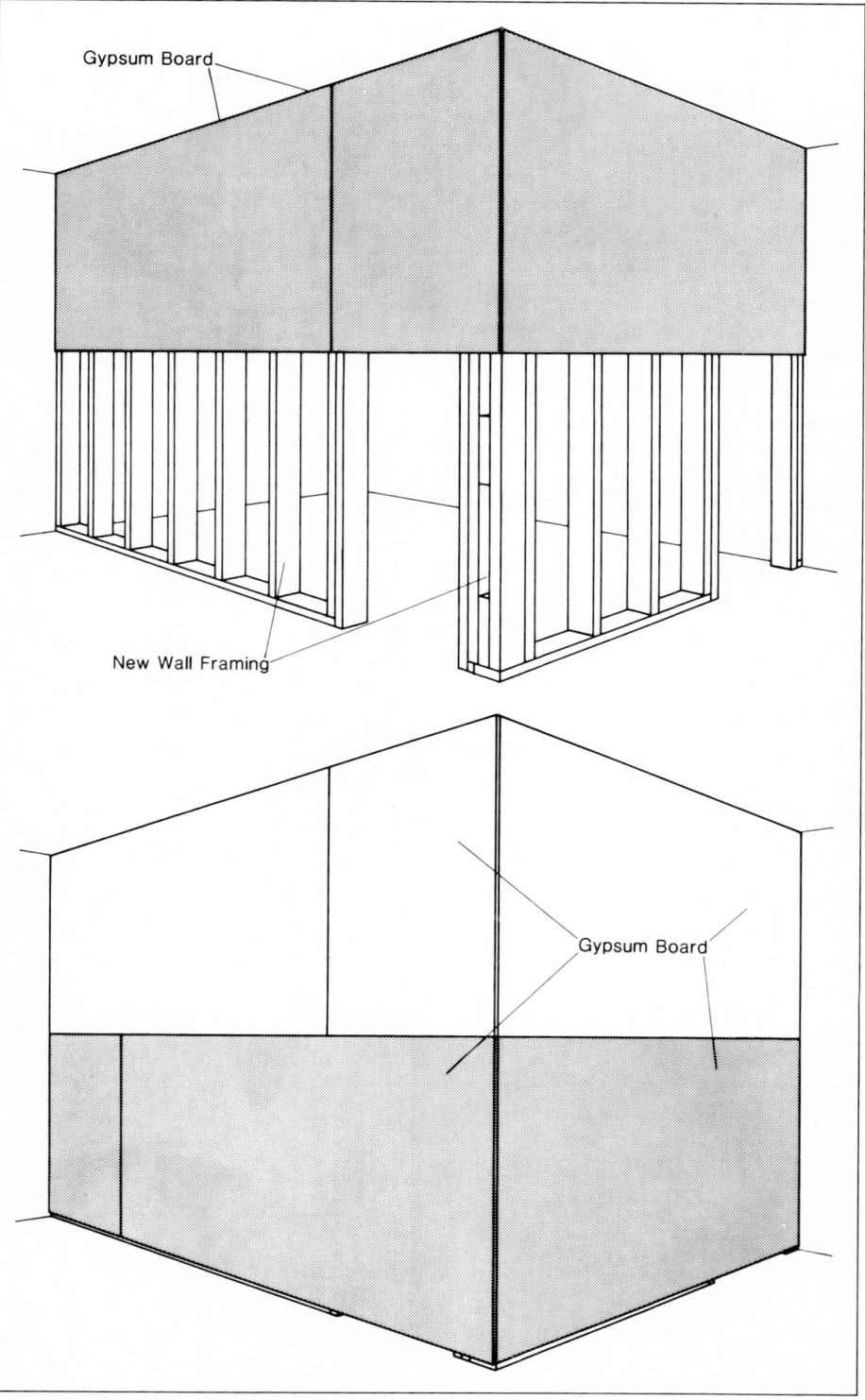

Gypsum wallboard is installed most easily by running the sheet horizontally. This puts the long seam at a comfortable height. Completely cover door openings and cut out board later.

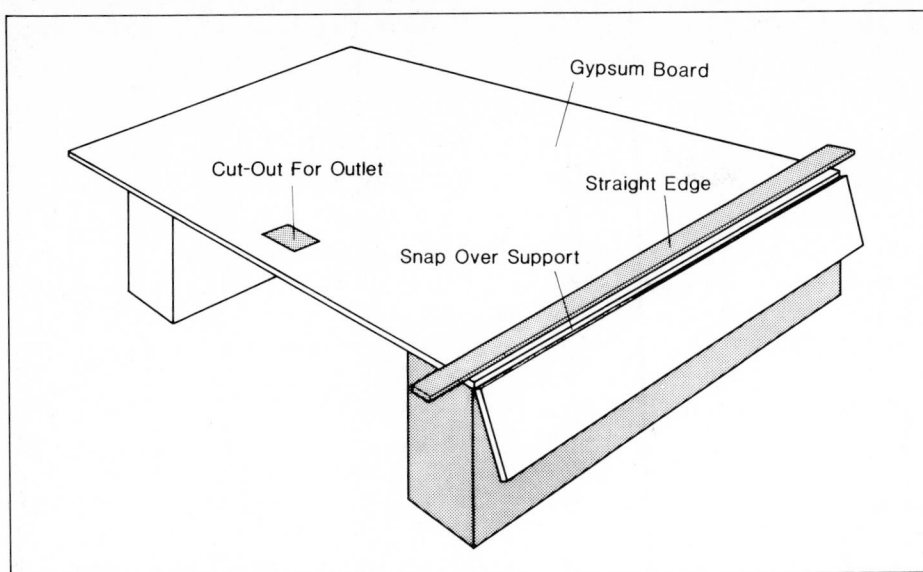

Make cuts in wallboard after careful measuring. Support the board, score and then snap. Cut paper on the back to free strip. Cut out small areas with a keyhole saw.

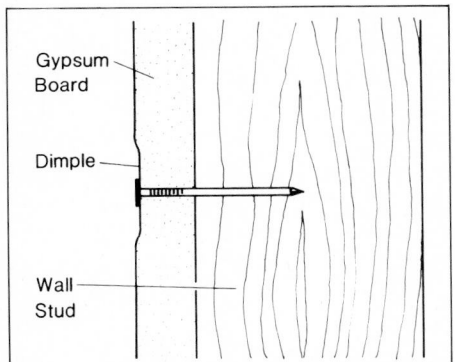

Drive nails to slightly below board surface. Dimple will be filled when seams are sealed.

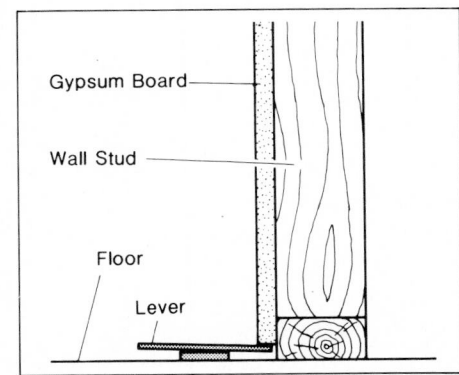

Use a lever to hold wallboard snugly in place. Gap at floor will be covered by molding.

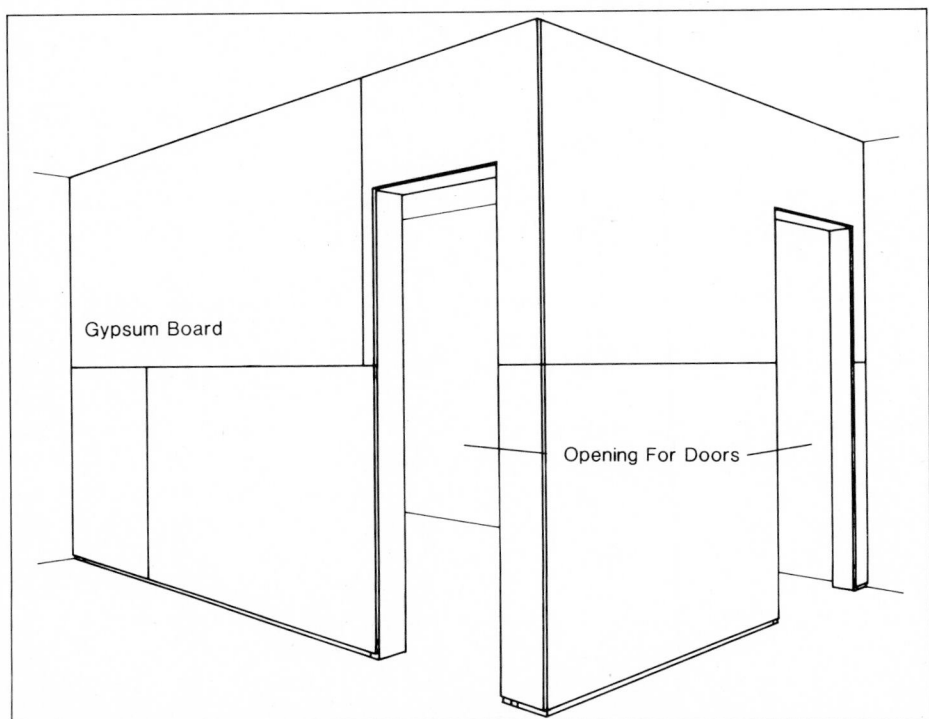

When all sheets of wallboard are in place, find the approximate center of the door opening(s) and drill a small hole. Cut over the frame and remove section with a sabre saw.

inches wide, over the tape on one side. Let dry; repeat on the other side.

Sealing seams and ceiling holes. It will require two spot coats of joint compound to cover the dimples where the board has been nailed. Let the first coat

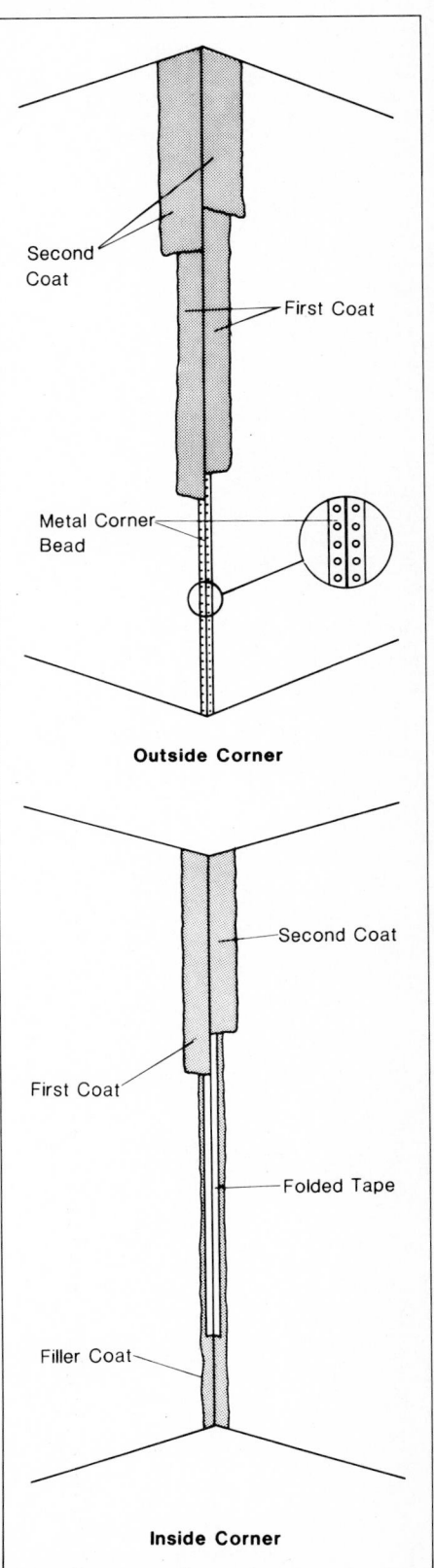

Outside corners require protective metal bead before applying joint compound and tape.

Repair small holes or dents in new, or old, wall-board with joint compound. Sand when dry.

Fill seams with compound, then apply seaming tape as smoothly as possible over the joint.

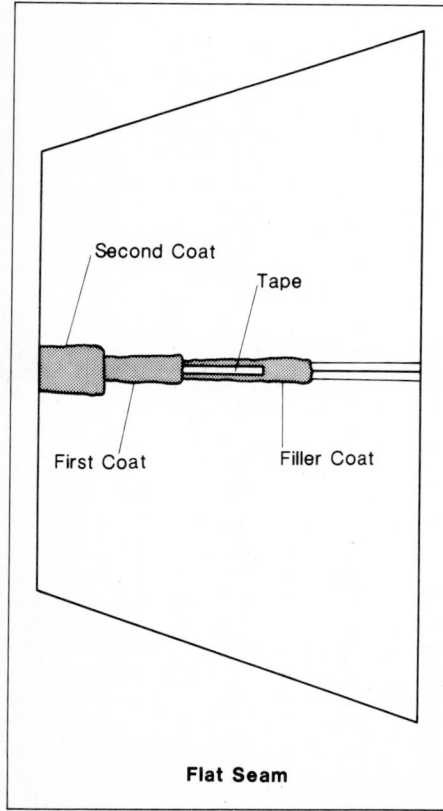

Second Coat

Tape

First Coat   Filler Coat

Flat Seam

Two more coats of joint compound seal joint. Feather the compound at edges. Sand smooth.

dry before applying the second. Apply compound to fill the channel formed by the tapered edge of the board at the joint. Place the joint tape on the compound while the compound is still wet. Let dry, then apply a 6- to 8-inch wide coat of joint compound over the tape. When this is dry, a final coat, 12- to 14-inches wide, should be applied. About 24 hours after applying the final coat, smooth the compound with a damp sponge. A light sanding may be required to smooth the seams completely. The walls are now ready for paint or wallpaper.

Plaster Walls

Because gypsumboard is easier to install and less expensive, plaster is rarely used today, even when the existing walls are plaster. Wet plastering is one of those jobs that normally is better left to the experienced professional. However, if you wish to use plaster and want to do the work yourself, you should carefully research the material options and the proper application methods, then work with plaster as practice before you start to plaster your new walls. Methods of application and mixtures vary with climate, so consult local experts before you begin. Instructions are given here only for repair of large holes in existing plaster walls.

Repairing Plaster

While it is easier to repair plaster walls with wallboard by creating a smooth edge to the cut-out plaster with a saw, taping and filing the joints, and finishing just as for a wallboard seam, you may wish to repair your plaster wall with the original material.

If you have been very careful in planning and the space cut out at the junction with a new wall has been kept to a minimum, you may have a rather narrow space to fill on each side of the new wall. Purchase new metal lath at your hardware store and nail it to the studs to fill the space between the members. If the lath can only be nailed on one side, slip it behind the existing lath on the other side, attach 6-inch lengths of string at two foot intervals to the lath and then attach dowels to the string. Twist the string on the dowels until the lath fits snugly against the existing lath and brace the dowels across the opening. Cut string and remove dowels when first layer of plaster has dried. Use a trowel or wide putty knife to apply the plaster, or

spackling compound, in a thin layer over the lath. Let it dry. Wet down the spackle and edges of the adjacent plaster before applying a second layer of plaster to bring the surface nearly level with the surface of the wall. After a day or two, repeat the moistening and apply a third layer of patching plaster. This layer may stand fractionally above the surface and be sanded down after it has dried.

Patching plaster and spackle have a tendency to dry out in time, so it is probable that you will have to sand down the areas that crack, moisten, and repair the surface every year or two.

Repairing a small hole. If you accidently chip or crack a section of plaster adjacent to the area that you have cut out, you may repair the damaged area with patching plaster or spackle. You should clean out any loose plaster with a small, stiff-bristle brush and carefully chip or sand away any rough edges. Moisten the edges of the crack or hole and apply patching plaster or spackle with a small trowel or putty knife. Make the surface as even as possible, bringing the fill material out over the edges of the crack or hole. Let the plaster dry completely before sanding the surface smooth.

Sheet Paneling

Prefinished paneling is probably the easiest type of wall finish for the do-it-yourselfer to apply. Panels come in 4x8-foot sheets, though a limited selection of other sizes are available on special order. Sheets ½ inch or thicker may be nailed or glued directly to studs. Thinner paneling will require a ¼- or ⅜-inch gypsumboard backing. However, the gypsumboard seams do not have to be filled before paneling is applied.

Preparing the wall base. Paneling can be applied directly to the new wall studs and over the plaster or gypsumboard of the existing walls. Where part of the existing wall was cut back for framing purposes, install a patch of gypsumboard or wood nailing strips to bring the surface even with the rest of the wall before applying the paneling.

Laying out the panels. Let the panels sit for 48 hours in the room where they are to be installed. This lets the wood adjust to the humidity level. Because the grain of real wood paneling will vary, stand panels against the walls and rearrange the panels until the desired pattern and appearance are achieved. Turn the panels over and number them in sequence on the back. Locate the studs in existing walls and mark them with a light pencil mark at the ceiling and floor.

Installing the panels. At a corner, begin nailing or gluing the panels. Make sure each panel is level and plumb. Use a spirit level, and if necessary, mark the wall with a chalkline/plumb bob suspended from the ceiling. Fit each panel in place against the last one installed. Align edges with studs from top to bottom. Because the corners in most houses are not perfectly true, the first panel may need to be trimmed slightly. However, if there is a slight gap at the corner, this may be covered with inside corner molding, just as the top will be covered with crown and the bottom with base trim. Spray-paint strips down the existing wall and on new wall studs, where the panels will meet. The color should match the color of the panel grooves. This will help hide slight gaps between panels.

Allowing for openings. To make cutouts for windows or doors, measure from the last installed panel and mark the opening on the back of the next panel. Measure and mark carefully. The old saying, "measure twice and saw once," is very good advice. An incorrect measurement will waste a panel. Cut out the opening using a sabre saw with a plywood blade, or with a handsaw that has a minimum of ten teeth per inch and minimum (narrow) set to the teeth. This is important. The wrong type of blade will splinter the panel's surface.

To position cutouts for electrical and other outlets, cover the surface of the outlet box with chalk, set the panel in place, and press against the box. The chalk outline of the box will appear on the back of the panel. Drill a hole in each corner of the box outline, about ¾ inch in diameter. Cut out the box opening with a keyhole or sabre saw.

Nailing the panels. There will be grooves on 16-inch centers; the nails can be driven into the groove. Regular small headed finishing or color-coded nails can be used. The nails should be at least 1¼ inches long if paneling is nailed directly to studs, and 2 inches long if paneling is installed over another surface. Countersink regular nails and fill each hole with a matching putty stick. Space the nails 6 inches apart on the edges and 12 inches apart inside the panel. You may also apply

You must nail sheet paneling to studs. You may use a stud finder to locate positions. Mark each stud location on the wall.

A stripe of paint, the same color as the sheet paneling, should be placed at joint locations to hide any irregular joints.

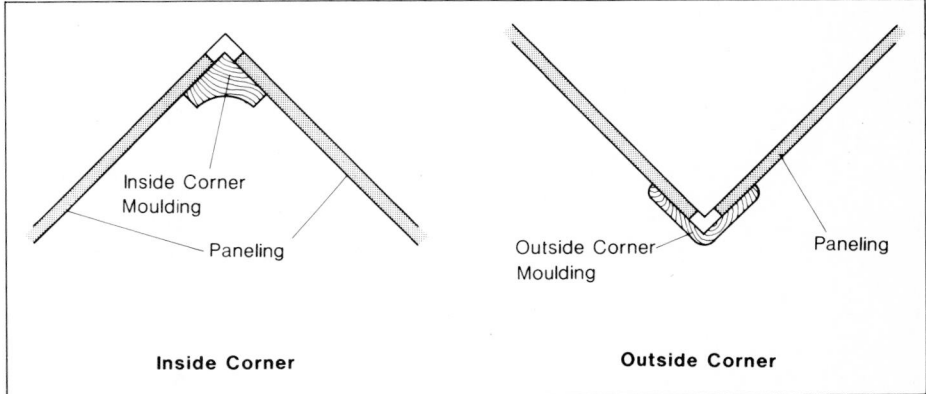

Inside Corner Moulding — Paneling — **Inside Corner**

Outside Corner Moulding — Paneling — **Outside Corner**

Corner joints do not have to meet exactly because inside or outside corner molding will cover these junctions and hide any gaps that may occur.

If you must cut openings in a sheet panel, measure carefully and drill a starter hole to allow cuts with either keyhole or sabre saw.

Cut openings with either hand or power tools. Choose the tool suitable for the opening. Be sure blade is sharp or panel will splinter.

the panels with a panel adhesive; follow the manufacturer's directions. Installation with adhesive may be best for application to plaster walls.

Leveling uneven walls with furring strips. If your walls have bad surfaces or are out of true, nail 1x2 inch furring strips to studs. Use a level and shims to bring the wall to true. You may also use furring strips on masonry walls, securing them with masonry nails, spacing them 16 inches on center.

Trim pieces. Once the paneling is up, apply the trim. Use a mitre box and coping saw to trim the molding to fit the installa-tion; make every measurement carefully. Joints in long sections of trim must be mitre cut for an overlay fit. Panel trim can be purchased unfinished or prefinished. Trim should be attached with the same type of nails used on the paneling.

Plank Paneling

A beautiful but more expensive paneling, (such as redwood) plank paneling comes in prefinished individual boards. It will take longer to install than sheet paneling because each plank is placed separately. Plank paneling requires special framing for both new and existing walls: new walls

Rough-sawn plank paneling is very attractive in casual settings such as recreation rooms.

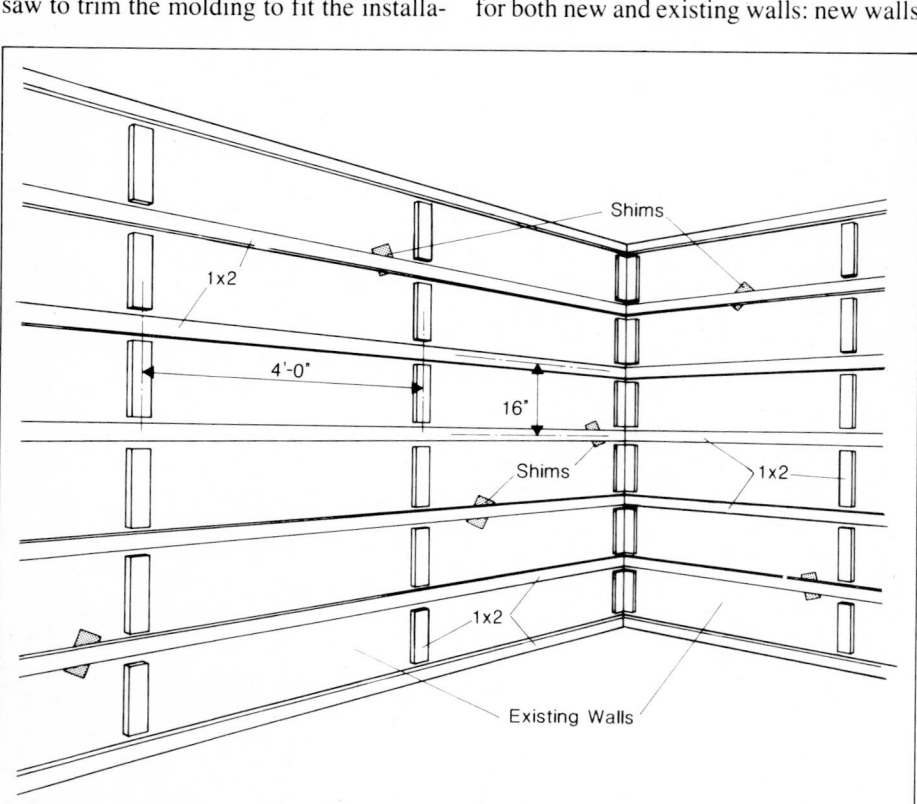

A wall that is out of plumb or that has an uneven surface must be leveled with furring strips before you attempt to install sheet panels. Shims may be needed to keep the wall true.

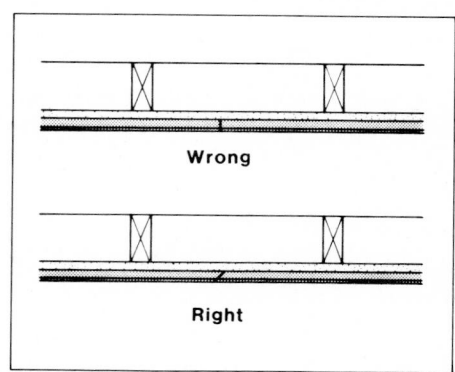

Cut base molding joints at a 45° mitre. This gives a smoother appearance and better fit.

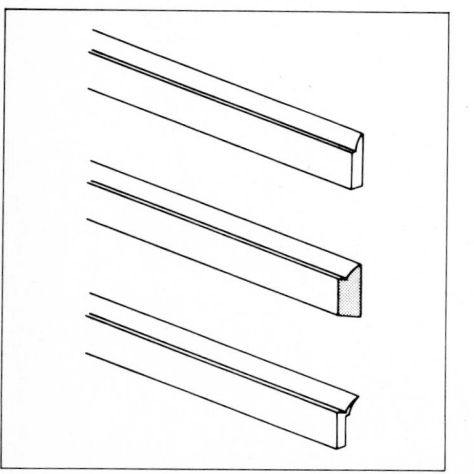

There are many types of base molding. Choose the style that is appropriate to your home.

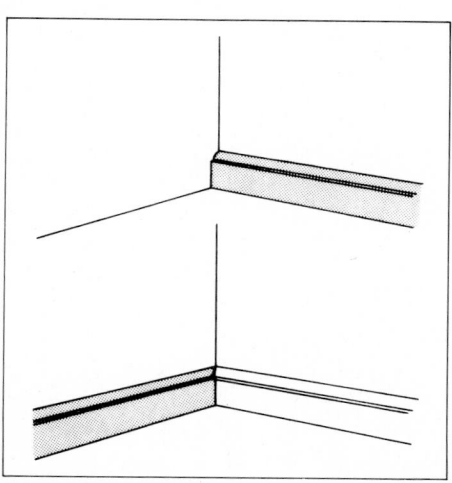

Place one base molding along one wall then cut the piece for the second wall to fit.

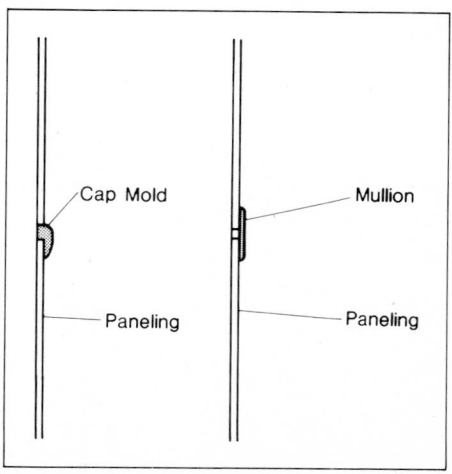

If sheet paneling requires a horizontal joint, use cap molding or a mullion to cover line.

need bridging between studs and existing walls must have nailing strips added. Follow the manufacturer's directions carefully when installing plank paneling, or you will see the nails in the finished wall. Use noncorrosive, best-quality, hot-dipped galvanized aluminum or stainless steel nails if using panels in a bathroom.

Installing board paneling. Measure all boards carefully and trial fit. Blind nail boards at tongue after tapping into place with a hammer and tapping block, a scrap with the groove edge intact to fit over board tongues. Check for plumb and, if

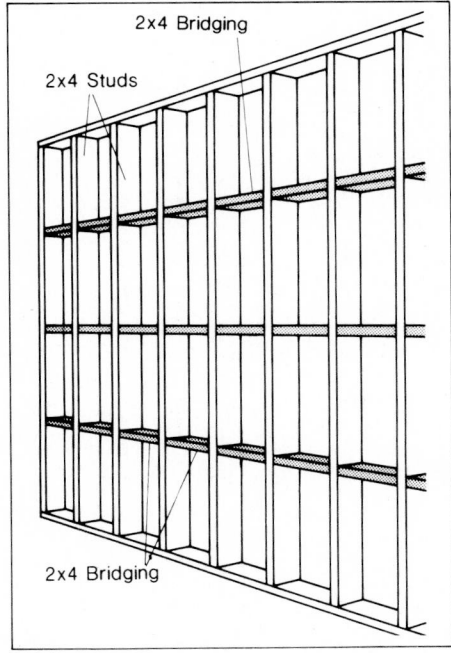

Plank paneling requires extra nailing surfaces. Add bridging between studs as nailers.

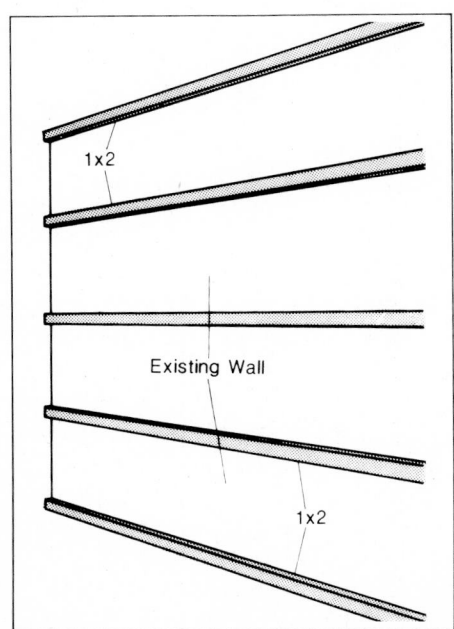

Nail furring strips to existing wall to provide horizontal nailing surface for planks.

necessary, slightly angle groove-to-groove fitting to make it square. When butt-joining short board ends together in the middle of a wall, be sure the joint falls over a stud or blocking.

At outside corner. Mitre-cut boards making 45° cuts on board edges, you can butt join. Trim off groove or tongue edges squarely, fine sand, and cover the joint with trim or molding.

Horizontal installation. Apply vertical furring strips to provide a good nailing surface. Space strips on wall studs about 24 inches apart. Nail additional furring strips around doors, windows, and any other openings.

To begin, nail a baseboard (a 1x6 or 1x8) with 6d finishing nails to each stud. Butt the groove edge of the first board against the baseboard, face nail the ends, and blind nail at studs. With wider lumber, face nail about ¾ inch from the baseboard, one nail per stud. Without a baseboard, place the first board tight against the floor and nail as above.

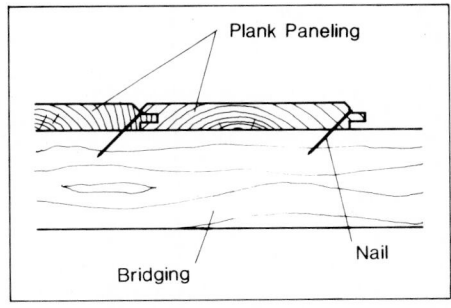

Blind nail plank paneling. Nail through plank at an angle just above the tongue.

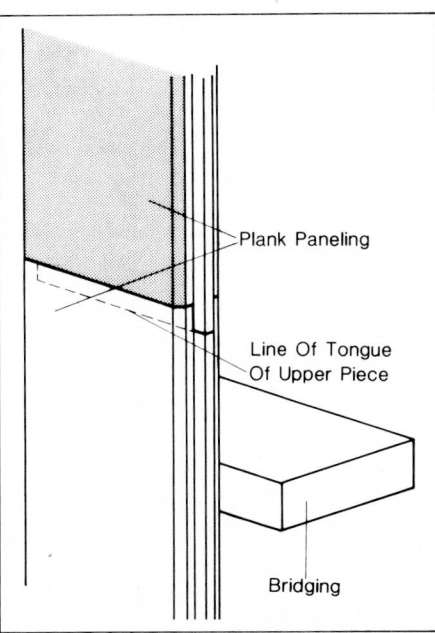

Ends of planks are cut with a deep tongue and groove so joints above bridging are tight.

On an outside corner, mitre the ends, cutting at greater than 45° to fit tightly. You may butt join boards, covering with molding or trim. Butt join inside corners. Handle baseboards the same way. Fit the last board at the ceiling by angle trimming the corner edge slightly with a block plane; set the wide part of the angle toward the wall.

Diagonal paneling. Diagonal paneling is often used on an accent wall. You need 15 percent more lumber, so that paneling 100 square feet of wall space requires 132½ board feet (115x1.15 = 132½), plus 5 percent for errors.

If walls need them, apply furring strips vertically. Start paneling at an inside corner, working left to right if you are right-handed, and right to left if left-handed, as for vertical paneling.

Arrange your first three boards flat on the floor so that on the wall, tongue edges will be up. Fit tongues in grooves tightly, position a carpenter's square and mark for a 45° mitre cut (see illustration) across all three boards. Saw and trial fit on the wall. Shaving the ends slightly will assure a tighter fit. Face nail the corner piece and blind nail the next at each end and at an intersecting stud or furring strip.

To butt join board ends in the middle of a wall, you can trim square or mitre cut. The joint should cover a stud, blocking, or furring strip. Butt join board at corners, covering outside edges with trim or molding.

Window and door trim. Before applying furring strips or paneling, remove any window and door trim or casings that will be replaced with plank boards. After finishing walls trim doors and windows, nailing build-up strips into jambs to cover board ends and/or furring strip edges where necessary.

Install vertical or diagonal paneling from an inside corner and work toward a window or door. To fit diagonal paneling at these openings, mitre-cut board ends. At corners of openings, position a board diagonally as it will be in paneling, mark horizontal and vertical edges of the corner, make a cut, and finish with a wood rasp for close fit. Horizontal paneling starts from the baseboard or floor and work up.

Hardboard or Plastic Panels

Hardboard panels covered in tough melamine plastic finish are a good choice for a bathroom or kitchen where walls need longlasting water resistance.

Melamine-surfaced hardboard panels installation is different from that for all-wood paneling. The panels are held in place by adhesives, not nails. They must not be applied over ceramic tile, fibreboard, or furring strips. Molding strips, for butt joints and corners are essential to the installation rather than just as trim. Since melamine-coated panels cannot be face or edge-nailed, the slotted moldings hold consecutive panels together. These moldings also provide edge-finish for the panels. It is essential to use the proper moldings.

Cap molding. This molding covers the top edges of a wainscot panel, or a horizontal edge where additional panels will be installed. Use it also as a finish strip around windows and doors, at wall-ceiling junctures, at floor (or baseboard) junctures.

Outside corner. This molding joins two panels that come together at outside corners.

Inside corner. Used where two panels come together at inside corners.

Divider. This molding joins two panels at a vertical joint.

Tub molding. Use this molding at the joint between wall panels and the bathtub.

Panels are sold in 4x8 foot sheets; most moldings come in 8 foot lengths. Use a backsaw (and mitre box) for cutting moldings. Use a keyhole saw for cutting openings within panels, such as those needed for electrical outlets, plumbing lines, faucets. Make pilot holes with an electric drill. Cut panels with a very sharp crosscut saw (8 to 12 teeth per inch) or a portable circular saw. To avoid cracks or breaks, cut panels as given in chart.

Saw	Panel faces
Keyhole	Up
Crosscut	Up
Portable circular saw	Down
Electric drill	Down

In addition to saws and electric drill, you will need a hammer, nails (for molding strips), tape measure, a plane or wood rasp (for dressing panel edges, a file (for use with moldings), a pencil compass (for scribing), pencil, notched trowel, base trim, adhesive, caulk, mineral spirits or turpentine, and rags for cleanup.

Preparation. Melamine-surfaced panels must be installed over a solid backing, such as plaster that is firm and smooth, or over gypsum wallboard. The existing wall must be sound, dry, smooth, and flat with no old loose paint or wallpaper, and free of dirt, dust, and grease. Let all new plaster cure for at least 30 days.

Caution. If you are paneling the inside of an exterior wall, install wood furring strips over polyethylene film and then cover the 3/8 inch or thicker wallboard. This gives a solid backing for gluing panels on and provides the vapor barrier that must be between the paneling and the exterior wall. Use this same method of furring strips and wallboard if you plan to panel a basement bath or shower room. Basements tend to be damp and often are not well-drained; a vapor barrier between paneling and existing wall is especially important.

Calculate how many 4x8 foot sheets you will need. Be sure to include lengths and type of molding strips you will be using. On graph paper, make a scaled drawing of each wall, noting size and location of fixtures, soap dishes, towel bars, electrical outlets and so on.

Order the material and supplies you will need. When materials and supplies arrive, let panels and adhesive, as well as caulk, adjust to the room temperature for 48 hours. Separate the panels and stand them, on long edges, around the walls while you prepare the room.

Remove all baseboards. It will make your job of cutting and fitting much easier. Mark on the wall the location of all moldings, which should be nailed onto the wall surface at stud locations.

Wainscot installation. Mark a level line that extends horizontally around all the walls. Leave the necessary gap between paneling and floor for later installation of the base trim. Measuring up from the floor, draw a line around the room that will indicate where the top of the base trim will reach.

Allow for a total of 3/16 inches between panels, to allow for a 1/16 inch expansion space between the panel edge and the inside of the divider molding. Never force the panels into position; always leave this small space for expansion.

To start paneling, begin at the inside corner. Nail cap molding along the line marking the top of the wainscot (use miter joints in corners). Nail an inside corner

molding in the corner, extending from top of the base trim line to the bottom of the exposed flange of the cap molding. It will be necessary to cut away a little of the wall flange where it overlaps the cap molding.

Now, check the corner to see if it is straight and plumb. If not, it will be necessary to scribe the edge of the panel and trim it to conform to the corner.

Fit, but do not yet install, the divider molding for the exposed vertical edge of the panel. (If necessary, remove part of the wall flange where it overlaps the cap molding.)

Full-height panel installation. Start at an inside corner and nail a strip of inside corner molding extending from the line at top of base trim up to ceiling.

Next, install a strip of cap molding along the wall-ceiling juncture. Slip a panel into position and, if necessary, scribe and trim panel edge to fit the corner. Check with level or plumb line to be sure that the edge away from the corner is plumb. Cut and fit a divider molding, but do not nail it in place yet.

Cutting and Putting Up Panels
Dry-fit the first panel to the molding, which has been nailed up. Lay it face down on a padded worktable (to prevent scratching) and dust the back with lint-free cloth. Using a notched trowel and recommended adhesive, spread adhesive over the entire back of the panel. A trowel with 3/16 inch notches is suggested unless otherwise specified.

For waterproof seal, put adhesive or a caulking bead (as recommended by the adhesive manufacturer) into the molding grooves.

Then slip the panel into position and press tightly against the wall. Apply adhesive into the groove of one of the divider moldings that has previously been fitted and set aside, and slip it into place along the panel edge.

Check to see that the divider is plumb, then fasten that edge of the panel to the wall by nailing through the exposed flange on the molding strip. Return to the panel and press it firmly against the wall, working from center outward toward edges. Repeat this after 20 minutes to ensure good contact. Remove excess adhesive as soon as possible, using a soft cloth and mineral spirits or turpentine. Install additional panels in a logical sequence, following the procedures just discussed.

Hardboard and plastic panels are flexible enough to allow bending into position.

Interior walls may be given a stucco-like finish that can then be wood trimmed.

Freshly applied texture compound will accept a variety of finishes from different tools.

Note. To put a prefitted panel into place when only one side is open — that is, surrounded by moldings on two sides and across the top — set the panel on the floor and bend the panel slightly, as shown. When the two opposite edges can be slipped into molding grooves along both edges, release the curved panel, and slide the panel upward into position, in the top molding groove. Finish the job by installing base trim at the bottom of the wall.

Masonry Walls

Adding a heavy masonry wall will require investigation of the bearing capacity of your foundation. It is possible that it will not support the extra weight of a true masonry wall. You should always consult an expert to determine this.

Stucco-like walls. There are easy and inexpensive ways to achieve the effect of real brick or stucco. There are acrylic-based compounds or textured paints on the market that are applied directly over wallboard. The materials can be given nearly any desired texture with a trowel, broom, paint roller, or even a piece of corrugated cardboard. The texturing material is applied to the wall with a trowel or wide putty knife (such as a drywall knife) and textured with whatever tools are required to get the surface finish desired. This simulated "stucco" and thin "bricks", discussed below, are suggested for interior use as a practical alternative to heavier and more expensive solid masonry wall construction.

Thin, face brick is fireproof and will give a masonry look to a prefabricated fireplace.

Bricks. For the appearance of brick, there are a number of thin "bricks" on the market that, when applied properly, create the appearance of a full brick wall. The brick units are installed in an adhesive mortar applied directly to plaster or gypsumboard with a wide putty knife. The brick units are pressed firmly into the mortar, wiggled slightly to get a good "set". Then a brush is used to smooth the mortar joints. Finally, the wall is given a coat of protective sealer to make the wall easy to clean.

An extra touch with wood. Whatever wall finish or combination of finishes you want, the impact may be heightened by adding wood. Whether you are using paint, wallpaper, acrylic stucco, brick, or a combination of finishes, a new and more dramatic appearance may be achieved when wood is included in the design. Any number of combinations is possible. Use your imagination to create your own personal design.

COVERING THE CEILINGS
Gypsumboard

The most common type of ceiling for new construction is gypsumboard. It is relatively easy and inexpensive to install, but is harder to install on ceilings than on walls because working overhead is awkward. Just as for walls, plan out the pattern for applying the gypsumboard to the ceiling. The actual work then is minimized. The installation can be accomplished in the same basic manner as wall installation — except that you are working at a difficult angle. The lengths of the sheets run at right angles to the ceiling joists.

Installation. At least two people are needed to install a gypsumboard ceiling; an inexperienced worker using 12-foot-long sheets may even need two helpers.

Climb a rung or two up a step ladder, until you can reach the ceiling comfortably for nailing. Have the helper hand one end of the gypsumboard up and then lift the other end, using a 2x4 to hold it in place temporarily. Keep the 2x4 brace against a joist so there is no chance of puncturing the gypsumboard. Hold the board in place with your head or one hand while you nail the end in front of you. A few nails are needed to set the end. Now move and set a few nails in the middle. Finally, set a few nails in the opposite end. Nail every 5 to 7 inches to finish.

Finish the seams exactly the same as the wall seams. The finished ceiling will be completely smooth.

Texturing the wallboard ceiling. You may prefer your ceiling to have a finish different from the smooth finish normally used on walls. To achieve this, first give the ceiling a coat of white paint. A number of effects can then be achieved with gypsum compound and various tools. For instance, the compound may be applied to the ceiling with a mop, or troweled on in swirls for the desired effect. Whatever design you attempt, practice on a scrap piece of gypsumboard before beginning to work on the ceiling. The gypsum compound design will not need painting once it has dried.

Another popular way to finish a gypsumboard ceiling is to have it "blown". This requires a blower to spray gypsum compound onto the ceiling to achieve a strippled finish. The result is very attractive, but the process does require a professional with the proper equipment. Unless you have experience and access to such equipment, it is not a do-it-yourself project.

Plaster

Plaster application is difficult for the do-it-yourselfer to master; working overhead only compounds the problem. Trying to patch an existing plaster ceiling is even more difficult than applying a fresh ceiling. Find a professional to install a plaster ceiling unless you can learn the technique from a technical or extension course.

Paneling and Wood

Sheet paneling, plank paneling, and tongue-and-groove lumber are not difficult for the do-it-yourselfer to install on a ceiling and can be very attractive in the proper setting, especially on a vaulted ceiling. The darker colors of wood can make a room seem smaller and make a standard height ceiling seem too low; a vaulted ceiling or high ceiling compensates for this problem. Installation of the sheets or planks on the ceiling is the same as application to the wall surface.

Installing Ceiling Tile

The easiest, and often the least expensive type of ceiling for the do-it-yourselfer to install, is the tiled ceiling. The application is completely dry — requiring no painting, pasting, or wet compound.

Nailing to furring strips. Tiles in one-foot squares can be applied to a level ceiling by nailing 1x2 furring strips at one-foot on center, perpendicular to the ceiling joists. Position the tiles and staple them into place. These tiles have a tongue and

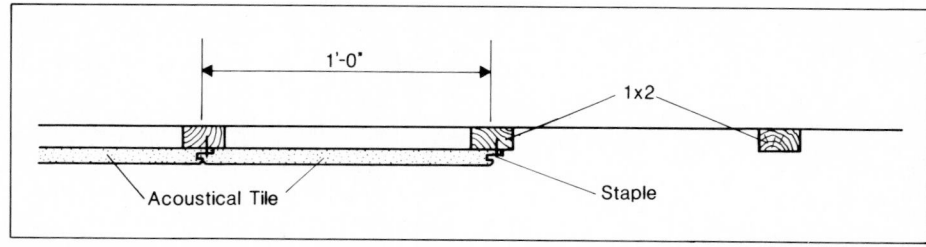

Acoustical tile is simple to install. You may staple into place to furring strips. You may also nail acoustical tile directly into a ceiling if it is smooth and flat.

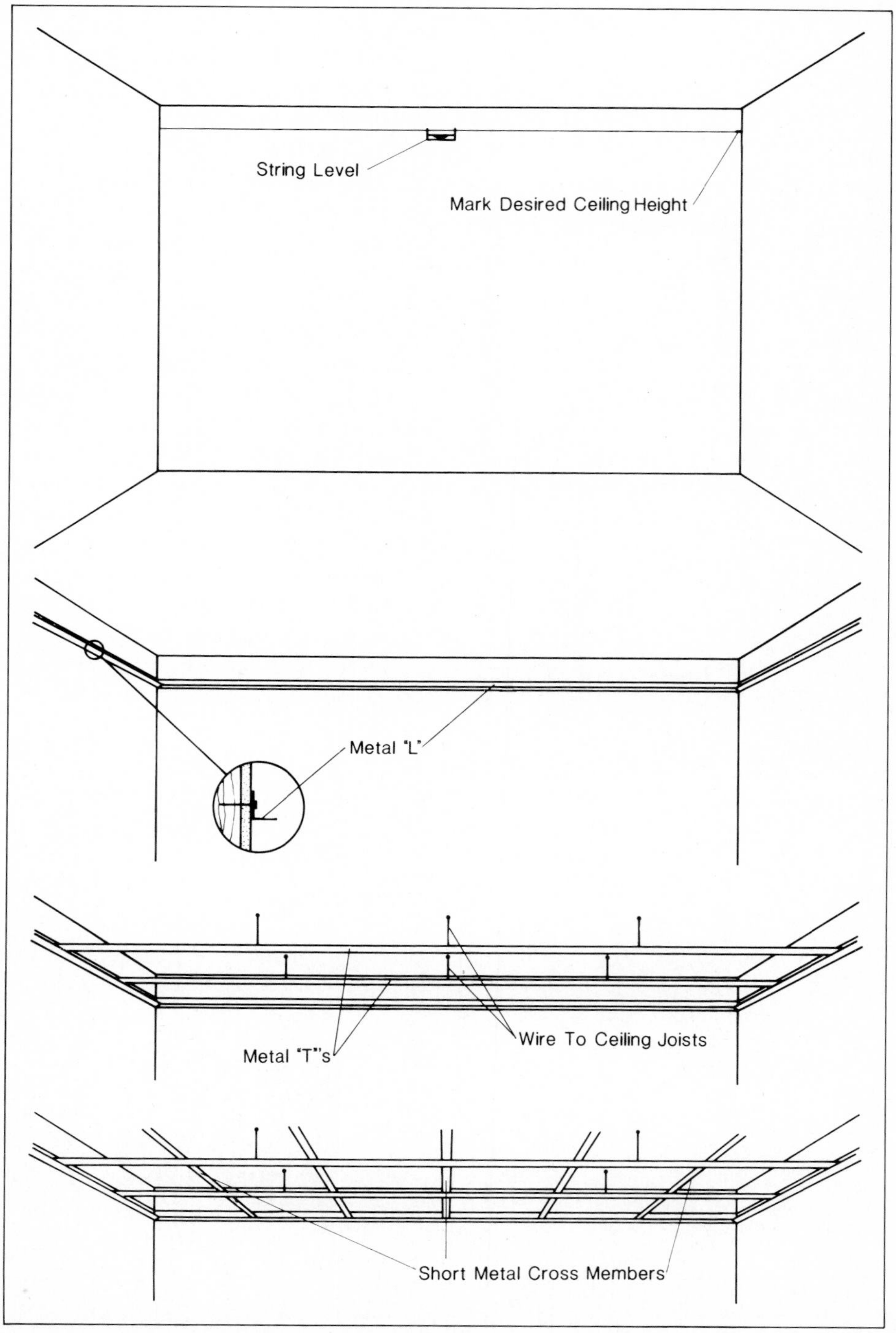

A suspended ceiling will create a new, level ceiling, hide ductwork, cracked plaster and uneven surfaces. Create level on the wall and install framework.

groove and should be stapled to the furring strips through the tongue so that the staples will not show. If the ceiling is both smooth and level; the tiles may be glued directly into place without using furring strips.

Suspended ceiling framework. The second system uses a framework of lightweight metal to hold 2x4-foot ceiling tile panels. This installation is especially good if the existing ceiling is uneven. Measure your room and plan the ceiling. Your dealer will help you determine amount and type of frame lengths and panels needed.

Mark the desired finished height of the ceiling in each corner, measuring up from the floor. However, if your floor is not perfectly level, mark only one corner. Then use a string and string level to mark the remaining corners. Nail the metal "L" channel pieces to the wall studs at the marks. Use a level to keep the "L" level and even.

Determine which way you want the 4-foot length of the panel to run and place screw-eyes in the ceiling joists every 4 to 6 feet to hold "Ts" with wire. Check the level at each tie to keep the ceiling even. Set the short cross members into the long "Ts". Center the short pieces every 4 feet. They will be perpendicular to the long "T" sections. When the metal frame is complete, lay the tiles in one after another.

FINISHING THE FLOOR

Installation of the floor is usually the last step in the job. Once the flooring is in place and finished, the remoldeler can relax and enjoy the results.

Wall-To-Wall Carpet

Wall-to-wall carpet is still the most popular type of flooring in use, even though its popularity has declined since the introduction of newer, easier-to-install materials. However, carpet comes in various types and there are different ways in which it can be installed. The two most traditional methods are explained here in detail. These are the methods most commonly used by the do-it-yourselfer: (1) the installation of separate carpet and pad stretched over tackless strips; and (2) installation of foam-backed carpet with double-stick tape.

It is suggested, however, that you leave most carpet installation to the expert. This is because the labor cost is small in relation to the cost of quality carpet. A mistake by a do-it-yourselfer could be very expensive, and most quality carpeting is sold on an "installed cost" basis.

The Tackless Strip Method

Step one: preparation. First, the base molding or "baseboard" is set so that it is ½ inch above the floor. This space allows the board to cover the carpet edge. If the baseboard is already in place and you don't want to remove it, you can add shoe molding ½ inch above the floor surface either before or after the carpet is installed. Applying the baseboard or shoe molding first is suggested; you can use a plywood spacer laid on the floor to ensure an even ½ inch space.

To remove original baseboard, or any other trim, insert a pry, a crowbar or similar tool, behind the board and pull a little at a time. Place a small block behind the pry to protect the wall. Try to pry at or near the stud locations; this is where the molding is attached. Careful work will not only avoid wall damage, it will permit you to reuse the trim.

Step two: fastening the tackless strips. With the baseboard or shoe molding nailed in the proper place, install the "tackless strip". This is a length of narrow, thin wood with scores of slanted tack points facing upward. The tack points hold the carpet in place. Several small nails are driven into the length of the tackboard to secure it to the floor. The same technique is used whether it is an existing

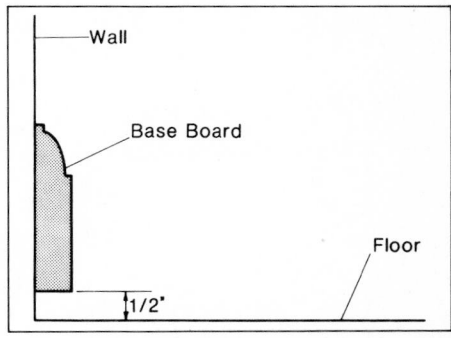
Wall-to-wall carpeting should fit beneath base molding. Allow ½ inch space.

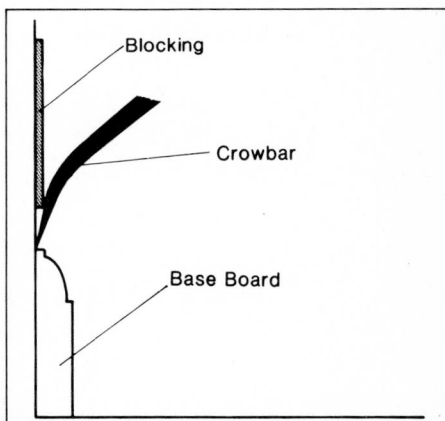
Use blocking to protect wall surface if you must pry base board free to raise it.

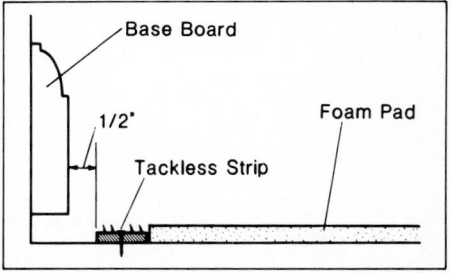
Nail tackless strip ½ inch away from the base board and lay padding up to the strip.

A suspended ceiling allows installation of recessed lights in this artist's studio.

Suspended ceiling panels drop into place with ease. They come in many styles.

wood, concrete or tile floor. Nail the tackboard along the walls about ½ inch away from the face of the baseboard, with the tack points aimed toward the wall. At doors or other openings, use a metal gripper bar.

Step three: laying the pad. Cut the foam or other type of carpet pad with scissors and lay in place. The pad can be pieced as necessary. Simply lay the pieces

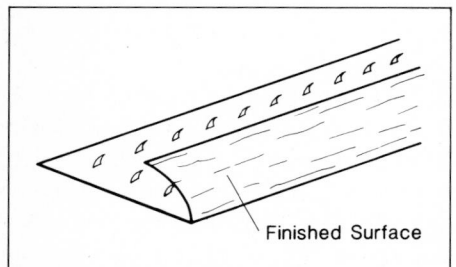

Use metal gripper bar at any door or opening. This holds carpet and protects the edge.

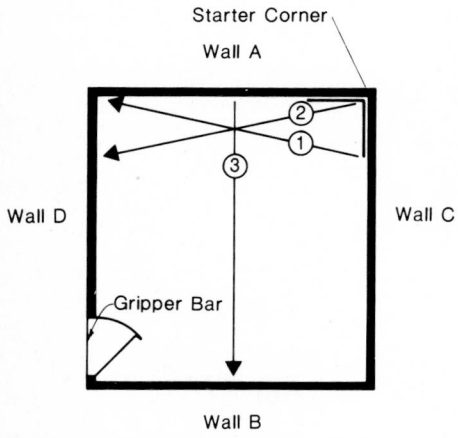

Set carpet at corners of one wall, set along that wall and then set along opposite wall.

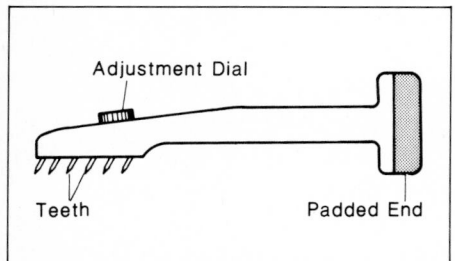

A knee kicker has adjustable teeth that grab and stretch carpet when padded end is pushed.

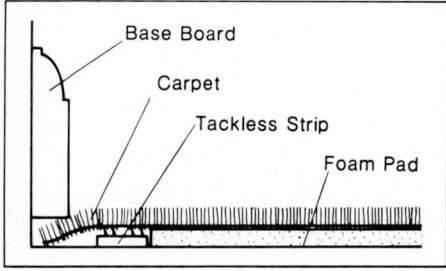

Strip will hold the carpet in place. Edges will be hidden under the base board.

side-by-side. It is not necessary to secure them to each other. The pad should go up to the inside edge of the tackless strip.

Step four: placing the carpet. Unroll the carpet in the room so that the carpet width (12-foot or 15-foot) is parallel to an equal or smaller dimension. (For rooms larger than 15 feet in both directions, the carpet will have to be seamed.) Roll the carpet out so that the excess lays against one or two walls. If the room is approximately the same width as the carpet, the excess will be at one end only. Otherwise the excess will be on two walls.

Be sure the carpet does not gap away from the wall where it fits flush. Use a carpet knife to cut away the carpet excess at the walls where it overlaps. Cut close to the corner, but leave a little extra along the wall — about ½ inch. This will ensure that the carpet is not too short.

Step five: permanently setting the carpet. When the excess is cut away, lay the carpet over the tackless strip and under the baseboard. Start in a corner. Use a "knee kicker", which can be rented, to place the carpet over the tackless strip. Install about three feet on each side of the starter corner. Be sure the teeth of the

kicker are adjusted for the thickness of the carpet you are using. Improper adjustment can tear through the carpet, pull the pad up over the tackless strip, or not grab the carpet firmly enough to stretch it. The knee kicker is placed near the edge of the carpet (about 1½ inches away) with the slant of the teeth toward the wall. Tap with the knee kicker from an "all-fours" position. As you hit the knee kicker, it pulls the carpet over the tackless strip. When the knee kicker is released the carpet springs back and is caught and held by the tack points. Then secure the remainder of the carpet, working all around the perimeter of the room. You may need to cut away small amounts of excess carpet as you go. This is all right. It is much better than to have to put excess stretch in the carpet and then discover that you do not have enough to cover the tackless strip.

Seaming the carpet. The carpet for a large room will need to be seamed. Overlap the carpet about two inches and match the pattern or nap. Then, using a straightedge as a guide, cut through both pieces with a carpet knife. You will need a roll of hot-melt seaming tape and a seaming iron. Rent a seaming iron; Do not use your reg-

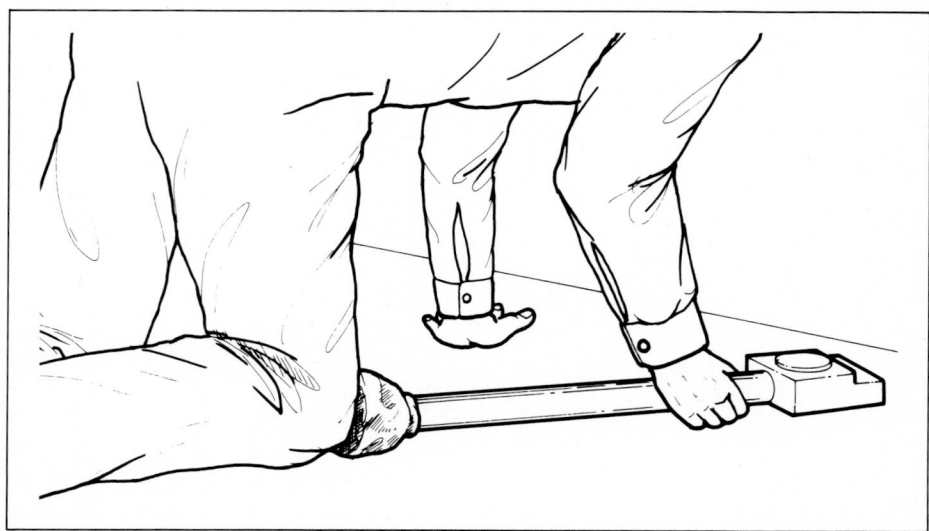

Kneel on the carpet and place the knee kicker so the end with the teeth is near the wall. Place your knee against the padded end and push. Carpet will stretch over the tackless strip.

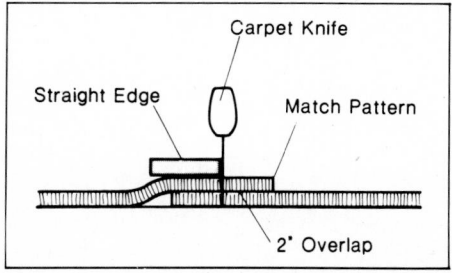

To seam, overlap section and cut through both layers. Use a straight edge as guide.

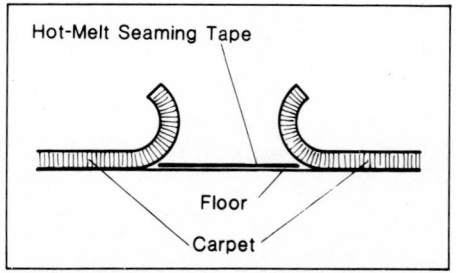

Place seaming tape on the floor under the cut edges. Use special iron to melt wax.

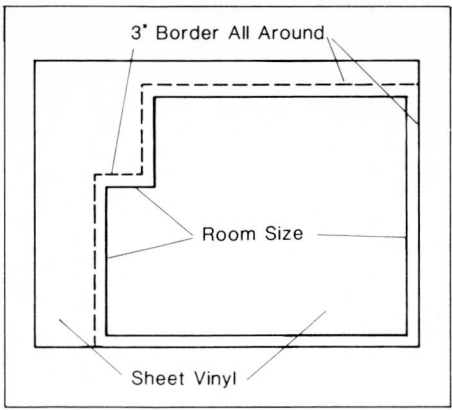

Cut sheet vinyl to approximate size; allow a 3 inch border on all sides to be trimmed later. Allow vinyl to lie in your room for 24 hours.

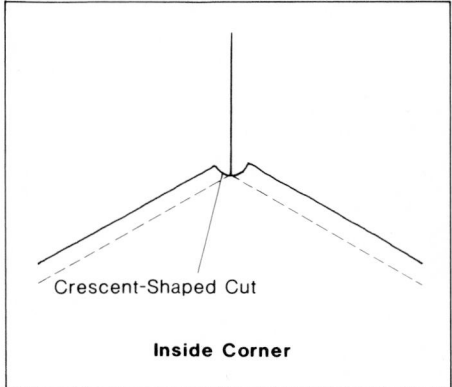

Cut a small crescent at inside corners to ease sheet vinyl flat before trimming.

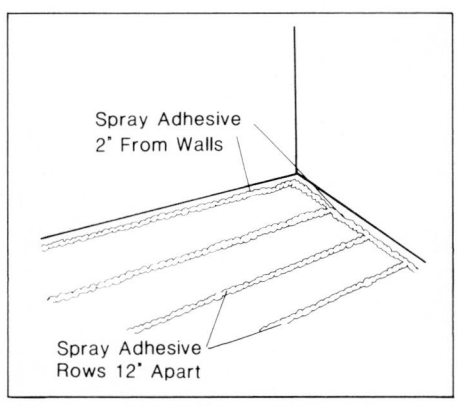

If you are using spray adhesive, apply in lines as shown to provide good coverage.

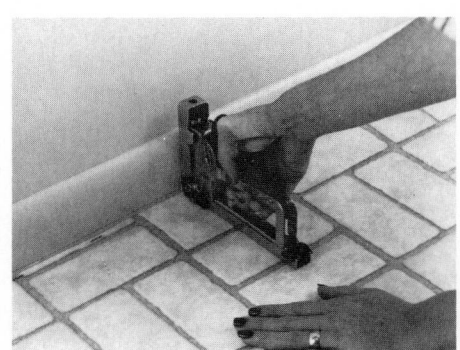

Sheet vinyl flooring may also be stapled down around the perimeter of the room.

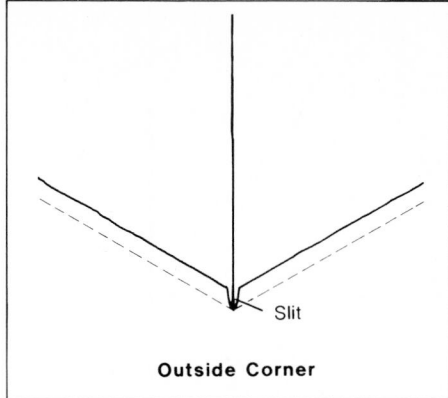

Slit sheet vinyl at outside corner to allow material to lie smoothly on the floor. Cut carefully so slit is slightly short of the floor.

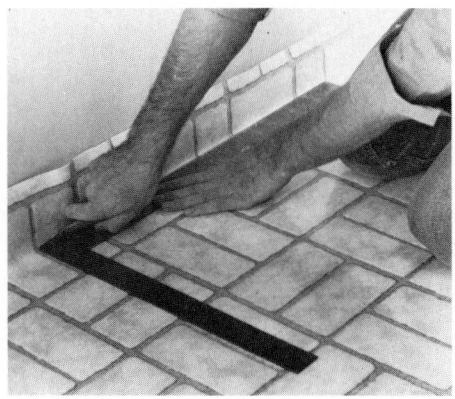

Use a metal straightedge to guide a knife when cutting excess away at the walls.

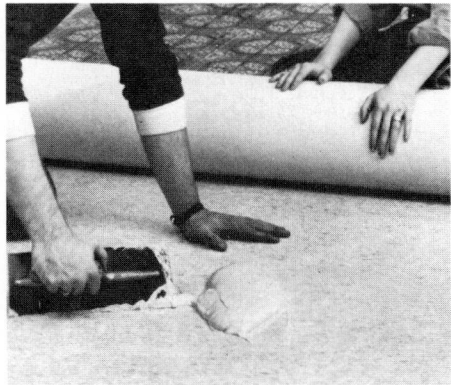

Bulk cement should be troweled down on one side of the room at a time.

Sheet flooring provides an attractive and usually seamless floor.

Sheet Vinyl

Today's sheet vinyls come in more colors and styles than ever before, in several widths and are made of materials that are easier to work with and to maintain. Most sheet vinyls, especially cushioned vinyl, are flexible and can be stretched slightly if required. Standard widths are 6 feet, 12 feet, and 15 feet. This allows you to place sheet vinyl in most rooms without seaming.

Preparing the sheet vinyl. Carefully measure the area to be covered. This is critical. An incorrect measurement could mean you to have to install with an unnecessary seam in the flooring. Lay out the sheet vinyl in a large area, then mark the room size onto the sheet. Add three inches all around to allow adjustment in final fitting. Cut this line; you can use a utility knife, another sharp knife, or ordinary shears. Place the flooring in the room where it is to be installed. The excess three inches will lap up onto the walls. At outside corners make relief cuts just long enough so the material will lay flat on the floor. At inside corners, trim the corner in a crescent shape. Do this gradually, cutting a little at a time, until the material lays flat.

Installing the sheet vinyl. Trim the excess along each wall, using a framing square as a straightedge and a utility or other sharp knife for the cuts. Small gaps that occur during cutting will be covered with shoe molding or quarter round later. When the flooring is cut to fit, roll back one-half and apply adhesive to the exposed floor with a trowel or, for easier installation, apply a recommended spray adhesive. Spray a line of adhesive about two inches from the walls, and interior lines about 12 inches on center. Roll down the flooring. Repeat on the other half. Run a push broom from center to sides to eliminate any air pockets. You may wish to apply additional pressure with a rented 50 lb. roller. Sometimes it is helpful to use staples to hold the flooring in place at the edges of the room.

Ceramic Tile — Pregrouted Sheets

The easiest installation calls for use of pregrouted sheets. For this job, mark a chalkline on the subfloor as for resilient tiles. The installation sequence is very similar, except that you must allow for grout lines between sheets. Trowel adhesive onto the floor in the area you are going to work. If the adhesive is a fast-setting type, spread only as much as you can use in the time limits stated. Press the tile sheets into place along the chalkline. A ceramic tile cutting tool is needed to chip the tile to fit around odd shaped fixtures. Along a wall, the sheets can be cut by scoring with a sharp glass cutter along a straightedge, and setting the sheet over a metal rod. Place boards along either side of the scored line for even distribution of pressure and snap at the scored line by stepping on the boards on each side. Curved cuts are made with a set of tile nippers. The nippers will bite into the tile and cut out small pieces.

Once the tiles are in place, grout between the sheets. A silicone rubber compound is applied using a caulking gun, with the tip cut to fit the joints. Remove excess grout by wiping along the joint with cheesecloth soaked in denatured alcohol. Do not wipe across the joint, only along it. There are also grout compounds that are spread with a squeege. The excess is wiped away with a wet sponge as soon as the grout has firmed.

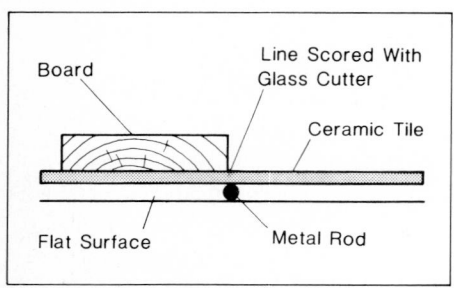

Tile that has been scored will break easily if pressed over a sturdy wire.

Ceramic Tile — Thin-set Installation

Room preparation. Since you will be raising the level of the floor itself, check bottoms of doors to check for adequate clearance. If necessary trim the door. To check the clearance, place two tiles, one on top of the other, against the inside door edge and mark a line above the top tile. Using a level to ensure straightness, extend this line across the bottom of the door. Remove the doors by tapping out the hinge pins. (If the hinge is an old style one, you must remove the screws holding it to the frame of the door.) Then cut along the line to provide sufficient space for the new floor. If you need to remove only a little of the door bottom, use a plane. If you must remove a fair amount, use a saw.

If you are tiling just the floor, remove the shoe molding at the base of the wall,

but leave the base molding in place. To remove the shoe molding, insert a thin pry bar under the molding.

Floor surface preparation. The surface must be clean and completely dry. Cement floors must be made level and free of holes or protrusions. Painted floors should be roughened by sand to insure a good bond. Old ceramic tile and linoleum must be removed or roughened, as long as the old surface is firm and unchipped. Use a floor or disc sander to roughen the surface. If any special problems exist — such as a surface that is soaked with oil, or one that is not level because of chipped concrete or cupped and warped floor boards — consult your tile dealer. In many cases, the best course is a layer of particle board or plywood, or a new concrete over the old. The subfloor must be level for a good bond.

Setting up the layout. First, snap the chalklines. You will want to cut as few

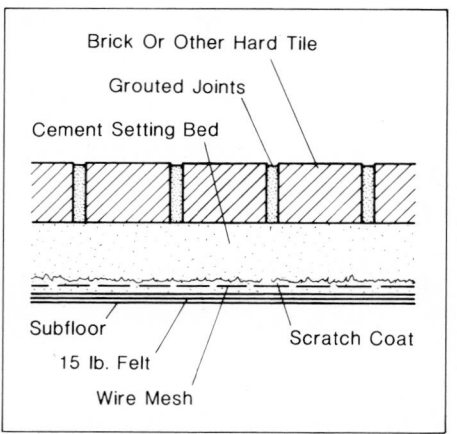

Thick-set tile needs professional installation.

tiles as possible. Working from the center, dry lay a row of loose tile along one working line. Do this carefully and be sure to leave spaces for your grout lines, since most floor tile does not come with built-in spacers. If you will need a finishing tile that is cut to less than half its size, make an adjustment. If the grout line for your installation is fairly wide, make the line smaller to add space next to the wall. If the grout line is fairly narrow, expand it to eliminate cutting the tile. If neither of these options is viable, you will have to move the chalkline over to one side or the other. Move it a space equal to half a tile. Then test the layout again. Check both chalklines in this manner.

Apply the adhesive. The working lines divide the floor into quarters. You will lay one quarter of the room at a time.

It is probably best to start with the corner that is farthest from the door. You can nail wood battens along the chalklines. Spread the proper adhesive, using the method and trowel size recommended by your dealer or tile manufacturer. Some adhesives set at an angle to the tile; others are spread in circles. Do a small area at a time so the adhesive does not dry out before the tiles are set. Spread only a little near the wooden guides, if you are using them. If your tile is extra thick and has a deep, ridged back pattern, also spread the adhesive on the back of each tile. (This is called "buttering.")

Laying the tile. Floor tile is laid either jack-on-jack (stacked vertically) or running bond style. The general principles for both arrangements are the same, and both start at the center of the room and work out toward the corners.

Technique guidelines. With a slight twisting motion, press each tile firmly into place. Do not slide tiles against each other, or you will wind up with excessive adhesive buildup in the corners. This will have to be cleaned out before you can grout the tile.

As you lay the tile, check the straightness of the courses with a straightedge and square. If they are a little out of line, wiggle the tiles until they are true. To set the tiles flat and firmly embedded in the adhesive, slide a flat board covered with carpet or felt across the surface, and tap the board with a hammer. The felt or carpet prevents scratching or marring the tile. The block should be large enough to cover several tiles at a time.

As you come nearer to the wall corners, your working space will lessen. Try not to walk on tiles you have just set. (Some adhesives dry fairly quickly; others do not.) If you must walk on the tile, lay flat, smooth boards over them to help distribute your weight.

Laying a jack-on-jack pattern. Take three tiles. Place Tile 1 in the corner created at the room center by the crossed working lines. Place Tile 2 next to Tile 1, and Tile 3 above Tile 1. These three tiles form the basis of the stair-step layout that will fan out to cover the quarter of the room on which you are working. Fill in, beginning at one working line and moving up and over to the other working line. When you come to the wall edge, leave the space open for cut tile. After completing one quarter of the room, repeat the process for each quarter. Make sure you clean the adhesive off the tiles as you go, because it is extremely hard to remove once it has set up.

Laying a running bond. For this, you will fill half of the floor at a time. In every other course, the working line will run through the center tile.

Applying the grout. You may prefer gray grout on the floor, since gray hides dirt better than white grout. You can buy the grout premixed, or you can mix it yourself. Allow the floor to set in place for 24 hours (or follow the directions of the adhesive manufacturer). Then clean all debris from the joints and, if necessary, remove any spacers. Work the grout between the tiles with the flat side of a rubber trowel or squeege. When the joints are firm, wipe the tiles with a damp sponge. Then polish with a soft cloth. Allow the grout to dry for another day or so. Then wash the floor with a clean mop and household detergent and water. Polish with a soft cloth and add a grout sealer.

A variety of tile was used in this bathroom. The floor is slate with dark mortar. White grout contrasts with the dark tile and blends with the white tile.

Wood parquet tile was applied to the floor of this room done in contemporary style.

Tile is both a practical and a decorative element in this European kitchen.

Tile floors may give a dramatic appearance to any room in the house.

Vinyl tile in decorative patterns will look seamless when it is perfectly installed.

Several different types of tile were used in this kitchen. The floor tile, in a pattern created with two different types of tile, is repeated on the counter.

7
BUILDING STAIRWAYS

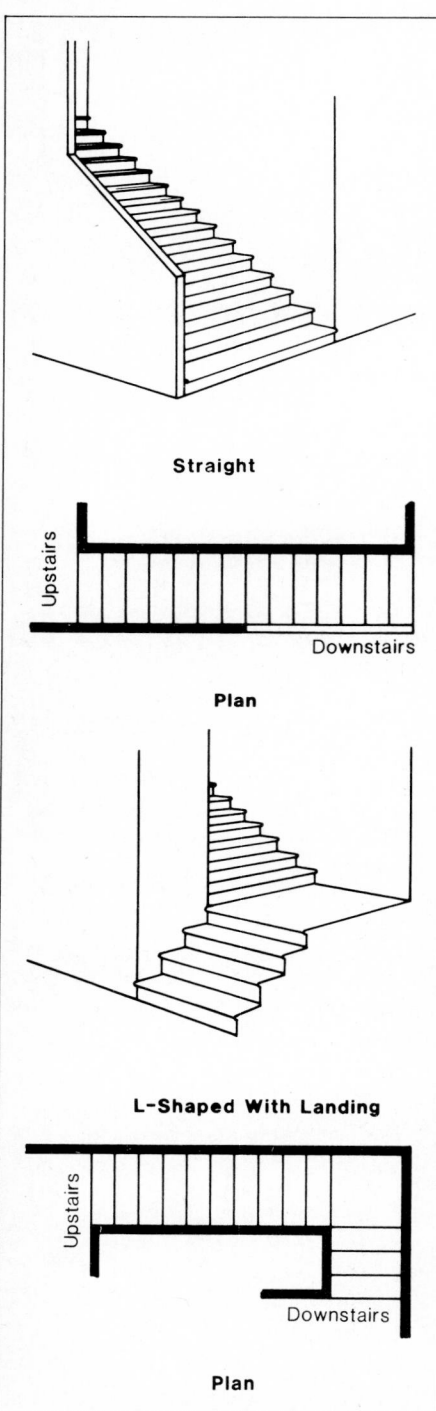

Straight

Plan

L-Shaped With Landing

Plan

Either a straight or an L-shaped run of stairs are common in spacious, older homes.

A set of stairs is needed for general access for any expansion into the basement or attic. If you already have a set in good condition, you may only need to add finish materials.

However, in many cases the steps or stairs entering the attic or basement area were built for occasional use only, so that they are not sturdy or attractive enough for the main living areas.

STAIR DESIGN

New stairs can be designed in a number of ways to take advantage of the available space. Stairs can be built on-site or, in the case of spiral staircases, can be purchased already constructed and easily installed where needed. The type of staircase you will use usually depends on the type of space you have available.

Straight-Run Stairs

A straight staircase may be located against a long wall. The stairway can be held to a minimum width and take up as little space as possible from a room, but will require a long, unobstructed run. However, the layout of your rooms on either end of the run may make it difficult to find enough length for a straight staircase. It is the easiest staircase to build on-site, except for the ladder type sometimes used with lofts.

Determine the length necessary for the straight staircase using the dimensions for

A straight run of stairs usually leads from the front door to an upper hall. This set of stairs was originally open, but the area beneath the flight was enclosed for storage space.

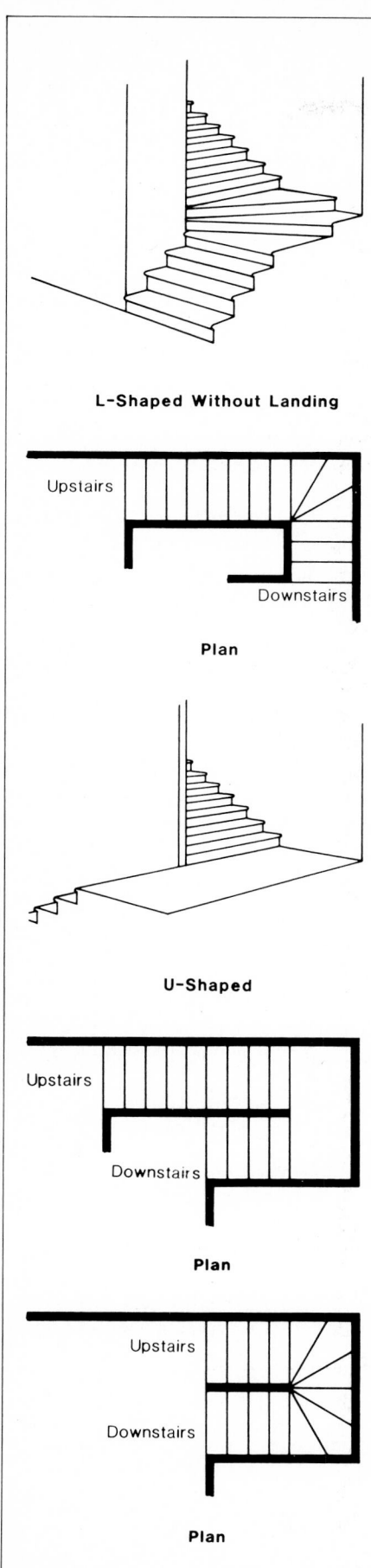

L-Shaped Without Landing

Upstairs

Downstairs

Plan

U-Shaped

Upstairs

Downstairs

Plan

Upstairs

Downstairs

Plan

Increase the rise in a run of steps by installing turning steps rather than a landing.

risers and treads given later in this chapter in "Staircase Dimensions". Divide the height from one floor level to another by the height of a single riser. This will tell you how many risers you will need. Subtract one for the number of treads needed. Then multiply this number by the depth of a single tread to get the total length of the stairs.

L-Shaped Stairs

Use the L-Shaped staircase if you do not have the length available for a straight staircase. These stairs at some point make a 90 degree turn, usually against a wall. A square landing equal to the total width of the stairs is located at the turn. If space is tight, two risers may be used at the stair turning instead of the landing.

U-Shaped Stairs

If your available space for stairs is more square than rectangular, the best choice is probably a U-shaped staircase. This is often the case if the new staircase will be built in a former storage area or small room. If the space you convert is larger than needed for the stairs, the remaining space can be converted to a closet, cabinets, bookcases, other storage, or perhaps a small wet bar.

U-shaped staircase can also be built without a landing, similar to the L-shaped staircase that does not have a landing; however, there will be a few more turning steps. This does result in a staircase that is more difficult to climb or descend. Use stair turnings only if space requirements leave no other alternative.

Do not overlook the storage capacity under the new stairs. You can make use of this often-wasted space by planning a closet and drawer storage. The storage area can be left unfinished to reduce costs.

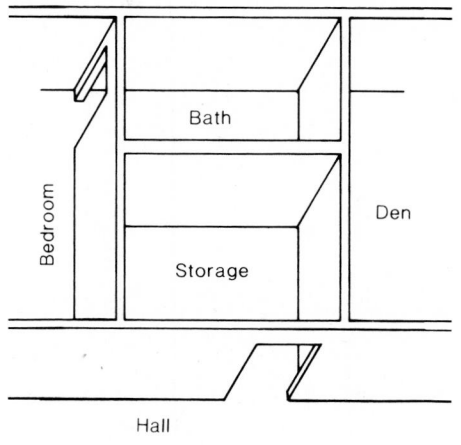

Before

It may often appear that there is no possible space for a new set of stairs, but careful study and design may reveal a location.

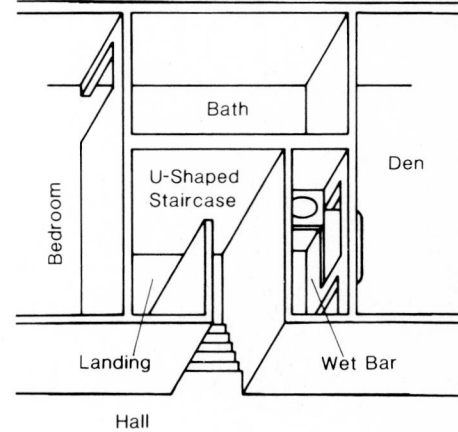

After

A storage area can be converted into a stair location. Extra room may become a closet or even a full wet bar.

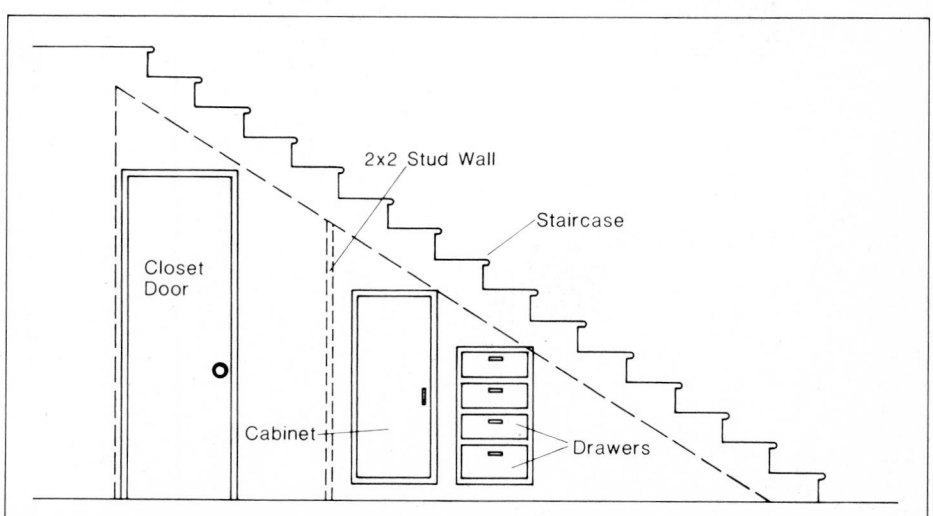

Space under an end-of-run staircase should be utilized. Very little extra construction is needed to enclose the space, support the drawers and cupboard, and make the closet.

A prefabricated spiral staircase gives access to a second floor without taking much space.

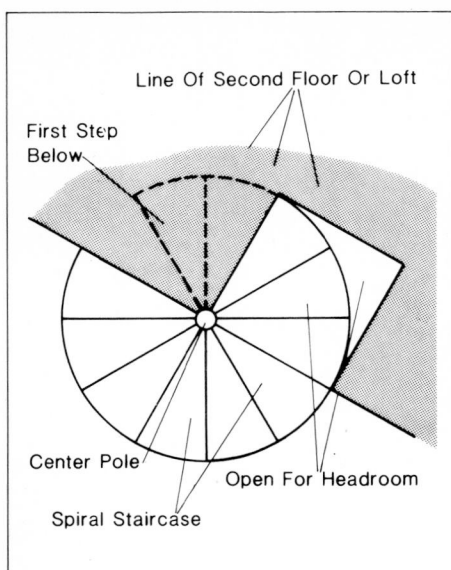

The curve of the spiral brings the steps into vertical alignment but provides headroom.

Spiral Stairs

You can use a spiral staircase where space is exceptionally tight, or for an architectural effect. Spiral stairs take up very little from the living area; but they are a little more difficult and potentially dangerous to go up and down. The spiral staircase is usually purchased as a complete unit. A spiral staircase can be built on-site, but this requires some very skilled carpentry. These units are commonly used for lofts and small areas where space for a more elaborate stair system is not available.

Using Ladders

Another, and much less expensive, type of stair system used with a loft is the ladder. A ladder takes up almost no space because it rises vertically. A ladder can be built in several ways, each relatively easy to construct. The ladder, however, is much more difficult to climb than stairs and should not be used as the access to major areas such as attic and basement conversions or rooms for preschoolers.

Building a loft-access ladder. To build a loft-access ladder, use a 2x6 (or 2x8) for each side piece. Using a router or circular saw and chisel, cut a ½-inch-deep by 1½-inch-wide dado on the inside of each side section 8 inches from the bottom and every 8 inches on center from the bot-

The wood treads of this spiral unit tie the stairs visually to the room itself. The area needed to achieve two floor access is very small. Note upstairs guard rail.

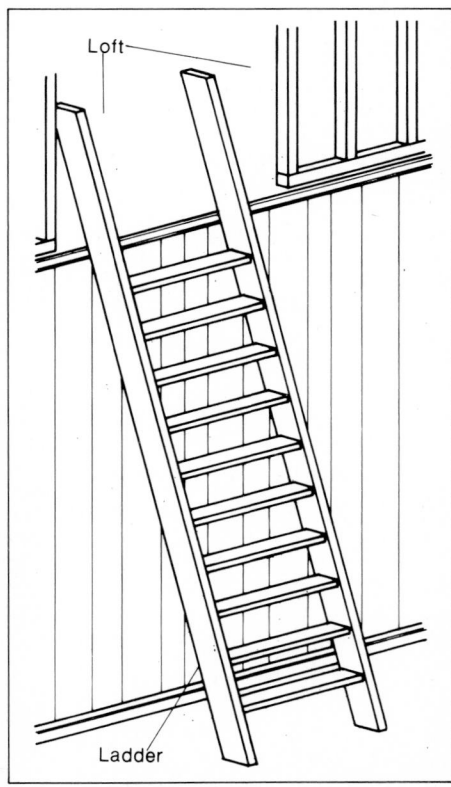

A ladder may be used for loft access, but this is not safe for constant use or use by toddlers.

tom. Set the 2x6 (or 2x8) rungs of the ladder into the dados and secure with 16d common nails or 3-inch wood screws.

The ladder shown is a straight ladder that should be toenailed to wall studs and to the floor with 10d common nails. If the ladder will be used frequently, attach it with L-brackets bolted to the ladder and attached to the studs with 3-inch wood screws. For a ladder that is slanted, essential if it is to be movable, cut the bottoms of the side supports and the rung dados at the same angle. The degree of the angle will depend on the slant that is desired in the ladder.

STAIRCASE DIMENSIONS

The following guideline dimensions for interior stairs are based on the average human size and do allow some latitude for adjustment. If your family members are exceptionally short or tall, you may adjust them even further. But do not make radical departures. A change of a few inches could prove uncomfortable and unsafe for both you and your guests. Also, a radical departure could hurt the potential resale value of your home.

> Riser: 7 to 9 inches
> Tread: 10 to 12 inches
> Nosing: 1 to 1½ inches
> Height of handrail: 2 feet 6 inches
> to 2 feet 8 inches from
> nose of tread.
> Height of handrail at landing: 2 feet
> 10 inches to 3 feet
> Headroom: 6 feet 6 inches minimum,
> 7 feet preferred
> Width of stairs: 30 inches minimum,
> 36 inches preferred

Staircase Location

Refer to your family living pattern, established in Chapter 2, to determine the best location for the new staircase. It should be in an area that is not well-used already, but it must also be convenient to the final design of both levels. You may need to rearrange the rooms slightly. Or, if there is a small room that can be eliminated or reclassified elsewhere, this might be the best location.

First, determine the amount and type of space available; then study the types of staircases to see which type will fit best in the space you have. Use the dimensions given above, adjusted to fit your individual situation, to determine the exact size of the staircase. This may be done by measuring the dimension from one finished floor level to the other, in inches, then dividing to see how many risers are required to reach the new floor level. The number of treads required will be one less than the number of risers. Multiply the number of treads by the depth of the tread to get the total run length of the stairs. For L-shaped and U-shaped staircases, the landing marks a division between stair runs and should be taken into account in your computations. A landing on an L-shaped stair will be a square, with each side equal to the stair width. The U-shaped landing will be a rectangle, with one dimension usually equal to the stair width and the other double the stair width.

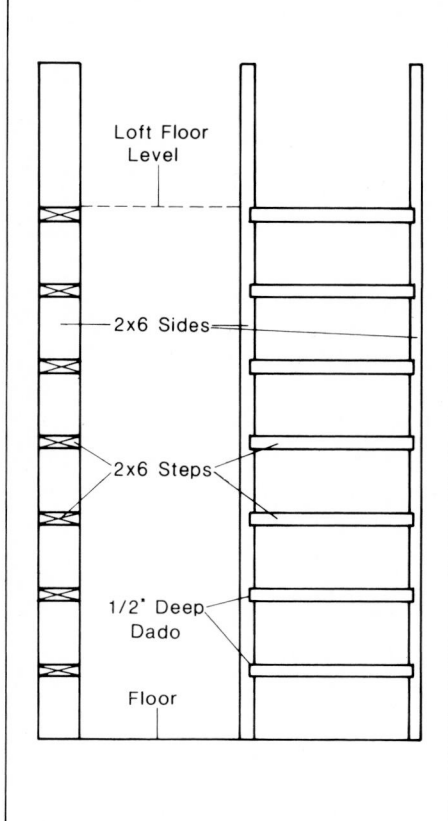

A sturdy, vertical ladder may be built of 2x6 members. The rungs are set into dadoes. For security use both glue and wood screws.

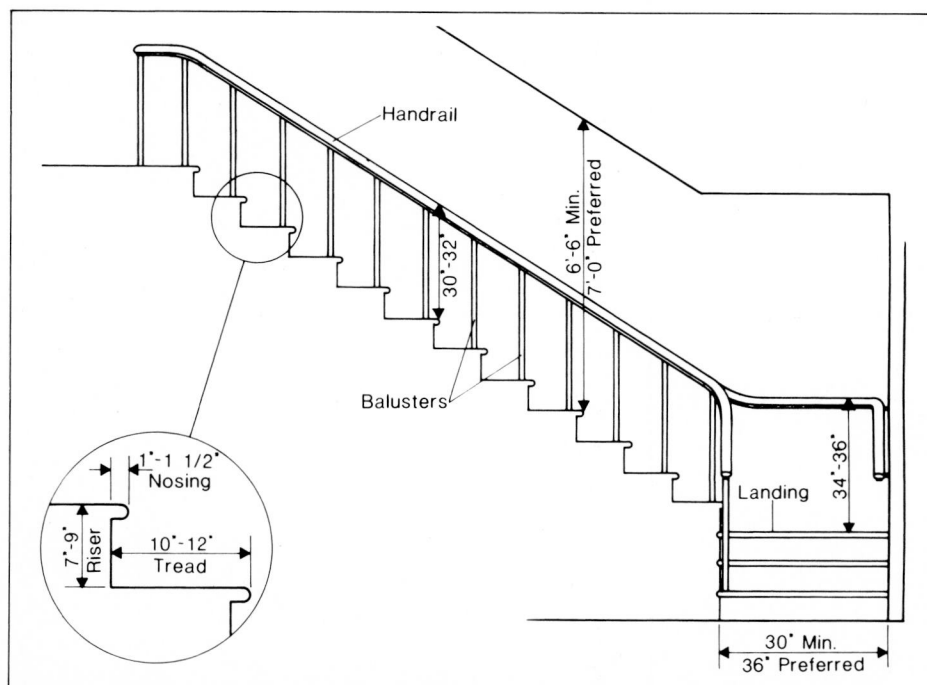

These standard measurements are good guides to use in stair construction. While adjustments are possible to meet individual limitations, a great variance will create a safety hazard.

Balusters are not necessary. A handrail may be top finish of a half-wall hiding stairs.

BUILDING STAIRWAYS

Begin by removing any existing stairs and/or walls that are not to be used. Before you remove any walls, however, make sure they are not bearing walls (see Chapter 4.) Then construct new stud walls to surround or support the stairs (see Chapter 4 for construction of new walls.) Construct a temporary ladder from 2x6s for access between levels until the new stairs can be used.

Cutting the Stringers

Cut three stringers from 2x10s or 2x12s, as necessary, to the exact dimensions of the treads and risers. The cuts in the stringers can be marked with a framing square, which has a ruler on each side. Find the riser height on one side of the framing square and the tread depth on the other, then mark the tread/riser cutout along the two sides of the square. The stringers can then be cut with a circular saw, but you must be careful not to run the cut beyond the marks. This will leave a small area of wood which should be cut with a hand saw. The point of the ''V'' cut out of the stringer should be at least 3½ inches from the straight, bottom side of the stringer.

Installing the Stringers

Place two 2x8 headers at the top position of the stairs, level with the floor framing. If the top of the stairs is in the attic, frame around the entire opening with lumber that is the same size as the joists. Notch the bottom of the stringers for 2x4 thrust blocking. Nail the stringers in place on either side of the steps and in the center; use 16d common nails. If the stringer is adjacent to a wall, nail it securely into the studs. Toenail the stringers into the headers at top, and nail the thrust blocking into the floor. Secure the stringer to a concrete basement floor with masonry nails or set screws. Use masonry nails or power-driven pins to secure the thrust blocking to concrete floors. Pieces of scrap lumber may be nailed to the stringers as temporary treads during construction.

For free-standing stairs (where sides are not against a stud wall), frame underneath using a bottom plate and 2x4s at 16 inches on center as shown. Install finish materials on walls adjacent to the steps before you add the treads and risers.

Attaching Treads and Risers

Nail treads and risers into the stringers with 8d ringshank nails. Drive the nails in at a slight angle to prevent squeaking. Use oak, yellow pine, or birch with a minimum thickness of 1¼ inch for the treads. The risers can be smaller stock, but use less than ¾ inch thick. Unless the steps

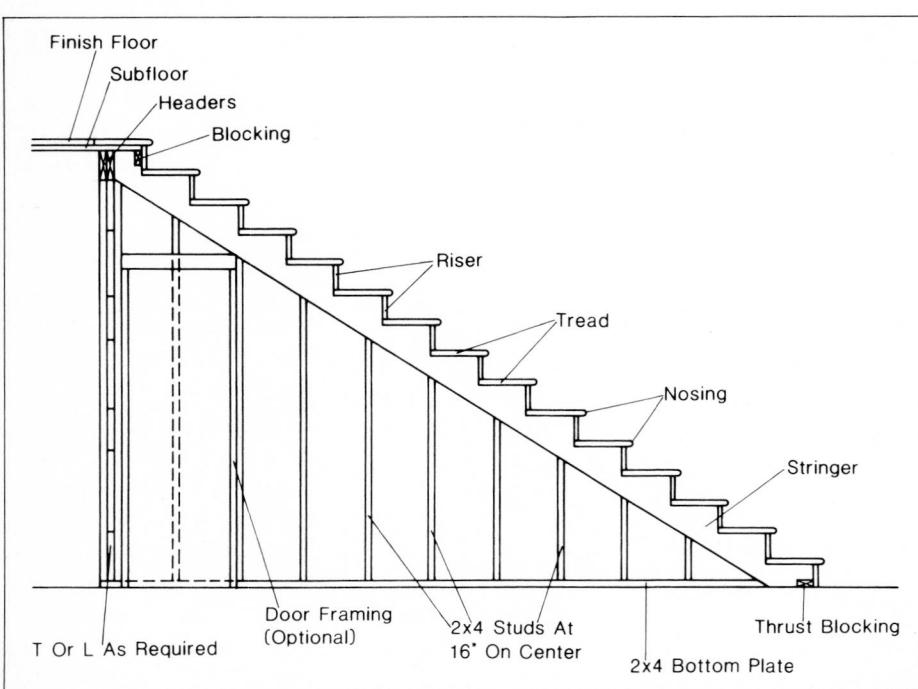

A straight run of stairs is framed with triple stringers and standard 16 inch o.c. studs. Thrust blocking nailed to the floor secures the base. Headers and support blocking fit at top.

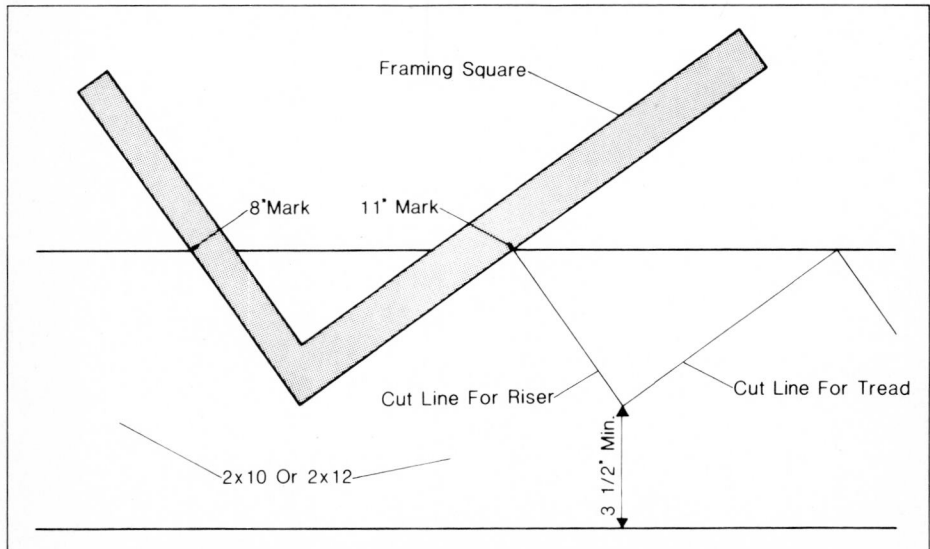

Mark stair cuts on the stringer by aligning the tread depth and riser height on a carpenter's square on one edge of the stringer. There must be at least 3½ inches uncut for strength.

Confined spaces may require relatively steep stairs. Secure carpet and pad firmly.

are to be covered with carpet, the risers should be of the same wood species as the treads. If you prefer, purchase risers and treads precut. You need only cut the material to proper width, nail into place, and stain and varnish as desired. Some come prefinished and will not require either stain or varnish. If the finish material is wood, countersink the nails and fill the holes with putty stick.

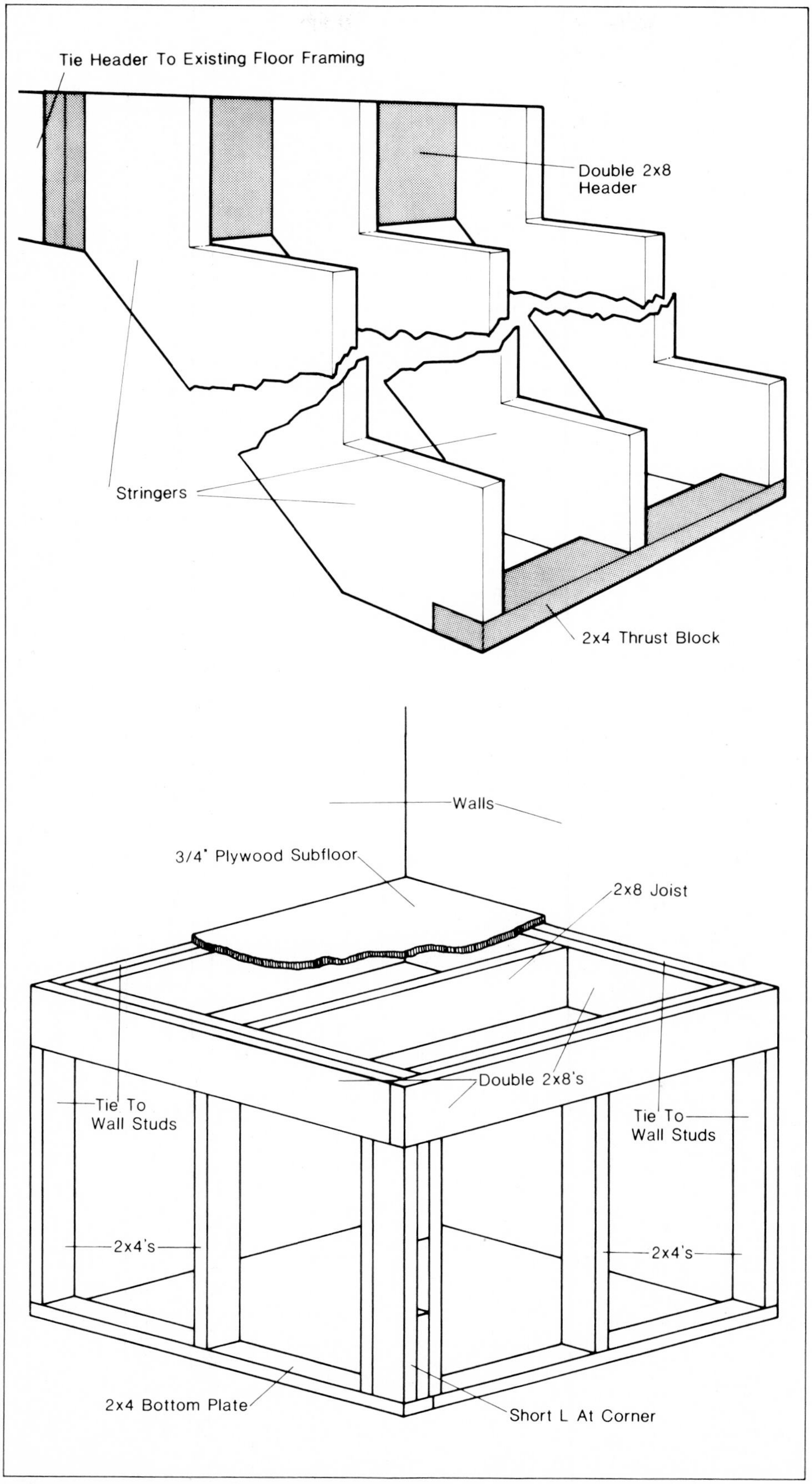

Adding handrails. The handrails can be added last. Because of the variety of handrail types and differing installation requirements, follow manufacturer's recommendations. Discuss installation with the building materials supplier before you purchase the handrails, so you will understand the proper installation of each type before you select one type. A very simple handrail may be created by attaching a large dowel to a wall with support brackets.

If steps are to be carpeted. Construction is slightly different for steps to be carpeted. The risers on the stringers are cut at a slight angle so that there is a solid surface (from the tip of the nosing to the tread below) against which the carpet can stretch. A tackless strip is nailed onto each tread about ¼ inch from the riser. Then the carpet is pulled one step at a time, starting from the bottom. Carpeted stairs are also commonly constructed with no nosing at all; the risers simply go up vertically. While this construction is easier, it is less desirable because there is no additional toe space on each tread. This type of stairs, however, is desirable if the flights are to be used by an elderly person or someone wearing a leg brace.

Tie Header To Existing Floor Framing

Double 2x8 Header

Stringers

2x4 Thrust Block

Walls

3/4" Plywood Subfloor

2x8 Joist

Double 2x8's

Tie To Wall Studs

Tie To Wall Studs

2x4's

2x4's

2x4 Bottom Plate

Short L At Corner

Nail stringers to headers by toenailing. Bottom rests of thrust block that is nailed to the floor. Doubled 2x8s serve as headers and thrust blocks in landing construction.

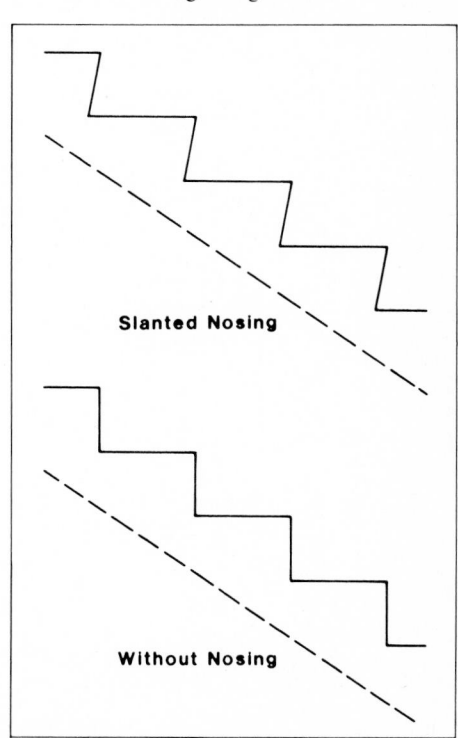

Slanted Nosing

Without Nosing

If you will carpet stairs, use continuous slant or straight nosing for safe installation.

8
CLOSETS
& STORAGE

It is a rare home that has enough closet and storage space to meet the needs of the average family. This is true for both the older home and in the new. In many older homes the function of the closet was served by furniture; closets were not built into houses. Even when the construction of closets and storage rooms became common practice, closets were small and unsuited to today's needs. Several decades ago, people simply could not afford the volume of material goods that we enjoy now. Today, because of the extremely high cost per square foot of construction, most of the space in a new home is devoted to actual living area, at the expense of closets and storage.

ADDING A CLOSET

While it is relatively easy to add a closet, it is not easy to decide where. If you examine each room separately and tack on a closet wherever it is convenient, the overall result may be less than desirable. You should consider the house as a whole. Closets should be added where they will be convenient but take a minimum of the living area.

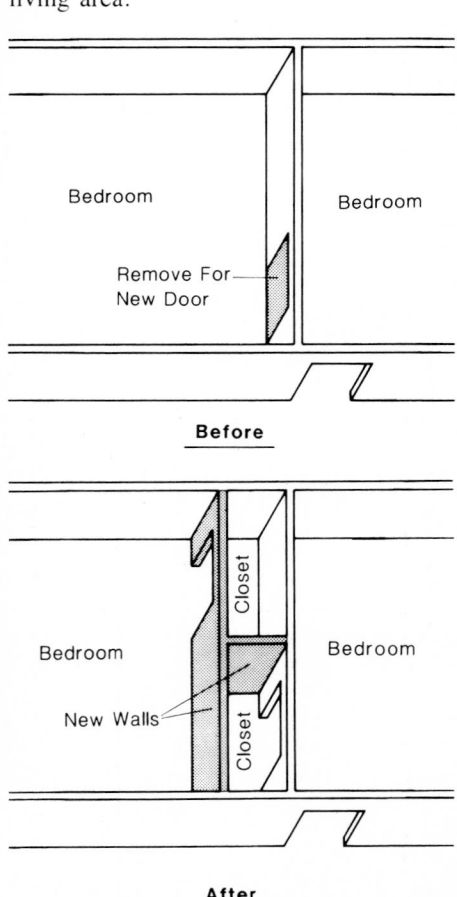

Books and other small objects need relatively little depth for secure storage. This shallow niche is filled with shelves that provide attractive and useful storage for many items.

Relatively little area need be taken from a room to provide generous closet space.

Planning Locations

Sharing between bedrooms. To get the most out of a closet addition, place a closet against a common wall of two adjacent rooms. Or, working with the existing wall between the rooms, add a parallel wall in the larger of the two rooms. Then split the space between the walls into two closets.

Locate doors to each closet to fit the layout of the rooms. In other words, place the door to each closet so the arrangement gives each room the maximum usable wall space.

Hall and bedroom space. If you have a hall that dead ends into a bedroom, this is an ideal position for one large closet and a linen closet opening to the hall or for two closets and a linen closet. Extend the wall of the hall into the bedroom space, relocate the bedroom door, and subdivide the closet space. When you are deciding which closet should open into which room, take a careful look at how the door openings will affect the wall space of the rooms.

Bedroom and Living room space. If you need a coat closet at the entrance to your home, this can be solved by adding a wall in an adjacent room, if space allows. This can give you a coat closet, linen or other storage, and a closet or cabinet space for the adjacent room — depending on the type of room it is.

Under the stairs. Another good place for a closet and/or storage is under a staircase. Often these areas will be only partially used or not used at all. By opening up the entire space a great deal of storage can be gained in the area where there is little head room. (See Chapter 7.)

If you are considering adding a fireplace, a dramatic effect can be achieved with a recessed fireplace. A partition brings the side walls level with the fire-

place and the spaces created at the sides can be used as closets, bookcases, cabinets, or any combination of these. If the fireplace backs up to another room, such as a bedroom, the side spaces can be used for closets that open into the other room.

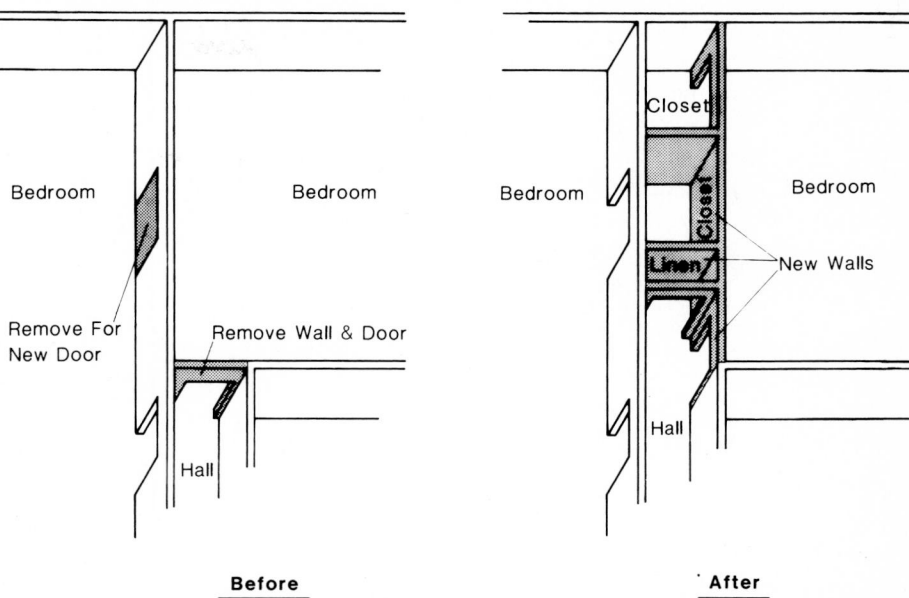

Repositioning a bedroom door allows the installation of new closets for adjacent bedrooms and the creation of a new linen closet in a small space.

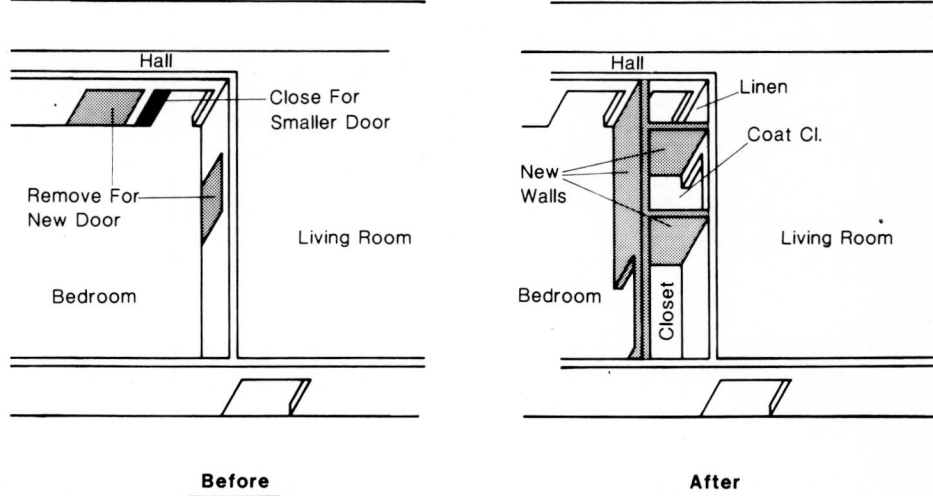

Changing an existing door and adding two new doors, allows for construction of a good size bedroom closet, a guest closet and a linen closet.

Existing storage facilities may be improved without major changes. Low cupboard shelves that slide out improve kitchen storage.

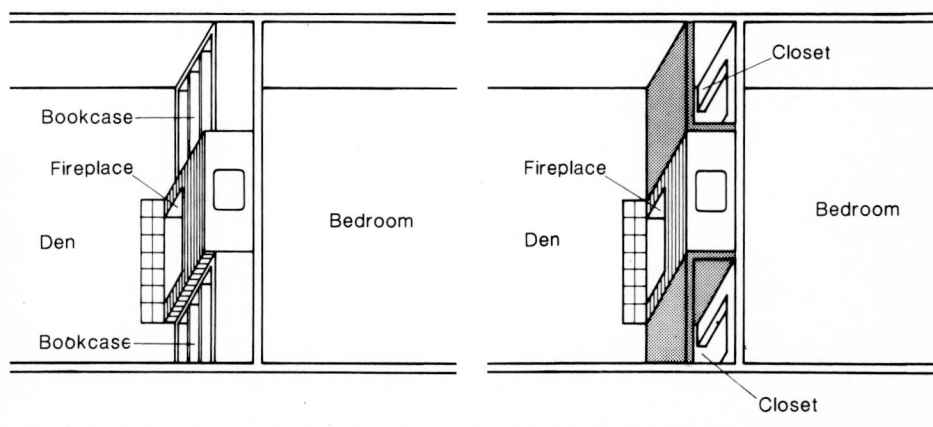

Installing a fireplace on an interior wall will leave spaces on either side that may be filled with bookcases or framed in to provide new closets opening to either room.

Walk-in and modular closets. You may also wish to consider adding drawers or open shelf storage in any closet in any of a number of arrangements. You can make your own custom arrangement, suited to you and your family's needs. Further information on modular closets is provided later in this chapter.

If you can spare the square footage; especially in an older, larger home, a walk-in closet will provide a great deal more hanging space for clothes. As with any closet, the walk-in closet should be de-

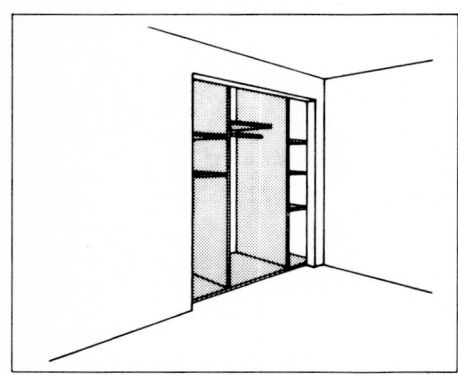

Adding plywood or particle board partitions to an existing closet will allow new storage.

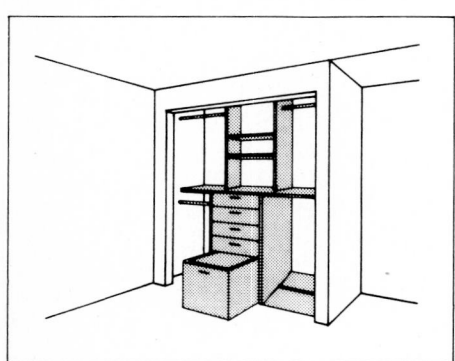

Closet rods may be set at various heights and built-in drawers added to meet your needs.

signed to maximize usable space. You may put two walk-in closets along a single wall or one, with a standard closet for the adjacent room and built-in book shelves beside the walk-in closet.

Typical Closet Dimensions

The typical dimensions of a closet may vary considerably. The depth of the closet, for instance, may be larger if it is an extension of the hall. The depth can also be reduced to as little as 1 foot-10 inches if space is extremely tight. The height of the rod and shelf may be adjusted several inches up or down to accommodate your own height. Do not make drastic changes, however, unless you make the levels adjustable. Permanent mountings at unusual heights could hurt the resale value of your home.

Walk-in closets should be, at the very least, four feet deep; five feet is more desirable depth. If a walk-in closet is too

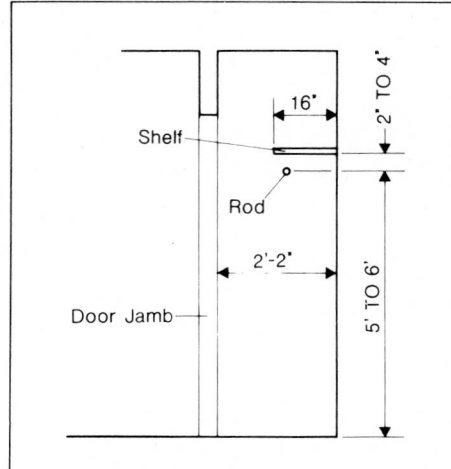

Closet rods and shelves should be located conveniently but within average positions.

shallow, any hanging space gained on the sides is lost in the corners. The width should be at least 5 to 6 feet to allow for a rod and shelf on each side and space to maneuver in between. If the closet is built wider than 8 feet, the middle space is too large, and precious room footage is lost. An ideal width is between 6 and 7 feet.

Closet Construction

The wall framing, fastening, and surfacing will follow the steps in Chapters 4 and 6. Center the middle stud in the short wall at the end of a closet. This will make it easier to find the stud when you are adding the rod and shelf. You may want to add a stud in the existing wall to align with the stud in the new wall.

Finish materials. You may choose a finish material other than wallboard inside

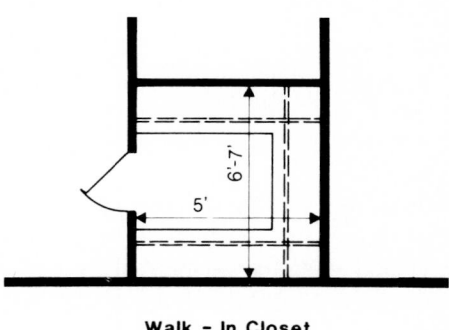

Walk – In Closet

A walk-in closet should provide at least 5 feet by 6 feet 7 inches or it is too small.

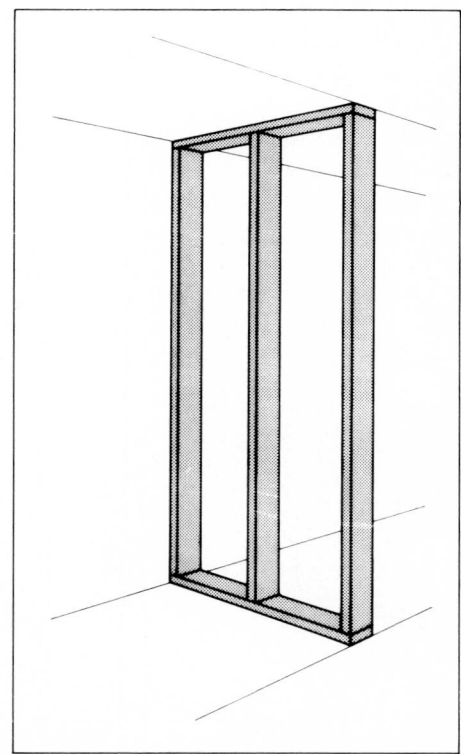

In order to secure a closet rod, locate a stud at the center of your new closet wall.

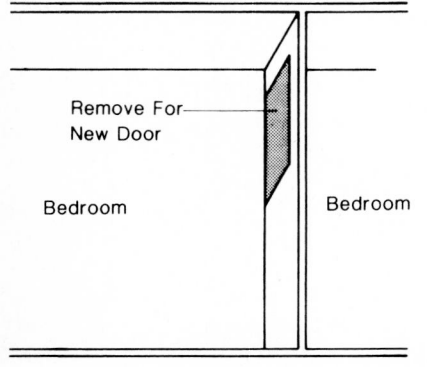

Before

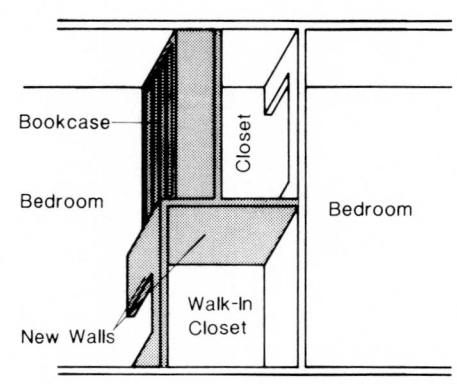

After

A large bedroom may have room to spare for more than a single closet. If their space is large enough, two types of closets and a bookcase or built-in dresser may be added.

the closet. Cedar chipboard, although it does not stop moths, does add a fresh scent to your clothes. Hardboard, while not suitable for room walls, is a durable, easy-to-install surface inside the closet. Pegboard is another popular surface.

Doors. Because of the wide variety of types and sizes of closet doors, you should select the doors you plan to use prior to beginning the framing. Then frame the rough opening for the door as suggested by the manufacturer. The door framing requires a header supported by jack studs and cripple studs above the header. If you plan to install sliding doors, you will have to install a double header. Choose a door or doors to fit your closet and select appropriate hardware to fit. Installation and framing specifications will be included.

Rods and shelves. The rod and shelf may be attached in a number of ways. There are several types of prebuilt units available. These should be installed according to the manufacturer's directions. The rod, wood or metal, can screw directly into the stud on either side, with the shelf supported by 1x2s. The rod also may

be removable; use a 1x4 or 1x6 on each end to support both the shelf and the rod.

Holes are drilled in each side for the rod with one side sawed to allow the rod to lift out. If the closet is more than 5 feet wide, one or more center support brackets should be installed. These can be purchased separately or may come as an integral support that holds both the shelf and rod.

Bath cabinets may have customized interiors that allow adjustable storage.

Any number of arrangements are possible in modular closets. Second pole doubles space.

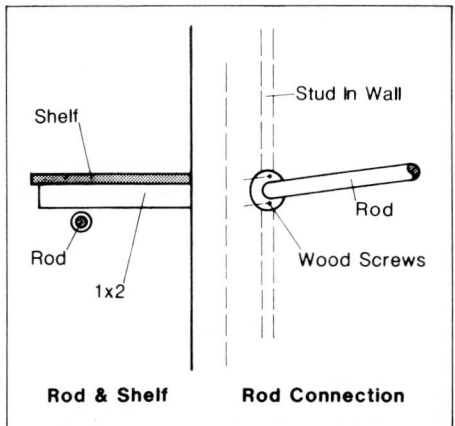
Shelf supports should attach to studs in back wall, rod to studs in end walls.

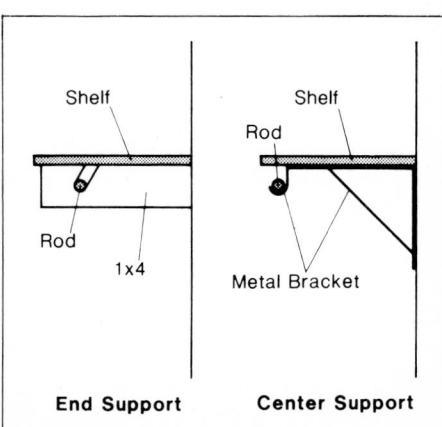
Long rods must be supported at the center by a bracket, like this metal one, and at ends.

This custom designed closet allows considerable adjustment to the interior without reconstruction. Lower shelves are adjustable. Short rods need minimum support and may be raised quickly.

Modular Closets

When properly designed and constructed, a modular closet can be a tremendous space saver. There are several rules you should follow in laying out the closet design.

1. The modular closet should be located where you get dressed. Since a modular closet will hold everything from underclothes to accessories, getting dressed is done in one area. If you use a mirror when dressing, consider adding

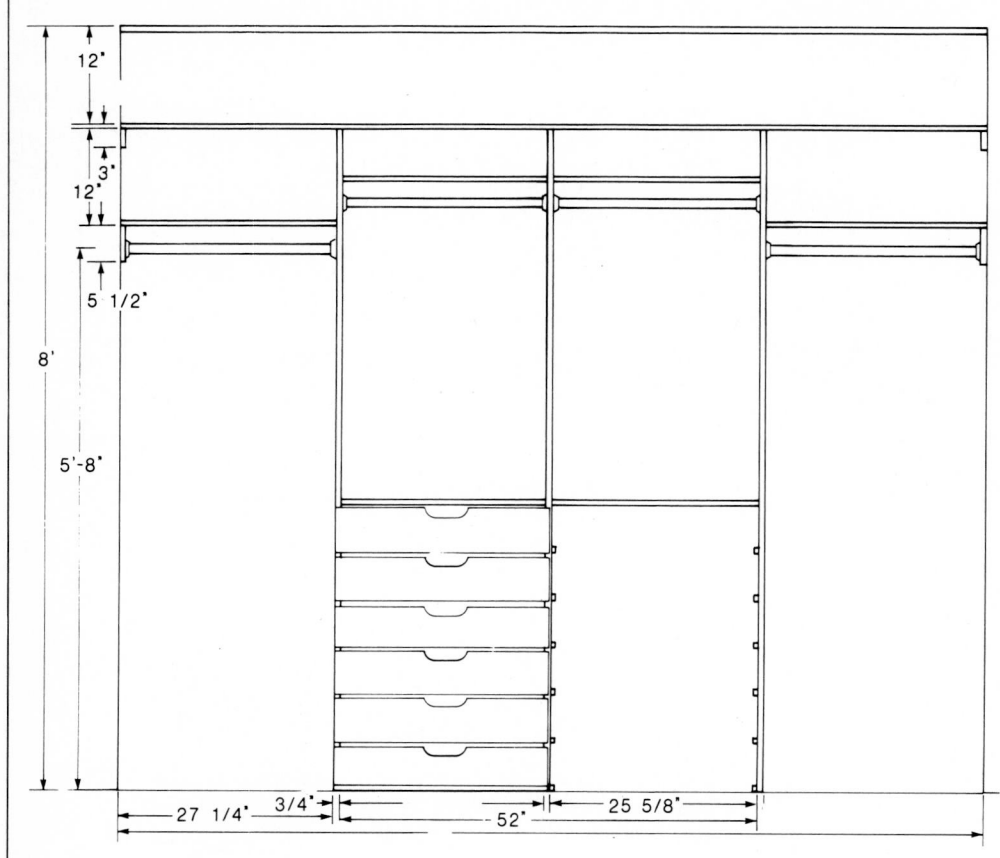

Here is one example of a closet adapted to the specific needs of the users. The measurements given are for the closet as shown in the photo at the bottom of the next page. The design takes into account all basic storage requirements of the husband and wife and the space available in this basic closet. The slide-by doors were removed for the photo to show the entire interior. The basic construction is shown in the drawing below. When you are planning your adaptation to your situation, take stock of the items that you have. Allow for long and short hanging garments, shoes, accessories and off-season storage.

In this arrangement there are drawers for sweaters, underwear, socks or stockings, scarves and other foldable clothing. These drawers were built so that they ride on plywood support strips; however, it is possible to build the drawers with edges that will fit into dadoes as shown at the top of the next page. Either of these methods may be used, but a drawer with the bottom set into dadoes in the drawer sides will be sturdier. Study your space and needs to develope the most successful design.

full length mirrors on the closet doors; or, if you prefer a more casual layout where the closet does not have doors, locate the mirror(s) on the adjacent walls.

2. Study the items to be stored in the closet and your preferences for handling them. Consider these questions: do you fold or hang your clothes? Do the clothes to be hung fit into general groups by lengths? How many pairs of shoes do you have? What types of accessories will be stored, and how will they be easily accessible?

3. Design the closet to suit the actual needs and habits of the person who will use it. Do not set idealistic goals that are at variance from lifelong habits.

Once you have established the types of storage needed for the modular closet, design it with open shelves, drawers, rods, hooks, and other compartments or features to suit. There are many inexpensive closet ''organizers'' on the market that help turn a small closet into a large storage area.

Open shelves can be added using 1x12 wood shelving, prefabricated metal shelves, ½ inch or thicker plywood, or ⅝ inch or thicker particle board. Simply cut and nail or screw the shelves to uprights of the same material. Rods may be attached as previously discussed. If you would like to add drawers to the closet, you can construct units in several ways. The drawers may be supported by guide strips, or side notches. You also may purchase drawer hardware kits that provide side-mounted guides. If, however, you would like cabinet quality drawers — but are not handy with woodworking — consider having a cabinet shop or cabinet maker build the drawers to your specifications.

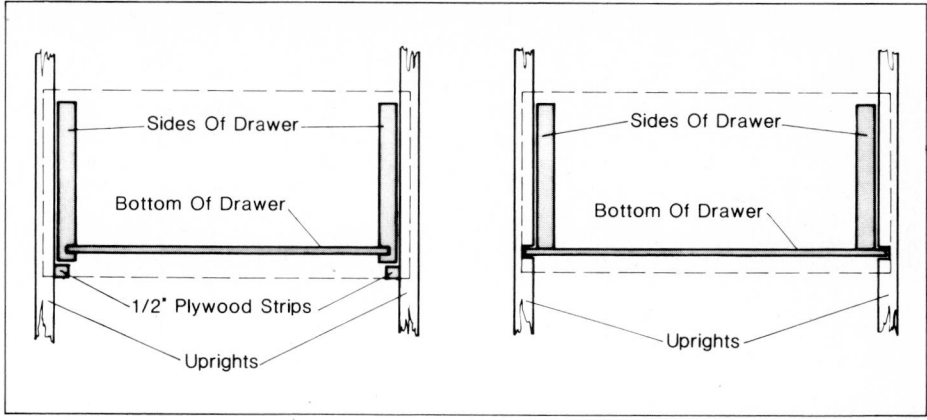

This detail shows the two ways to build drawers and support them at the sides. Either method may be used, but the drawer at the left is stronger.

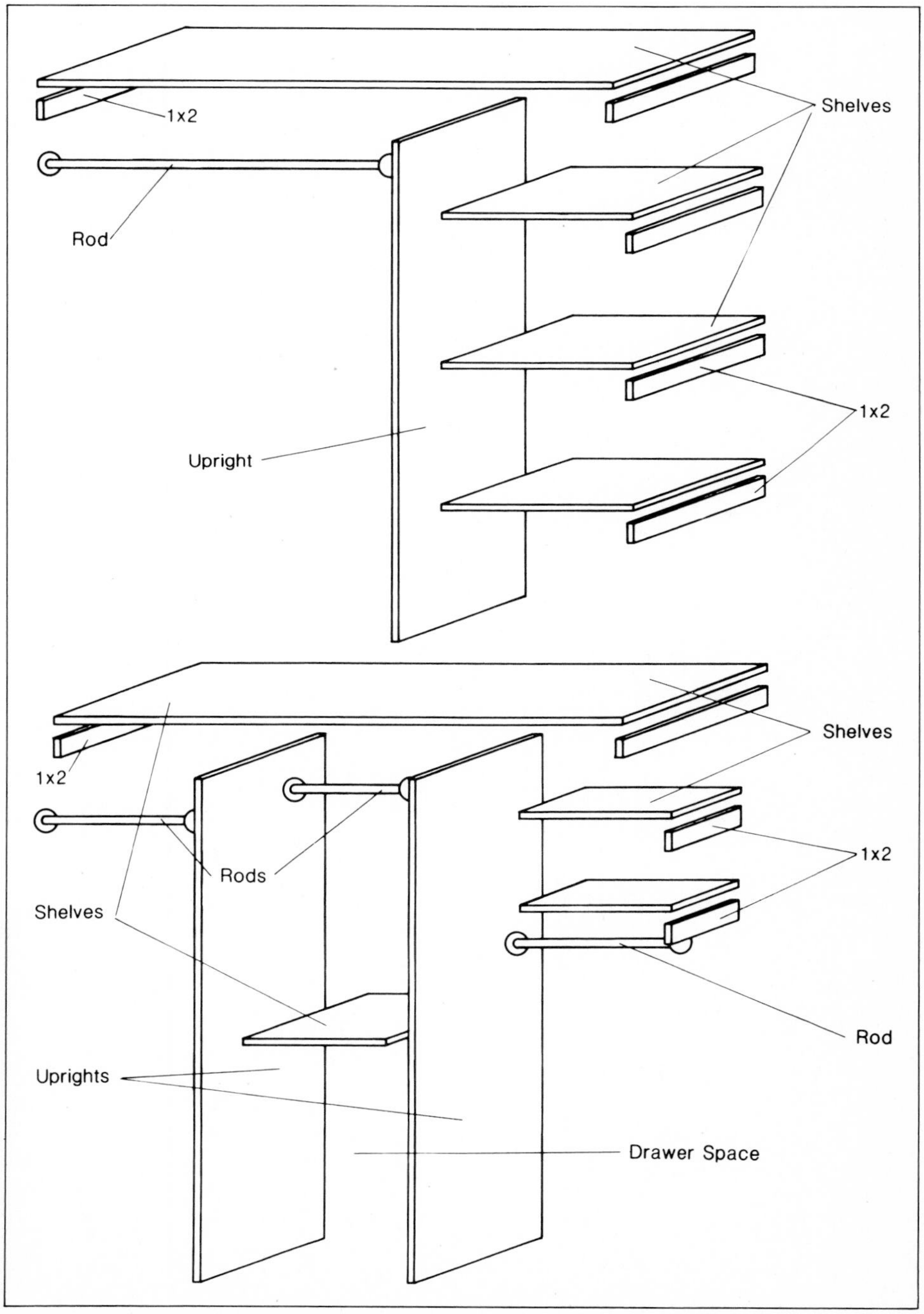

A place for everything in this closet means that it is neat and everything is at hand.

Provisions for adjustable shelves are usually standards that allow supports to be moved up or down in ½ inch increments, or 1x2 strips that may be pried off and renailed.

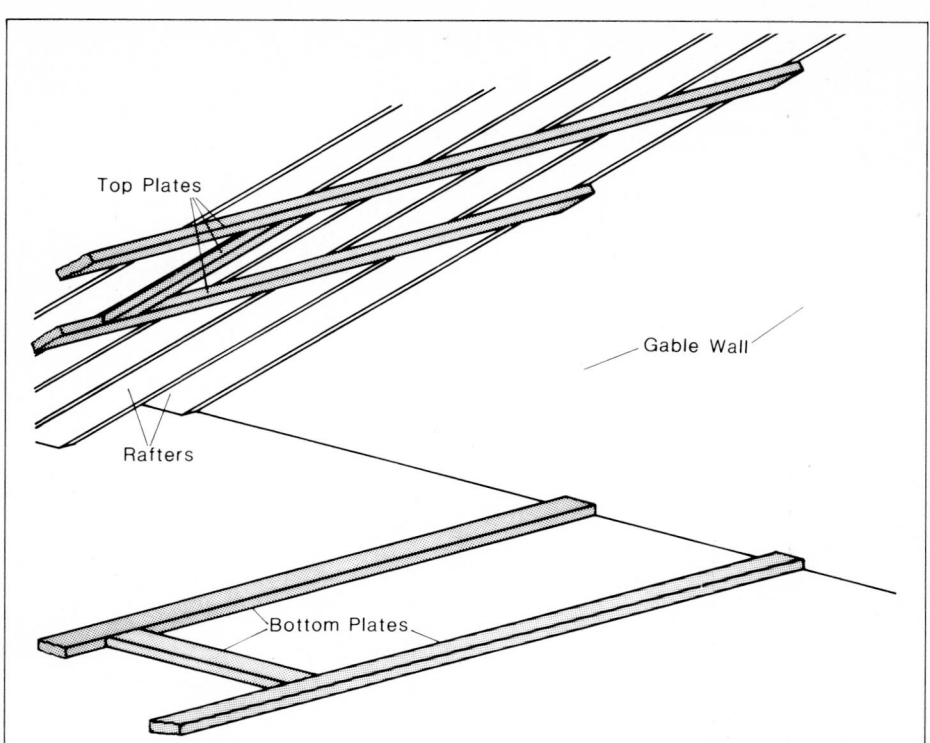

Handy towel storage was created by using part of a vanity counter area.

To build a closet under attic eaves, begin by nailing top and bottom plates in position. Location is determined by the slope of the roof and the length of garments to be hung.

These closets, located under attic eaves provide good storage. Louvered doors help ventilate closet area to keep clothing fresh.

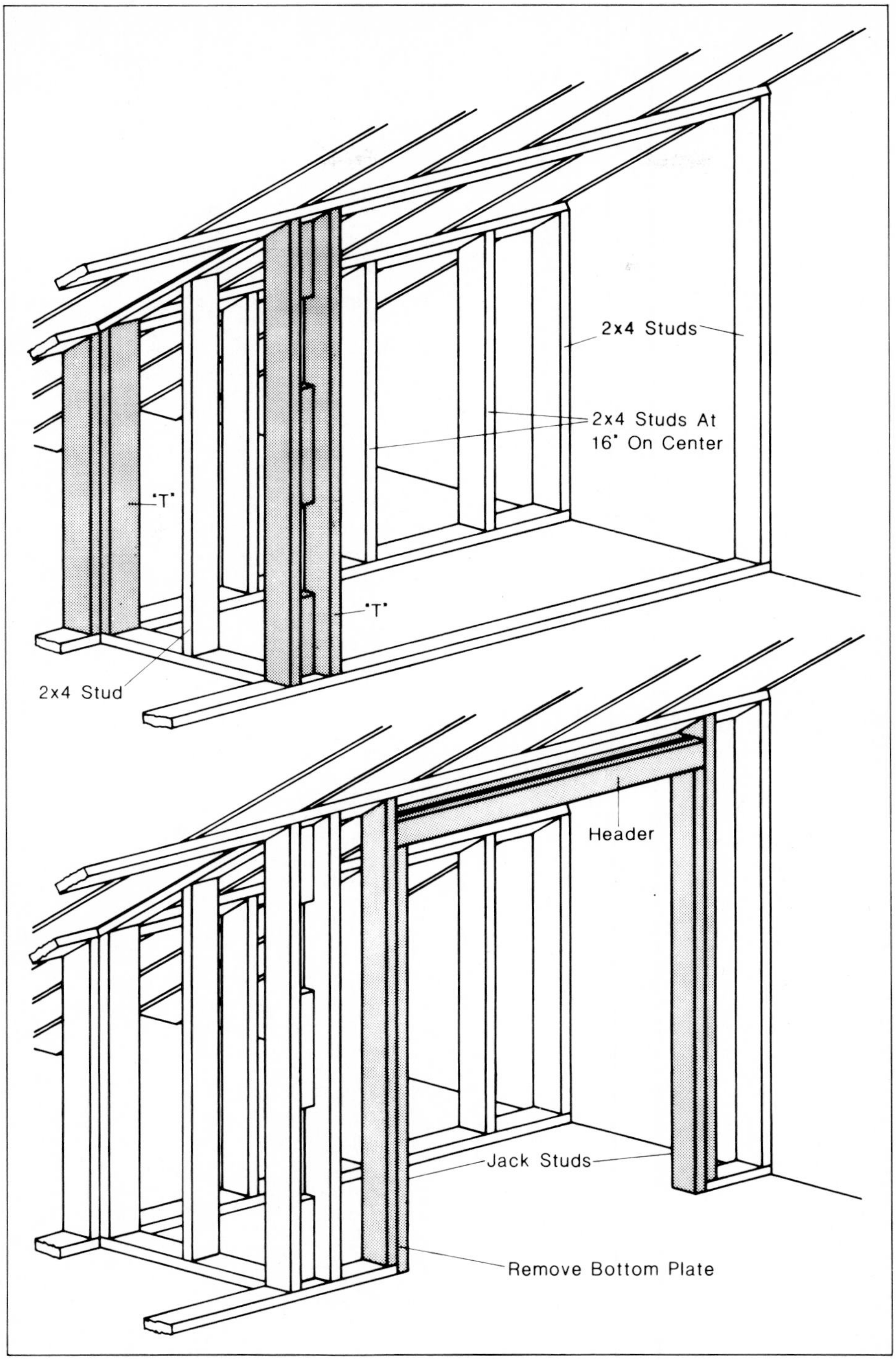

2x4 Studs

2x4 Studs At
16" On Center

"T"

"T"

2x4 Stud

Header

Jack Studs

Remove Bottom Plate

Vinyl covered metal wire shelving will support considerable weight and allows ventilation. Cedar chipboard adds pleasant smell.

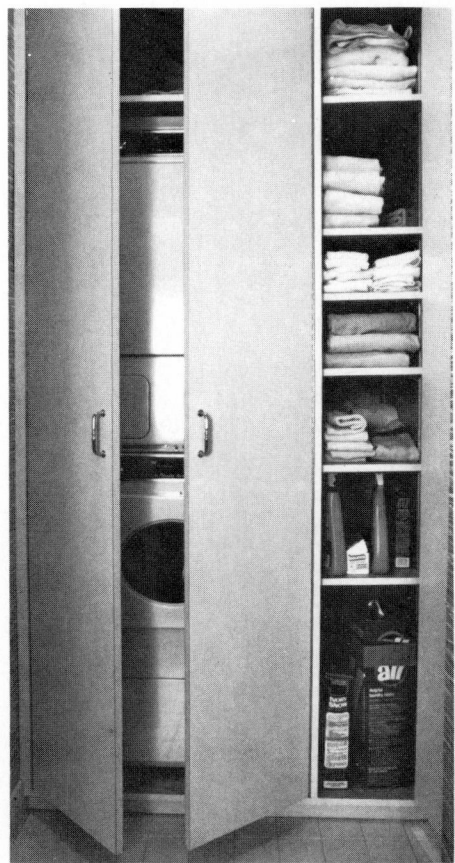

This cupboard is at the bottom of a clothes chute. Height is good for handling laundry.

A large closet may be converted to hold a full wet bar. Tile counter cleans easily.

There was enough room at the end of a hall to "stack" the washer and dryer and build an open cupboard for all needed supplies.

Full-length Mirrors

The most logical place to install a full-length mirror is in or near a dressing area so one's appearance can be checked before going out. Often such mirrors are hung on the back of bedroom doors. However, it is useful to have one or more doors of a wardrobe closet mirrored.

When you are shopping for mirrors, look for good float or plate glass mirrors with a smooth finish. While regular glass mirrors are much less expensive, the surfaces may contain flecks, bubbles and waves. These distortions may not seem important when you are purchasing a mirror, but each time you look into the mirror after it is installed, the distortion will be very annoying.

Because of the fragility of glass, handle all mirrors with care. Use gloves and wear goggles or safety glasses when cutting and installing.

Installing mirrors on regular doors. As mentioned in Chapter 5, a good full-length mirror usually comes with the mounting hardware. If the hardware is separate, the dealer will advise you on the type to buy. If you are mounting a mirror on a hollow-core door, you will have to use molly bolts or other anchoring screws to ensure a firm installation. However, when mounting a heavy mirror on a hinged door a problem may develop due to the pull of the added weight on the hinges. Most bedroom doors, especially modern, lightweight hollow-core doors, are hung on two hinges. Before hanging the mirror, install an extra hinge halfway between the upper and lower existing hinges. If you have any doubt about the stability and strength of the existing hinges or the door, replace the whole unit — or at least replace the hinges with strong, case-hardened steel hinges.

Installing mirrors on sliding doors. If you are planning an entirely new installation of slide-by doors on an existing or a new wardrobe closet, then you must purchase heavy-duty track hardware to support the weight of the mirrored surface. Mirrored doors are too heavy just to hang free. They should have base rollers and support track at the bottom just as if they were glass patio doors.

You can install a sheet mirror on the outside of the slide-by door, but if the clearance is limited, you may have to pry the face of the hollow-core door off the frame and plane down the interior bracing

and exterior frame. This should allow the mirrored door to pass by the other door and frame easily. Reglue and renail the face back on the frame. Always try to attach the mirror to the frame and bracing, not just the wood surface.

Mirror tile. You may be more comfortable with the simpler installation of mirror tile to a door or a section of a wall. Directions were given in Chapter 5.

REMOVING CLOSETS

For the rare house that has an overabundance of closet space, you may want to remove one or more closets to provide additional living space. This can be done easily if you follow the steps for wall removal detailed in Chapter 4. First, determine how you can use the space best. It may be that other wall and/or door changes will be required to get the extra space into the room where it is needed.

MAKING SPACE IN THE KITCHEN

One of the most common space problems in the home is a cramped kitchen. Making the kitchen larger, however, may not solve the problem. In fact, a kitchen may be too large to be efficient and may overwork the cook, because too many steps are required to get from one work area to another. Instead of tearing out a wall to increase the size of the kitchen, consider some easier and less expensive changes that will make better use of the space you have and will keep everything you need within easy reach.

Open Shelf Storage

Open shelf cabinets (no doors) offer storage with a casual attractiveness. Space is conserved because none is needed for the door openings, and it is easier to get items in and out of open shelves. Open shelves can be intermixed with regular cabinets, so you can either add shelves where you have extra wall space or convert some of your existing wall cabinets by removing the doors and refinishing the scars from the hinges.

Adjustable Shelves

Adjustable shelves will maximize your storage capacity. This is true whether the adjustable shelves are in standard wall cabinets or are open shelves, because the shelf can be adjusted to the height of stored items, reducing wasted space, and this allows future changes.

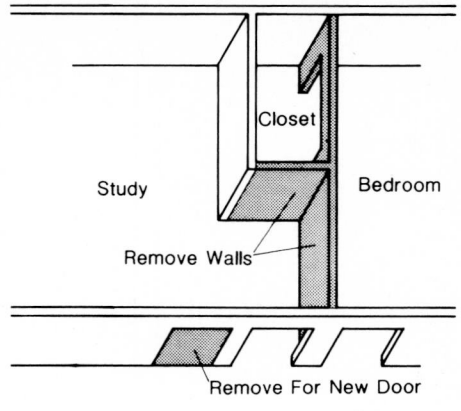

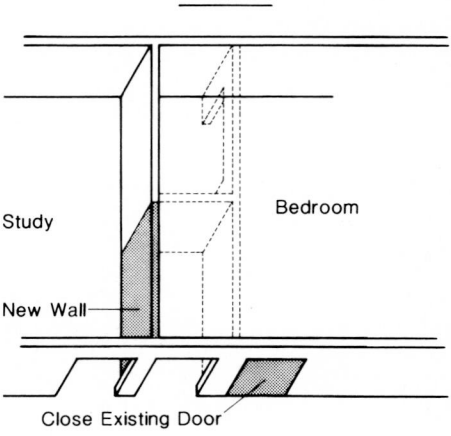

Before

After

If you have more closet space than you need, or if closets are in the wrong location, remove them; add space to room.

Open shelves may be added for additional storage and display space. Here, range hood and window frame are part of the support.

Base Cabinets

Your base cabinets, with a little reworking, can be adapted to suit your needs much better. First, shelves do not provide the best storage in base cabinets. In order to reach anything, particularly on a bottom shelf, you usually must get down on your knees.

Adaptations to base cabinets. Convert the stationary shelves to pull-out shelves or, better, to deep drawers; it will provide easier access and much better storage space in the base cabinets. A "lazy Susan" should be provided in the corners to make the formerly inaccessible storage space usable. However, these units must be installed while the corner is open, usually during initial construction or a major remodeling. If you are short on counter space, add pull-out work tops just above the drawers to solve the problem.

Kitchen Hangers

Another way to create more storage space in your kitchen is to use utensil hangers on the underside of the wall cabinets or on open walls.

Free-Standing Cabinets

If your kitchen adjoins another room, without a separating partition, such as a kitchen-dining or family room, additional storage can be obtained by installing sections of free-standing cabinets. This could include a peninsula or "island" base cabinet and a ceiling-hung wall cabinet as well. If you already have a peninsula, regular or open shelves, add free-standing wall cabinets. To install base cabinets, tonail the base frame to the floor. Set the cabinet unit on the base and attach with wood screws driven through the floor of the cabinet into the base frame. A ceiling-hung cabinet is installed with 4-inch lag screws driven through top framing and into ceiling joists.

Adding a Pantry or Storage Wall

If you have or can make the space in the kitchen, a pantry or storage wall is an ideal addition to a kitchen. The shelves can be from 12 to 24 inches deep and be installed from floor to ceiling. The pantry may be as wide as space allows. If you add doors, the storage wall becomes the perfect storage for canned goods and other non-perishables. Open shelves are more appropriate for storage of your utensils, dinnerware, and bowls.

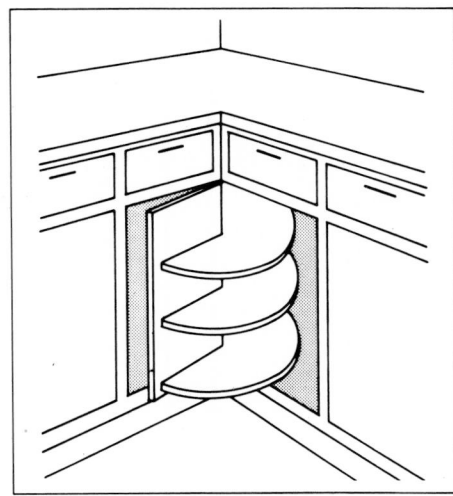
A corner lazy-susan unit makes storage more accessible and converts wasted space to use.

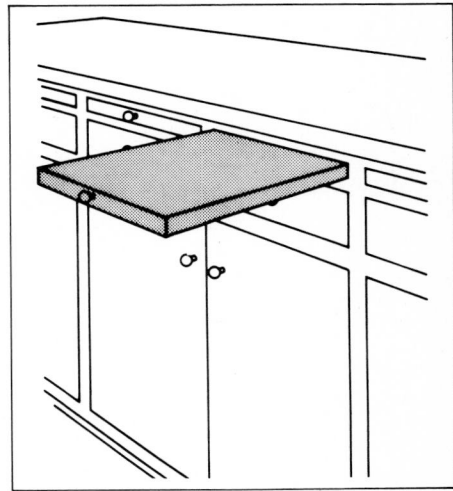
A small, pull-out shelf gives more working space, taking room from drawers below.

Excellent pantry storage may be provided by adding shelves to a closet.

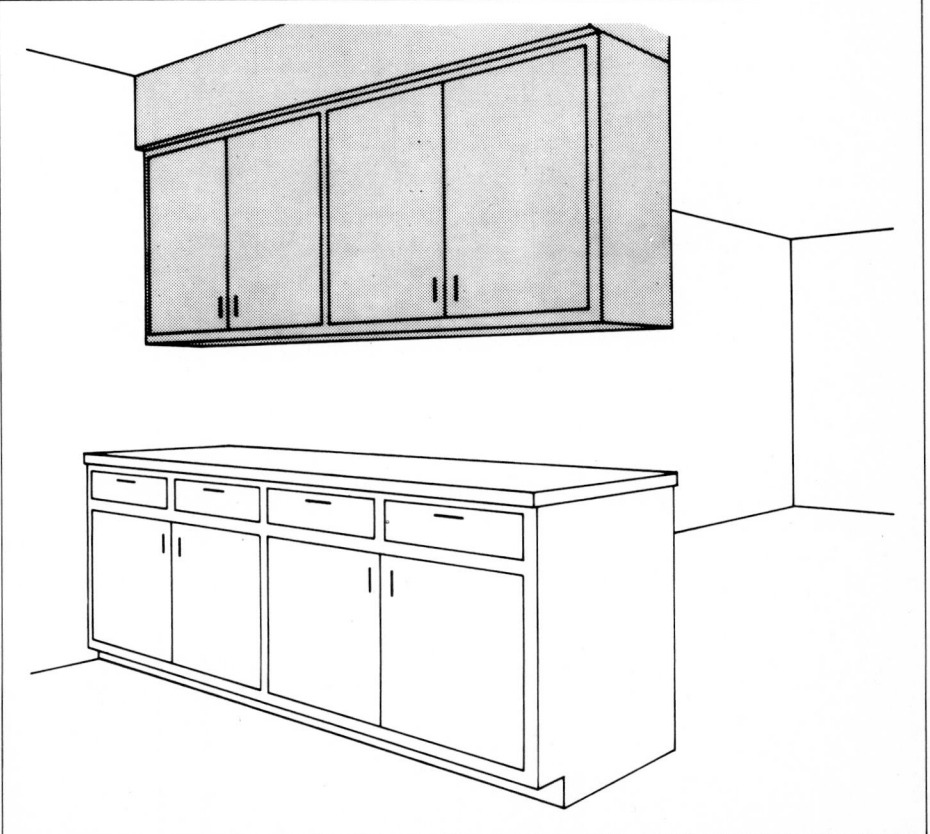
A peninsula cabinet will add storage. If more storage is needed, suspend a cabinet from the ceiling. You may use soffit or additional section of cabinets.

HOUSEHOLD STORAGE
Linen Closets and Other Cabinetry

Just as they usually lack enough closets, most homes also lack sufficient general storage to hold all those things that are used rarely but cannot be done without, as well as all the things that are used almost daily. There are, however, many good and efficient solutions to this storage problem.

Liberal use of built-in cabinets allows for ample storage and may add beauty and value to the home. A linen closet, because it can be as little as 12 inches deep, can be placed easily in a bathroom or in the hall. Cabinets in the dining room, provided with open wood or glass shelves, a mirror, and/or a wine rack — gives additional storage and, potentially, a touch of elegance.

Bookcases will go in almost any room and often can be combined with base cabinets. A built-in desk is an attractive addition to almost any room, including the kitchen. A desk not only provides storage but also helps to keep things organized.

Adding a Storage Room

Refer to your family living pattern, as established in Chapter 2, to see what areas of which rooms are rarely used and can be spared for a storage/utility room. Ideally, the space should be close to the kitchen and be partially along an exterior wall so that outside access is available. If no easy solution presents itself, you may need to examine your overall plan. It could be that a simple change in another area could open up the spot for the storage room.

Combining uses. The storage room can be combined with other functions such as a laundry area and a mud room, or the areas may be separate, depending on your requirements and the availability of space. If the new storage room is to contain plumbing for a washer or sink, it should be located adjacent to an area that has existing plumbing so that the hookups can be made easily and inexpensively.

Space requirements. The size of the storage room can vary greatly, depending on your needs and/or available space. A minimum width and length of 5 feet, however, should be maintained. If the washer and dryer are included, these minimums should be increased to 6 feet by 5 feet 6 inches.

Door framing. Any walls of the storage room can be constructed as outlined in Chapter 4, with one exception. If the storage room is to have outside access, an exterior door must be installed. This will be similar to the door installation explained in Chapter 4, except that a double 2x6 header should be used above the door; use 2x8s if the door is wider than 3 feet. This is required because all outside walls are load-bearing walls. You must follow all directions for removing a section from a load-bearing wall. In addition, you will have to patch the exterior wall surface. Chapter 12 contains a full discussion of exterior wall construction.

Storage Space Alternatives

Window greenhouse and storage. If you have been giving serious thought to installing a greenhouse window in the kitchen or dining room, consider carrying the project one step farther and adding storage cabinets beneath the window bay with an opening to the outside for small lawn and garden tools and supplies. This arrangement is attractive both inside and out, and gives a sense of ''opening up'' the inside of the house. The cabinets can be built just off the ground and tied into the wall framing in simple construction.

Other built-ins. Built-in beds and bunks provide additional possibilities for storage. The space beneath can be used for deep drawers.

The attic can be used to store the items you rarely use if you provide some flooring. Place ½-inch plywood decking on the joists (⅝ inch if the joists are spaced at 24 inches o.c.). Paint the plywood with a sealer so that it will resist moisture and

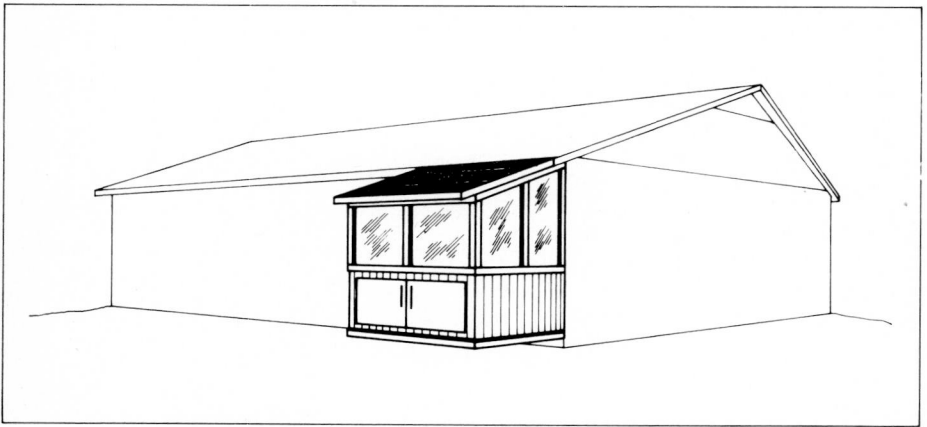

A small greenhouse added to the back of a kitchen will add light to the room. Garden equipment can be stored below and reached from the outside of the house.

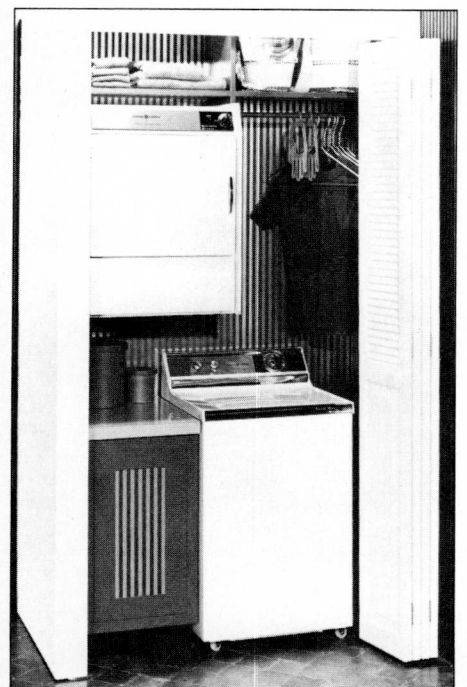

Kitchen or back hall closet shown has been converted into an entire laundry room.

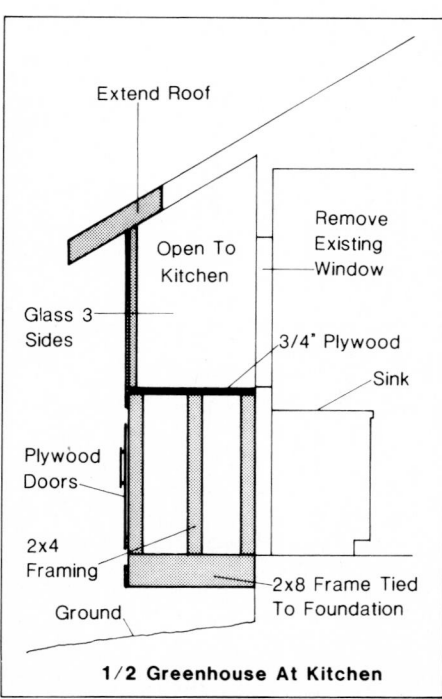

1/2 Greenhouse At Kitchen

Extend Roof

Open To Kitchen

Remove Existing Window

Glass 3 Sides

3/4" Plywood

Sink

Plywood Doors

2x4 Framing

Ground

2x8 Frame Tied To Foundation

Framing for greenhouse unit ties into the house. Top is glassed in; heat warms kitchen.

withstand use. You also may consider adding a set of steps that fold out of sight into the attic.

Another good storage area for rarely used items is overhead — in the attic, the basement or the garage. A wood frame, suspended from and secured by bolts to rafters, will support a plywood or particleboard base. Coat the frame and base with sealer so that it will not warp or crack from moisture and heat.

Every small niche in a home that is wasted space can be put to use, eliminating storage problems. A small, unused, recessed corner area can be converted into useful space with the installation of shelves for book or other items. Some space can be used for heating equipment such as a wood-burning stove or even a small central furnace. You can build in a linen closet or other cabinets that do not require more depth than the space available.

Framing an arch for a niche. If you have a small area you would like to make more attractive, you can build an arch without too much difficulty. Open the wall as explained in Chapter 4 and place a 1x4 top plate between the 2x4 studs at the height desired for the arch. Use a 2x4 if you make the opening wider than 4 feet. If you want the arch to reach the ceiling, the top plates of the framing can serve as the top piece of the arch. Nail all 1x4 framing with 8d common nails. Use 12d common nails for 2x4s.

1. Measure ⅓ the total length of the top piece from each end and mark.
2. Measure down a distance equal to ⅓ the length of the top piece and mark each side piece.

3. Fit a 1x4 with ends mitred at a 45° angle from one mark on the top piece to the mark on the nearer side piece to form a triangle.
4. Repeat on the other side.
5. Subdivide the remaining center third of the top piece into thirds. Do the same with the newly installed, angled side pieces.
6. To finish the arch, cut four pieces to fit from the vertical side members to the angled pieces, and from the angled pieces to the top piece. The ends of these boards will be mitred at 22½°. Nail all lumber into place and cover framing with finish material.

Creating a smooth curve. Cut saw kerfs on the back of the finish material. Set a circular saw blade at slightly over one-half the thickness of the finish material and saw a series of cuts every ½ to ¼ inch across the back of the material perpendicular to the length of the wallboard or paneling. Set the kerfed surface material to the frame, bending the curves slowly. Nail through the finish material into the framing. Cover the front faces of the framing and finish the joints.

In-Wall Storage

When storage space is extremely short, consider using cavities in interior walls for storage. You can create very shallow storage between studs or by subdividing closet space with access from different rooms.

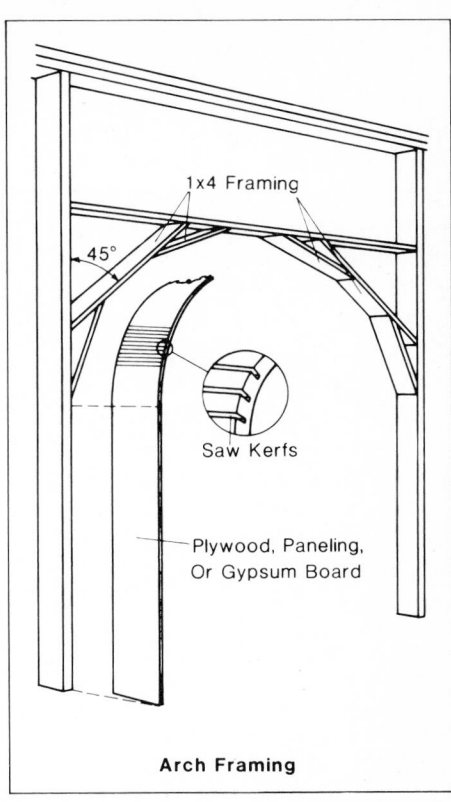

Instructions for building this arch are at left. Principle may be applied to adapting any door opening to an archway.

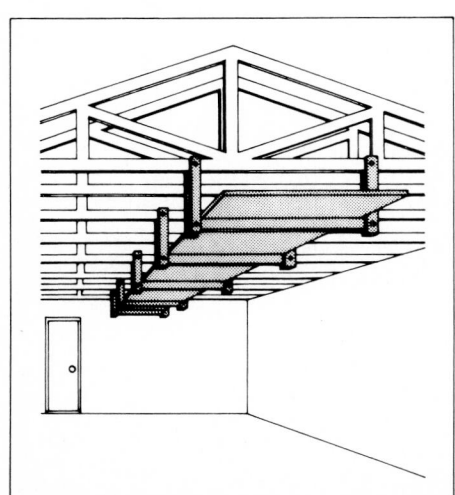

Storage for screens or storm windows is created from plywood and braces attached to joists.

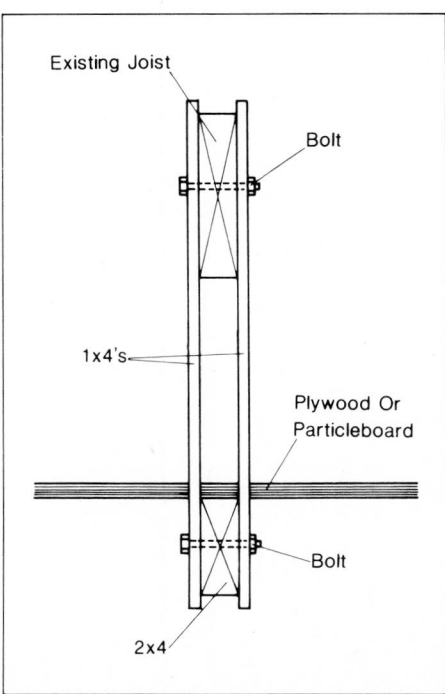

Bolt 1x4s to joists and 2x4 supports. Lay plywood on 2x4s. Nail in place for security.

Shallow, in-wall storage is used to display many items in this attractive room.

But be careful. This type of construction will transmit sound more readily than any standard construction. Place the in-wall storage unit between two rooms where sound transmission would not be a severe problem, such as between a bath and a closet or other storage area, or between a master bedroom and master bath. A plumbing wall usually will be thicker than a standard 2x4 stud wall, because of the extra space required by the pipes.

Opening the walls. Locate the studs and remove wallboard or plaster and lath even with the inside face of the studs. You can cut through the surface with a circular saw set to the thickness of the surface material, but be sure you do not cut farther than the area you wish to remove. Follow directions given in Chapter 4.

Creating the storage space. You may open the wall to expose the space between two studs or between several studs. The opening may reach to the full height of the wall or be as small as two feet. Line the back of each stud recess with hardboard, plastic laminate or wallboard. Determine the spacing of the shelves and nail 3-inch long 1x1 cleats to the sides of the studs to support the shelves. Make sure the cleats are flush with the back of the stud, level and perfectly matched so the shelves will be level. Cut shelves from 1x4 stock, ½-inch plywood, or particle board. If you wish to hide the cleats, face each board with a strip of ¼-inch plywood or other facing material. You may paint the studs and shelves or cover all the exposed surfaces with hardboard or laminate.

Finishing the area. The shelf units will be more attractive if you frame the opening with the same molding used else-where in the room. A simple molding is half-round cut with mitred corner joints. If the objects to be stored are attractive, you need not cover the opening. However, if you are planning to use the space as "catch-all" storage, you may want to install doors. These can be simple plywood panels, but louvered shutters can be used to create an attractive covering for the opening.

Both magazine and book storage were created when this bookcase unit was built into the wall between two tall windows.

Almost any wall will accept custom-designed bookcase units. Plank paneled walls make these wood shelves appropriate to the room.

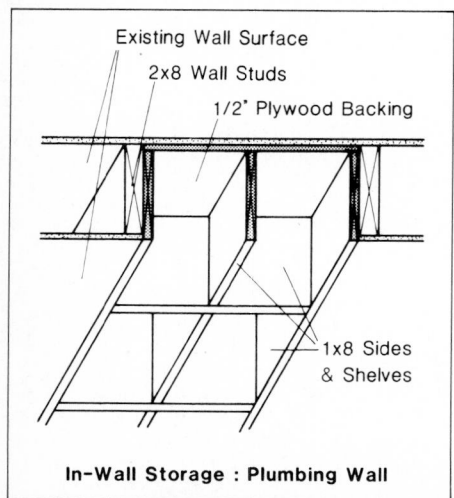

In-Wall Storage : Plumbing Wall

Plumbing walls have more depth and have more adequate between the wall space for storage.

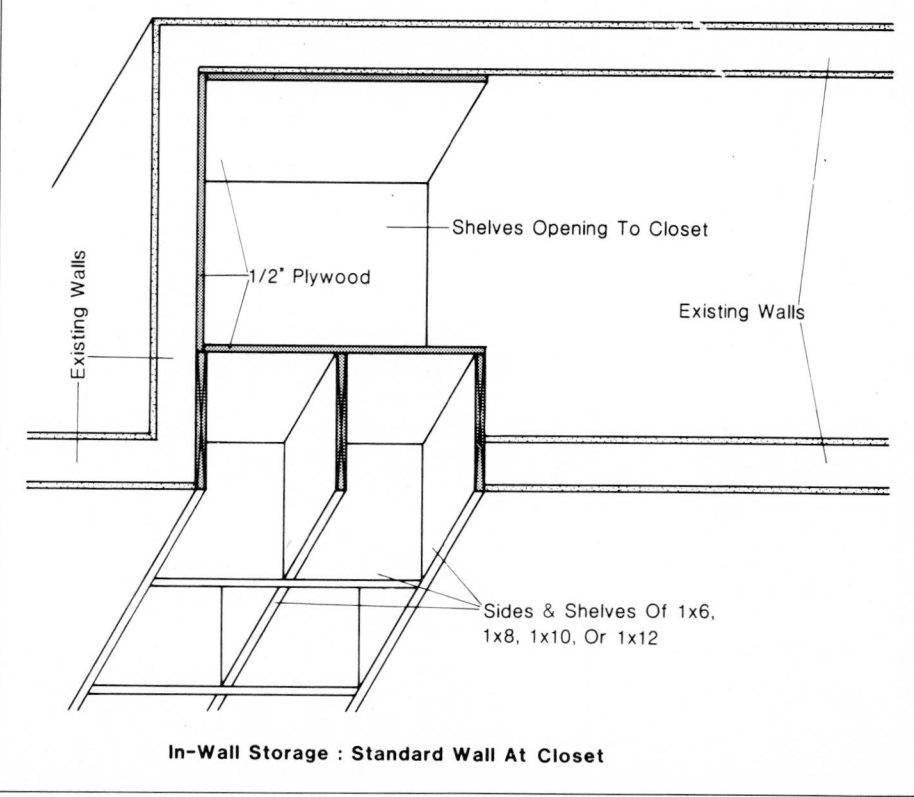

In-Wall Storage : Standard Wall At Closet

This in-wall storage fits between studs and borrows space from a set of closet shelves on the other side of the wall to bring storage into the other room where it is needed.

9
BASEMENT CONVERSIONS

The basement, because of its location, may not be the ideal place for living area expansion. However, it usually is not fully utilized and could be the easiest and least expensive part of the house to develop. The floor, wall, and ceiling structures are all in place, so that all that is needed is construction of interior wall framing and installation of finish materials. The most effective use of the basement is for a purpose suitable to a downstairs area, which will free rooms on the main floor.

BASEMENT DESIGN
Do not adapt the space to a room that is heavily used, such as a family or great room. This could lead to excessive trips up and down stairs. It should also not be used as a room for elderly or handicapped persons. Consider the basement for rooms that are either used infrequently or for rooms in which the user will remain for long periods of time.

Plumbing
If plumbing is readily accessible in the basement, a bath, wet bar, and/or kitchen-

Frequently overlooked basement spaces can become very attractive and useful to the family that does a lot of entertaining.

ette can be added easily. Remember, however, that there is always a possibility that the basement is below the sewer that drains the house. If this is the case, a pump will be required to lift plumbing waste so that it can flow out the house sewer by gravity. If the cost and maintenance requirements of such a pump are more than you can accept, then assign uses that do not require plumbing.

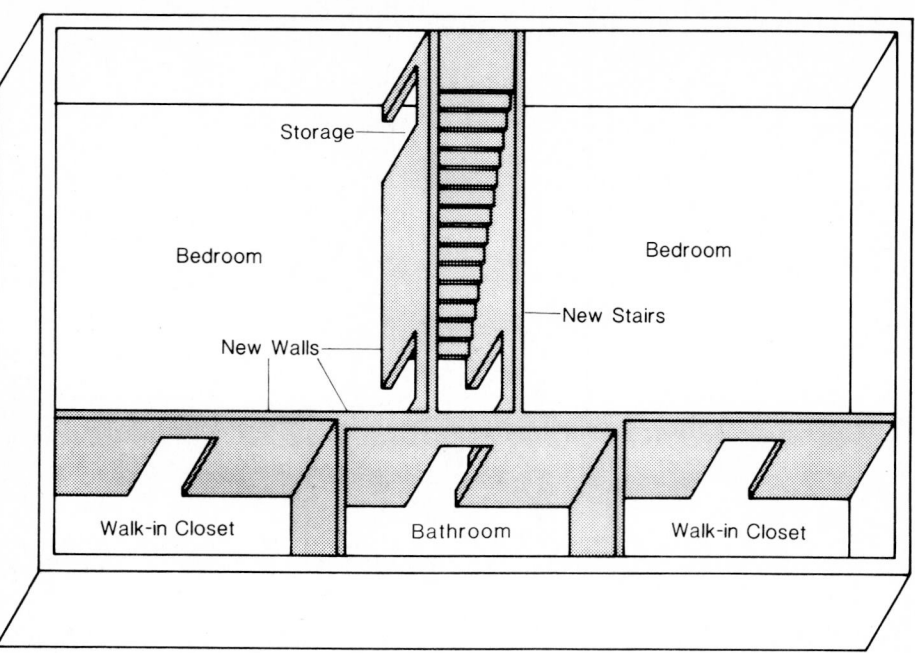

A basement naturally divided by a center stairway can be adapted to use in several ways. Two bedrooms and bath are one option that will work in a dry basement with a low sewer.

An unfinished basement may seem an unlikely prospect, but good design will change it.

Recess and table lighting brighten an area finished with paneling and new flooring. Meant to be a game room, there is still space for a desk.

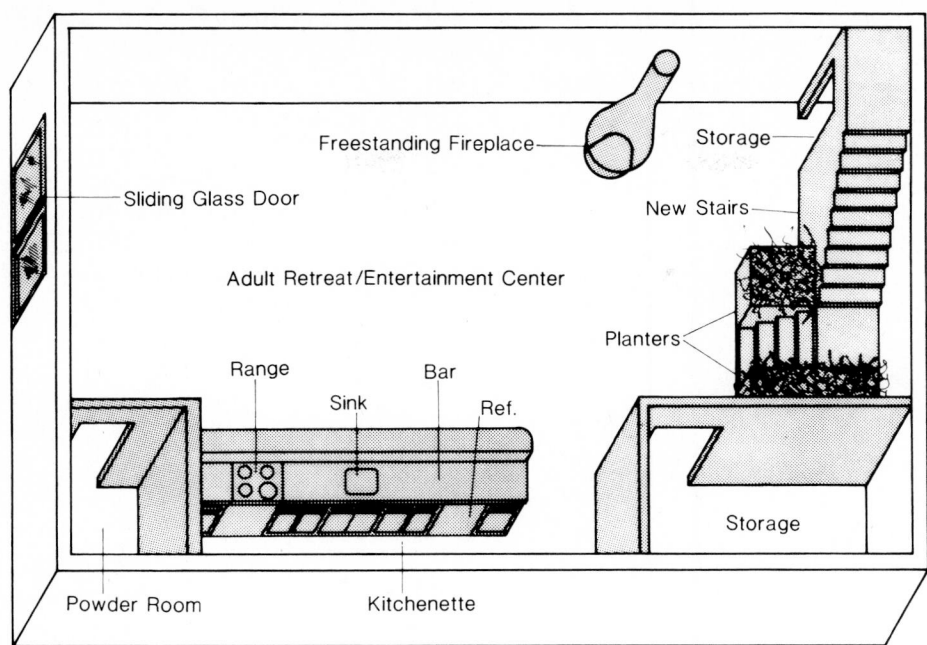

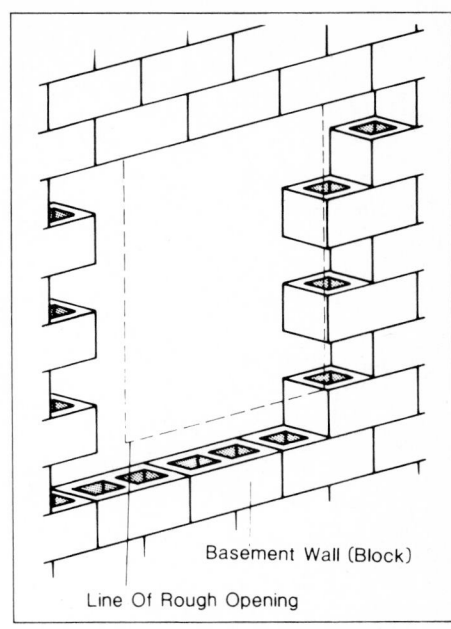

Remove block to create a rough opening for a new window in a basement wall. See Chapter 4.

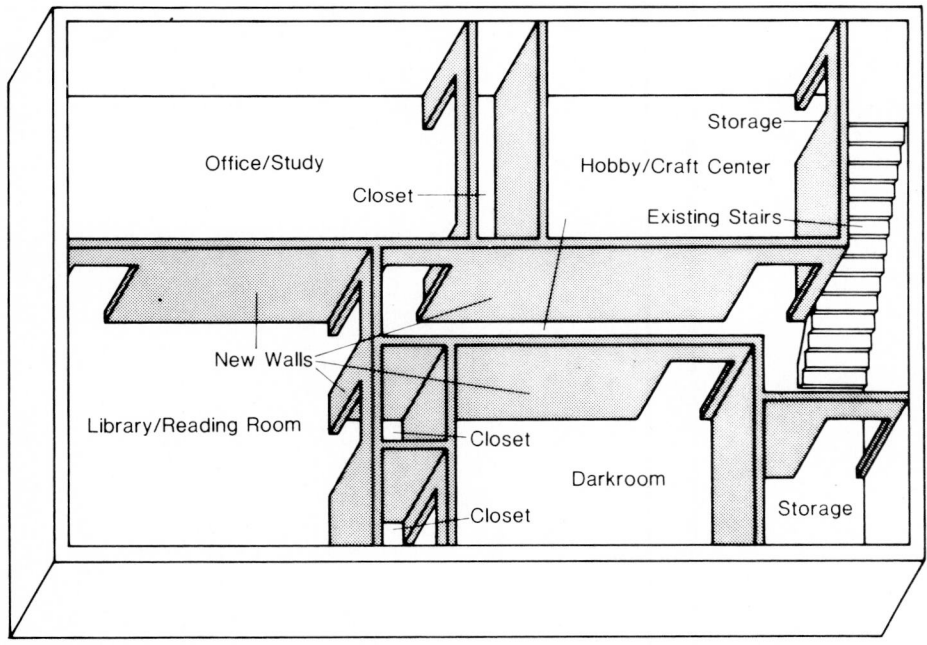

This basement is shown with two entirely different uses designed for different families.

Use as a Bedroom

The basement is not often used as a bedroom. This is probably because we usually imagine the basement as a damp, cold, and musty place, lacking windows and natural light. Most of these problems, however, can be overcome. You may add or increase waterproofing, ventilation, insulation and heating, and lighting, then decorate with light, bright colors, add a bath and create comfortable basement bedrooms.

Recreation Areas, Dens, and Hobby Centers

These are the most common choices for basement conversion because these rooms call for a minimum of extra construction effort. Usually, there is enough space for a well-equipped recreation room, far enough from the main living area to keep recreation room noise from becoming a problem. A cozy adult retreat can be built with a bar and/or freestanding fireplace. If a sloping lot permits access to the outdoors on one side, and a door can be added (if one does not already exist), the adult retreat can become a party and entertainment center. The entertainment room would be complete with a small refrigerator or kitchenette.

The basement is a good location for an office or a hobby or craft center. Hobby areas could include a photographic dark room, a children's television room, a stereo room, a library/reading room, and any other convenient use that will not require repeated trips upstairs. Lighting, counters, and cabinets or desks will be needed. Carpeting will make the area more comfortable.

SOLVING PROBLEMS IN THE BASEMENT

Most of the problems associated with basement development can be overcome. First, you must determine the exact problems or combination of problems before you can match up the problem with a solution.

Adding a Window for Natural Light

Because the basement is underground, there will be few, if any, windows; most windows will be small. If your home is built on a sloping lot, you may have one wall, or a section of one wall, that is substantially above grade. If this is the case, windows may be added to brick or even concrete block walls without too much difficulty.

Supporting the wall. Because foundation walls are load-bearing, removing a section may weaken the wall. Have an engineer check the wall and your plans before proceeding. The cost of an hour or two consultation is very small compared to the potential costs of repairing a collapsed wall. Even if your window is to be

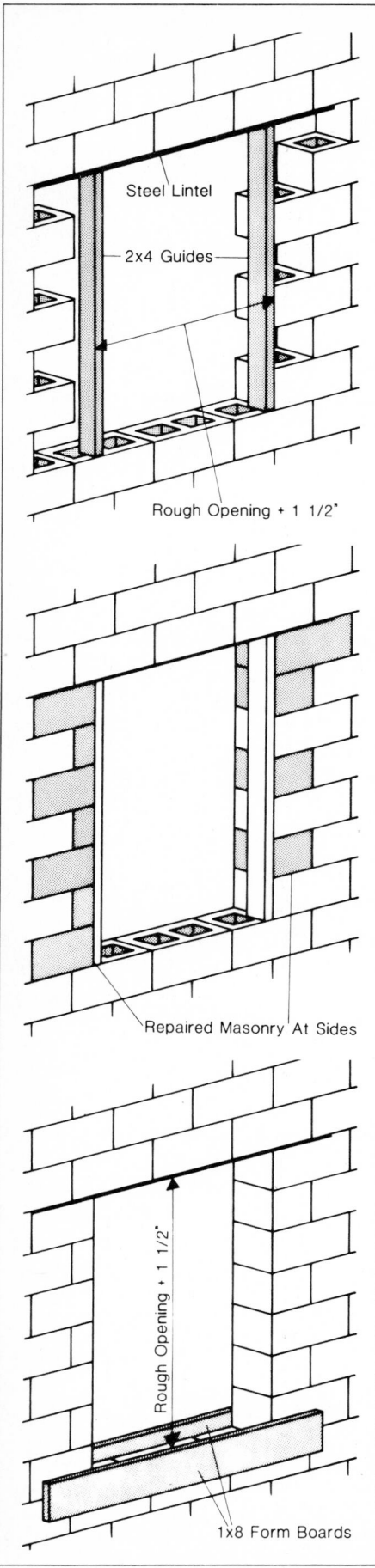

To create window, install support lintel and guides. Repair masonry and set forms for sill.

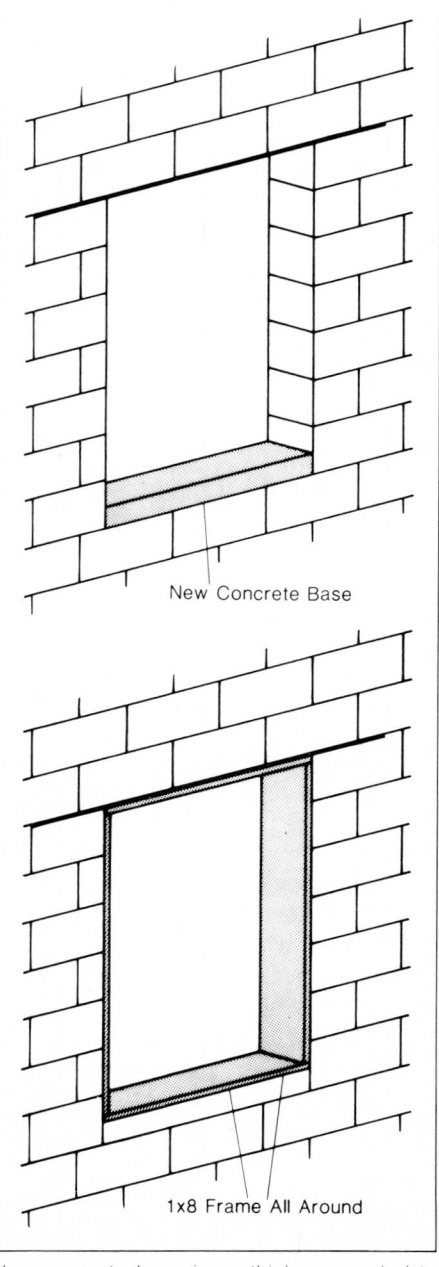

New concrete base is as thick as needed to bring opening to size for the new window frame.

quite small, it is necessary to prop the ceiling joists for support of upper floors while you are doing the work. Place a 2x4 across the joists and support it with vertical 2x4s wedged in place with shims.

Opening the wall. Locate the desired position for the window. Wear protective goggles. Remove the section of wall with a hammer and cold chisel (see Chapter 4). You can also use a circular saw with a masonry blade to saw through the mortar joints. Make the opening slightly larger than the rough opening needed for the window you have selected, because you will have to install new masonry, a lintel and sill. Be sure the window is not so large that the sill will be below the ground level.

Placing the lintel. Place two 2x4 guides in the rough opening and set a mortar-buttered steel lintel across the top of the opening against the last full row of brick or block. Wedge the temporary 2x4 braces so the outside faces reach ¾ inch beyond the rough opening. Be sure the braces are level. The lintel should extend a foot or more on each side of the window opening. Remove additional brick or block at the sides as necessary to fit the lintel in place. Temporarily brace with pieces of block and/or wedges on each side. To maintain the integrity of the wall, the lintel should be positioned and secured as soon as possible after the opening is completed.

Relay the masonry on each side, from the bottom up. Piece as necessary so that the masonry just touches the 2x4s. When the mortar has set, remove the 2x4s.

Creating a sill base. From the lintel, measure the length of the rough opening for the window. If the measurement reaches just to the bottom row of masonry, you need only to install the wood frame. If it is within an inch of the bottom row, you can use a mortar joint to close the gap. If the sill space is larger than an inch, you will need to pour a concrete sill base. Use masonry nails to nail 1x8 formboards to both sides of the opening. The formboards must be level at the top and 1½ inches lower than the rough opening. Place newspaper in the cells of the concrete block so that the concrete will go no more than 3 or 4 inches into the cells. Pour the concrete level with the top of the formboards.

If the window unit you will install does not have an integral sill, the concrete base must project one inch beyond the outside face of the wall. The top must slope away from the house to provide good drainage. This will require building special forms to provide the proper shape.

Framing and installing the window. Build a four-sided frame of 1x8s to fit the opening. When the concrete base has set up, place the frame into the opening. Level, shim as needed, and nail into the blocks on the side and the concrete base on the bottom with concrete nails. Flash the opening, then install the window unit following the manufacturer's directions. (If you have not chosen a window unit with integral sill, you will have to create a sloping concrete base, described above. Level the window, using shims if required, and nail into the frame you have set into the opening. Liberally caulk around the window and 1x8 frame.

Even if your basement walls are solid concrete, the window can be installed in much the same way, but creating the opening will be more difficult. Consider professional assistance because to do this yourself, you will have to rent a power chisel or jackhammer. Removal with hand tools will be almost impossible. When rebuilding the sides of the window opening, add a bonding agent to the cement mixture to assure a firm bond between the new concrete and the old concrete wall.

Adding a Door

Doors can be added in the same manner as a window, but with different framing requirements (see Chapter 4). However, you may need to adjust the grade away from the basement to allow for the door opening.

Adding a Large (or Bay) Window
Creating and supporting the opening.

For larger openings, such as for a bay window, a slightly different approach is needed. Place a substantial temporary brace of 4x4 posts under the floor joists near the

opening. Wedge the posts with 2x4s at the top and bottom.

Remove the masonry at the opening all the way up to the wood sill plate. Make the opening at the top about a foot wider on each side than the rough opening. Cut and remove the sill plate the full width of your opening. Remove the ends of the floor joists to create space to add a beam of nailed two 2x10s to the boxheader with 16d common nails. (Add three 2x10s for a two-story home.) Toenail the floor joists into the new beam. Next, replace the sill plate with a board wide enough to extend a

A standard double-hung window comes in many sizes. Choose one before remodeling.

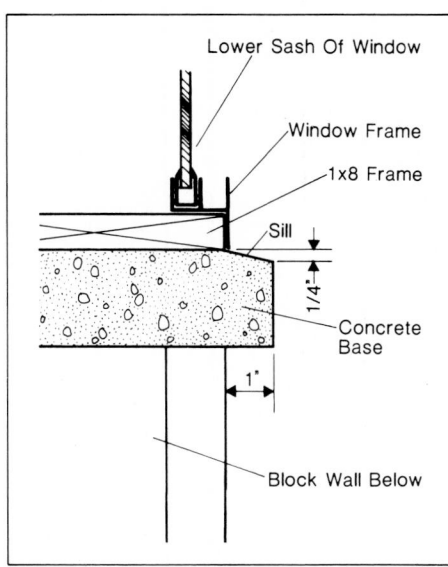

Slope concrete sill away from window and have it overhang wall to prevent drainage problem.

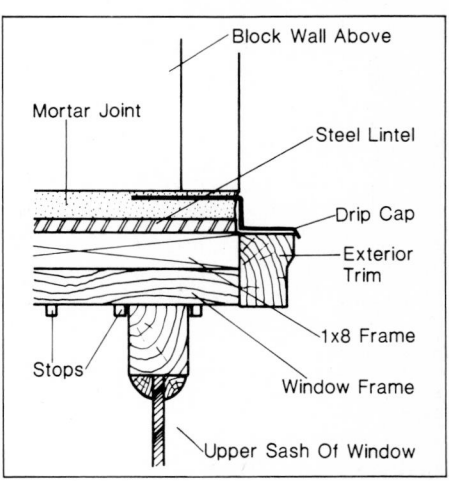

Flash top of the window with drip cap over exterior trim that covers rough frame and window.

If the ground slope of your lot permits it, an exterior access door may be added to a basement wall. This will increase usefulness of the basement area, especially for summer entertaining.

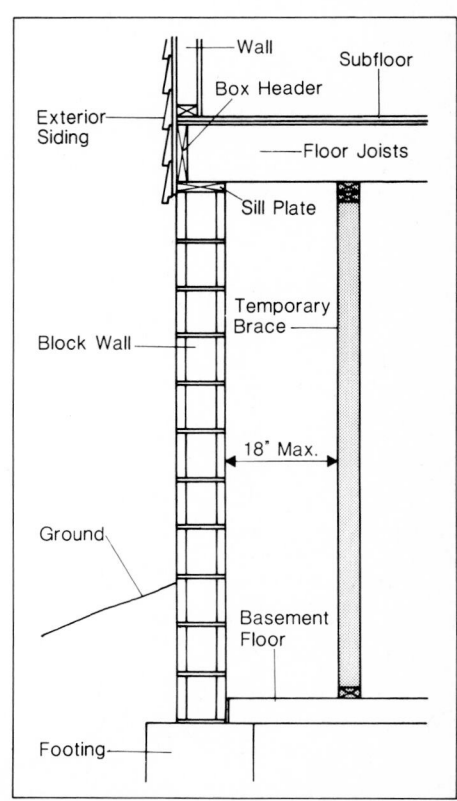

A temporary brace is required to support floor joists before removing any area of the wall to create the new door opening.

minimum of two inches under the floor joists. All nailing is done with 16d common nails.

Remove any exterior finish material in the rough opening below the level of the sill plate. Carefully repair the masonry on the sides; the new masonry is what supports the new wood beam. Allow the masonry several days to set firmly before you remove the temporary brace(s). Install the window unit as previously described: providing a concrete base, frame with 1x8s and flash the opening. Use galvanized steel or copper flashing on top. To place anything as large as a bay window, you will need one helper for every three feet of width.

Using Artificial Light and Color
Use light, warm colors to paint, paper, or panel the walls in the basement. Select light-colored finish materials for the floor and ceiling. Provide liberal quantities of artificial light. Track lights, a series of recessed spots, fluorescent lights, and lighted ceiling panels all work well in the basement. Plan to use a combination of lighting patterns if the basement will be a multi-use area.

Providing Ventilation
Because basements usually contain few openings, increased ventilation is a must in the remodeled basement. If you do not already have them, provide closable vents all around at the top of the wall. These

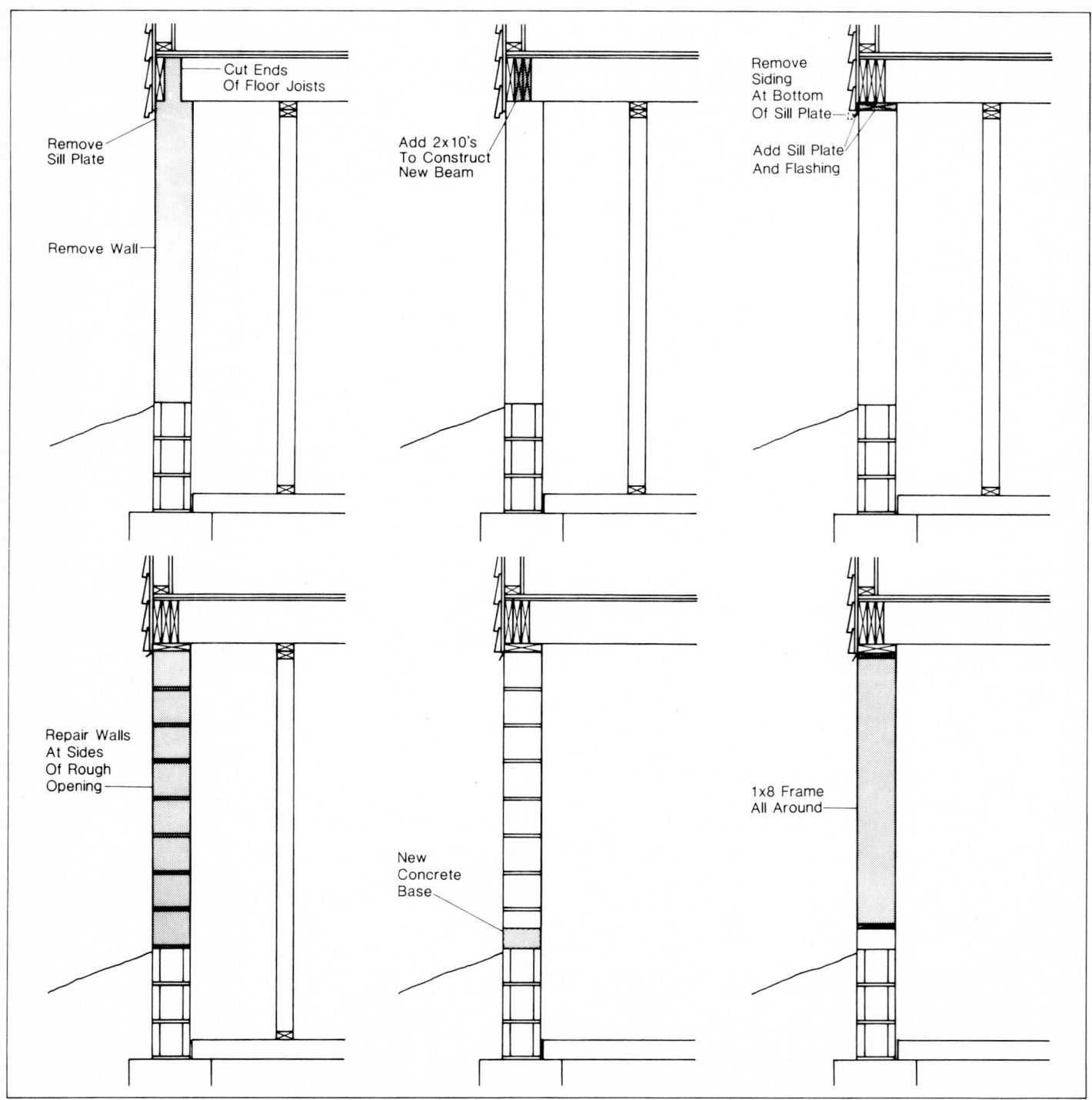

Addition of a door or large bay window requires considerable reconstruction to provide support for upper floors. Additional beams must be added to carry weight of the walls, and a new, wide sill plate is needed to carry joists. Sill base and window framing are similar to small window.

should be located about every 8 to 12 feet. There should be enough space from the grade level outside to the level of basement ceiling inside to allow for a vent at least 6 inches high. The air circulation can be increased by adding a fan to one or more of the basement vents. This fan should have a baffle over the back, so that it will pull air under the baffle and create a more positive air flow through the basement.

New bay window with double-hung sash will bring light and air into the remodeled basement.

Small basement windows provide adequate ventilation if small dehumidifier can keep air dry.

Pumps for Plumbing Needs

As previously mentioned, if the basement is too low and the plumbing cannot drain through the house sewer by gravity flow, a pump will have to be installed to compensate for this. Such a pump should be located near the point the pipe leaves the house. Small, relatively inexpensive pumps are available for this situation, but regular maintenance is required.

Insulation Needs

Basement insulation could, in some parts of the country, actually be a disadvantage. Because the earth lying against the outside of the basement walls has a high capacity to store heat, insulation is only about half as useful in a basement as it would be in exposed walls. In the summer the earth stays cool for a long time and actually absorbs heat from the basement and keeps the area cooler. Insulation would only inhibit this heat absorption process and reduce the advantage of the natural cooling capacity of the earth.

In warm climates, where air conditioning is more of an energy concern than heating, insulation of the basement walls usually is not necessary, except where basement walls are exposed. If you live in an area with severe winters, then insulation of the basement walls is advisable. Use 2-inch rigid insulation or foil-covered foam sheathing. Apply them directly to walls, following manufacturer's instructions.

Heating and Air-Conditioning

Because a basement is usually a sizable area, you may find your present heating and air-conditioning system will not accommodate the additional load. Separate units, such as wood-burning heaters, wall heaters, or fireplaces, can be used to warm the basement space. If you need additional air conditioning, install a window unit but place it in the wall. Use the techniques given in the previous section on adding windows. A wall installation is advised because there are usually few basement windows and they should be left to provide light and ventilation. You may prefer a combination heating and air-conditioning unit that will mount into the wall just as a window unit air conditioner does.

For a very large basement (800 square feet or more) that will be divided into several rooms, you should consider adding another, smaller central unit. This unit should operate independently from the existing system to save energy and to keep utility bills down. Run ducts across ceiling, strapping sections to joists. Install a suspended ceiling for camouflage.

HOW TO DAMP-PROOF A BASEMENT
Interior Waterproofing

Identifying the problem. Basements are often damp; some basement walls are actually wet. This makes many homeowners reluctant to use the basement for living-area expansion. With the multi-

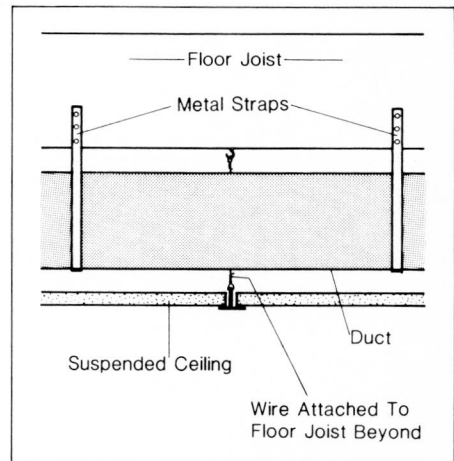

Ductwork in the basement can be hidden by a suspended ceiling. Ts are hung from joists.

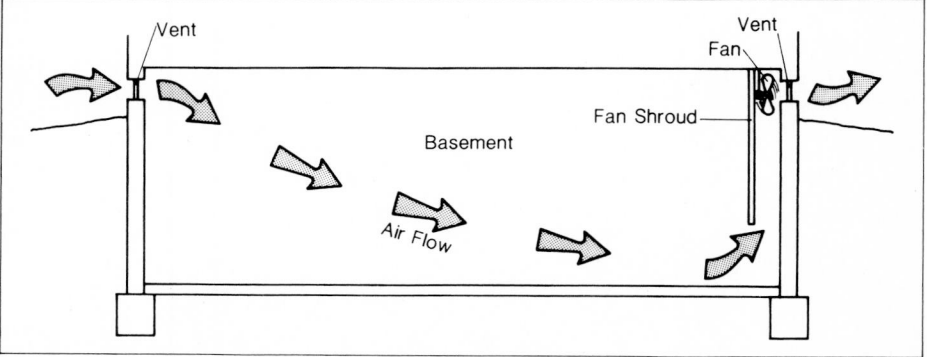

A fan protected by a shroud or baffle will pull air from one vent and out another. The shroud will mean the air is pulled down and then up for best circulation.

tude of products available today, a damp basement no longer need be a problem.

The two reasons for water accumulation in a basement are seepage and condensation. Seepage occurs when water comes through the walls from the outside. Condensation occurs when warm, humid air in the basement hits the cool masonry walls, and the water vapor condenses on the walls. A simple test will determine which problem you have. Place a pocket mirror or a piece of aluminum foil on the wall and leave it overnight. If water collects on the wall side, your problem is seepage. If it collects on the room side, the problem is condensation. Both problems can be corrected, although the solutions involve procedures that are quite different.

Dealing with condensation. To eliminate condensation you need a vapor barrier between basement space and the masonry wall. The best way to do this is with a finished wall construction; painting the masonry wall will not correct the problem. Nail 2x2 furring strips to the walls, on 24-inch centers, with masonry nails. Then apply a vapor barrier to the furring strips. One of the best types is a foam insulation and board with a foil vapor barrier. The vapor barrier faces the room side. This will provide both insulation and a vapor barrier. Other vapor barriers available are polethylene and asphalt-saturated felt. Finish wall materials may be applied directly over the vapor barrier.

There are some specifically formulated coatings (paint) that are designed to control moisture, but these are not very effective when applied directly to the masonry walls. It is best to use these paints on a finish material, such as gypsum wallboard, that has been nailed directly to the furring strips without a vapor barrier. If a vapor barrier is installed behind the finish wall, regular interior house paint should be used.

Controlling seepage. Solving seepage problems may be a little more difficult. Begin by checking the grading around the basement. The ground should slope away from the house for at least 10 feet. Flower beds often cause a flattening of the grading. If the ground does not slope properly, you must regrade it. Also make sure all downspouts divert water away from the

house. If finding and correcting these problems do not solve the seepage, walls will have to be waterproofed.

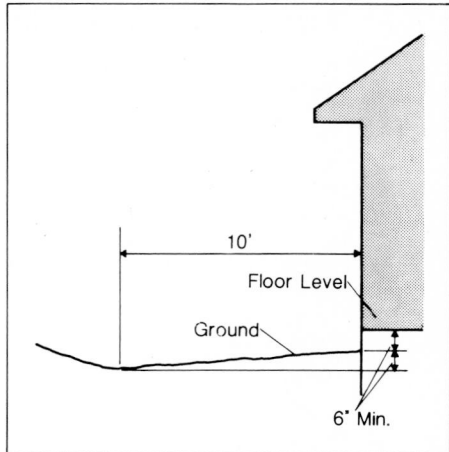

Slope ground near the house away from the foundation for at least 10 feet, with 6 inch drop.

Some insulating sheathing comes with a vapor barrier attached. Install furring strips over the sheathing and attach wallboard or paneling to furring strips. Paint or paper the wallboard.

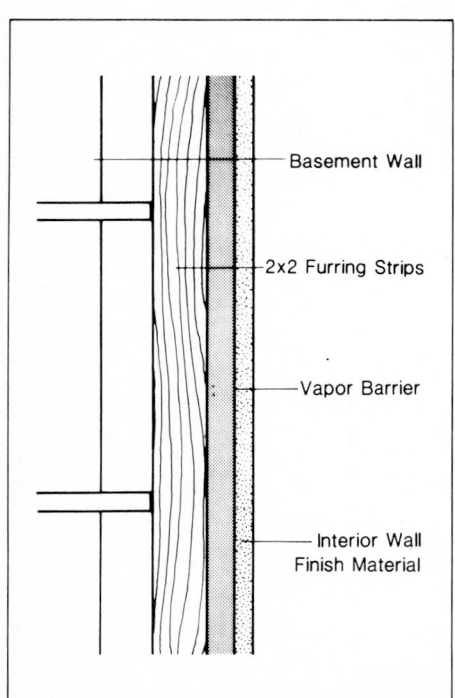

A vapor barrier is needed when finishing walls over cold concrete or damp block foundation.

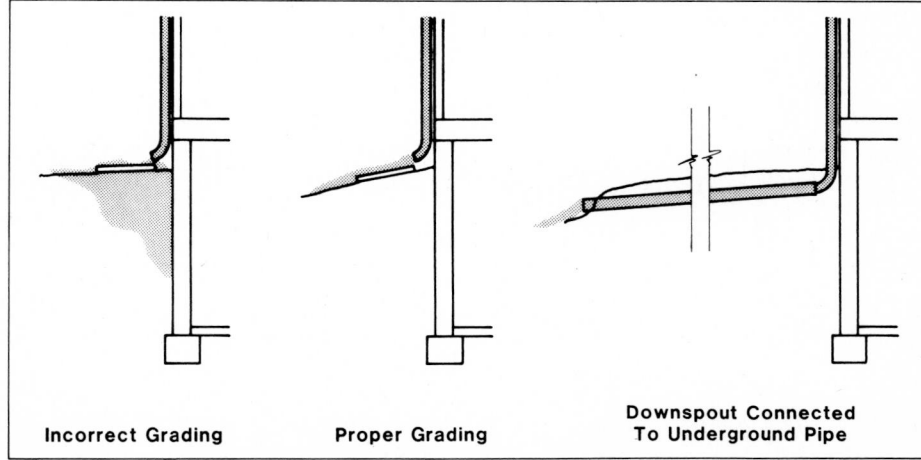

Incorrect grading means water will build up near the foundation. Direct runoff away from the foundation by grading or use of a drainpipe to carry water away from the house.

Waterproofing basement walls

First, remove any excess cement from the interior basement walls with a hammer and chisel. Then chisel a grove about ¾ inch wide and ¾ inch deep between the wall and floor. Do not cut a "V" shape. Instead, chisel the space out squarely so that the top and bottom of the notch will each be ¾ inch wide. This process is necessary because concrete shrinks as it cures and the floor slab may have pulled away slightly from the walls and allowed water to seep in. Also chisel out all cracks in the floor and walls. You may prefer to rent a power chisel or jack hammer to make the work go more quickly. Create small holes at the bottom of concrete block walls every 4 or 5 feet to allow internal condensation to drain.

Now fill the notches you have made with a nonshrinking grout. There are sev-

A foundation with serious water problems must be repaired and the basement dried before any remodeling may be done in the area.

Begin by cleaning the concrete block walls of any excess mortar, cement or any mineral deposits left on the surface by leaking water.

Make holes every 4 or 5 feet along the base of the wall to allow water, trapped in the block wall, to drain out and relieve pressure.

Chisel notches ¾ inch wide and deep along the base of the wall and floor joint and along any cracks in the wall and floor.

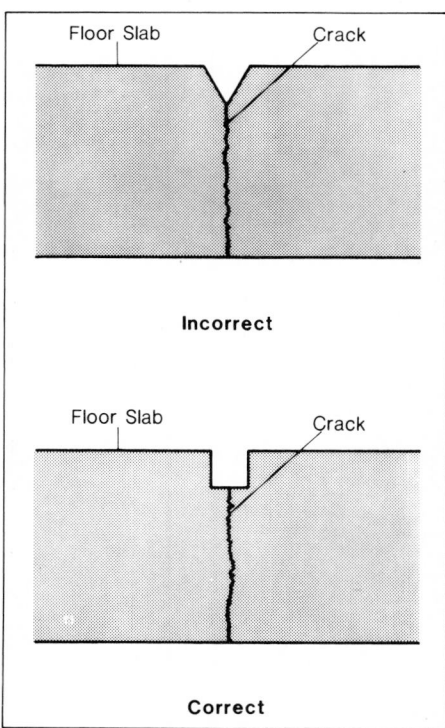

Floor Slab   Crack

Incorrect

Floor Slab   Crack

Correct

The chiseled notches must be nearly square in order to provide a good base for the repairs to be made with the patching material.

Fill the notches with a waterproof, non-shrinking grout. Fill exactly as directed by the manufacturer to prevent failure of the grout.

Use a sealer over the grout according to directions and patch any small holes. Reexamine the floor and walls for any cracks that you may have missed before applying paint.

eral brands on the market made specifically for this purpose. Follow the manufacturer's application directions carefully. Improper application will probably result in continued water seepage. Paint over all the patched cracks with a sealer designed for this purpose. Extend the sealer several inches on each side of the patch. Following the manufacturer's recommendations, paint the entire surface with the sealer. When the sealer has dried, patch and seal the holes you have made at the bottom of the walls. The walls may now be painted. Some sealers come in several colors so that additional painting is not necessary. You may wish to fur and finish the walls with wallboard or paneling.

Note: If you are waterproofing the outside as explained under "High Water Table" below, no waterproofing of the inside walls will be necessary unless seepage continues after the outside work is complete.

Apply waterproof paint over grout as an extra seal before painting the entire wall surface.

Next apply a full coat of paint over the damp areas of the wall to seal out water.

Coat of waterproofing paint should extend over the line of grout at the base of the wall.

Bring waterproofing paint up on the wall far enough to cover area of dampness.

Fill holes made for drainage with non-shrinking grout and paint over the area.

You may paint the entire wall and use no other finish if you like the look of the surface.

How to Add Exterior Waterproofing to Control Exterior Leakage

High water table problems. During heavy rains, usually in the spring and fall, the water table (level of underground water) rises. If your basement has footings that extend below the floor on all sides, it may result in trapped water under the floor and inside the footing when the water table rises above the level of the basement floor. Hydraulic pressure forces the water through any small cracks in the floor. If there is sufficient pressure, water can seep through concrete even if there are no cracks. Hydraulic pressure has been known to build up enough force to crack open a concrete floor and spew water into a basement.

This problem usually can be solved by waterproofing the outside of the basement wall and adding a 4- or 6-inch diameter perforated pipe — concrete, metal, or plastic — at the base of the wall.

Step one: digging the excavation. Excavate the earth against the basement wall. Make the excavation wide enough to work in. Slope the trench back, away from the wall, to prevent an earthslide that could trap you or others while working at the base of the wall.

Step two: applying the waterproofing. Cover the exterior of the basement wall with two coats of black asphaltic material. Apply the sealer from the grade down to and including the top of the footing. Next apply a layer of polyethylene or lapped fiberglass fabric. Finally, apply another coat of the asphaltic material.

Step three: installing the drain pipe. Lay perforated drain pipe in a gravel bed. Place the pipe along the side of the footing, sloping it at least ¼ inch per foot toward the pipe that will connect to the city storm sewer or town drainage ditch system. Place a one-foot-wide by one-foot-high bed of gravel around the pipe and backfill over the gravel. Grade the earth away from the house for at least ten feet. Provide a minimum drop of six inches in the ten feet, and much more on any side where there is a large slope draining toward the house.

Step four: connecting the pipe. Connect the perforated pipe to regular pipe at a storm sewer connection (if code allows), a drainage ditch outlet or a lower part of the lot. Keep all pipe steadily sloping downward to the outlet, at least ¼ inch of slope per foot. When the water table is high, the

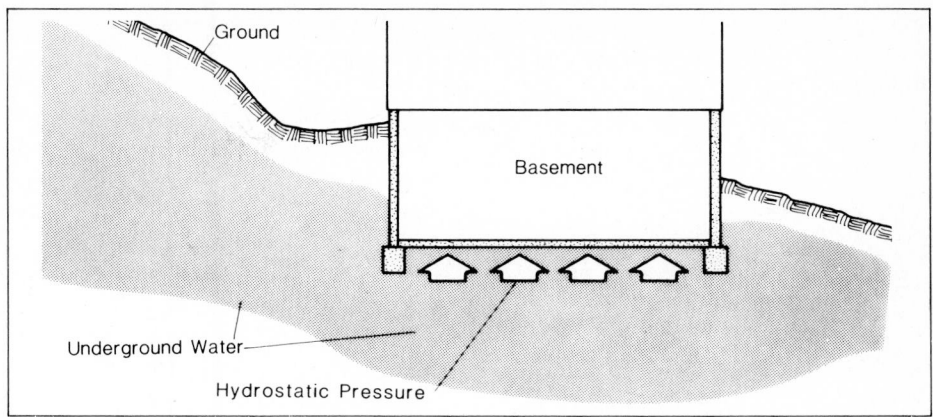

When the level of the water table rises above the level of a basement floor, water is trapped by the footings and water pressure builds enough to crack the concrete.

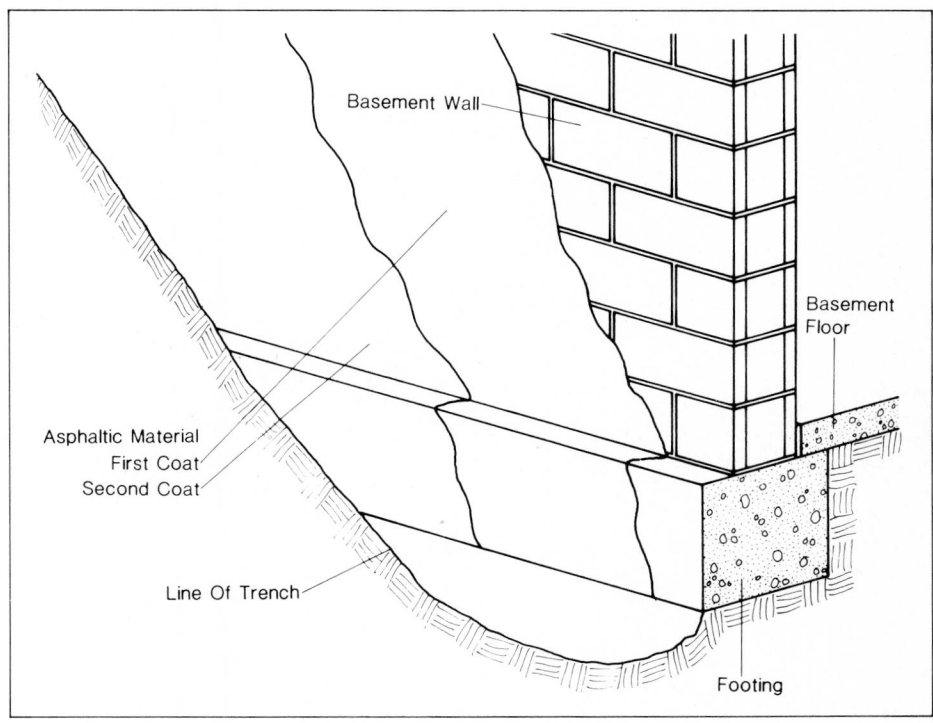

Water leakage from exterior pressure requires major work on the foundation. Dig a trench around the basement to below the footing and apply asphaltic waterproofing to the outside walls.

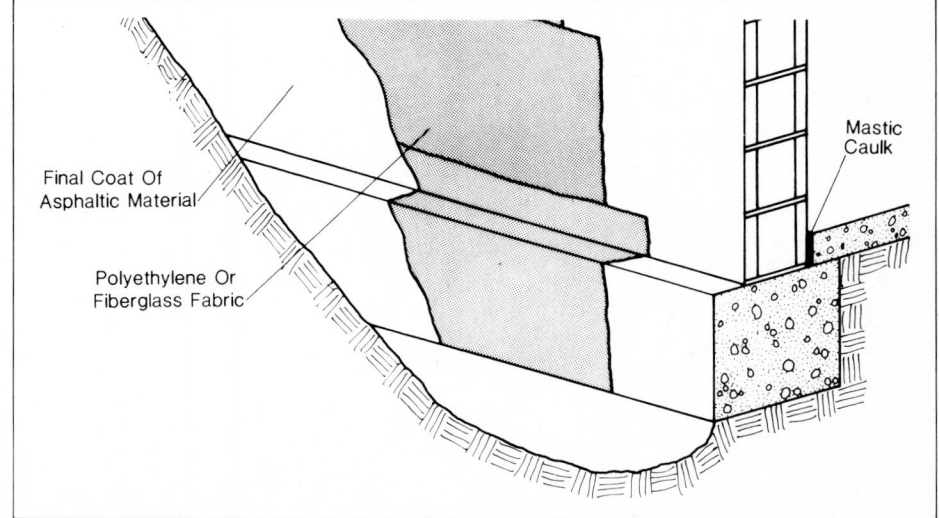

For a complete seal, apply a layer of polyethylene or fiberglass to the exterior of the wall. Notch interior wall/floor joint and fill space with mastic caulk or non-shrinking grout.

water under the basement floor will seep into the perforated pipe and flow away through the outlet.

Step five: allowing for drainage. Chisel small holes every 4 or 5 feet along the base of interior block basement walls to allow any trapped water to drain. After a few days' drying time, patch the holes with nonshrinking grout.

Using a Sump Pump

If there is not enough slope to your lot for natural drainage to a positive outlet, the solution is more expensive. The perforated pipe at the footing will have to be drained to a sump pump. The pump should be placed on a concrete base with concrete block walls. Add metal footholds on one wall, setting them in the mortar bed every second course. This provides access to service the pump. The perforated pipe is laid through the wall to drain into the sump pump area. As the area fills with water, the pump turns on and the water is lifted high enough so that it can drain out of your lot by gravity flow. While a pump is somewhat expensive, and does require periodic maintenance, the cost is usually

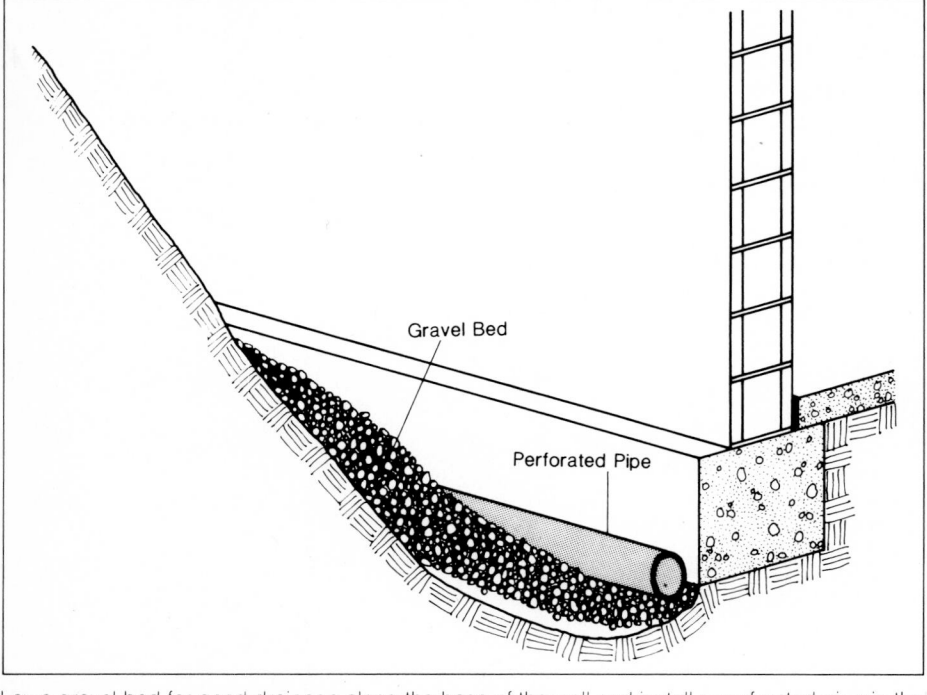

Lay a gravel bed for good drainage along the base of the wall and install a perforated pipe in the trench to carry away the water so that it does not remain against the foundation.

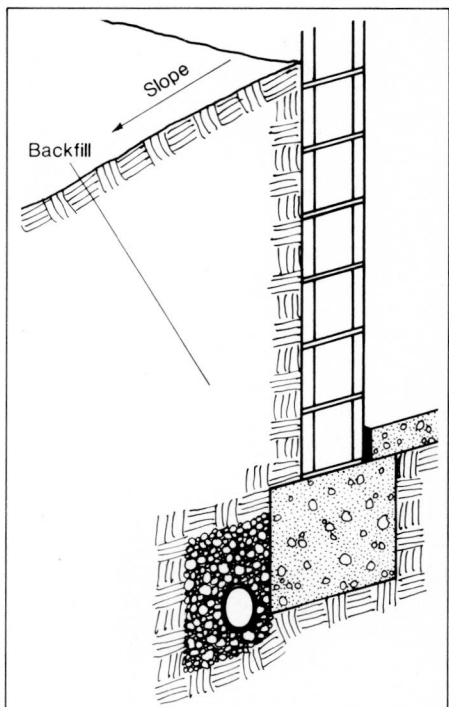

Grade backfill away from the house so that surface runoff is directed away.

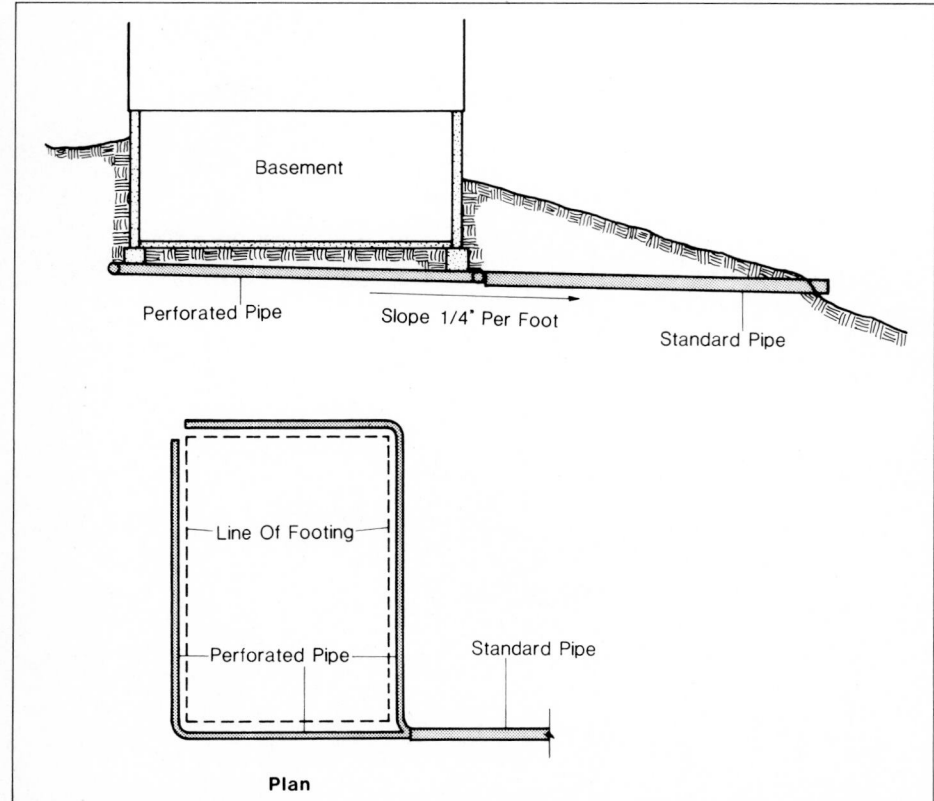

Pipe should surround the foundation and be sloped to carry the water away from the house and to a storm sewer or drainage ditch. Be sure that slope is consistently away from the house.

Drainage may require the assistance of a sump pump. Battery power backup is ideal.

far below that of a full addition. The cost of a pump also will save the expense of serious reconstruction of walls and floor destroyed by water pressure.

CONSTRUCTION WORK

Frame interior walls as discussed in Chapter 4. The finish materials may be installed as explained in Chapter 6.

Adding Finish Materials

If you have solved all water problems and your walls are smooth, you may wish only to paint the walls. Finish materials, such as gypsum board and paneling, may be applied directly to the masonry or stud wall using construction-grade glues manufactured for this purpose. Furring strips will not be required. If you wish to nail

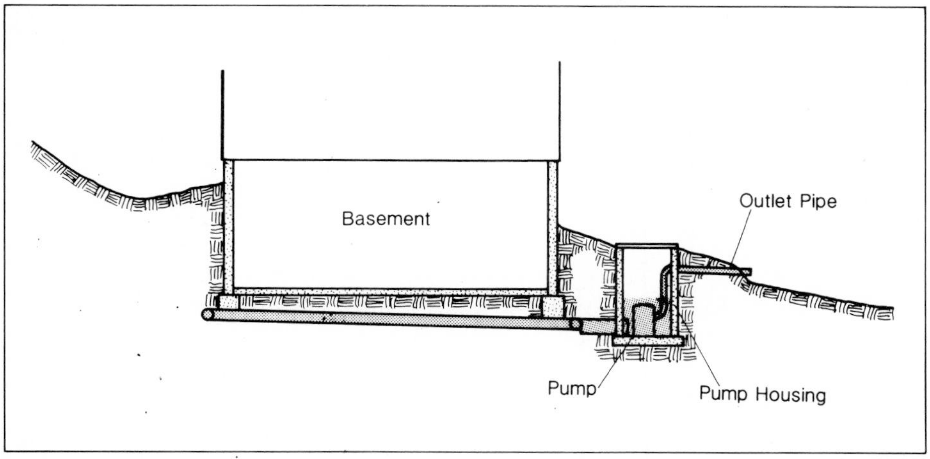

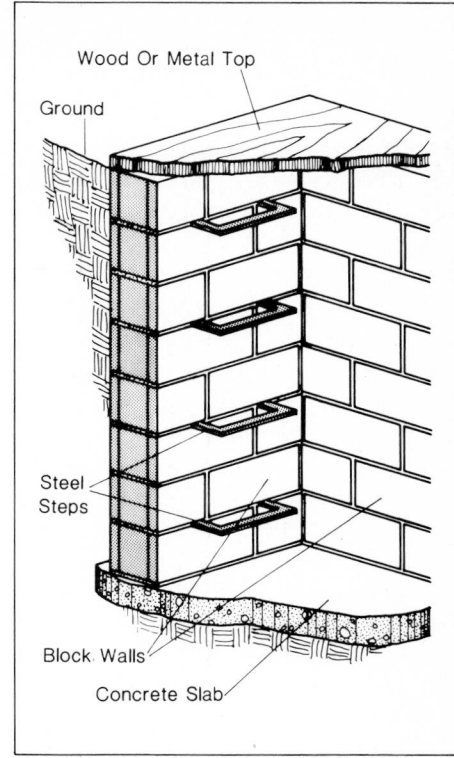

Sump pump is needed in this home site because the positive outlet is higher than the level of the collection pipe at the foundation. Pump must lift water to drainage outlet.

Provide permanent and durable access to outside sump hole for pump maintenance work.

A dry basement can be finished and furnished and put to any use the family requires. Materials are in no way limited by basement location.

finish materials to the walls, place furring strips on the walls with masonry set screws or concrete nails to add the finish materials. Nailing to masonry walls always requires installation of furring strips. Apply finish materials only after all water problems have been solved.

Working Around Support Columns

In larger homes, basements may have columns to support the floor joists of the main floor. These must be taken into account not only when planning the basic design of the basement, but also in relocating the stairs so they will fit between posts and still be convenient on both levels. Whenever possible, leave the staircase in the original location. However, you should always try to incorporate the columns into your basement redesign. Their removal or relocation could be, and probably would be, very expensive. They can become part of divider partitions, or can be boxed in to disguise their utilitarian nature. Avoid removing the columns, if at all possible. If you must make such a major structural change, consult an expert, such as an architect or structural engineer, on what must be done to guarantee sufficient support once the columns have been taken out.

Thin brick units may be applied to a basement wall for a decorative look. These units are fireproof and are a good backing to a wood stove or fireplace installation.

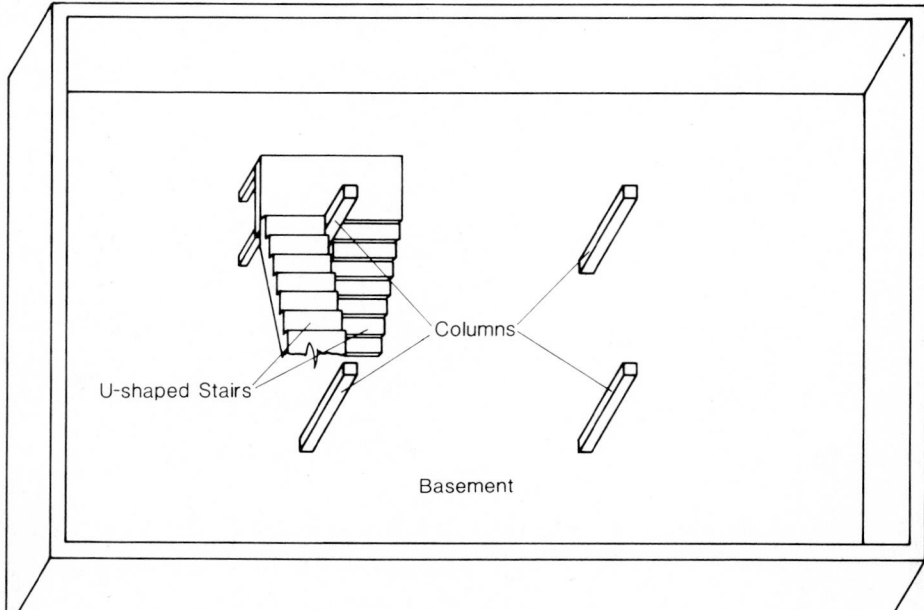

Support column was used here as a partition between basement kitchen and other space.

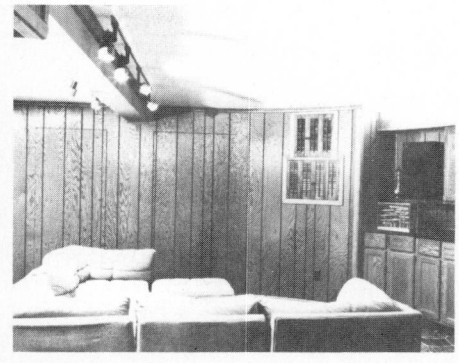

Track lighting on either side of beam brightens the basement sound room.

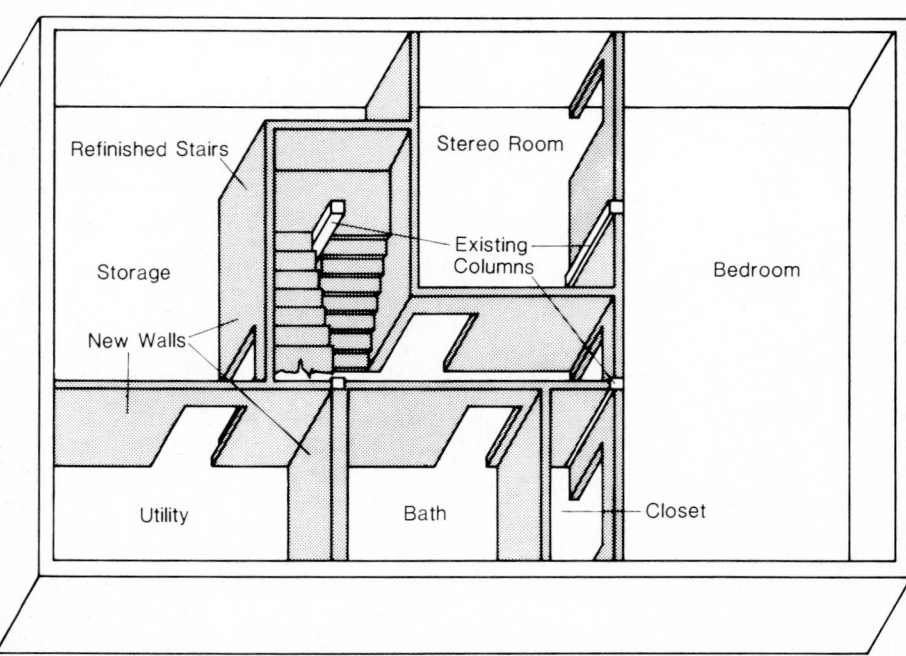

Support columns should be left in place whenever possible. Design construction or remodeling so they are made part of the partitions. Trim out with finish lumber to disguise them.

BASEMENT CONVERSIONS

This apartment was developed in the basement of a turn-of-the-century home in a Midwestern city. A dry area, it was ideal for conversion to a more practical use than catch-all storage. The area uses a comparatively open plan that allows available light to pass from one area to another to compensate for the naturally lower light levels in a basement. Smooth-finish knotty-pine boards were used for walls and ceilings in most of the apartment. This material works well with the natural brick of the basement walls. Smooth plaster walls are used in the kitchen area because they are easier to maintain.

Optimum use of the space is evident. Storage space is provided under the bed. There are open bins on the living area side near the fireplace. On the bedroom side, the storage is in the form of drawers built under the raised bed. Note the small ladder near the bed for access.

Lighting is provided by the basement windows and various ceiling and recessed fixtures, as well as other lamps. Many of the ceiling features include lighting fixtures and storage shelves. The small trestle desk sits under a storage shelf. The box shelf contains a recessed lighting fixture that illuminates the desk.

The plan was well thought out and executed to make the most of the space, provide an attractive and comfortable living area, and sufficient storage that the person living in the apartment would not have to feel limited in what he or she could have.

Not all basements are as large or as usable as this one; however, the possibilities of conversion of any basement are limited less by the physical problems of conversion than by the imagination of the person doing the design and planning.

BASEMENT CONVERSIONS

Recreation/entertaining areas are one of the most common uses of basements when converted. A unified plan that coordinates colors, materials and functions can lead to a dramatic and inviting environment that is warm and comfortable.

LOFTS

A home that combines vaulted ceilings and lower ceilings provides many visual contrasts and interesting design possibilities. A kitchen is protected by a partial wall that is open at the top to emphasize the height of the room.

LOFTS

The exterior of an urban carriage house was left virtually unchanged when the upper level was converted into living space. Because of the height of the upper level, it was possible to add a loft structure that essentially doubled the use of the space. The kitchen is contained in the base of the loft. An office/studio, with a dramatic view of the rest of the apartment, sits on top of the loft. The original hayloft door remains in the dining area. Additional windows were installed just below the roof, under the eaves. An enclosed area at the back of the loft is the bedroom. Privacy is gained while the open feeling remains.

LOFTS & STAIRWAYS

The word "loft" also describes a building with each floor containing one open space. This type of loft usually has considerable appeal for those looking for an expanse of living area. Privacy is a problem that one loft dweller solved by building a complete room on wheels that serves as a bedroom. The entire room can be moved about the loft space as needed.

A more conventional loft is shown here and on the cover. This type of loft maximizes the use of rooms with high ceilings. The use of the lower area was not lost when the library was placed above the usual level. Details of construction are given in Chapter Eleven. This type of loft is used very effectively in buildings that have ceilings of 12 to 14 feet of height. This type of construction is not longer common, but it was standard in the late 19th century. Many older homes that have been converted to apartments have ceilings of this height and the usable space in the apartments is radically enlarged by the construction of lofts along one or more walls.

Although few people would consider them lofts, open foyer/stairways have much the same visual function. The person standing on the upper level has a clear and unusual view of a lower area. From the lower vantage, the stairway is the center of attention; from the upper vantage, the leaded glass window is the focus. The area was designed with an understanding of the visual impact as well as the use of the staircase. Try for the same coherence in your design of space.

VAULTED CEILINGS

Vaulted ceilings, whether part of original construction or created by removing an upper room or opening a part of the attic, substantially enlarge the appearance of space, even if not really creating more space. Sometimes beams or joists must remain in place for structural reasons, or they may be added for decorative reasons.

GARAGE CONVERSIONS

A garage conversion makes use of existing walls and roof, so it may be relatively inexpensive to add this to your living space. Exposed collar beams in the vaulted ceiling are part of the necessary and unremovable construction, so they have become a part of the overall design in this well done conversion. Completed conversion, when finished, blends with the rest of the house and adds substantially to it.

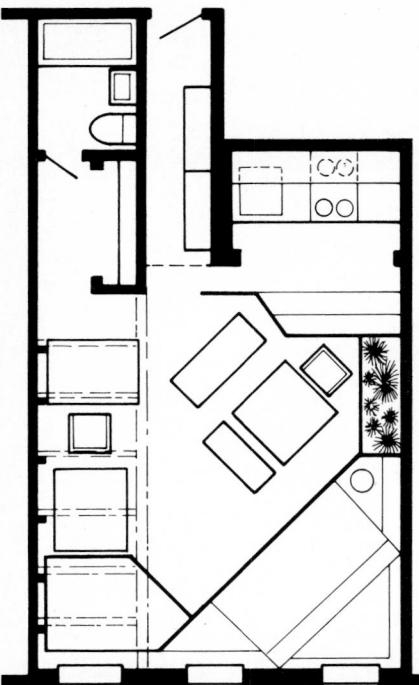

COMPACT LIVING SPACE

The principles used in this very small apartment can be applied by anyone converting a space to another use or possibly converting a garage or other space into an income producing apartment. The space here is very small. The main living area is approximately 18 by 22 feet. Careful planning has made the most of this space, making a usable, apartment out of an area scarcely larger than a master bedroom.

A two-level kitchen counter with open shelves provides work surfaces and serves as a room divider. The other wall of the kitchen contains the appliances, scaled to the available space. Cupboards above the appliances provide more storage space.

Because the walls are white, the space looks large and is as bright as possible. The sides of the window spaces have been mirrored to enlarge the appearance of the space and to increase by reflection all light that comes through the windows.

To simplify activities, the owner has wired lights and the electrically controlled shades so they are controlled from the panel on the end of the bed platform. This platform and the benches in the dining space were built especially for the apartment. There is extra storage space in the benches.

The bookshelves were also specially designed for this space. A new box beam was installed in the ceiling. Lighting was added behind the beam. A series of 2x12s were cut to fit between the box beam and the wall. These were installed at an angle to allow easy access to all the shelves and to allow the light to spill into the room. Holes were drilled in the 2x12s to accept shelf brackets that span the space between the 2x12s and support the shelves.

The area below the shelves is used as a small lounge space and a small office/work space. A walk-in closet and the bath are just beyond the desk and are placed parallel to the entrance.

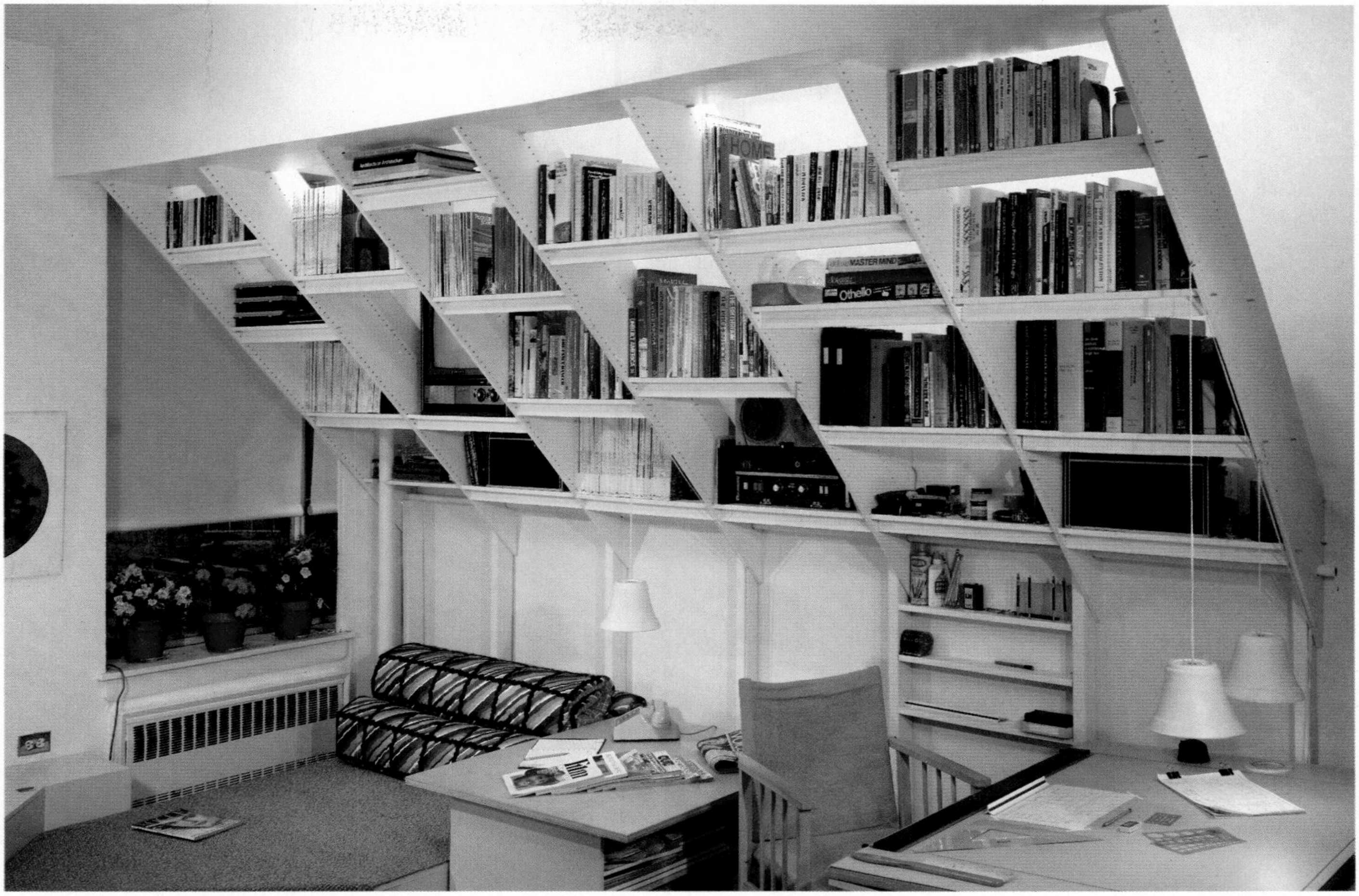
MASTER MIND
Othello

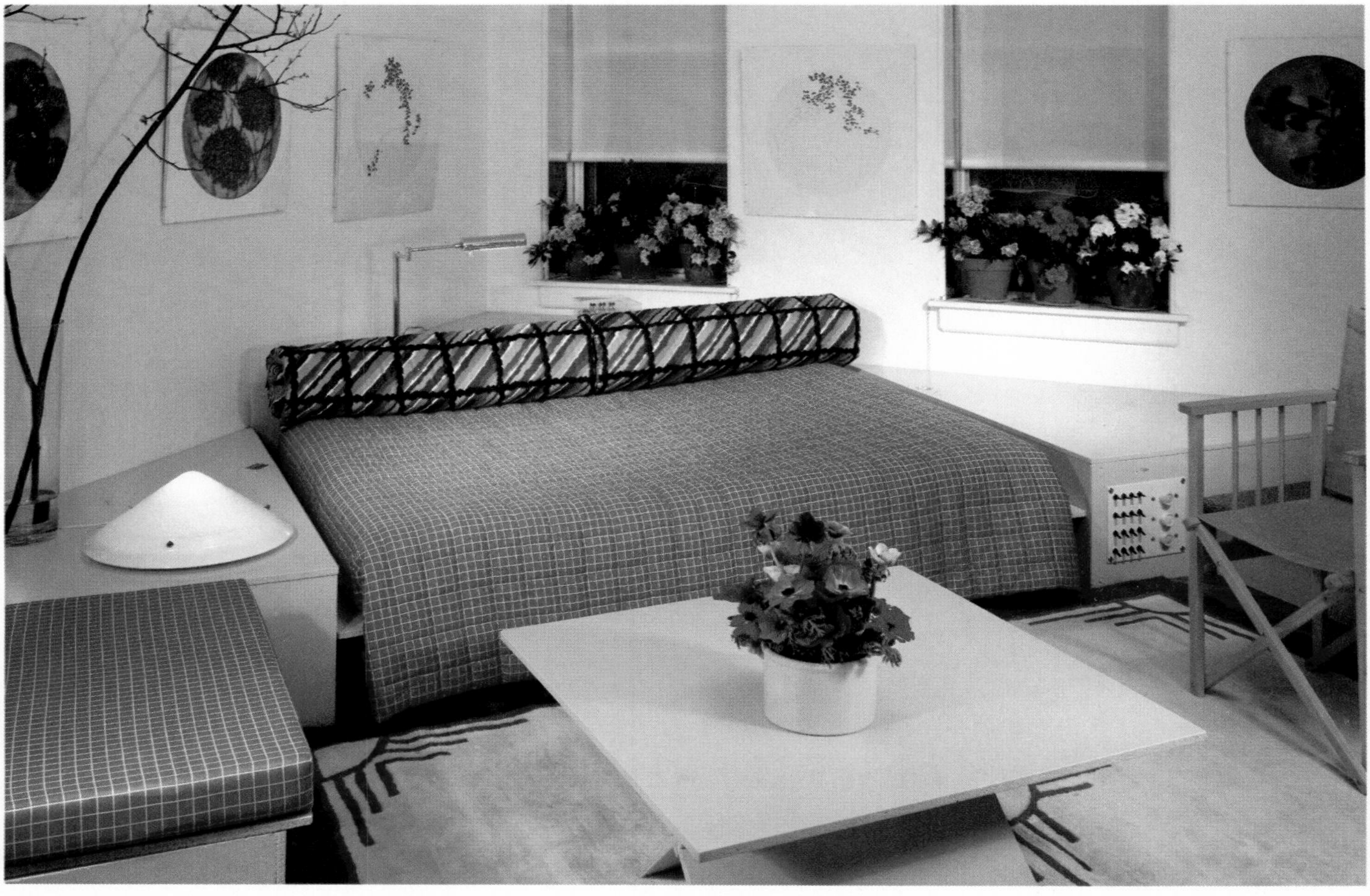

ATTIC CONVERSION

A stairway had to be added for access to an attic that was converted into a bedroom with a full bath and study. Additional storage areas were developed in the spaces where the slope of the roof was low. Large windows at each end provide considerable natural light.

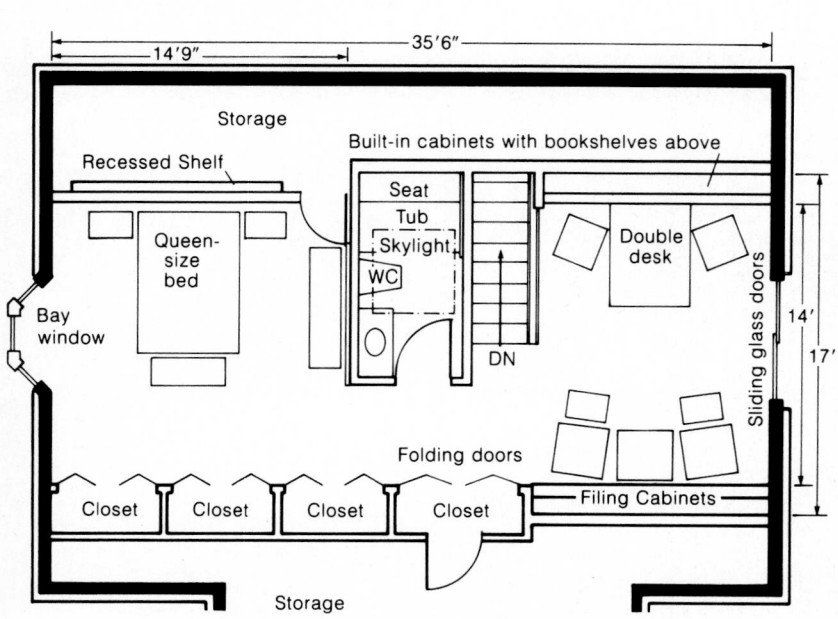

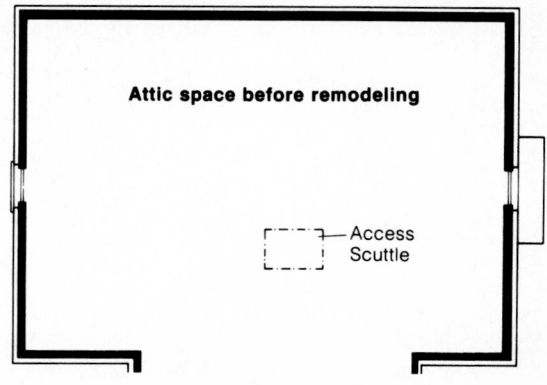

Attic bedrooms often have oddly shaped ceilings that can be either obscured or emphasized depending on how they are handled when decorated.

10
ATTIC CONVERSIONS

Attic expansion usually is less expensive than a basement conversion, especially if that area has water problems, but you also could encounter problems in the attic that cannot easily be solved. You will have to do some investigating before making firm plans to use this area.

IS AN ATTIC CONVERSION FEASIBLE?
Evaluating Structural Support
First examine the type of construction used in the attic. Take some wide boards, or sheets of plywood at least ½ inch thick, up to the attic for temporary footing. If you try to walk around in the open attic and miss a joist, you easily could put your foot through the ceiling below. Do not walk near the edges of the temporary footing, either. If the board is not supported by a joist on each side of your foot, it could tip, throwing you off your feet.

Truss construction. Look around at the type of construction. If your roof framing consists of trusses, it will be obvious; the many framing members will be tied to the joists and rafters with metal truss

plates. A truss is a scientifically designed framing member. Each piece of a truss unit has a purpose and provides part of the strength of the entire member. A truss section cannot be cut and removed without destroying the load-bearing capacity of that section of the roof. The first heavy snow or strong wind might cause your roof to cave in. There are ways to expand into an attic built with trusses. However, each situation is different. You must have an expert — an architect or a structural engineer — design the solution necessary for

your individual situation. If you do, it is possible that the cost could exceed that of a full addition. Restructuring of a truss system probably will exceed the cost of expanding into any other enclosed space.

Conventional framing with braces. It could be that there is a framing member on each side, tied to the rafters and joist with nails. This is not a truss. The extra framing members you see are either wind braces or braces designed to reduce the span of the rafters so that smaller size lumber is used. If there is enough space be-

This boy's bedroom was created in an attic space that is quite large. A hanging bunk bed allows access to the closet. Built-in desks along the walls leave room open.

Place temporary footing material over joists when examining attic. Do not step near edge.

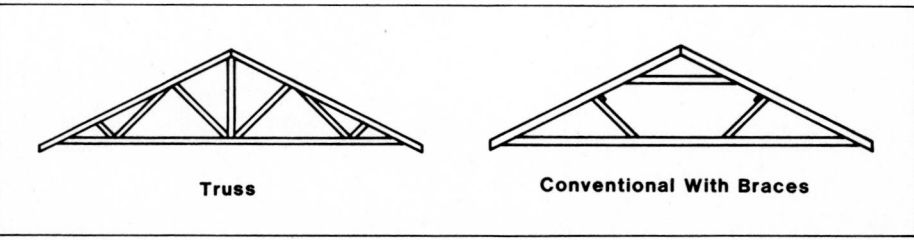

Both trusses and conventional roof framing with braces will limit space available in the attic. Neither should be removed or changed unless approved by a structural engineer or architect.

tween these braces, then expansion may be feasible as long as the roof is high enough to allow you to walk upright. In no case, however, should you disturb the integrity of the braces without professional advice. They must be left intact, uncut and unmoved, unless you have the roof redesigned by an expert. If your roof is conventionally framed, as most homes are, with ceiling joists, rafters, and collar beams that only tie the rafters, there is a very good chance your attic can be used for more space at a minimum of cost.

Joist sizes and centers. Before you plan to use the attic for expansion, be sure all the floor joists (the ceiling joists of the level below) are of adequate size and spacing to support the use planned. Even if the attic is already floored, check the construction. Locate the interior bearing wall and measure the span from outside wall to bearing wall. Check the proper size and spacing against the chart provided here. If the span of your joists is greater than the maximum span listed, you will have to increase the strength of the joists. If the

span is equal to or less than the maximum span given, the joists will support normal activities.

How to Increase Joist Strength
There are three ways to increase the strength of the joists. First, you may add a joist of equal size between each existing joist. The only place to nail these is into the top plate of the outer wall; other methods of adding joists allow you to nail into adjacent joists. The slope will make it hard to nail joists into exterior wall framing.

The second method, adding joists of

equal size next to the existing joists, may be easier. Nail the new joists into the existing joists every 12 to 18 inches along the run with 12d or 16d common nails. This is easier because, if you cannot reach the ends, you can nail into the existing joists almost to the end. Keep the top edges of the joists level and nail carefully. Heavy blows might crack the ceiling material below.

A third method is used only if the joists are far smaller than needed. Nail each new joist to an existing joist as described above. The new joists, however, will be of

Maximum Span for Floor Joists — 40 lbs. Live Load Per Square Foot

Nominal Size Of Joists	12 inches On Center	16 inches On Center	24 inches On Center
2x6	10' 8"	9' 8"	8' 6"
2x8	14' 1"	12' 11"	11' 4"
2x10	17' 9"	16' 3"	14' 3"
2x12	21' 4"	19' 7"	17' 3"

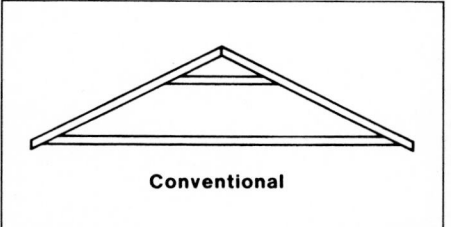

Conventional

Conventional framing with beams is more easily adapted to attic expansion and reframing.

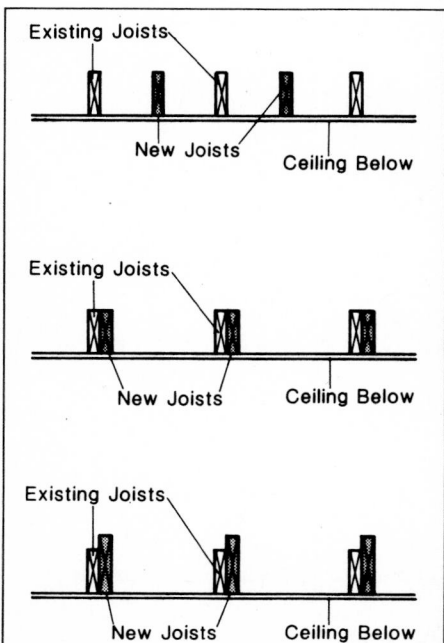

If you have to add joists, choose from any of the three methods shown to meet your needs.

A prefabricated, free-standing fireplace is a focus of attention in this attic converted into a full apartment that also features a small sleeping loft.

a larger size. This will raise the finished floor slightly and subtract some from the available headroom.

When considering joist centers and strength, allow for extra joists in areas where you plan to install heavy appliances or unusual loads, such as a cast iron wood stove.

Standard Space Requirements

Headroom. The generally accepted minimum height to provide adequate hedroom is 7 feet. Lack of headroom is the most common problem in attic spaces.

A very small attic space may not be suitable for a bedroom, but it can be converted to a very special, private retreat.

This is true even if your family members are all under 6 feet tall. A ceiling lower than 7 feet will make the area appear cramped and feel uncomfortable. If you have family members well over 6 feet tall, you may need to provide minimum headroom of 7 feet 6 inches, or even 8 feet, or you may discover that you have gone to a great deal of labor finishing an area only to find it is uncomfortable to use. You may minimally increase headroom in small areas by adding dormers.

Normally you will have the necessary headroom, and more, near the roof ridge. The problem develops if the width of the area in which you can still keep the minimum headroom is too narrow. If the space is 12 feet or more wide, there is no problem. This width will provide enough room for many possible uses. Of course, the wider the space, the more versatile the design possibilities are. If the usable width is less than 12 feet, you become severely restricted in how you can adapt the area. If it is only a few feet wide, the area becomes useful for little more than storage.

TAKING ADVANTAGE OF ATTIC SPACE

There are several ways to take advantage of an attic space without disturbing the roof.

Building Standard Walls

You can build side walls to standard room height, and then you can add a ceiling. Adding a ceiling makes the room feel like a standard room, obscuring all the lines of the attic. This only works effectively if the attic area is spacious. If your attic is not very wide, or if you like the appearance of a vaulted ceiling, you may want to leave the ceiling open to the rafters. This gives a more open feeling to the room. You may add a storage loft in part of the area.

Knee Walls for More Room

Another way to make the area feel and be larger is to build shorter "knee walls" at the sides, instead of standard height walls. The area looks larger because it is larger. The space near the low ceiling, along the knee wall, can be used for desks or other

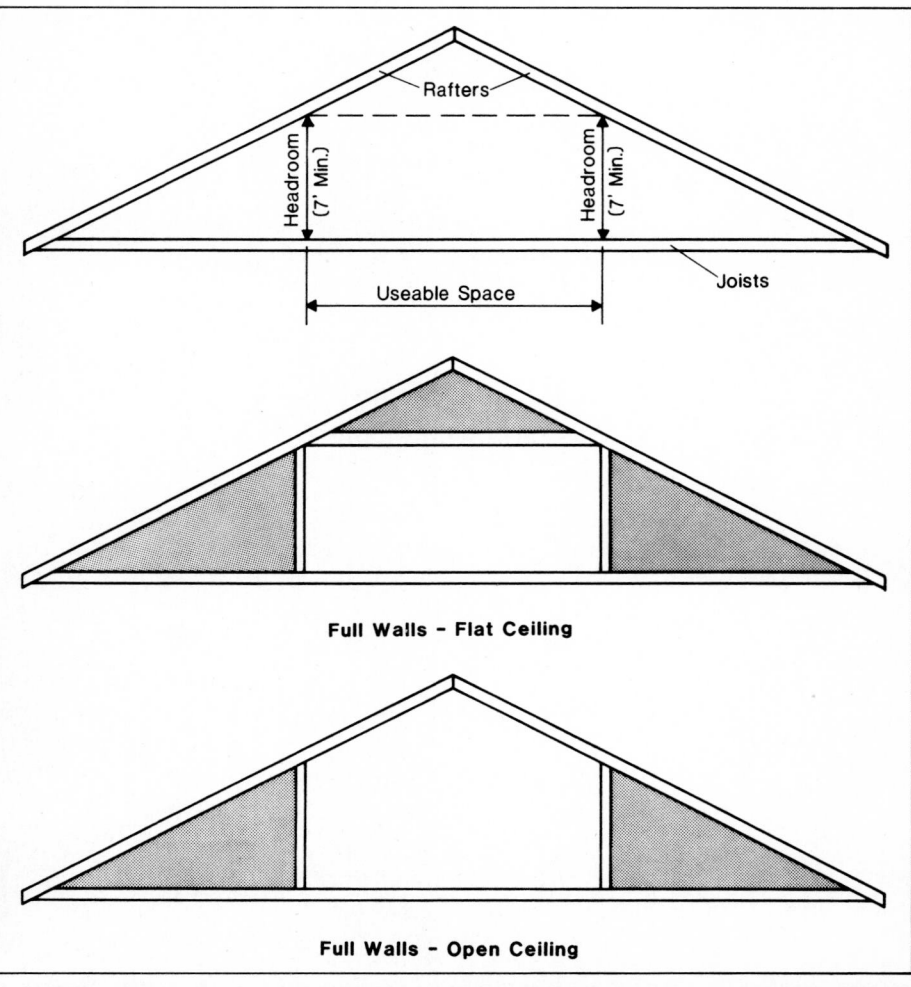

Rafters

Headroom (7' Min.)

Headroom (7' Min.)

Joists

Useable Space

Full Walls - Flat Ceiling

Full Walls - Open Ceiling

For full sides walls, you must have seven feet of headroom. The space between these walls may be finished with either a flat or an open ceiling, depending upon your preference.

work surfaces and seating, because these uses do not require full headroom.

Establishing knee wall height. The usual height for knee walls is 4 feet. However, this height was established at a time when roof slopes were generally steeper than those of roofs built today. To determine a useful height for a knee wall, locate the point at which the headroom decreases to 6 feet, or the point where headroom is equal to the tallest member of the family over 6 feet. At this point, draw a line for the knee wall that is 3 feet farther toward the outside wall.

If your roof slopes 8 in 12, the knee wall will be 4 feet high. If the slope is less, the knee wall will be higher. If the slope is steeper, come back out to the point where the knee wall is 4 feet high. Establish the location of the knee wall on both sides of the attic, then measure between the two knee walls to find the width of the usable area. Now you can visualize the real space available for the attic conversion.

The knee wall construction is the same as a standard wall with the exception of the placement of the top plate. Instructions follow later in this chapter.

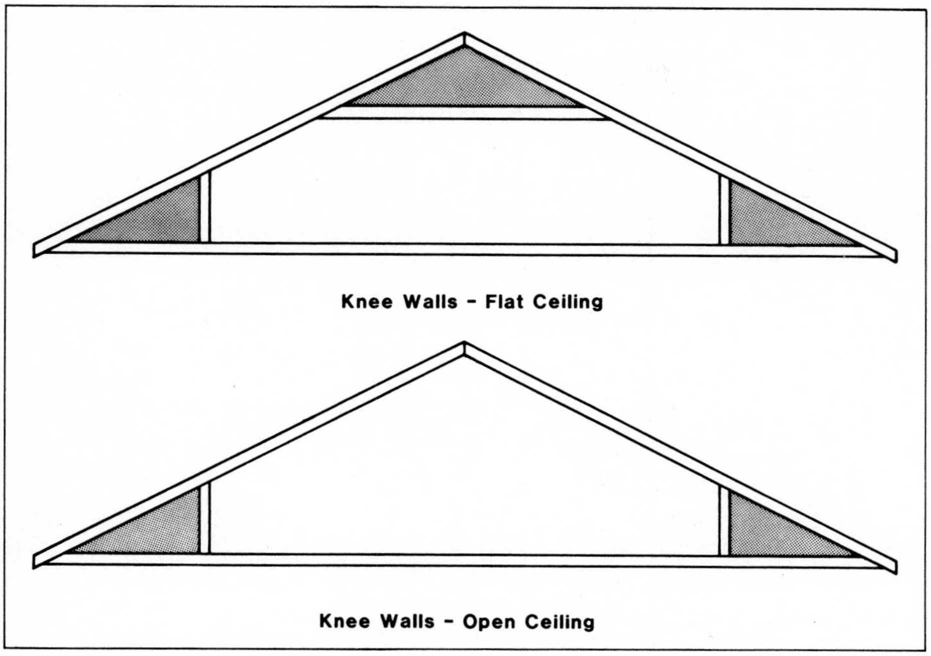

Knee Walls - Flat Ceiling

Knee Walls - Open Ceiling

Knee walls will provide more room area, but the sides can only be used for seating or low work spaces because no one can stand up straight near these walls.

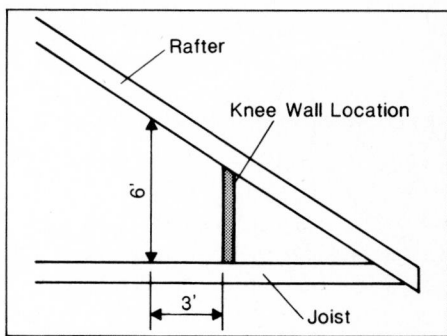

Position knee wall no more than 3 feet back from a point where ceiling slopes to 6 feet.

The spaciousness of this bed/sitting room is possible where the roofline allows the addition of windows and the slope of the roof is slight.

SUITABLE USES FOR THE ATTIC

The attic is a more versatile space than the basement for several reasons. It does not have the stigma of being cold and damp like the basement; it is easier to add natural light and ventilation; there usually are no problems with plumbing. The single disadvantage is that the construction usually will be a little more costly because of the expense of side wall framing, greater need for insulation, and a more complicated ceiling construction. However, this cost is minor compared to the usefulness of the developed space.

You are free to create almost any type of room from the attic conversion. The uses may include, but are not limited to: standard bedrooms, master bedroom suite, bath, recreation room, entertainment room, kitchenette, adult retreat, den, office/study, hobby/craft center, library/reading room, stereo/music room, dark room, artist's studio, garden room, and playroom. Some of these uses have special design and construction needs, any of which can be met in a properly planned attic conversion.

Problems in Attic Use

The handicapped. There are some space uses that do not work well in an attic under any normal circumstances. But even these can be especially designed and possibly be placed in the attic. Because of the stairs, it is not a good idea to plan this area for use by an elderly or handicapped person; however, there are electrically operated lifts available to allow access. The lifts can be attached to the wall of any staircase and will carry a rider up or down the stairs. Installation of this type of equipment will add to the cost of conversion, but it is not prohibitively expensive and may not raise the cost of conversion to the cost of a full addition.

Active and heavy-use applications. The main kitchen and busy family or great room are not logical choices for an attic. Such installation would lead to excessive stair-climbing. However, either room can be placed in an attic conversion if you want to make the upper floor the main level of the home. The greatest disadvantage to this placement is loss of easy access to the outside, unless you add a deck and exterior access stairs.

Plumbing additions. Since the attic is above the main level of the house, there is no problem getting the waste lines to drain

Attic, or even second floor, bedrooms tend to be warm because heat rises. A ceiling fan will circulate the air and help keep the users more comfortable and cool.

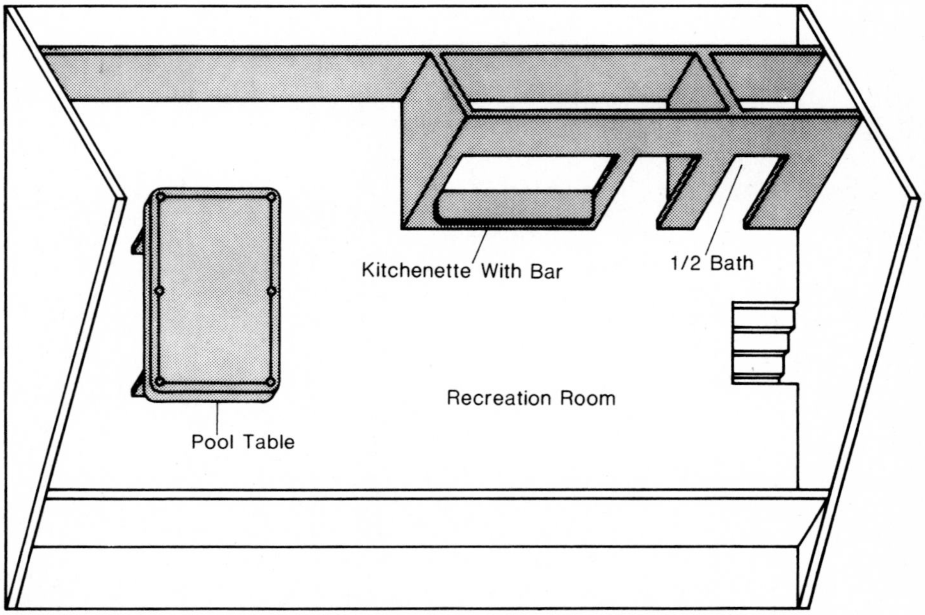

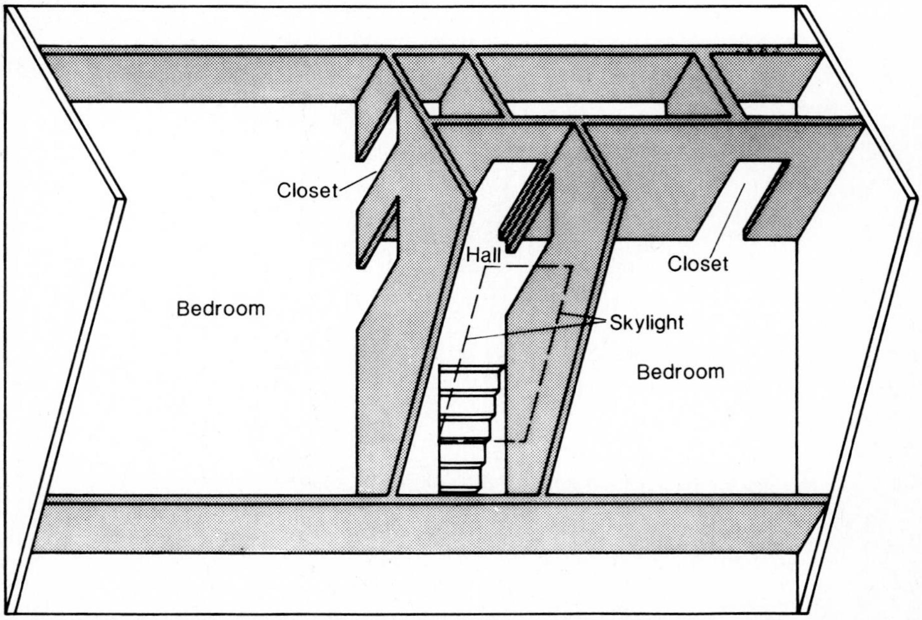

Kitchenette With Bar

1/2 Bath

Pool Table

Recreation Room

Closet

Hall

Closet

Bedroom

Skylight

Bedroom

Stair location dictates possible uses of an attic. A central location means that there will be more range to your uses, but an end location gives uninterrupted space.

by gravity flow; you may design any type of plumbing you wish to. The only limitation is that the walls containing the plumbing should be directly over the walls that contain plumbing in the main floor level. (See Chapter 5.) This arrangement will greatly simplify and reduce the cost of plumbing hookups. It also will be less expensive if you keep two spaces requiring plumbing — such as a bath and kitchenette or two baths — back to back. Both uses will draw from the one new connection to the existing plumbing.

HOW TO MAKE THE ATTIC LIVABLE

Except for structural problems that require virtual rebuilding from scratch, most solutions to attic usage problems are relatively simple, and easy to build or design around. Some problems can turn into assets. Others, however, may prove too costly to overcome, making it more practical to use a different area for expansion.

Increasing Space

You probably have a conventional frame roof that can be converted, but it could be that the area with acceptable headroom is too narrow for general use. You may be able to compensate for this by the construction of large dormers, either gable or shed style, for a very little more space.

Adding Natural Light

Usually an attic is dark because there is only a small window at the end of each gable, or you may have no windows at all. Additional light may be provided by installing larger gable windows or dormer windows or skylights. You can use any of these methods, but do not add too much glass. The attic naturally is one of the warmer areas of the house; too much glass could allow considerable heat gain, making the attic intolerably hot in the summer. Although this is not too great a problem in moderate climates, heat gain can be severe in the extreme south, especially if most of the windows are on the south and west sides.

Gable windows. These windows are limited in their application. Gable windows only go in gable end walls. You must create a dormer to put a window in a hip or other roof plane. If you have a gable roof, there already may be a window in one or both of your gables. The probability is that these windows are too small.

This attic bedroom receives quantities of light from skylights set into the roof just above the knee walls. The impression is of open space, but there is total privacy.

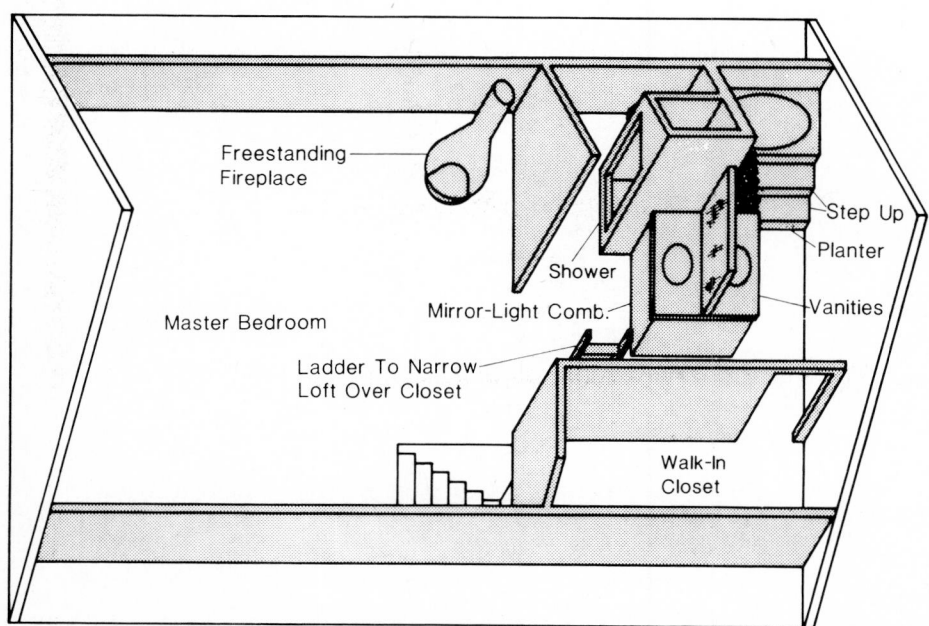

Freestanding Fireplace

Step Up

Planter

Shower

Mirror-Light Comb.

Vanities

Master Bedroom

Ladder To Narrow Loft Over Closet

Walk-In Closet

A master bedroom suite with a full bath and walk-in closet is an excellent use for an attic space. The area will be private, and the space is usually large enough to provide sitting room space.

You will have to replace the windows to provide adequate light and good ventilation for your conversion. Remove the old window and the framing around it to install the new window. Installation of a new gable window uses the same procedures discussed in Chapter 9, "Framing and Installing a Window". You may add extra windows on the side.

Dormers. Small gable or shed dormers are a little more difficult to install because they require some roof removal, additional framing, and new roofing. Dormers, however, do add a modest amount of extra space to the attic. Dormers also affect the architectural appearance of the outside of

your home. For this reason, you may prefer to add dormers to the rear of your house. If you add gable dormers to the front, add at least two, equidistant from the ends of the house.

HOW TO CONSTRUCT A SMALL DORMER

The size of the dormer is based on the size of the window it will hold. The shed and gable dormers for which we give instructions here are designed to be no more than four feet wide. A larger dormer would require the cutting of too many rafters. This cutting lowers the strength of the roof and necessitates extensive reframing to restore structural integrity. The width of the dormer opening should be equal to the inside dimension between either 3, 4, or 5

rafters, depending on the window width and the rafter spacing. The dormer must be at least 6 inches larger than the rough opening of the window.

Cutting the Rafters

The upper rafter cut should be made at a point even with the ceiling height of the attic (7 feet minimum). Then allow an additional 3 inches for the framing header. The cut is perpendicular to the rafter. To determine the lower cut, subtract the height of the rough opening plus 9½ inches (the usual distance from the frame to the ceiling) from 7 feet (or the exact headroom). After you have determined this figure, measure up this amount vertically from the floor to the upper edge of the rafter, mark and cut the rafter at this point. The cut is vertical to the joists. Be sure you measure to the upper edge of the rafter, not to the bottom. Remove the rafter and the roofing between these cuts, and between the remaining rafters on each side, so that the rafters are exposed. Keep a sheet of polyethylene or other weatherproof tarp handy to cover the opening when you are not working. Use wood battens to hold the edges in place.

Installing the Lower Framing

The framing for a small shed and a small gable dormer are the same, except for the roof framing.

Cut and nail a double header at the top of the opening. Use the same stock as the rafters. This ties the upper rafter sections together to restore strength. Nail through the sides of uncut, flanking rafters into the ends of the new header boards. Nail

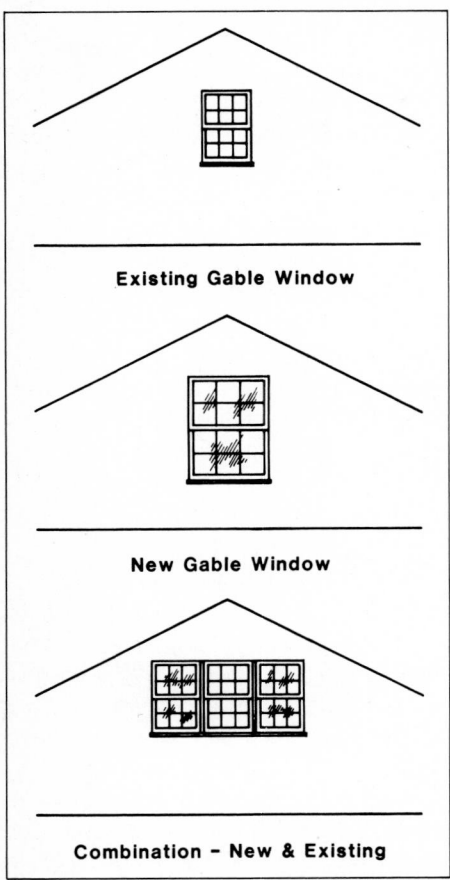

Replace or augment existing gable window to bring more light and air into attic.

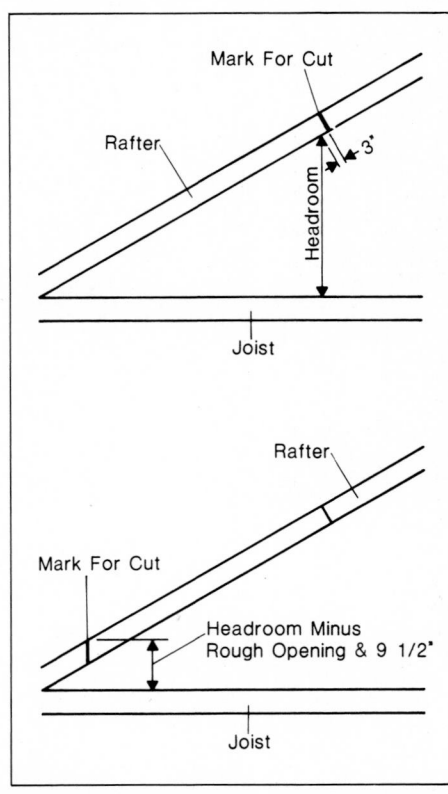

Upper dormer cut is made at right angle to the rafter; lower cut at right angle to line of joist.

Gable dormers will provide additional light and ventilation to an attic space. Take care in placing gable dormers to that they look suitable on the exterior of your home.

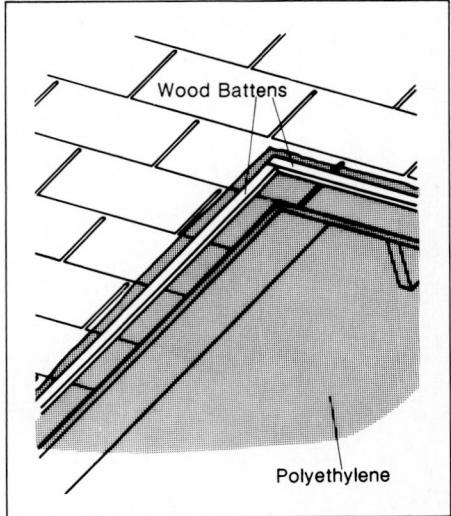

If you leave opening for several days, cover hole with polyethylene nailed through battens.

through the header boards into the ends of the cut rafters. Trim back the cut rafters as necessary to keep the edge of the header from interfering with finishing the interior at the proper ceiling height. The cut rafters at the bottom of the opening will be nailed into the cripples that support the sill plates for the window.

Double the rafters on each side of the opening; use lumber of the same stock as the rafters. Install a bottom plate on each side, from the knee wall to the face of the

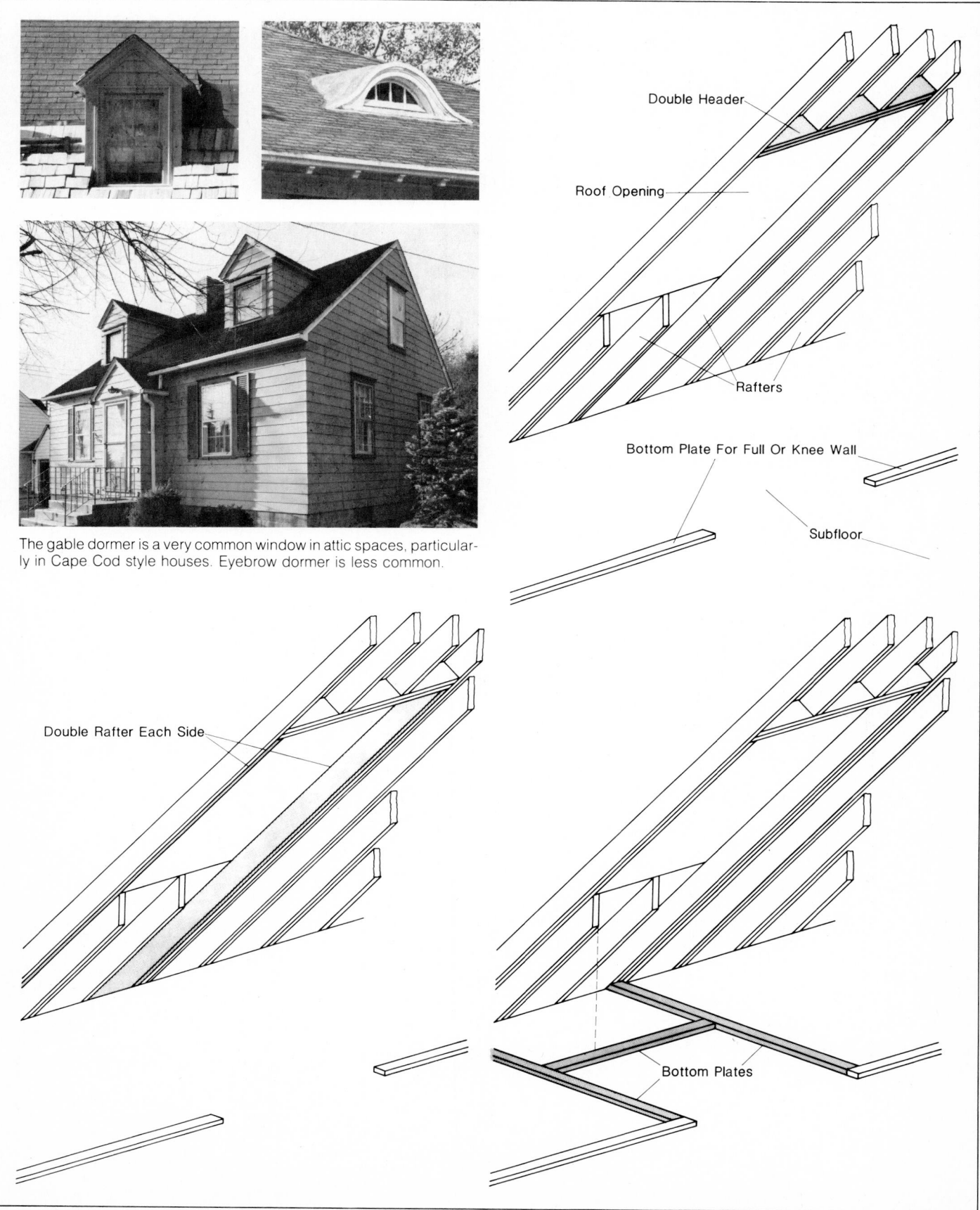

The gable dormer is a very common window in attic spaces, particularly in Cape Cod style houses. Eyebrow dormer is less common.

Double Header

Roof Opening

Rafters

Bottom Plate For Full Or Knee Wall

Subfloor

Double Rafter Each Side

Bottom Plates

dormer. Add another bottom plate parallel to window sill between the side bottom plates, directly under the window. Install double studs at the corners of the knee wall and at the corners of the dormer window location.

Toenail the window's bottom sill plate into the doubled rafters on each side. Nail a cripple at each end of the sill plate, and at

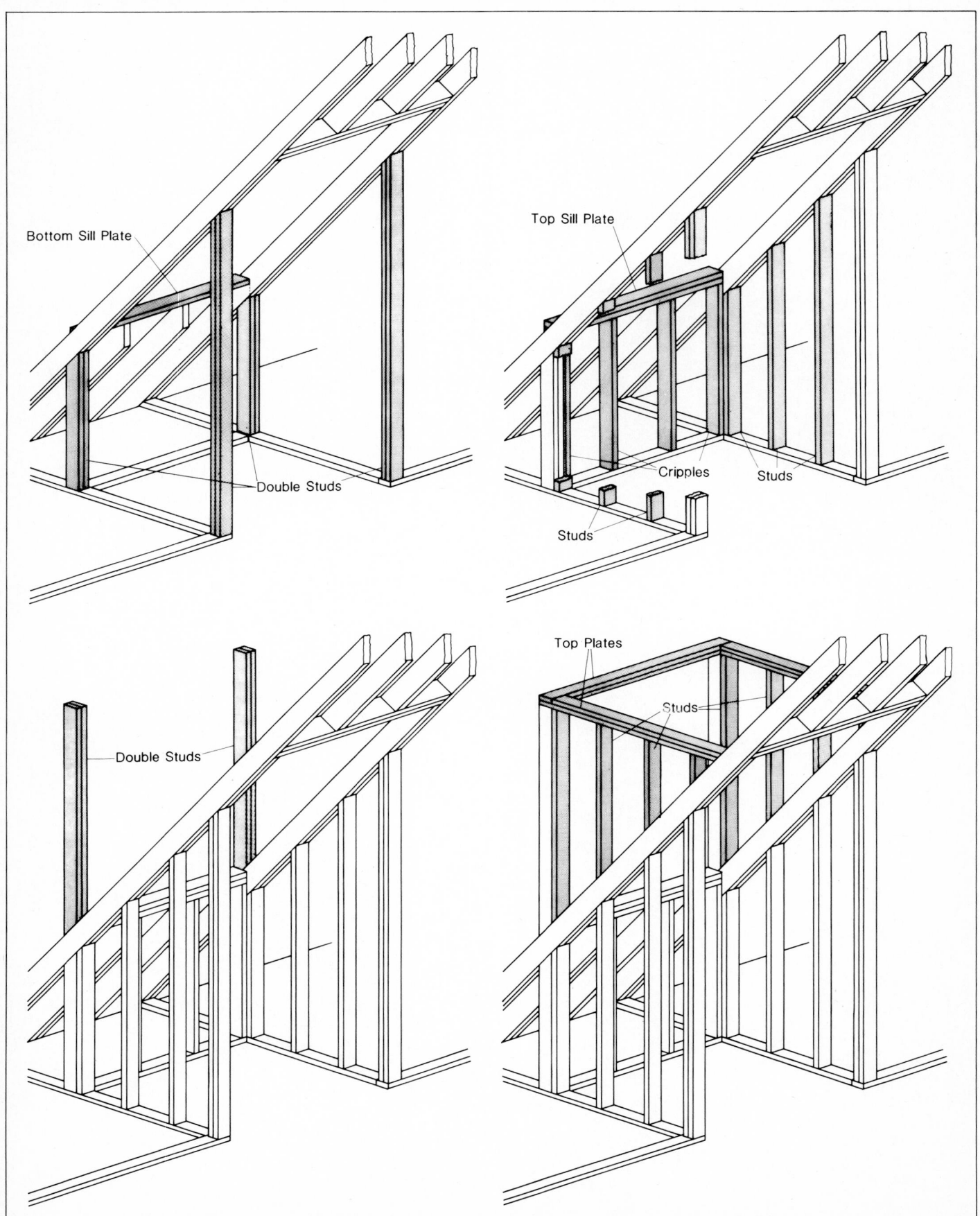

each point the plate meets a cut rafter. Toenail the cut rafter(s) into the cripples. Add the second sill plate. Add studs at 16 inches on center between the knee wall and the window sill wall. Toenail to doubled rafters and bottom plate. Place double studs at the outside corners of the dormer; toenail into the double rafters. These studs should be in line with the sill plates and directly above the double studs below the rafters. Set level and plumb.

Installing the Upper Framing

Place a full set of double top plates, one at a time, from the outside corner studs to the double rafters where they meet the header at the top of the opening. The top plates must be level and even with the bottom edge of the header. Next, place studs at 16 inches on center between the side top plate and the double rafters. Place a full-length stud on each side of the front corner, spaced so that the distance between them is equal to the rough opening plus 3 inches. The double studs already placed at the corners can be used for this purpose if the opening is the right size. Now add jack studs from the sill plates to within 3½ inches of the height of the top plates. A header of two 2x4s, turned on edge with a ½-inch plywood spacer between, goes on top of the jack studs. Place ceiling joists across the opening, reaching from side top plate to side top plate, at 16 inches on center. For such a narrow width, a 2x4 will be sufficient for each joist. If you do not want a flat ceiling, and prefer to show the line of the roof, omit the ceiling joists.

Framing the Roof

As mentioned earlier, a shed dormer and a gable dormer require different types of framing.

Shed dormer framing. A small shed dormer has rafters of the same stock as the existing rafters. The dormer rafters run from the front top plate back to the roof.

The shed dormer may be a small, single window unit or a longer unit with several windows.

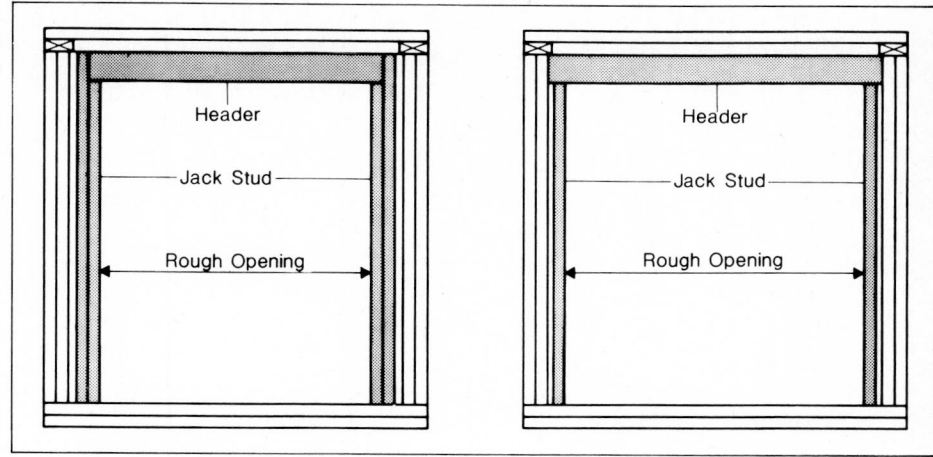

If dormer opening is nearly the correct size for the window, add jack stud and header only.

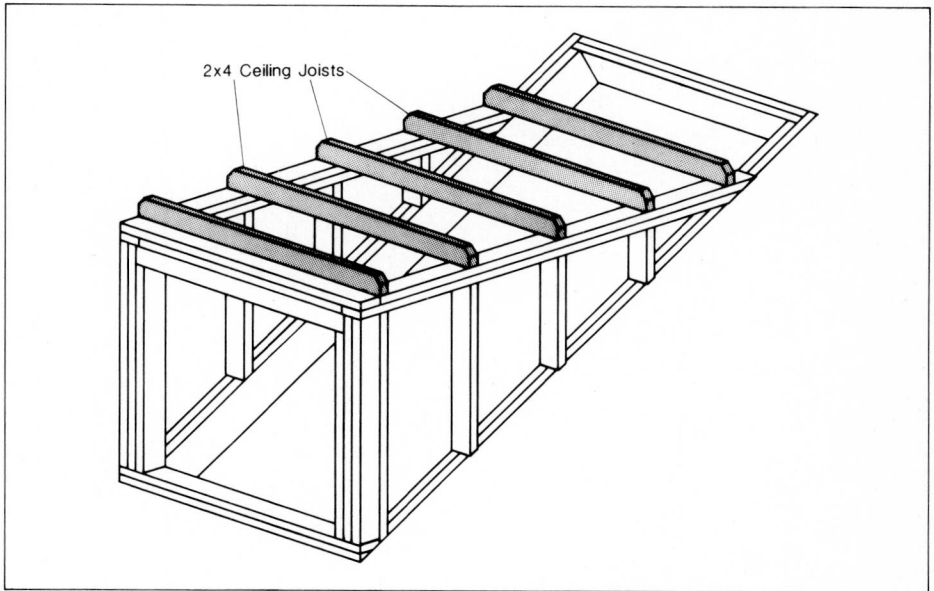

If you want a flat ceiling in the dormer, add ceiling joists across the dormer framing.

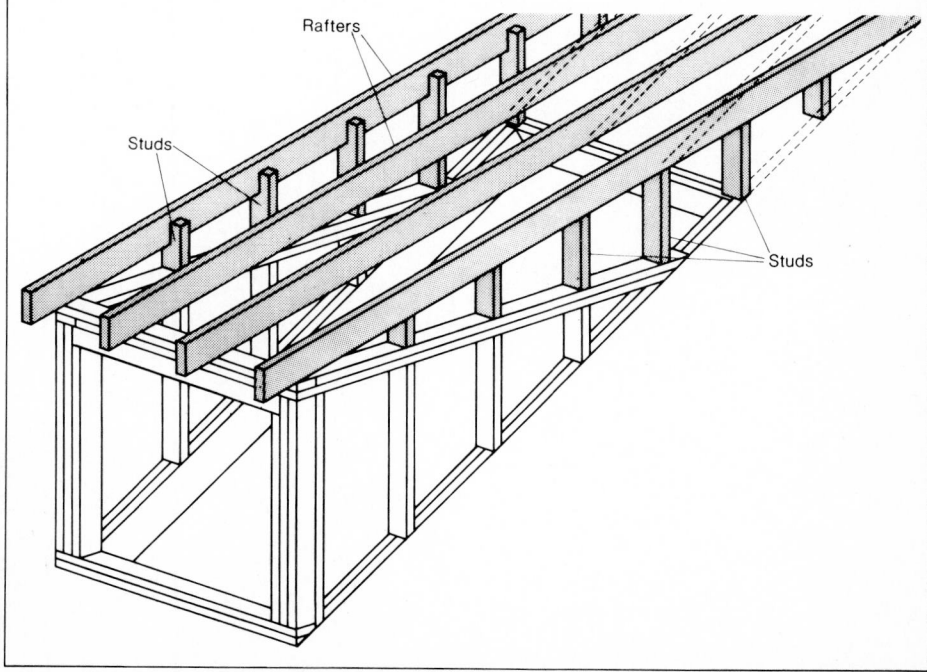

Shed dormer rafters parallel attic rafters. Toenail them and set on short studs for support.

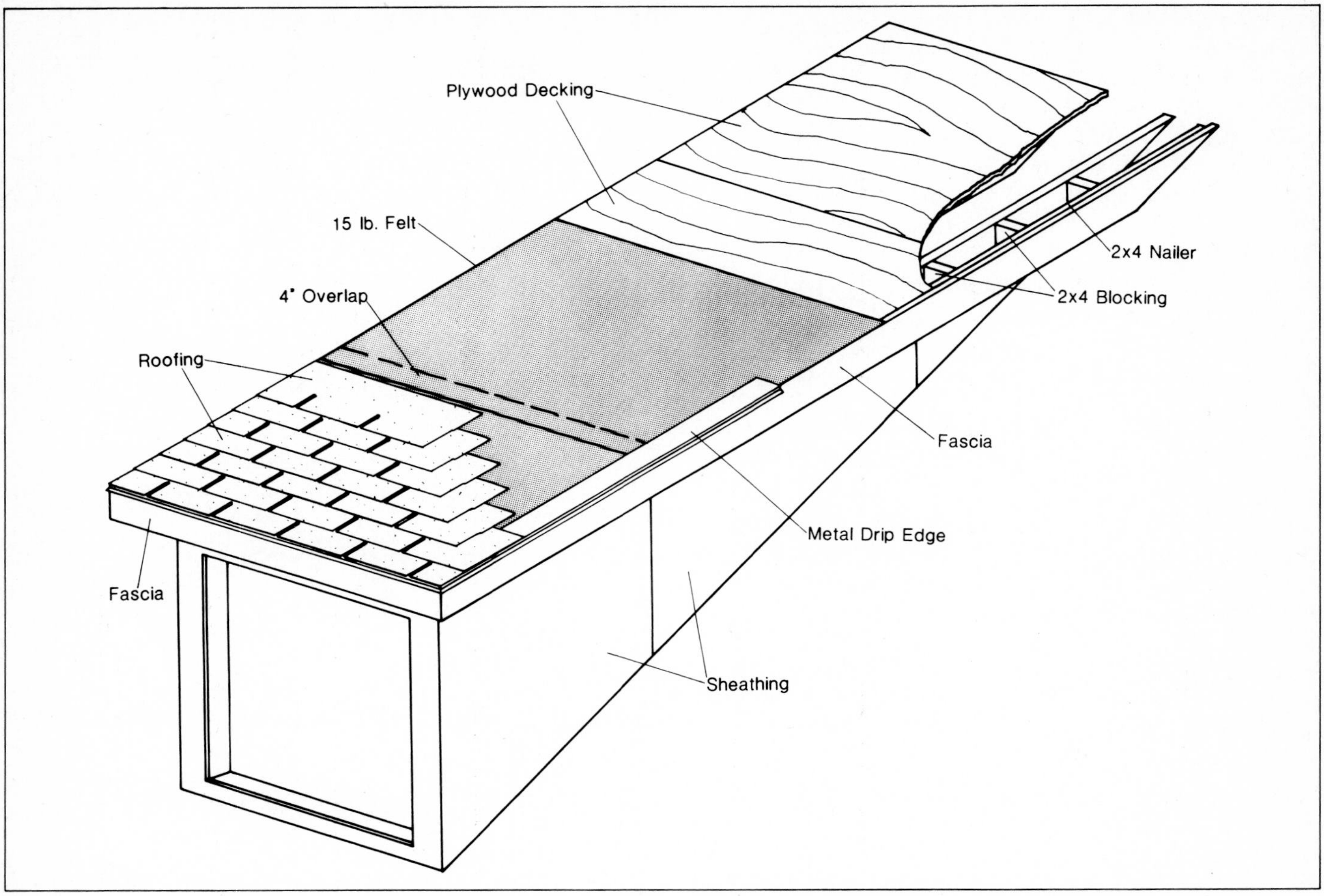

Plywood Decking

15 lb. Felt

4˝ Overlap

Roofing

2x4 Nailer

2x4 Blocking

Fascia

Fascia

Metal Drip Edge

Sheathing

Add plywood decking, overlay with 15 lb. asphaltic roofing felt overlapped at seams by 4 inches, add drip edge then shingle.

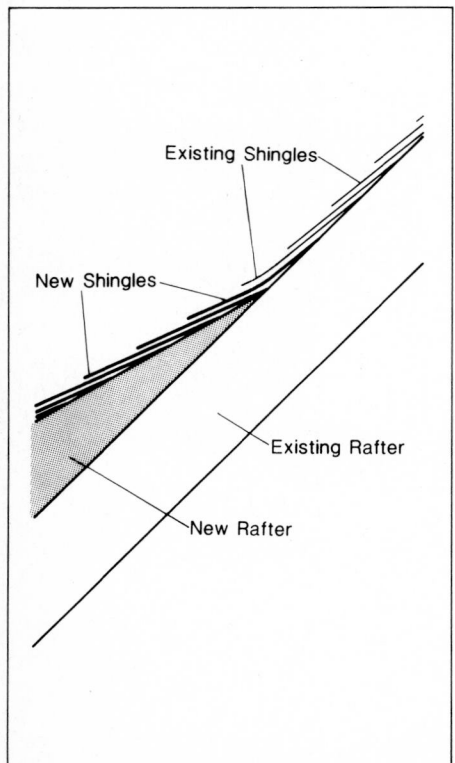

Existing Shingles

New Shingles

Existing Rafter

New Rafter

Existing shingles overlap new shingles at rafter joints. Flashing and caulking are also advisable at the joint to prevent damage from water backup and leaks.

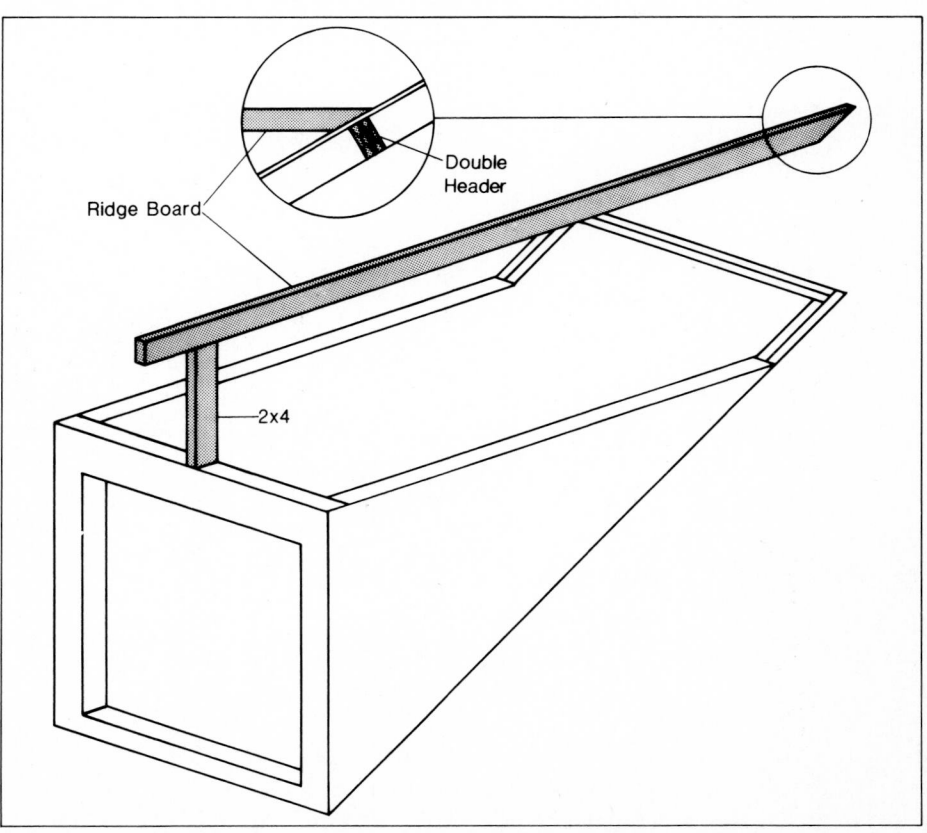

Ridge Board

Double Header

2x4

Gable dormer roof installation begins with attaching ridge board parallel to rafters. Nail into doubled header in roof and 2x4 support stud at front framing.

These rafters should rise at a minimum pitch of 3 in 12.

Place the rafters in line with the existing rafters. Nail dormer rafters in the existing rafters, through the roof. The overhang on the front may be as long as desired, or match the existing roof overhang. Add 2x4 cripple studs at 16 inches on center on the sides, between the top plates and rafter. Next, add sheathing to the walls.

Attach 2x4 blocking to the side rafters to add a 2x4 nailer along the sides, forming the side overhang. Attach the side fascia to this nailer. Nail the front fascia directly to the rafter ends. Apply ½-inch thick exterior plywood decking over the new rafters.

Cover the decking with 15 lb. asphalt felt. Lay from the front edge and overlap each seam by 4 inches. Apply the roofing material. Use the same type as on the existing roof, applying it from the front edge up. Start with a row of shingles with the tabs removed, laid with the edges toward the roof peak. Nail through shingles above the adhesive strip. Stagger courses so that joints do not align on successive courses. The final row of roofing must be overlapped by next row of existing roofing.

Gable roof framing. The roof of a gable dormer is a little more difficult to frame than that of a shed dormer. Center a 2x4 ridge board in the opening. Support it in front with a 2x4 set on end on the front top plate. The back end of the ridge must be cut to fit against the roof. If you have cut an odd number of rafters, the ridge board will meet the center rafter and should be nailed to it. If you have cut an even number of rafters, install a doubled header, between the rafters; attach the ridge board to the doubled header. Level the ridge board carefully, and nail with 6d or 8d common nails. The smaller nails are acceptable because the ridge board only separates the rafters rather than providing support. Although this ridge is not a load-bearing part of the structure, it must be correctly centered and leveled.

Cutting rafters for gable dormer. Cut and place rafters on each side of the ridge at 16 inches on center. To cut the rafter to the proper angle and length, you will have to measure from the top of the ridge board to the building line. Now measure the difference in the height of the side top plate and the ridge beam. If the distance from the ridge to the building line is four feet and the difference in the height of the top

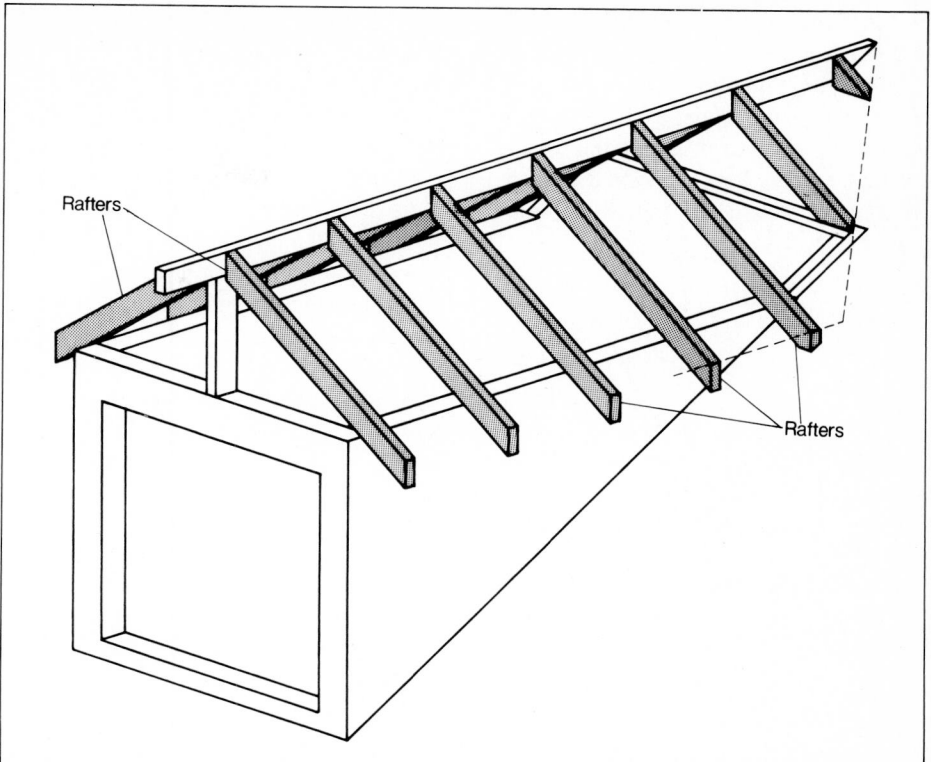

Gable rafters run from the ridge board to the sides of the dormer. Cut rafters to fit full width and, at back, to fit the valley line where two roof planes join.

This is an example of a very large dormer that was added to create an enlarged room. The windows occupy only part of the dormer that adds considerable space to the home.

plate and ridge beam is one foot, the rise is three inches per foot of run.

Place the long arm of a carpenter's square along the upper edge of a rafter board. The short arm, called the tongue, should be on the left and point away from you. Pivot the square at the 12-inch mark

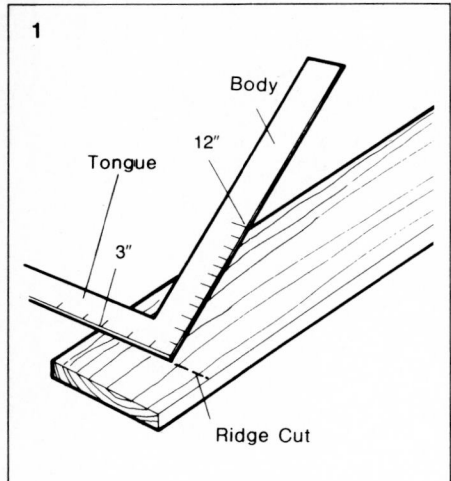

Align long arm with the upper edge of board. Pivot on the 12-inch mark until 3-inch mark on tongue intersects the edge of the board. Mark along tongue to show angle of the ridge.

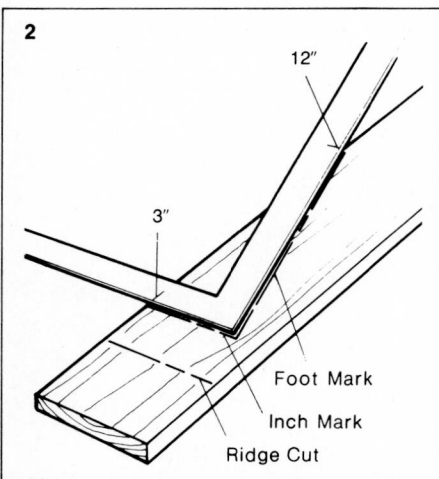

To determine the rafter length, lay the framing square along the board with the rise per foot on the tongue and the foot mark on the long leg, aligned with the edge.

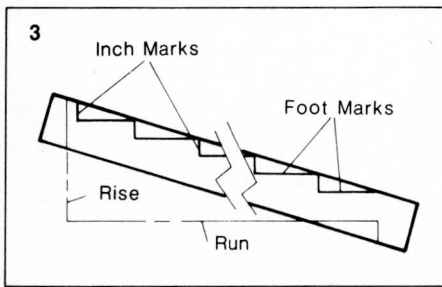

Finally, place the 3-inch mark on the tongue and the 12-inch mark on the arm against the edge. Starting at your last mark, repeat for each foot in the run.

on the arm until the 12-inch mark on the arm and the 3-inch on the tongue mark are aligned with the edge of the board. Draw a line from the top of the board to the bottom along the tongue of the square. This will create a cutting line that will make the board fit against the ridge beam.

Mark the 12-inch point where the arm crosses the upper edge of the board. Slide the square along the edge until the 3-inch point on the tongue aligns with the mark on the board. Repeat until you have sequentially measured and marked this dimension four times. You have now reached the building line. Place the 3-inch point on the tongue at the building line mark. Draw a line to the bottom of the board, parallel to the one made to fit the rafter against the ridge board.

Now reverse the position of the square

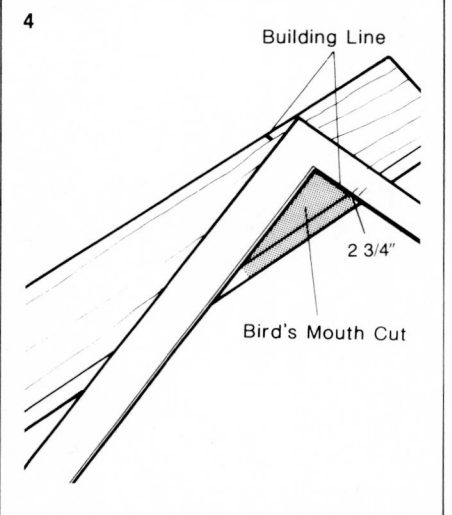

Mark the point where the rafter reaches the wall; align the inside of the tongue with the mark to draw the building line and the bird's mouth.

so that the tongue is on the right and points toward you. Align the inside of the tongue with the building line and position the 2¾ inch mark even with the bottom of the board. Draw a line along the inside of the arm from the tongue to the edge of the board. This marks the "bird's mouth" that is cut out so the rafter will fit over the top plate.

Slide the carpenter's square back toward the top edge and align the 12-inch mark of the arm with the building line and the 3-inch mark of the tongue on the upper edge. Draw a line down the tongue to mark the end of a one-foot overhang.

Finishing the gable surfaces. Apply decking and felt as for the shed roof. However, before you apply the shingles, place galvanized flashing in the newly created roof valleys between the old and the new

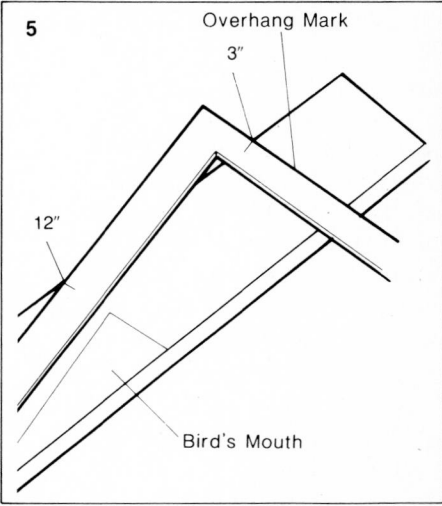

Place the 12-inch mark of the long arm on the building line. Align the 3-inch mark on the tongue with the same edge to find the length of the overhang and the cutting angle.

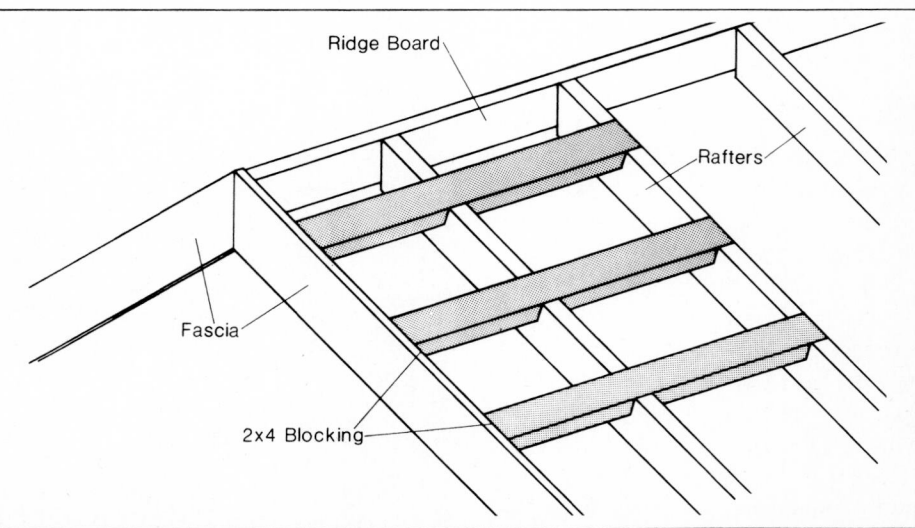

Notch rafters to accept 2x4s that serve as blocking as nailers for fascia. The fascia and blocking can create an overhang and soffit to shade the window from direct sunlight.

roof. The flashing should extend at least 8 inches on either side of the center of the valley. Slide the new flashing under the existing shingles and nail in place in a bed of roofing cement. Install a drip edge along the sides of the roof. Lay the new roofing according to the manufacturer's directions and trim along the valley on both sides. There should be two inches of flashing exposed on each valley side. Only nail along the edge of the flashing.

Now finish the outside of the dormer walls. Nail wall sheathing to the studs, cutting out the window opening. Install the window unit according to the manufacturer's directions. Apply flashing along the joint where the dormer walls meet the existing roof. The flashing fits against the sheathing and over the shingles. Place drip cap flashing above the window after the exterior trim is in place. Finally, nail the siding (see Chapter 12) with galvanized finishing nails. Caulk around the window and at the wall joints.

There are dormer kits available. These come complete with instructions and materials. Though a kit will be easier to install, it will also be a little more expensive.

Providing Ventilation

Installing any of the types of windows mentioned should provide good ventilation, as long as there are at least two on opposite areas of the attic and they are types that can be opened. However, if your plans do not include any windows or skylights, either install louvered vents in opposite ends or sides of the attic, or make

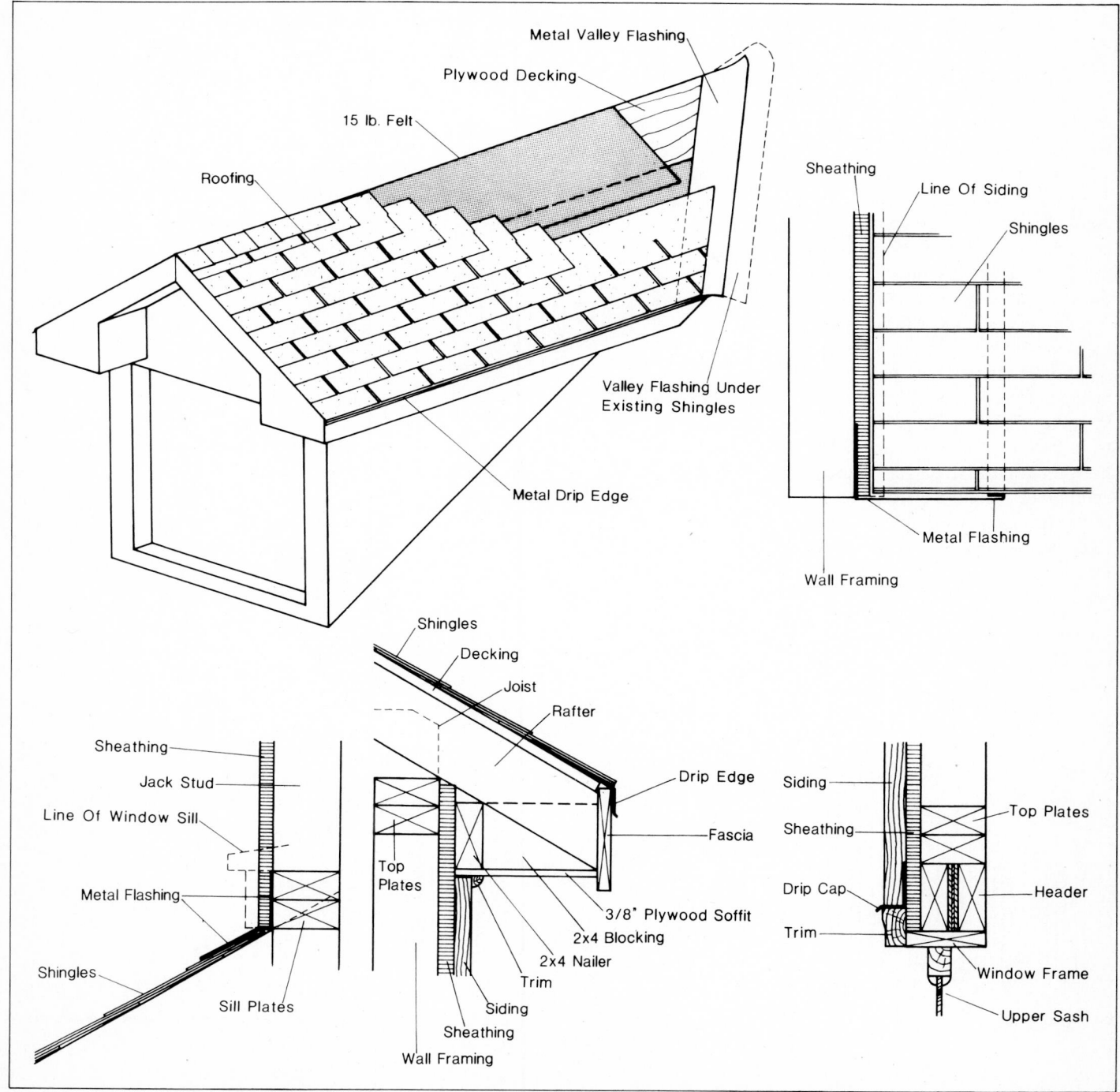

Finishing the gable dormer entails sheathing roof and sides, applying flashing to roof valley and side sheathing, covering surfaces with roofing felt, adding drip cap to window and drip edge to roof, then applying shingles and siding. Seal joints with caulk to prevent leaks.

sure the area is ventilated, heated and cooled with a forced air system. A vent with a fan is a good investment to maintain good ventilation and to pull air through the rest of the house.

Chimneys, Vent Pipes and Ducts

There may be a number of pipes and ducts rising through your attic. Vent pipes and ducts are usually small and, as a rule, can be enclosed as part of a new partition. If necessary, they can be removed without too much difficulty. If the vent is a plumbing stack, and you are adding an attic bath, it will be within any new plumbing wall needed for the attic conversion.

A chimney presents a different problem. A chimney cannot be moved, but it can be turned into a decorative asset. You may use a chimney as a room divider, painting the brick to blend with the other walls. Even without a fireplace, the chimney can be the focal point of a room. It is possible to place a wood stove or freestanding fireplace in front of the chimney, but you will have to run the stove pipe or prefabricated chimney through the roof. You cannot patch into the chimney at this point unless there is an unused flue contained in the chimney. If the brickwork in the attic is too ragged to look attractive when painted, build a frame wall around the chimney and cover the framing with appropriate finish materials. The wood framework must have at least 2 inches of clearance from the chimney. Where possible, work the framing into the wall system you are building.

Including a Fire Exit

Many municipalities require that any attic used as living space have two exits, especially if any part is used for bedrooms. Even if your community does not have this requirement, you may still want to provide an alternate escape route for the safety of your family. If you do not want to install a second complete set of stairs, which would greatly reduce usable space, add one of the many types of emergency ladders. Place the ladder near a window that is large enough to get through easily. Secure the ladder exactly as recommended by the manufacturer. **Be sure every member of the family understands how the emergency escape ladder is used.**

Stair Location

A common problem in converting the attic is locating the stairs. Unless your attic is

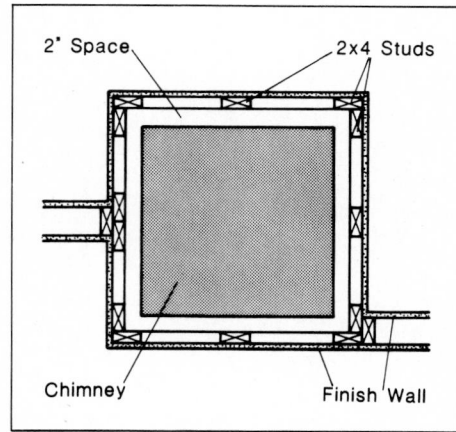

When framing around a chimney, codes require a 2 inch gap between masonry and framing to reduce fire hazard from overheated wood.

unusual, it has no more than a square access door through a ceiling. The door is probably hidden in a closet; if you are fortunate, it hides a fold-down staircase. Fold-down stairs do not give sufficient access. If the attic staircase is not reasonably convenient, expansion work will be wasted and the area will not be used. Try to install a standard staircase or, if space is very tight, a spiral staircase, but nothing less. See Chapter 7 for help in designing your stairs.

CONSTRUCTION WRAPUP
Safety Precautions

Before you begin working in the attic, take several safety precautions. The unconverted attic is usually poorly ventilated and can become extremely hot. Anyone is susceptible to heat stroke; do not work in the heat of summer. If the area is uninsulated and without a cooling system, temperatures can reach more than 140 degrees. After you have laid temporary flooring, add windows or vents to ventilate the area. Always wear a breathing mask when doing any work that creates dust, such as sawing. Do not take safety precautions lightly, especially when working alone and away from quick assistance.

Hoisting and Handling Materials

There may be problems in getting large materials into the attic. Try hoisting long boards and large panels from the outside, up through a window or other opening. This will probably require the use of a pulley or pulley system. You may find it easier to cut the pieces and take the pieces up as they are needed. Record all measurements carefully, so you do not waste expensive materials.

Installing Subflooring

Once you know that the joists are strong enough or you have strengthened the

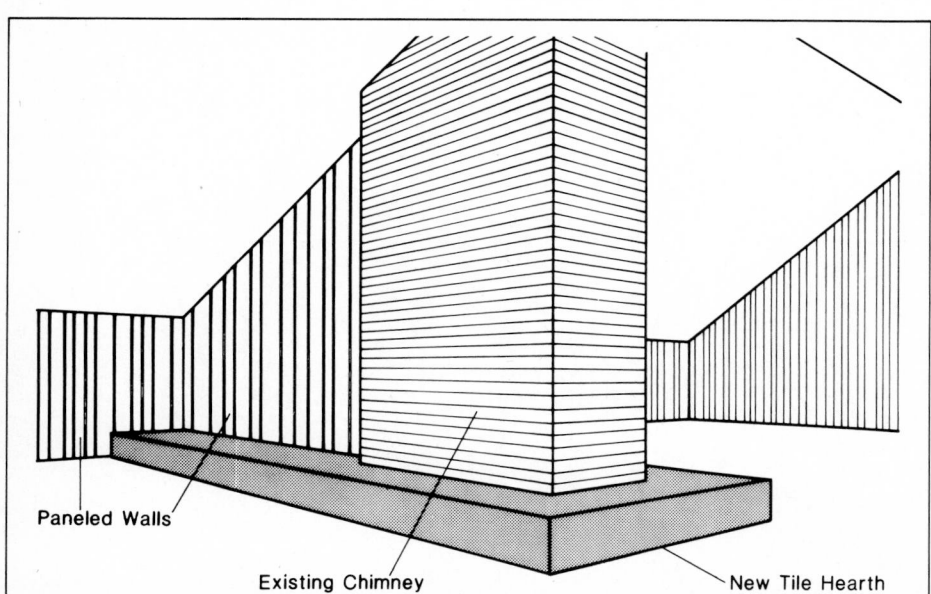

Even if there is no fireplace opening in an attic conversion, the chimney may be treated decoratively with a hearth ledge or framed up and hidden by paneling or wallboard.

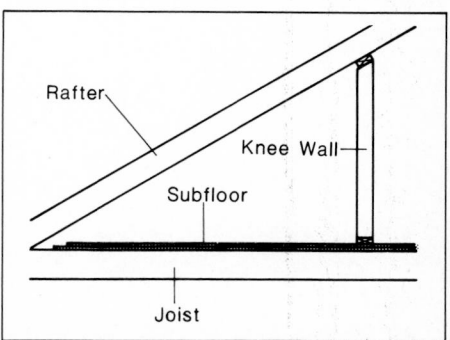

Install subfloor before partitions. Flooring should reach to exterior walls if possible.

joists, you can install the subfloor. Do this before putting up any wall partitions. Either special plywood subflooring or double layers of regular plywood may be used. Nail at 6-inch intervals along edges and at 10-inch intervals into other joists. Regular plywood joints must be staggered. In the attic, nail the subfloor carefully, so you do not crack the ceiling below. If you glue-nail the subfloor, there will be less nailing and less chance of damage. Carry the subfloor beyond the location of the knee walls, as close to the eaves as possible. This will allow you to use the space behind the knee wall for storage and closets.

Heating and Insulation

Leave any existing ceiling insulation in place and simply lay the subfloor over it. The insulation will offer a little sound baffle. However, it will continue to isolate the heating and cooling loads; the attic should be on a system separate from the main level. A consistent winter warmth cannot be maintained with heat from lower floors. There simply will not be enough heat. If you run vents from one level to another to allow the heat to rise more easily, there still may not be enough heat. You could also create an overload on the main level heating system. Sound will travel through the vents from one level to an-

other. You need, in most cases, a small additional heater.

To protect the lower level from annoying sounds use thick carpet and pad to absorb most low-frequency sounds such as footsteps. To further insulate against sound, construct a "floating floor" by laying a full covering of insulation or other sound-absorbing material over the joists or existing decking. Place 2x2 battens at 16 inches on center, perpendicular to the joists. Do not nail, just lay the battens in place. Nail the subfloor to the battens. This will greatly reduce noise traveling from one floor to another.

Finishing the Ceiling

Flat ceilings. To create a flat ceiling, add joists between each rafter at the proper level. Use the table given earlier in the chapter to determine joist size. If you have collar beams, usually on every third or fourth rafter, they should be retained. However, they can be moved up if the present level will make the ceiling too low.

The existing collar beams can serve as the ceiling joists, with joists added between where there are no collar beams. Provide an access to the crawl space you have created and ventilate it at the gables. Use roof vents or a ridge vent for a hip roof.

Insulation. Insulate between the joists, creating the required R-value for your locality. The attic is the hottest area of the house in summer and the coolest in winter, so proper insulation of walls and ceiling is critical.

In an open ceiling, and in the area between a knee wall and a flat ceiling, insulation can be handled in two different ways. As one alternative, you can place insulation batts between the rafters and hide the insulation with finish materials

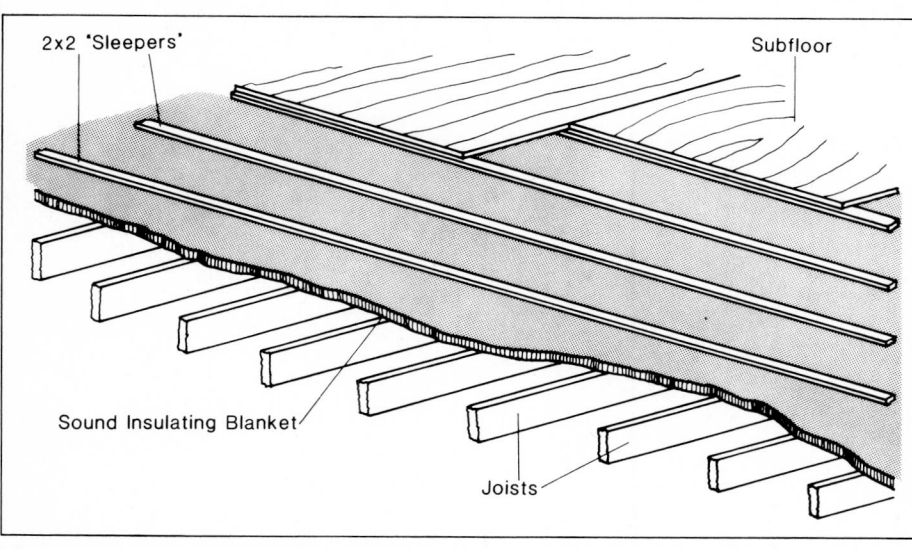

To keep sound from reaching lower floors, lay sound insulating blanket on joists, lay 2x2 sleepers loose on insulation and nail subflooring to sleepers. Stagger subfloor seams.

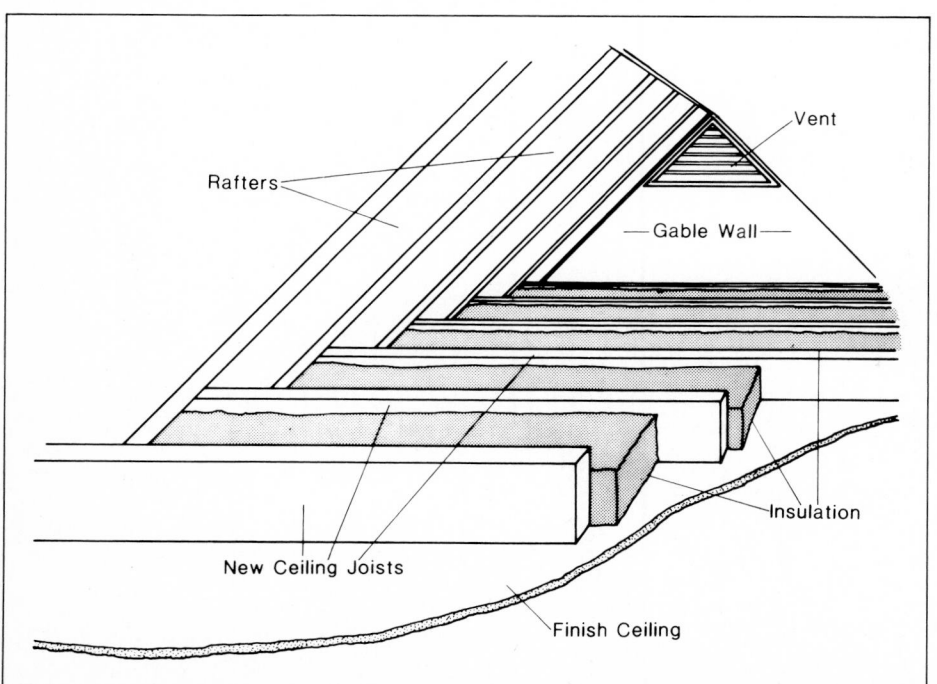

If you create a flat ceiling in the attic space, add required insulation for your area between new ceiling joists. Be sure there is adequate ventilation to move air through ceiling space.

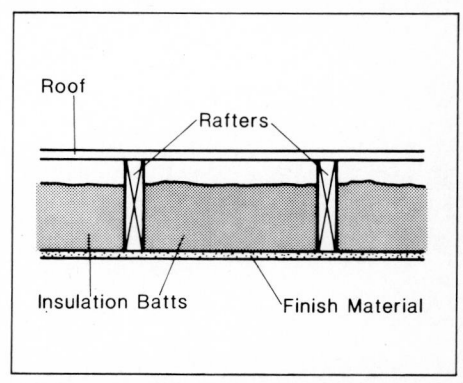

If rafters are behind finish material, insulation rests on ceiling; leave air gap at roof.

nailed to the rafters. The second method is used when you want exposed rafters. Provide blocking on each side of the rafter and secure rigid insulation to the blocking. Apply finish materials directly to the insulation between the rafters. Leave a space of at least 1½ inches deep between the insulation and roof decking. Add 2x2 blocking as a spacer. Place the 2x2s against the roof decking but nail the blocking into the rafters.

In an open ceiling, there is no crawl space to be ventilated, but the air pocket between the decking and insulation must be ventilated. To do this, install a vent at the ridge and grilles in the soffit.

Collar beams and the open ceiling. In an open ceiling, the collar beams could detract from the appearance you want.

The purpose of the collar beams is to tie the rafters together to ease the pressure that the rafters apply to the outside walls. However, the attic floor joists also hold the walls against this pressure. If the joists are strong enough to withstand the pressure on the walls, you can remove the collar beams. Have an expert determine the effects of removing the collar beams. They are necessary in areas of high winds and heavy snow loads. If you live in an area subject to these weather conditions, you may have to work the collar beams into your design.

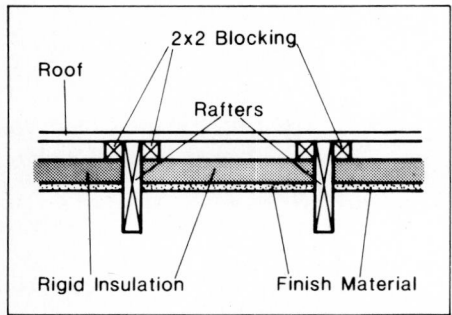

If you want beams to show, nail 2x2 blocking to rafters and attach rigid insulation to blocking and cover with finish ceiling.

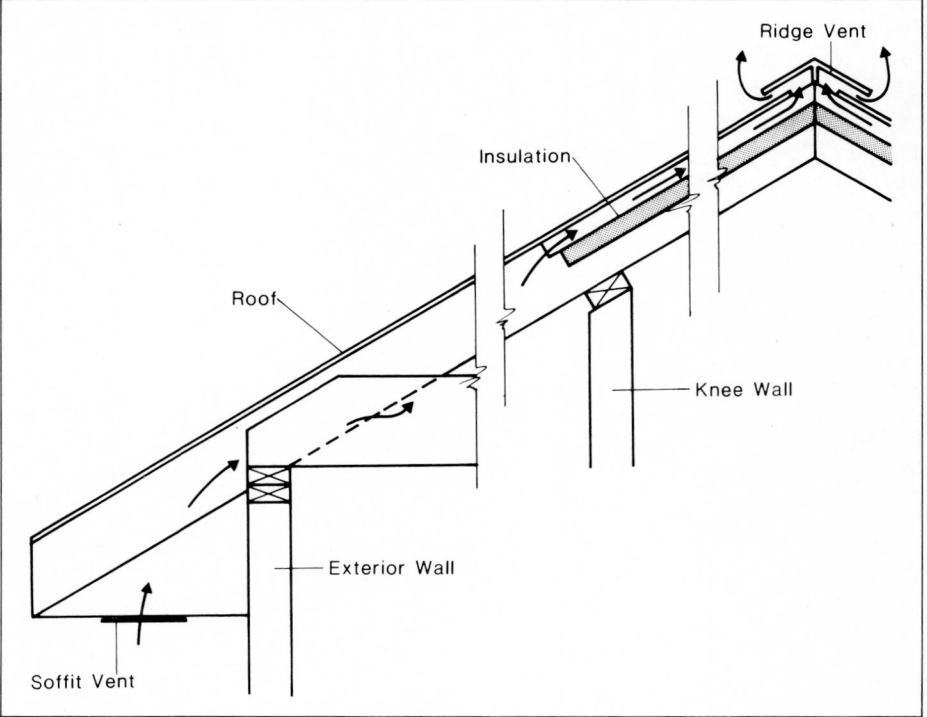

A ridge vent should be installed if you finish at attic and close off end vents. The ridge vent pulls air up through soffit vents to minimize condensation.

Rafters or ceiling joists can become a part of the decorative scheme of a room without making any structural changes in them.

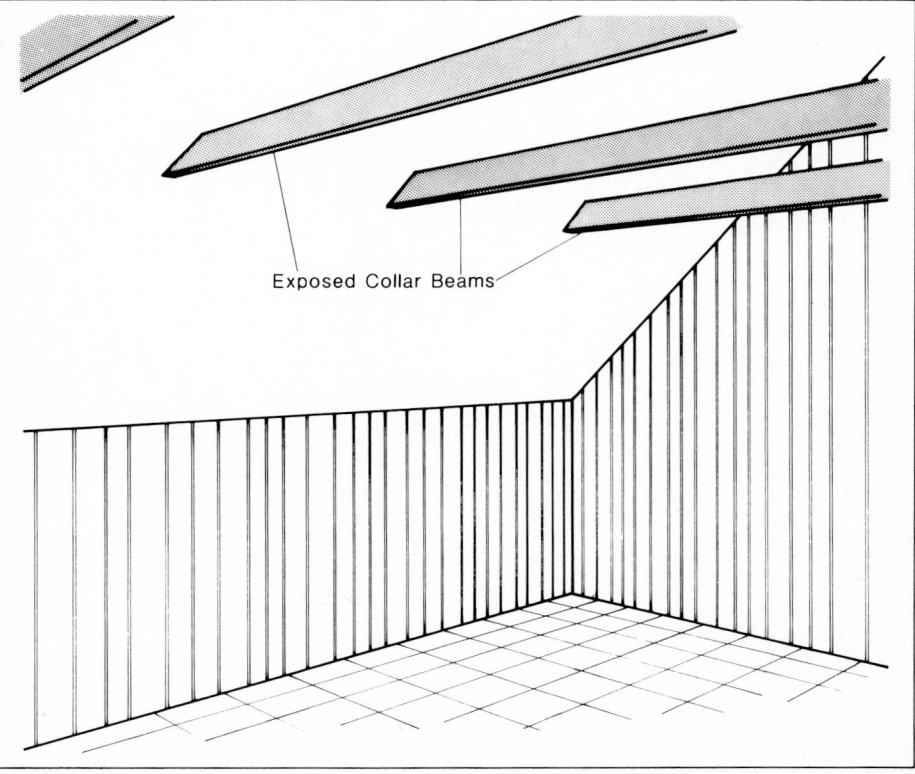

Collar beams hold rafters against stress of the outward pull of the house walls. If they must be left in place, they are usually above head level and are not in the way.

The collar beams can be left in place; if trimmed out with finishing lumber, the result will be a neater appearance and unique look.

Adding Knee Walls

Knee walls are constructed with a single top plate, single bottom plate, and studs at 16 inches on center. The top plate, however, will be at the angle of the rafters and the studs will have to be cut to fit against the top plate. If you will be covering the rafters with finish material, place a 2x4 nailer between the rafters. For exposed rafters, the nailer will fit directly above the top plate and be toenailed into the rafters. If you have a partition running parallel to the rafters, with an open ceiling, provide blocking between the rafters as a nailer for the top plate.

Provide doors or drawers in the knee wall, to suit your taste, in order to take advantage of the storage space behind. (See Chapter 8 for details on how to build drawers and other storage compartments.) Problems to be solved include working with the slant of the rafters and installing insulation. If the storage area is to be compartmented with divider walls, provide insulation in the outside walls and between the rafters above the storage area. If space is left continuous with door openings to the space behind the wall, cover the back of the door(s) with 2-inch thick rigid insulation.

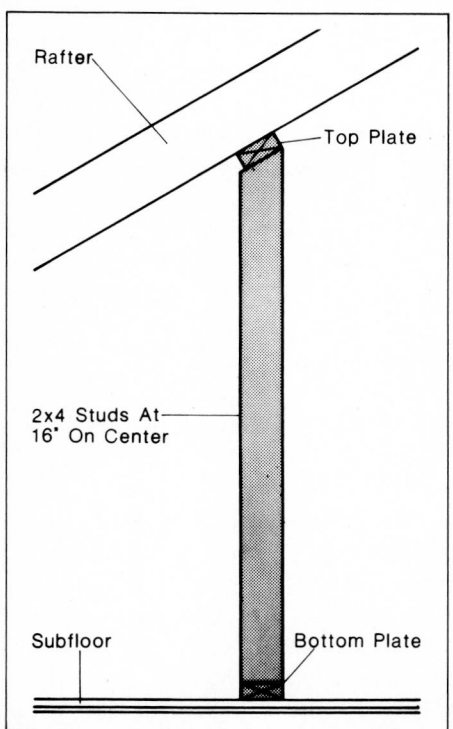

Knee walls fit between flat floor and angled ceiling. Studs must be cut precisely to fit the space and angles involved.

Collar beams support small loft in attic apartment. Beams and ceiling are finished alike.

Chimney rising through attic space is used as a divider between kitchen and other space.

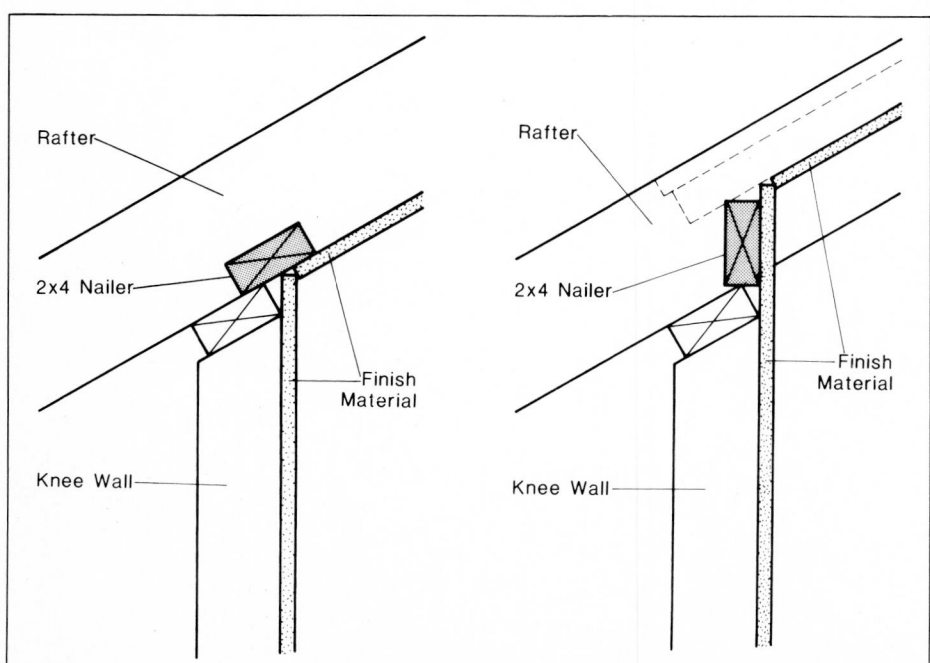

In order to provide necessary support and a nailing surface for finish materials, 2x4 blocking is needed between rafters. Position will depend upon desired layout of finish materials. Blocking may be toenailed into rafters, but it must be secure to hold wallboard nails.

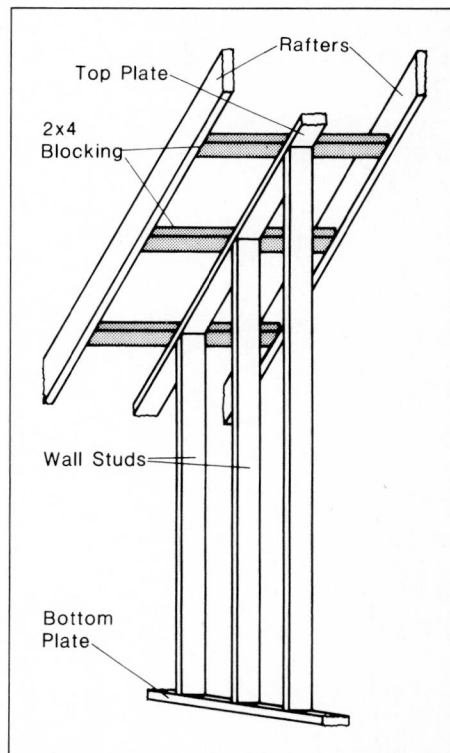

Install 2x4 blocking between rafters to support top plate of attic side wall (partition). Blocking can be nailed through the rafters.

11

GOING UP
INSTEAD OF OUT

This chapter will present several ways to take advantage of your attic space other than the straight-forward conversion discussed in Chapter 10. Two of the projects use the attic space to make the main level a more dramatic living area by opening up the attic to form a vaulted ceiling over the main level and by constructing a loft to overlook the main level. Some of these ideas will be relatively easy for the do-it-yourselfer, depending upon previous experience, but others will require professional help.

CREATING A VAULTED CEILING

A vaulted ceiling, open to the rafters, can produce a dramatic change in any room. Even though the actual square footage of the room remains the same, the height makes any room feel more open and spacious. In summer, the taller room should be cooler because warm air is allowed to rise above head level. A venting skylight or clerestory window near the top increases this effect. In winter, however, the vaulted ceiling may create a heating prob-

lem. Because the warm air rises, you will be heating air far above your head. The addition of clear skylights will increase solar heat gain during the day. The best solution is probably a slow-turning fan near the top of the room. The fan will help push the heated air down into the lower parts of the room.

The rafters of the vaulted ceiling can be left exposed or covered with finish material. If the climate where you live requires the installation of substantial insulation, you may have to cover the rafters completely to provide support for the insulation. If you still want to finish the ceiling with exposed rafters or beams, add false beams created with finish grade lumber.

Structural Evaluation

A vaulted ceiling can be simple, if you have standard roof construction. If you have a truss roof, the problem is complicated. It will require an expert, an architect or structural engineer, to redesign the truss system to allow removal of a portion of the trusses. He will have to study your

home carefully, since each situation is different. Discuss the methods of construction with your expert to determine if you can do the work yourself, if you must hire a professional to do the work, or to determine if anything can be done to change the ceiling line.

Standard roof design. If your home is conventionally framed, you may remove the ceiling joists, ceiling finish material, and insulation to create the vaulted ceiling.

Creating a new loadbearing wall. The interior wall near the center of the house automatically becomes a loadbearing wall as soon as the joists are cut. The cut ends of the remaining joist sections rest on the interior wall.

If this wall was originally a loadbearing wall, then there is no problem, but if the wall was not constructed for this, have an engineer or architect check your basement footings and foundation to determine if additional structural support will be needed to handle the shift of bearing walls. Because the removal of the joists lessens the weight of the actual structural load, you probably will not have problems. The roof load itself will still be carried by the length of the rafters to the exterior walls. However, an expert will see if proposed work will create enough shift in the weight distribution to put too much stress on the existing framing and foundation. The en-

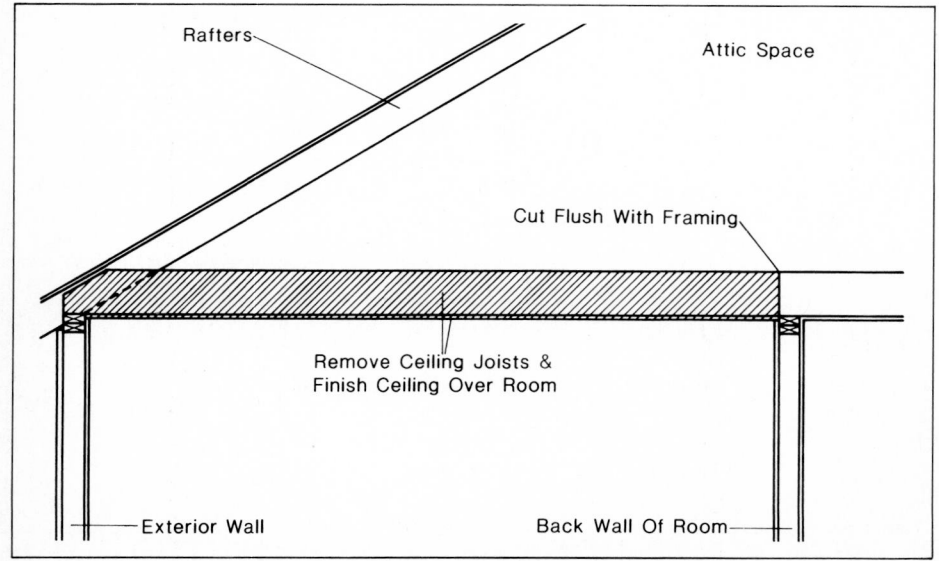

Creation of a vaulted ceiling begins with the removal of existing ceiling finish materials so you have access to the joists that will have to be cut and removed.

A vaulted ceiling gives room a look of strength; low ceilings give room an intimate look.

gineer or architect will be able to design new piers or other supports needed. Have the new supports installed before you begin removal of the ceiling joists.

Extending Walls to New Ceiling Height

Once you have removed the ceiling finish material, insulation and joists, your room will be open to your attic space. You now must extend the walls to the height of the vaulted ceiling to enclose the attic area and

to reestablish the finished appearance of your room. To do this, you will have to frame the space between the rafters and the existing walls. There is a slight difference between framing walls parallel to the rafters and walls perpendicular to the rafters. In both cases the first step is the same.

Step one: cutting the ceiling joists. After cutting away the ceiling finish material and removing the insulation, cut the joists at both sides of the room. Provide

temporary support with 2x4 braces so you can take each joist down after it has been cut. The cuts should be even with the inside faces of the walls.

Step two: adding top and bottom plates for wall perpendicular to the length of joists and rafters. Place a 2x4 bottom plate across the ceiling joists, directly over the top plate of the wall in the center of the house. These two plates should be flush so that finish materials will be even. Nail the plate to the joists with 12d common nails.

Use a plumb bob to locate the line of the bottom plate on the rafters. Mark this point on each end of the span of rafters, and snap a chalkline between the points. Nail a 2x4 top plate into the rafters along this line using 12d common nails.

Step two, variation: adding top and bottom plates for walls parallel to the length of the joists and rafters. The structure of a wall that runs parallel to the joists and rafters is the same as for the previously described wall. However, unless the wall falls exactly on a joist and exactly under a rafter, you will have to provide blocking as a nailing surface. Cut blocking to fit between the rafters and joists at 16 inches on center. Nail through the rafters and joists into the blocking with 12d common nails. The position of the rafters and joists to the new walls may be close enough that you may need to add only 2x4 nailers to the rafters and joists.

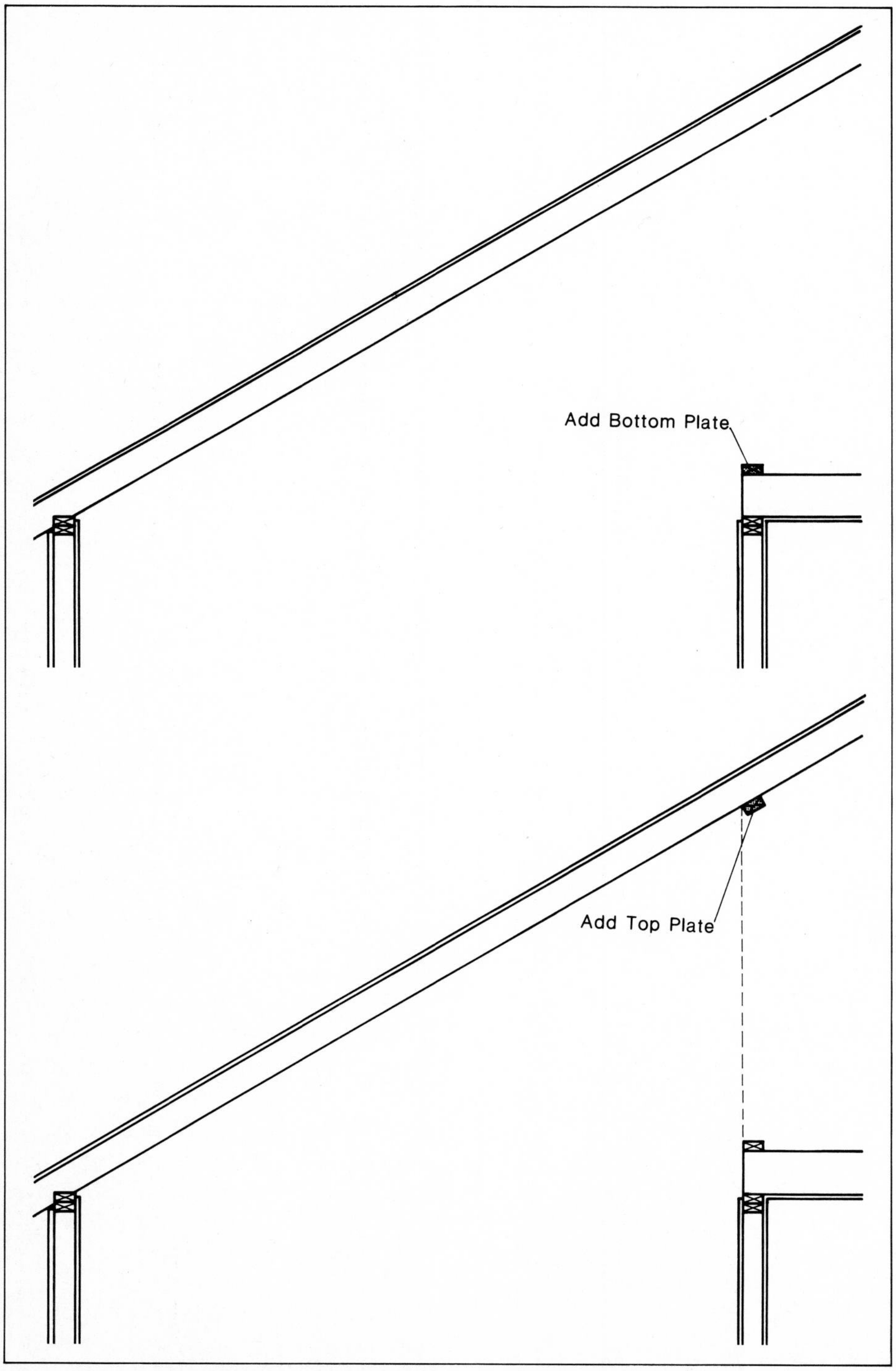

Add Bottom Plate

Add Top Plate

To finish the interior wall to the new open ceiling, install a bottom plate on the upper floor and a top plate across the rafters. Construction is like knee wall construction.

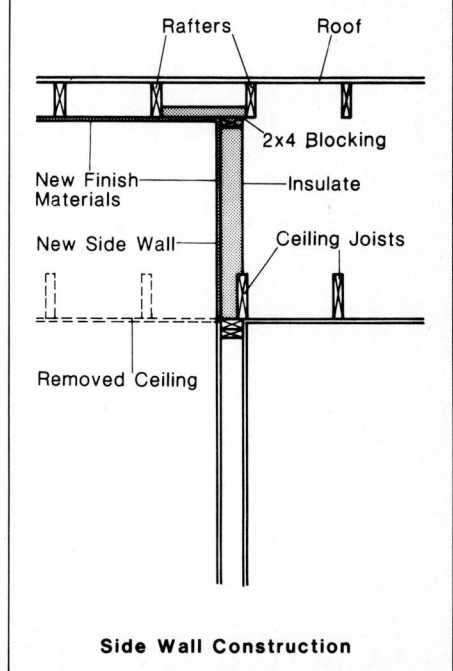

Side Wall Construction

Side wall construction, needed if you vault part of a room, needs blocking between rafters.

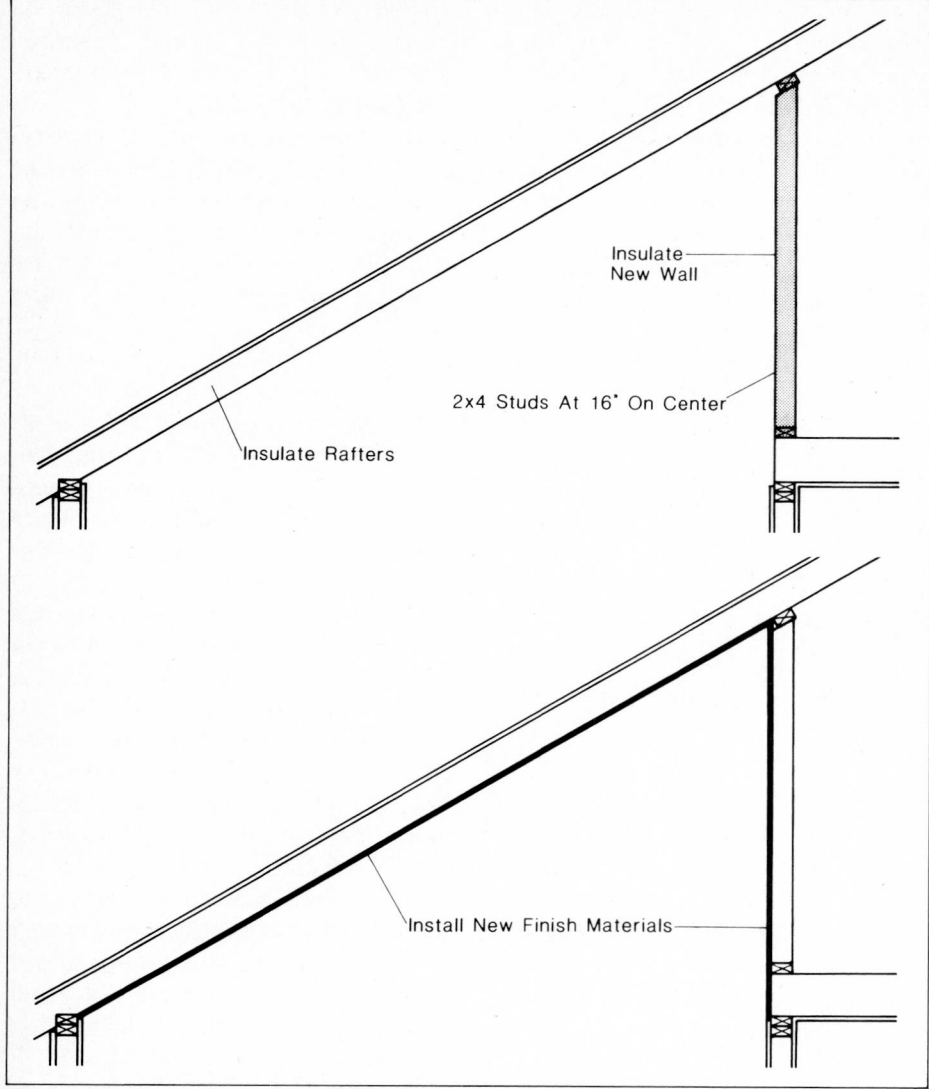

Because you have opened the room to the roof, you will have to provide new insulation in the roof and in the new attic wall. Cover with wallboard or paneling as is suitable for your design.

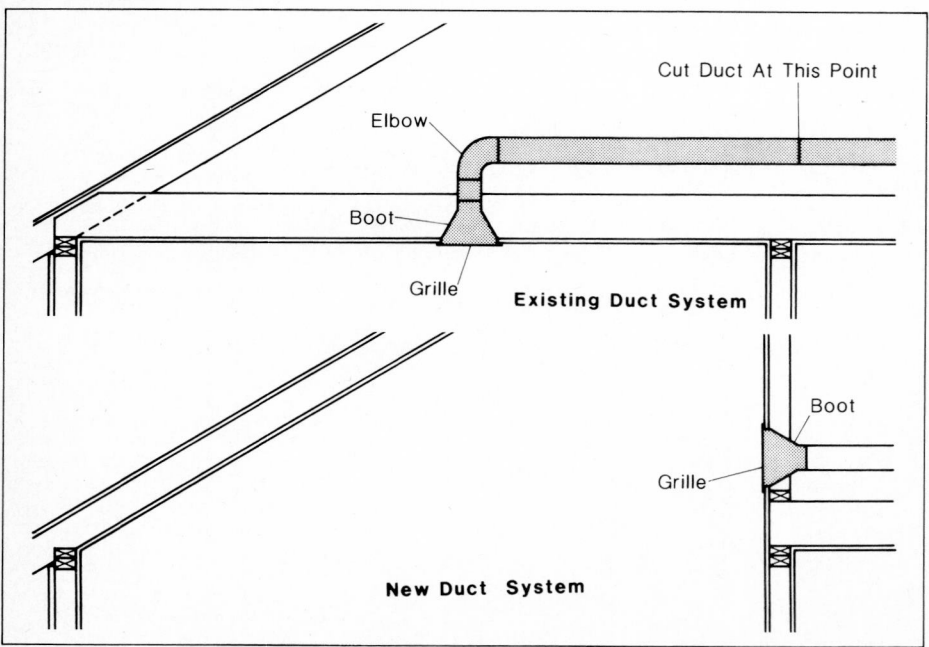

If a forced air system duct passes through area to be vaulted, you will have to cut the duct and relocate the boot opening in the new attic wall you create on the interior of the room.

Set a bottom plate in place and nail into the joist or blocking or nailer. Find the top plate position with a plumb bob, snap a chalkline as a guide and nail the top plate into position with 12d common nails.

Step three: nailing in the studs. Nail 2x4 studs between the top plate and the bottom plate, 16 inches on center. Toenail the studs into both plates with 10d common nails.

Step four: completing the walls. Insulate between the studs of the new walls. The type of insulation you use in the rafters will depend on the type of construction you are using. Refer to Chapter 10 on how to insulate rafters. Finish materials may be installed as explained in Chapter 6.

Moving Vents, Pipes and Ducts

Any vents, pipes or ducts that pass through the now-open attic space will have to be moved. You will probably have no vent pipes since they usually run directly up through walls. However, if you have a forced-air heating system with ducts in the attic, there may be one or, possibly two ducts, in this area. Cut the duct off where you have framed the new wall and reuse the same boot and grille in the new wall. You may have to reroute some of the ducts to insure heat in all rooms. If the main trunk duct runs through this space, it will have to be moved. Unless you are experienced with this type of sheet metal work, have a professional do this for you.

Handling Exposed Collar Beams

Joists tie the rafters together to counter the outward force caused by their slope. When you remove a portion of the joists, the collar beams, which also tie the rafters, become more important. These beams could be above the area you opened for your new vaulted ceiling hidden in the attic space. If so, you do not have to do anything. If the collar beams extend into the new open space, you must leave them in place; however, you may trim the beams with finish lumber to make them more attractive. If you feel that you must remove the collar, consult an expert and act on his advice, especially if the new vaulted ceiling is very wide.

Creating False Ceiling Beams

The vaulted ceiling is substantially higher than a normal ceiling. In order to work overhead at this height, you should set up scaffolding to provide safe access to the ceiling and a secure place to stand while nailing beam boards.

Creating false beams. Beams are built around a 2x4 nailed through the finish material into a rafter. Use 16d common nails driven approximately every 8 inches. If the false beam runs perpendicular to the rafters, use two nails driven into each rafter. Nail one-inch stock finishing lumber into the sides of the 2x4 nailer, using 6d finishing nails. The width of the side pieces may be whatever you wish. Nail a 1x4 bottom of finishing lumber between the side pieces, using 4d finishing nails. A good flush fit will be very difficult; if necessary, set the bottom board about ½ inch in from the edges of the side pieces. If it is hard to get a good fit between the edges of the side pieces and the ceiling, or if you like the design effect, add quarter-round trim where the sides of the beam meet the ceiling. Nail the molding into the side pieces with 2d finishing nails driven at a slight angle. Stain or paint the beams as desired. The size of the beam can be varied by changing the width of the 2-inch stock nailer and one-inch stock bottom piece.

Beam placement planning. Determine the location of any false beams you want to add. Avoid placing beams too close together. Crowded beams will give an uncomfortable, heavy appearance, especially in a smaller room. Place small beams 4 feet on center. Place larger beams at 6 feet (or even 8) on center.

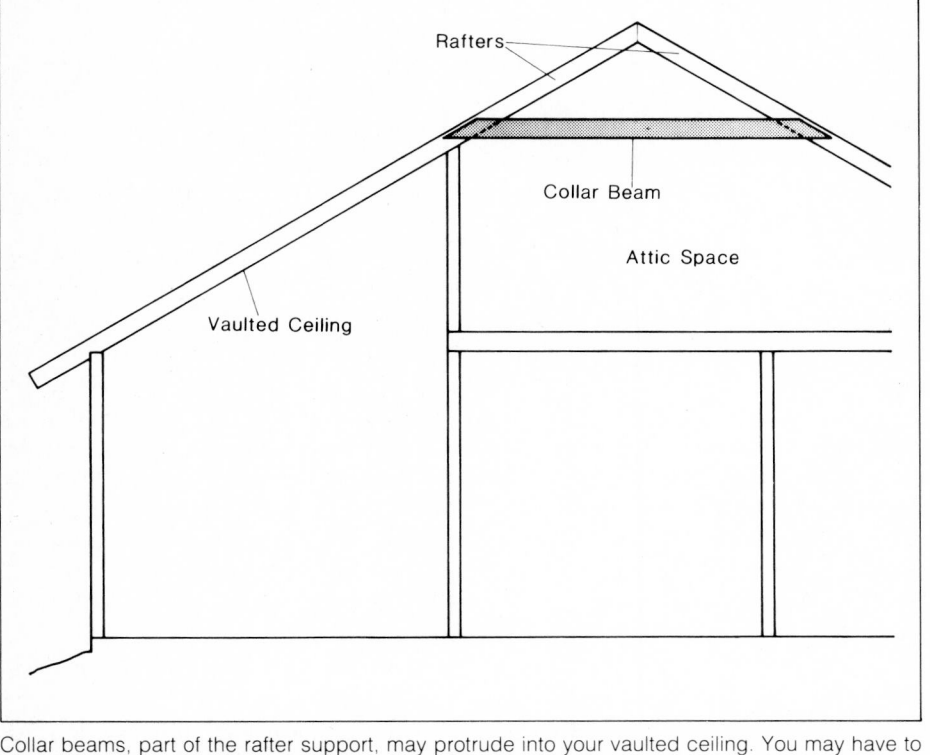

Collar beams, part of the rafter support, may protrude into your vaulted ceiling. You may have to install new beams closer to the ridge board or frame the beams to match your room.

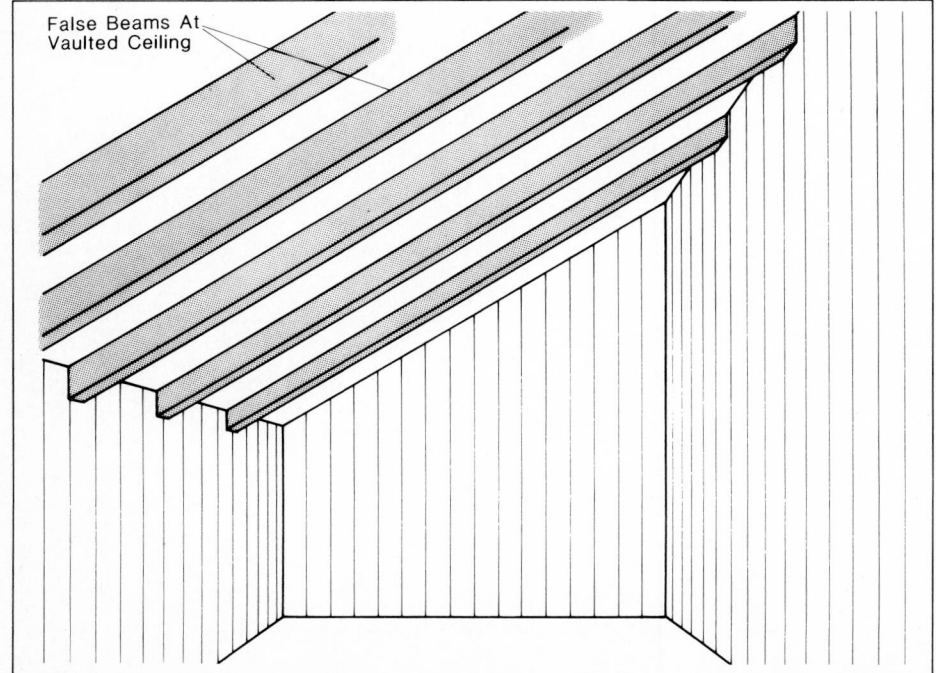

If a smooth, uninterrupted ceiling line looks uninteresting in your space, create false beams. You may use prefabricated beams or construct your own to match your paneling or furniture.

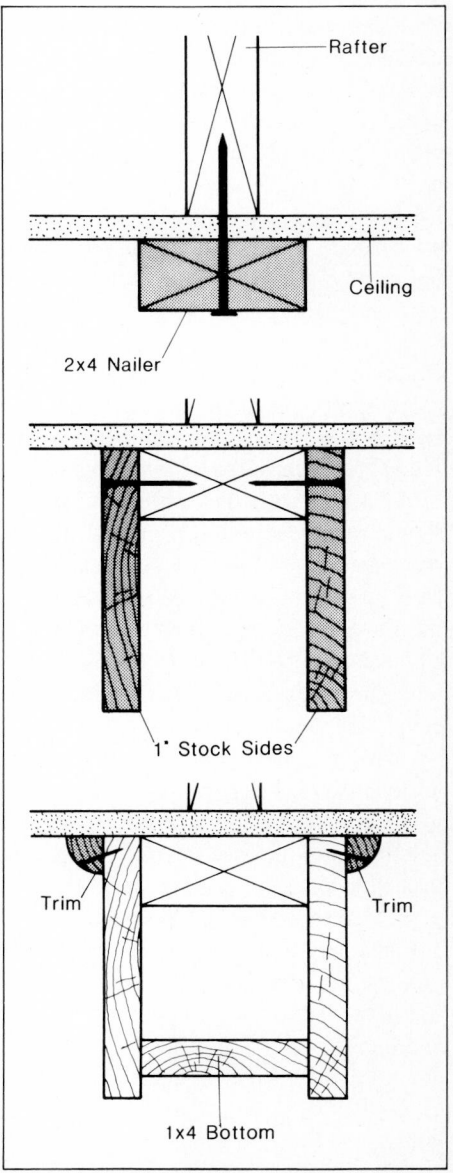

False beams are created around a 2x4 nailer attached through finish materials to the rafters. Beams and trim attach to nailer.

BUILDING A LOFT

In the past, small homes and cottages had lofts with a definite function, usually for sleeping space. A loft was a space-saving device normally built in the smallest homes, such as frontier log cabins. Today, lofts are built in some of the most expensive homes and are especially popular in vacation homes. While many lofts serve a necessary function, some exist just for the fun of having an extra hideaway or reading nook.

The loft is not a room of its own, but an extension of the room below. While the two areas may serve quite different purposes, the loft is still a part of the lower, larger space. A loft adds attractive, unique space, and a new dimension to the room.

The long, narrow loft on the cover of this book was added to provide space for extensive bookshelves, unavailable in the lower part of the room without sacrificing some of the seating space. The usefulness of the design is enhanced by the attractiveness of the arrangement. A wider loft can be a comfortable and functional office overlooking the master bedroom suite, a hobby/craft center in a teenager's bedroom, or a cozy retreat, overlooking almost any room.

Choosing the Best Location

A loft can be placed in any room that has enough headroom to provide the space needed for your purpose. If you plan a loft in the room with the vaulted ceiling, it should be placed on the wall that has the most headroom. You cannot build a loft if there is not sufficient room height to accommodate it. The headroom of the loft, however, can be held to 6 feet unless your family is exceptionally tall. The feeling of being closed in, usually associated with a low ceiling, is not a problem in a loft since it is open to the larger room below. Before you carry your plans too far, check the attic space in the area where you wish to locate the loft to be sure you can open it up to provide enough space. If your attic does not have any type of footing, use temporary footing as explained at the beginning of Chapter 10 so that you can move around and investigate the attic safely. The room over which the loft will open must have a vaulted ceiling or other high ceiling, whether existing or new.

Since the loft is usually a small area that serves only limited purposes, you do not want to waste a lot of precious space with

an elaborate staircase. Install a spiral staircase or a ladder of one type or another (see Chapter 7).

Construction Alternatives

Although basic construction of a loft uses methods similar to those explained for a vaulted ceiling, there are more structural considerations since you are creating an area that will carry a ''live'' load (people). This load will bear on the ceiling joists in the area of the loft. The loft can be constructed so it opens onto an adjacent room, or it can be constructed completely within the room, directly over a portion of that room. There are advantages to both situations. A loft open to an adjacent room will usually be easier and less expensive to build because you take advantage of existing walls and joists. The loft completely within a room has several space advantages which may make it feasible when the first type is not possible.

Building the Loft over an Adjacent Room

A loft over an adjacent room calls for the same steps as a vaulted ceiling, except that the wall perpendicular to the joists and rafters is not located directly over the existing wall of the room but is located at a point where the loft is as wide as desired — or where the headroom space becomes limited. This back wall of the loft is built like a knee wall (see Chapter 10); however-

er, the loft wall usually will be taller than a knee wall. The joists on which the loft will rest must be strong enough to accept a live load. Check the size and spacing of joists, then refer to the chart in Chapter 10 to determine if the joists are strong enough to accept the new load. If necessary, increase joist strength as explained in Chapter 10. The back wall of the loft should be located within 3 feet of an existing wall on the main floor. This will help keep deflection (bending) of the joists to a minimum.

Step one: constructing the loft walls. When the ceiling and joists have been removed, as given previously for a vaulted ceiling, establish the position of the back wall of the loft. Frame this wall and the side walls as above.

Step two: covering the floor. Apply the subfloor in the area of the loft. Sturd-I-Floor or other specialty subflooring plywood is suggested for the subfloor because no additional underlayment is needed. The suggested thickness for specialty subflooring is ⅝ inch for 16 inch on center framing. A standard plywood subfloor should be ½ or ⅝ inches thick with a ¼-inch plywood underlayment (the material directly under the finish floor) or a ½ inch or ⅝ inch underlayment of particleboard.

Step three: finishing the walls. Insulate behind walls and between rafters (see Chapter 10), and add finish materials (see Chapter 6).

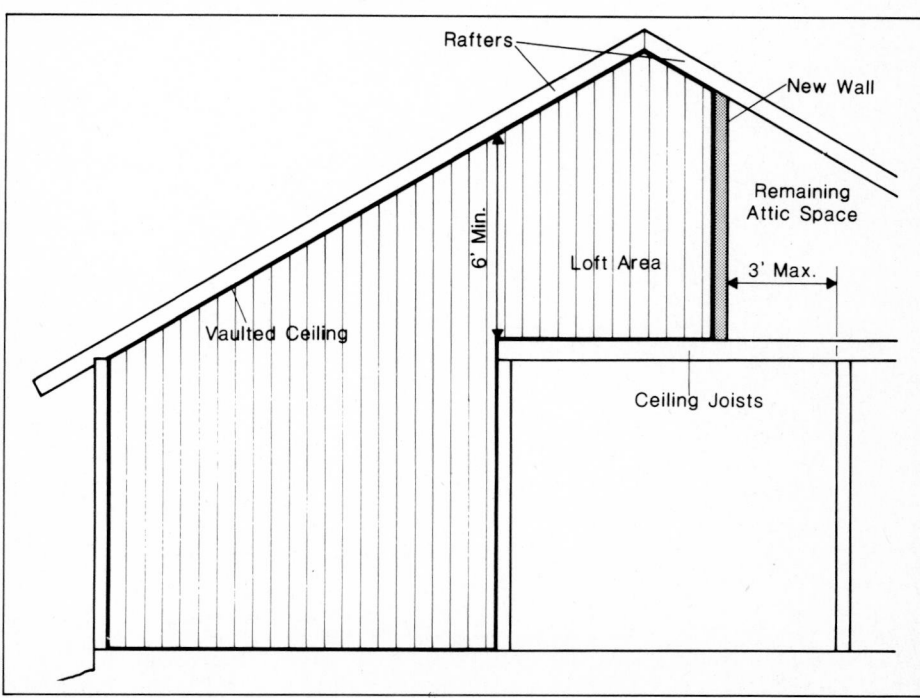

Newly opened attic space may become a usable loft if you place your new wall back from the edge of the cut joists. Back wall must be within 3 feet of wall below.

Building the Loft within a Room

If there is not enough headroom in the attic space to create an adjacent room loft, you may be able to build a loft that is completely within a room that has a vaulted or other high ceiling. This type of loft is essentially an interior deck. If the room has a vaulted ceiling, the loft within the room will be easier and less expensive than a loft over an adjacent room, which requires building and finishing new walls and finishing the ceiling.

Step one: laying out the dimensions. Determine the location and size of the loft, based on your room scale and available headroom. You can set the level of the loft so that the clear headroom under it is as little as 6 feet. With a total joist and floor thickness of 9 inches, you will need a total height of 12 feet 9 inches.

Step two: setting support posts. With the location established, place 4x4s at the points chosen for corners. Nail a wood or metal base plate to the bottom of the 4x4 with four 12d common nails, then attach the plate to the floor with 10d finishing nails or wood screws, or concrete nails if you are installing the deck on a slab. In the case of a slab, use a metal plate instead of wood. Both wood and metal base plates can be purchased. You can also make a wood plate by cutting a square out of a 2x6 or 2x8 and adding trim around the edges after the base plate is installed. The 4x4 posts should be long enough to extend to the height of the handrail around the finished loft.

Step three: setting ledger board. Install a 2x8 ledger board on the wall. The bottom of the ledger should be even with the line of headroom for the space below the loft. Nail the ledger into the studs with 16d common nails, two in each stud. Be sure the ledger is level. Then complete the outside framing by nailing 2x8 headers between the ledger and the posts and across the spans between the posts. Level the headers carefully as you work. Nail the headers to the ledger with 16d common nails, then attach headers to the posts with 3/8 inch bolts. Nail headers to each other through butting ends.

Step four: installing joists and rail. For the deck, lay 2x6 joists at 16 inches on center from the ledger to the front header

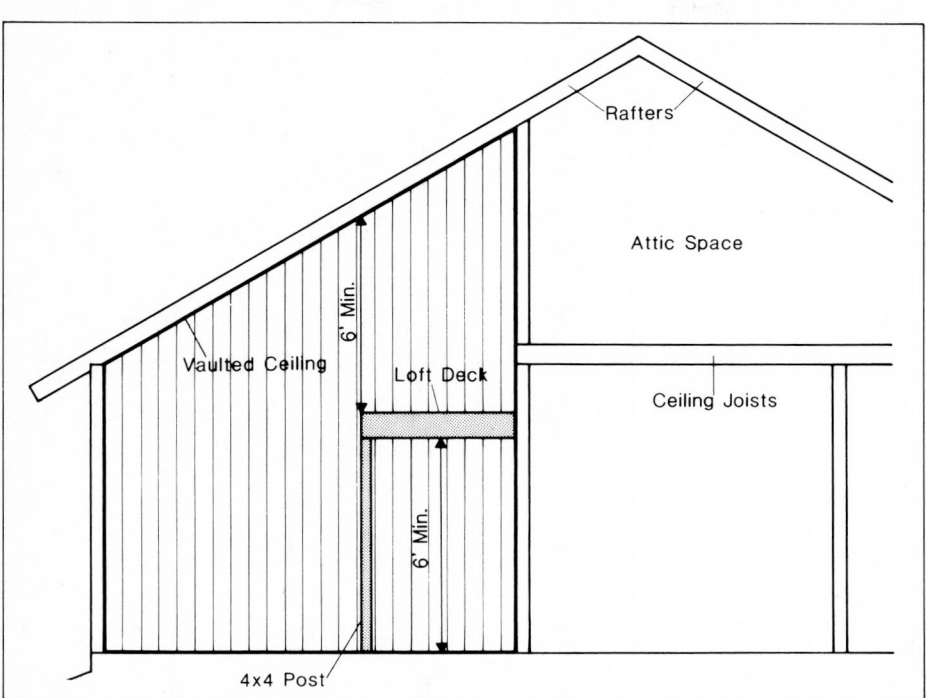

If your room with a vaulted ceiling is large enough, you may construct a deck-style loft within that room. This will increase the usable area of the room without major construction.

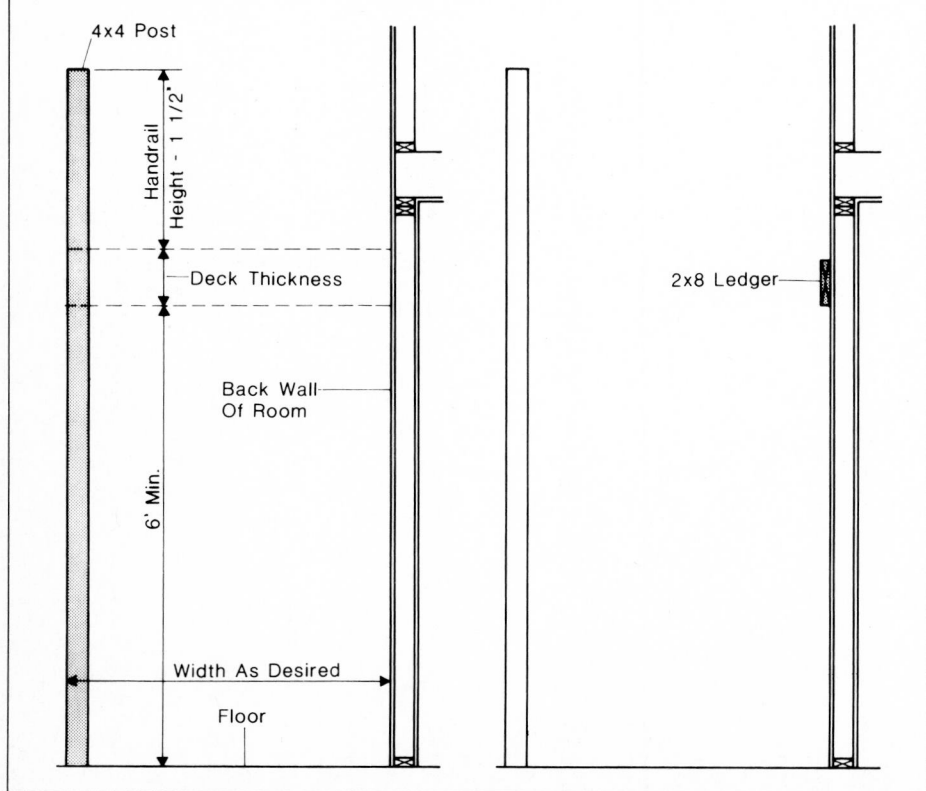

Locate posts at the desired width of the loft. The height should provide no less than 6 feet of headroom above and below the loft. Set ledger board accordingly. Allow for deck thickness.

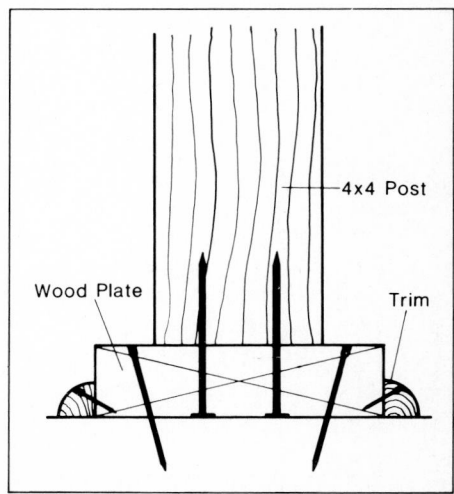

Support for deck loft is made with posts. Plate is nailed to posts and then into the floor.

across the width of the loft. Use 2x8s if the loft is more than 9 feet wide. To make it easier to hold the joists in place for nailing, first nail 2x2 ledgers even with the bottom of the 2x8 header and/or the ledger. Then toenail the joists to the ledger and header with 10d common nails. Nail from the inside so that the nailheads will not show. Additional 4x4 posts to support the hand rails must be installed on the upper level between the corner posts. The posts should be no further than 6 feet apart. Attach them to the header with bolts or 16d nails. The posts should sit on the 2x2 ledger and extend to the rail height.

Step five: completing the decking. Place a deck of 2x4 or 2x6 stock over the joists, in any pattern you want, and nail with 8d finishing nails. Complete the handrail to your taste, nailing members with 8d finishing nails, then stain or paint.

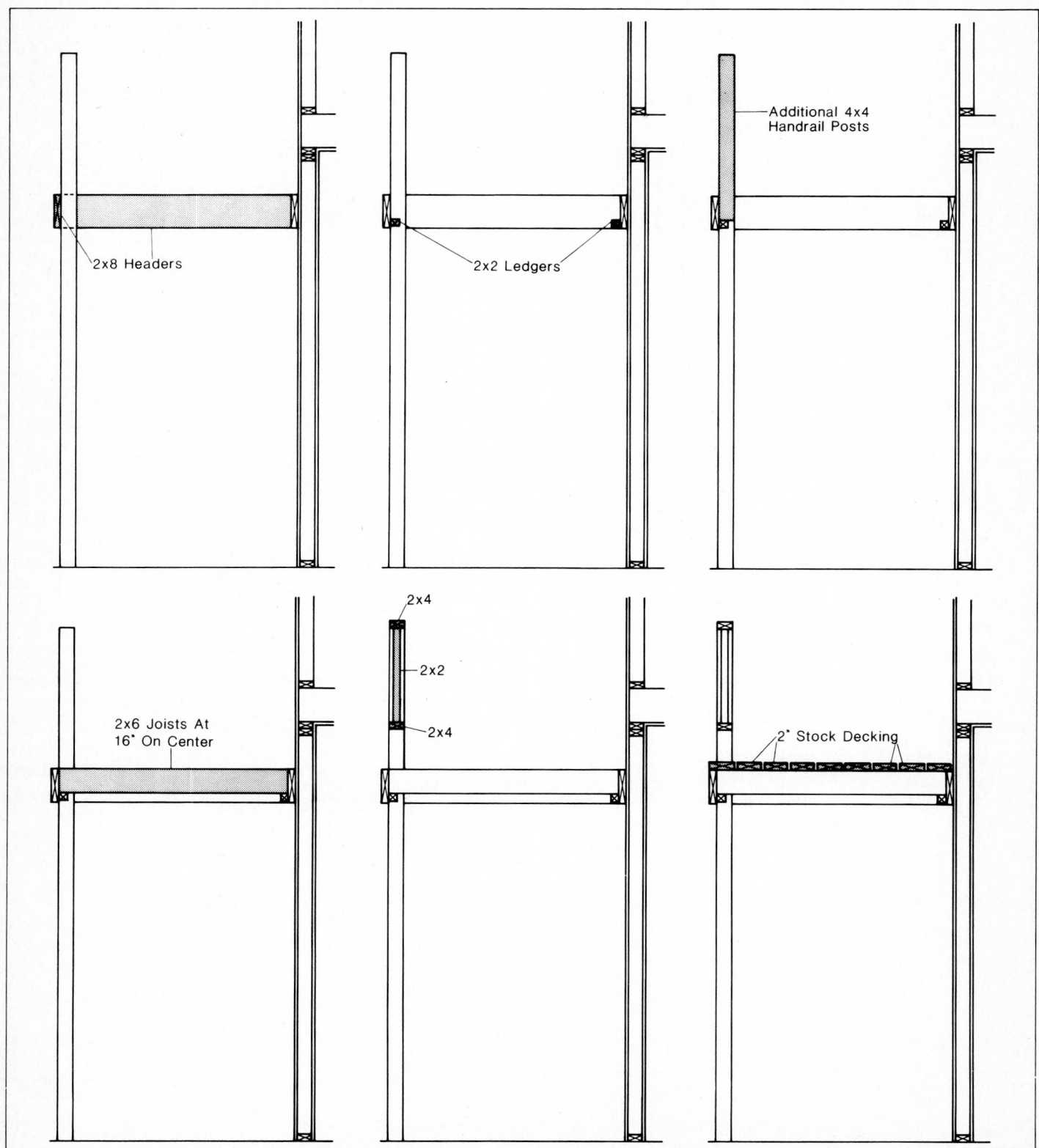

The construction of the loft is not difficult, but it does require care and accurate measurements to produce the secure construction you desire. Check for level and plumb as you install each section. Headers and ledgers that support joists must be even or your loft will not be level.

Alternative: installing finished flooring. If you prefer to finish the floor of the loft so that it has a standard floor above and a standard ceiling below, use a 2x6 ledger at the wall, 2x6 headers, and 2x6 joists without the 2x2 ledgers. Use metal joist hangers to hold members. Or, instead, use standard construction and nail through the header into the joist ends with 12d common nails. The nailheads will be covered with finish material. The rail may be constructed as described above, or you may build a partial wall with studs at 16 inches on center. Cover the partial wall with finish materials so that the project looks completed. However, this partial wall will reduce the open feeling of the loft area. Add a standard subfloor, then finish floor over that, finish wall materials on the side, and finish ceiling on the underside of the loft.

Creating a combination loft. You can also build a combination loft. This loft, which includes a deck extension from a loft in an adjacent room, will expand the loft space. The floor level of the loft should remain the same in both sections. A change of level would require a step or set of steps, which could be awkward and potentially dangerous. The floor finish in both sections should also be the same.

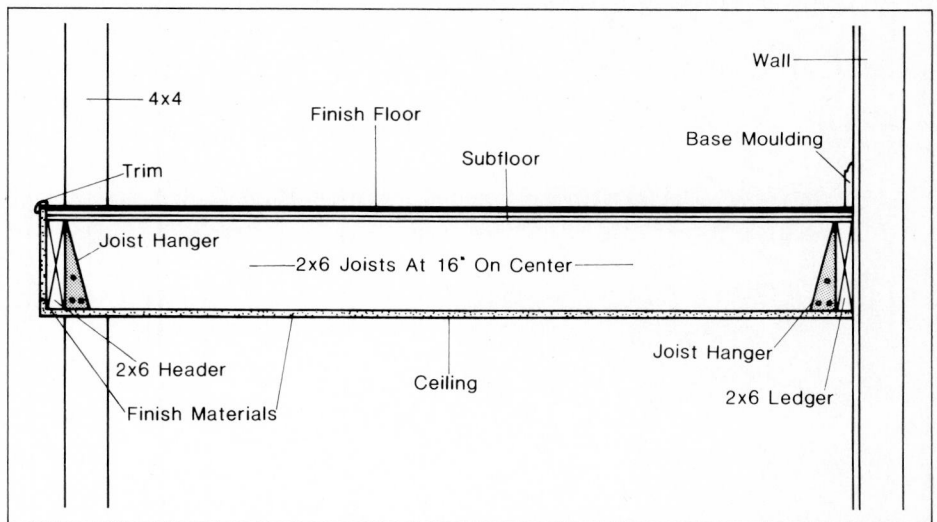

You may build loft with a finished ceiling and floor. Use joist hangers if you prefer them to small ledger boards. However, some attention to level and plumb is required for construction.

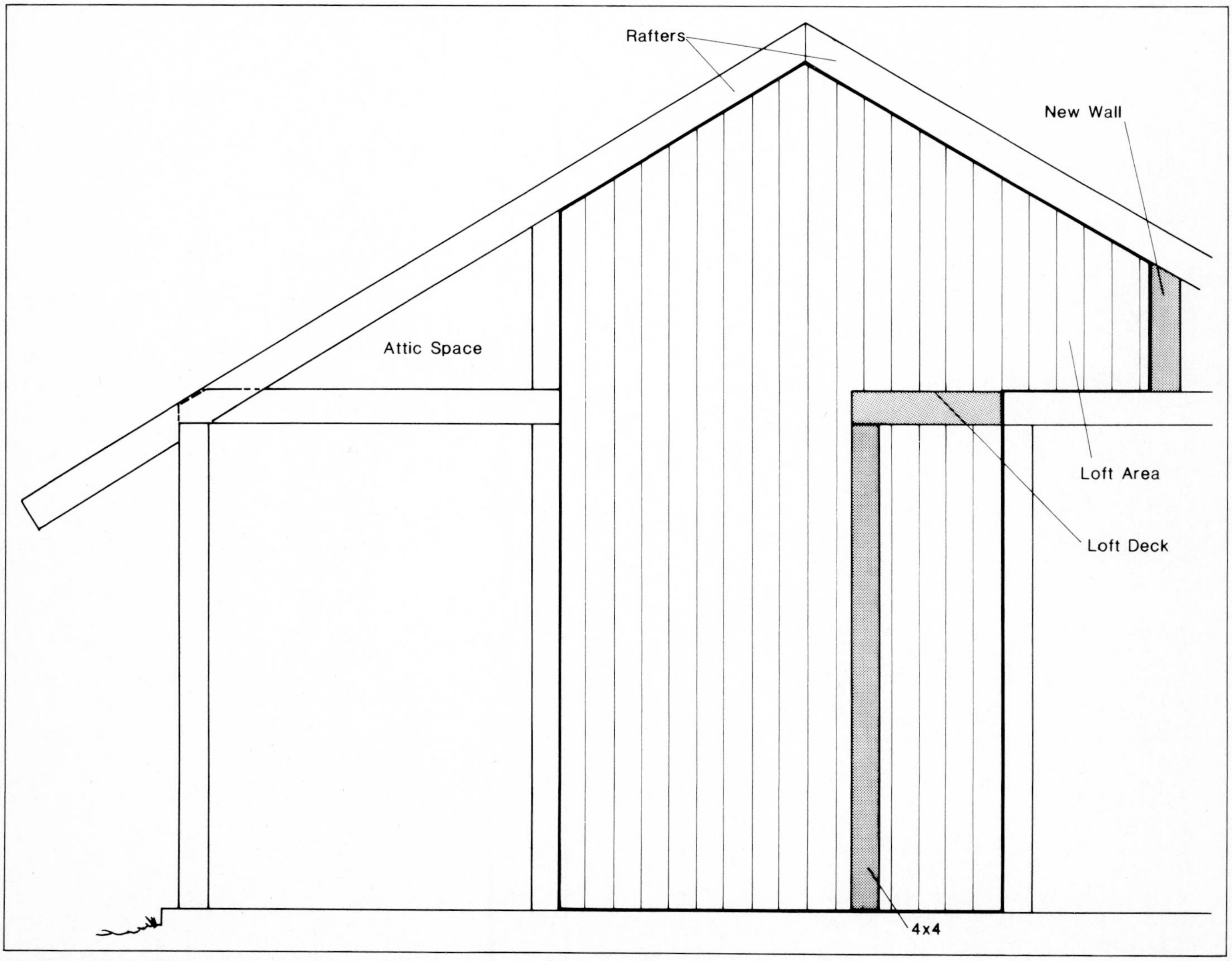

You may also build a combination attic/deck loft that allows you to create a good size loft without sacrificing too much space in either area.

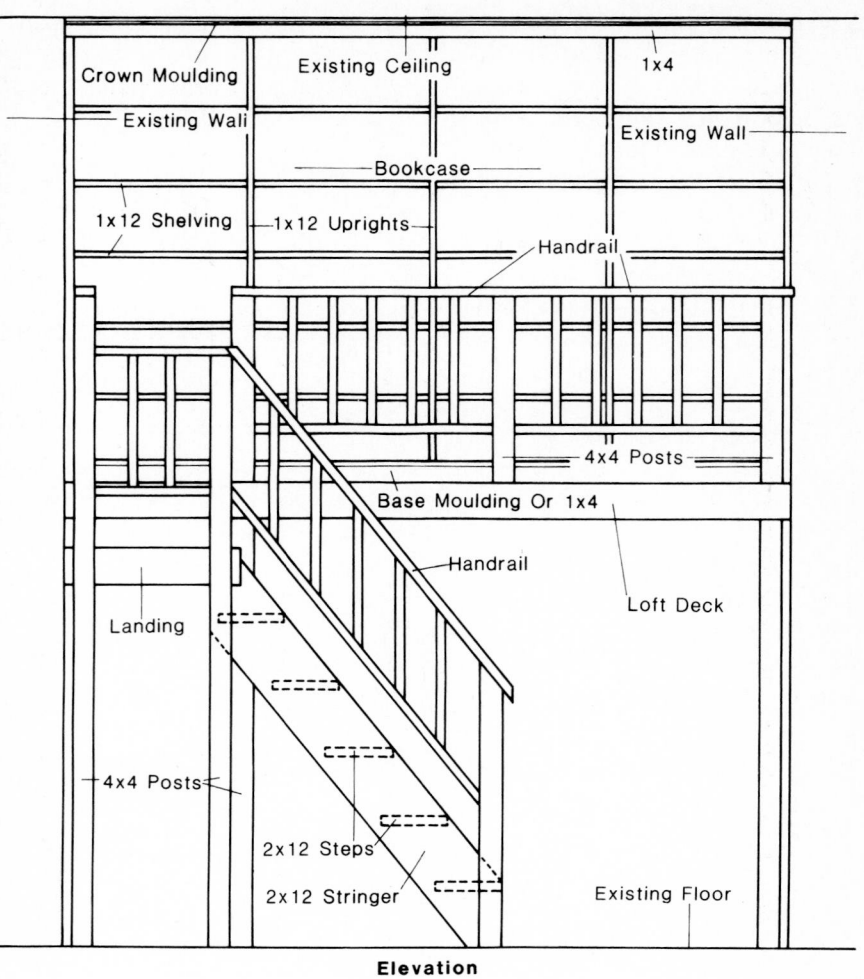

Elevation

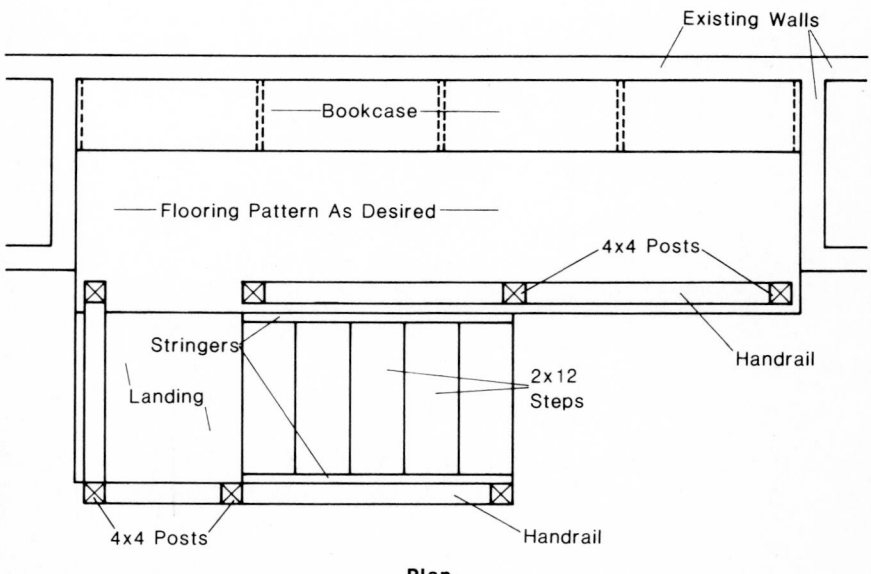

Plan

This loft, also shown on the cover, was designed to take advantage of the ceiling height in the apartment. The bookshelves are as high as can be reached by the owner. The space below is used for extra seating and as an indoor garden area. The loft was constructed from pine with 2x6s used from framing and bracing. The ledger board at the back is attached to a solid brick wall with masonry anchors and lag screws. The same construction on a stud wall might require additional support posts at the back because of the weight of the bookcases. Posts are 4x4; stringers and steps are 2x12s.

ADDING A SECOND FLOOR

It is almost always possible, and even economically feasible, to add a second floor over part of your home. However, construction is difficult and the work lengthy. It is strongly advised that the homeowner hire professionals for both the design and construction of a complete second story addition. The professional designer will be able to assess the capacity of the existing walls and foundation to carry the extra weight of a second floor. Walls, in most cases, will be substantial enough to support an increased load, but the existing windows and door headers usually will have to be strengthened, A professional contractor will be able to get the job done as quickly as possible. Adding a second floor to all or even a substantial part of your home will be beyond the ability of all but the most experienced and capable do-it-yourselfer. Adding a second floor over a garage, if the remainder of your house already has two stories, is a far less difficult job. It can be handled by the willing and able homeowner. Nevertheless, it is still a good idea to have a professional at least look at your home.

Protect the working area with sheets of heavy plastic. Use duct tape to attach sheets to the house wall and tack down other edges to the framing.

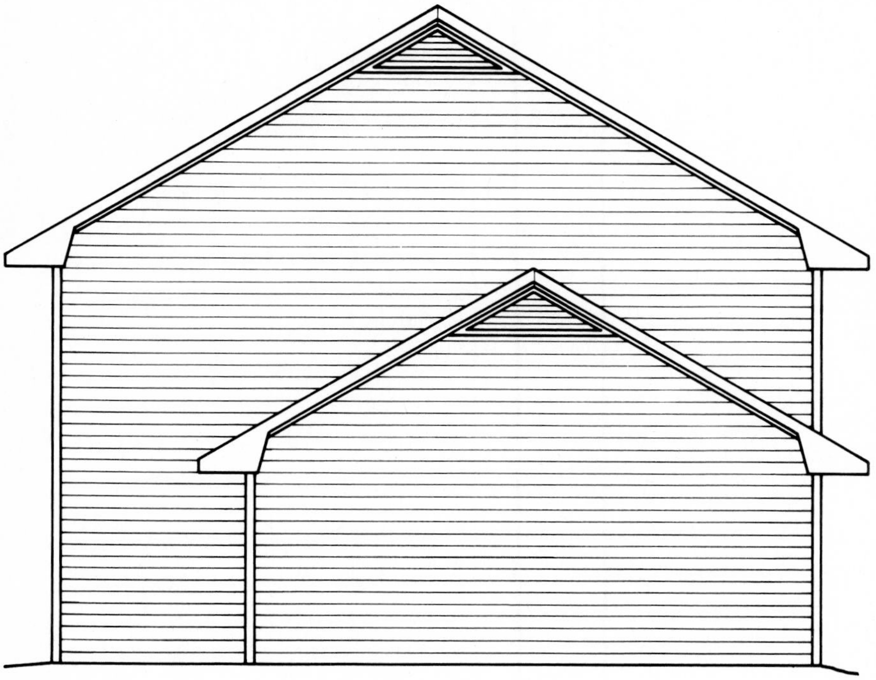

BUILDING A SECOND STORY OVER THE GARAGE
Structural Evaluation

Consult a professional, an architect or a structural engineer to determine whether the headers will have to be strengthened and by how much. The advisor can also tell if the foundation will have to be strengthened; generally, the existing foundation will support an addition. If the foundation must be reinforced, have him explain how the job is to be done. A slab foundation, as in a garage, should not be any problem. You may need to add one or more piers for a wood frame foundation. The professional's time will not be extremely expensive, usually between $20 and $50 per hour of consultation. This relatively small fee will save many dollars in construction costs and avoid a possible construction failure after the work is completed.

Before

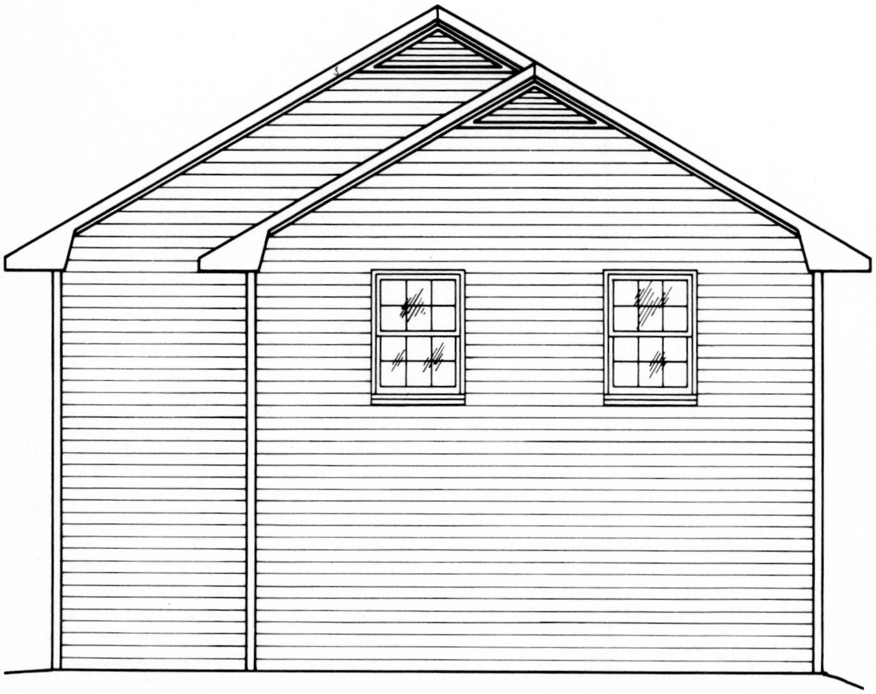

After

Setback lines may prevent extending the perimeter of your home, but the possibility of adding a room over the garage should not be overlooked. This can be done without extending the house.

A second-story addition over a garage provides new space and a new look to a home.

Step-by-Step Construction for Walls

Step one: strengthening the headers. Remove the interior finish material above any existing window or door so the header is completely exposed. Remove all door or window trim. Do not perform this work if there is a heavy load of snow on the roof; even with temporary support in place, the stress may crack the walls. Measure the length of the existing header, and build an additional header of two 2x4s with a ½ inch thick plywood spacer between. This unit will provide the needed additional strength.

Step two: providing temporary support. Place a temporary support a little wider than the header within 18 inches of the opening. Place a protective mat on the floor to prevent damage to the finish. Build the support unit by nailing a 2x4 bottom plate, a 2x4 top plate, and 2x4 studs at 24 inches on center with 8d com-

mon or box nails. Place a piece of carpet or quilted fabric over the top plate and wedge the unit into place and hold it tight by driving shims between the bottom plate and protective mat on the floor.

Step three: installing the new header. With the brace installed, cut out the cripples above the existing header. Now, slide the new header into place. This header will be directly over the existing header. Toenail the headers together with 16d common nails every 3 or 4 inches so they

will exist as a single unit. Trim the cripples by 3½ inches, the height of the new header; then nail them back in place between the new header and top plates. Toenail in position with 8d or 10d common nails. Finally, remove the temporary brace. Repeat for each door and window. Finish materials will be repaired when all structural work is complete.

Step four: opening the roof. Remove the roof shingles and felt above the exterior walls in the area where the second story

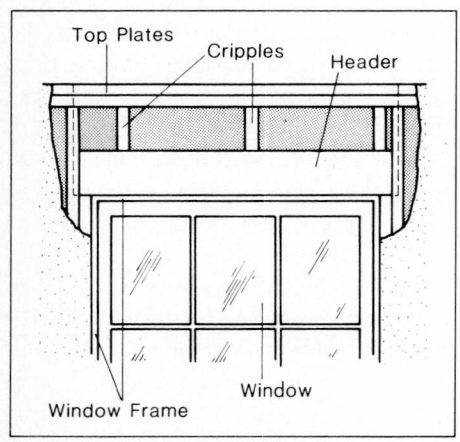

Exterior framing of a one-story garage will not be heavy enough to support a second story unless door and window framing is strengthened.

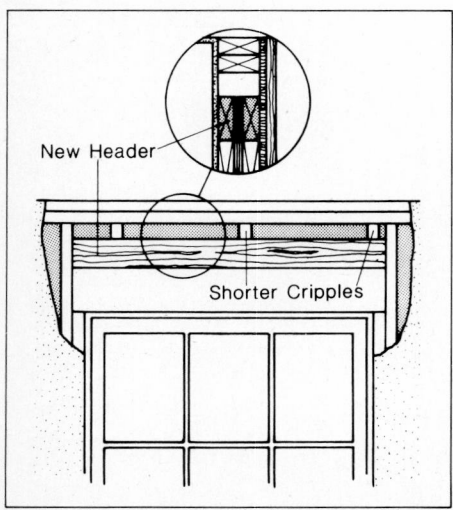

Additional doubled headers must be added above window and door frames. Cripple studs will have to be shortened to fit.

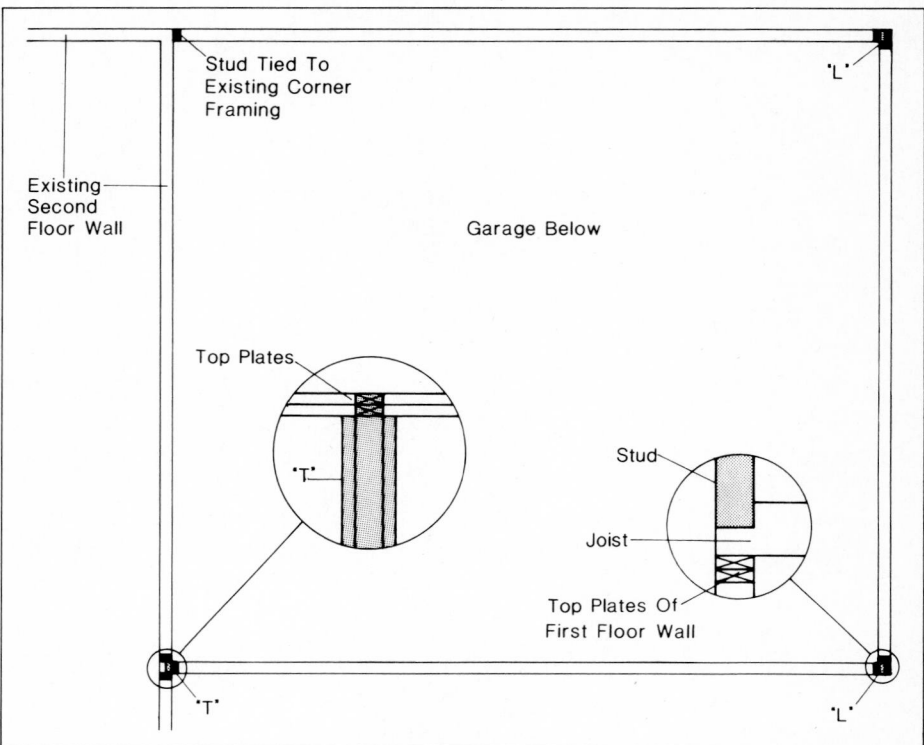

Framing of new second floor begins in the same way as framing a new interior wall. Install Ts and Ls at corners. A single stud may be tiled into corner framing of the existing house wall.

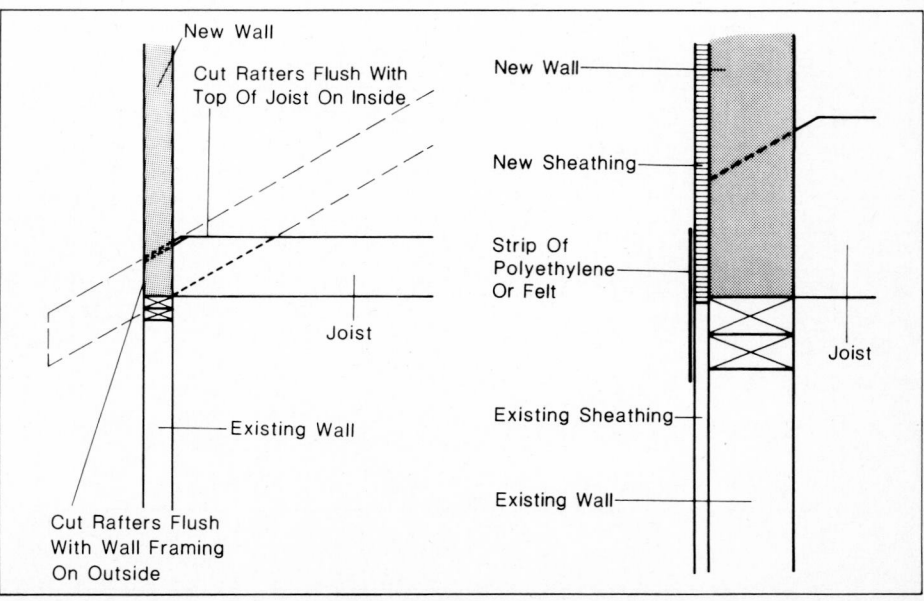

Rafters must be cut even with the wall and the joists and new studs set into place. Old and new walls must align vertically so that sheathing and siding will match. Seal joints as shown.

will be added. Carefully take off the sheathing by removing the nails. Pry out rafter nails and remove the rafters, collar beams and ridge board; they can be reused if they are not damaged. Unless you are planning major changes to the roofline, existing rafters may also be used as guides for cutting new rafters.

Step five: building the outside walls. Place an "L" (see page 39) at outside corners of the walls directly over the top plates of the wall below. Toenail into place with 10d common nails. Trim any part of the "L" as necessary to fit over any existing ceiling joist without disturbing that joist. Add 1x2 braces, leveling the "L", from the joists to near the top of the "L". Where the line of the new wall meets the existing second-story wall, remove the siding and sheathing to expose the framing, then construct a "T" intersection (see page 39) with the existing wall. The studs should be long enough to match the full length of the studs in the second story. Toenail the "T" at top and bottom with 10d common nails. The "T" must be level and plumb.

Place studs every 8 feet between the corners, toenailing into the existing top plates of the garage with 10d common nails. Use 1x2 braces to support sections. Add the first top plate, then complete the stud and window framing for the walls; finally, add the second top plate.

Providing a New Roof Structure

The easiest way to construct a roof is to order premanufactured trusses, and then set them in place as directed by the truss manufacturer. If you do not want to use trusses, consider these structural needs.

Step one: structural evaluation. If the new ceiling joists will span the entire width of the new second floor, refer to the joists span chart to see what size joists will be needed. Check the existing joists over the first floor to see if they will be strong enough to support the live load of the second floor. If not, strengthen using one of the methods given in the construction section of Chapter 10. Then add the subfloor.

If you want to break up the span of the second-floor ceiling joists, so that smaller size lumber can be used, a bearing wall will be needed. However, a bearing wall on the second floor must be located directly over a wall on the first floor. If you do not have a wall on the first floor, the joists will have to be large enough to span the

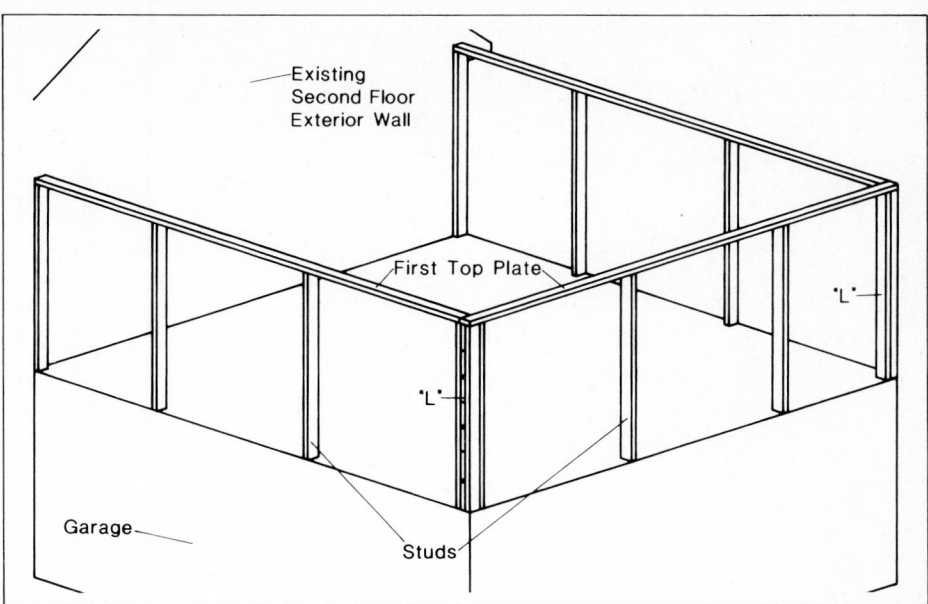

Garage top plate serves as second floor bottom plate. Install first top plate and studs.

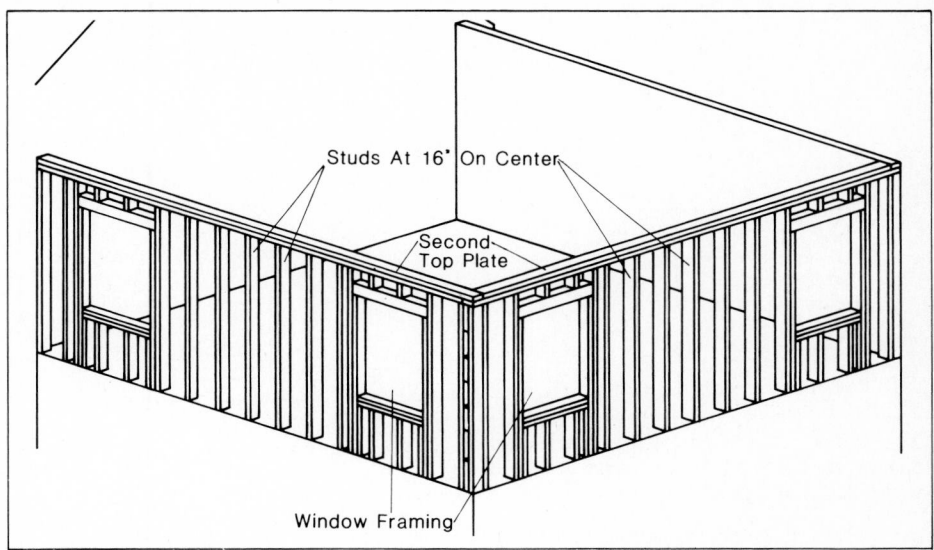

Place wall studs 16 inches on center. Add extra studs to provide solid framing for windows.

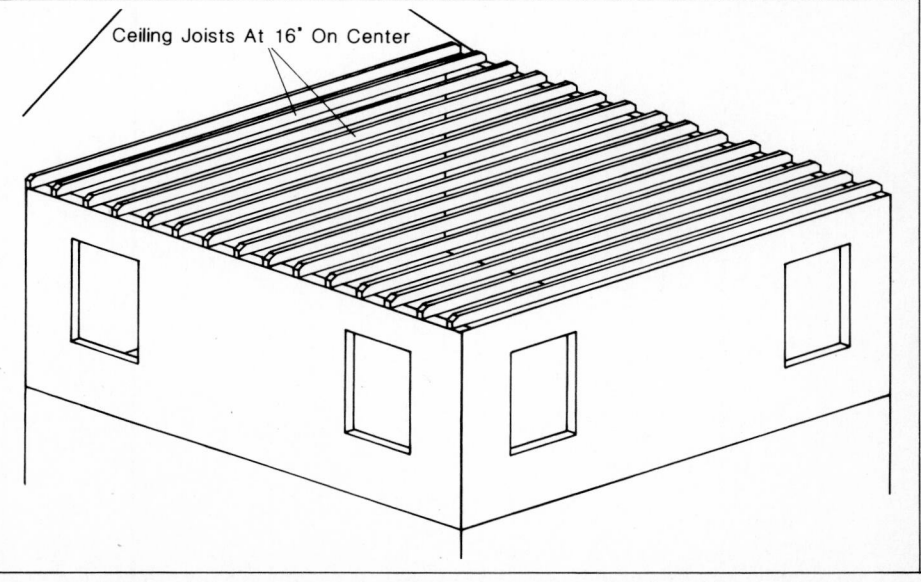

Set ceiling joists at 16 inches on center. Cut joist ends to match the angle of the rafters.

entire width of the second floor without extra support.

Step two: building a bearing wall. If you are using a bearing wall, construct it

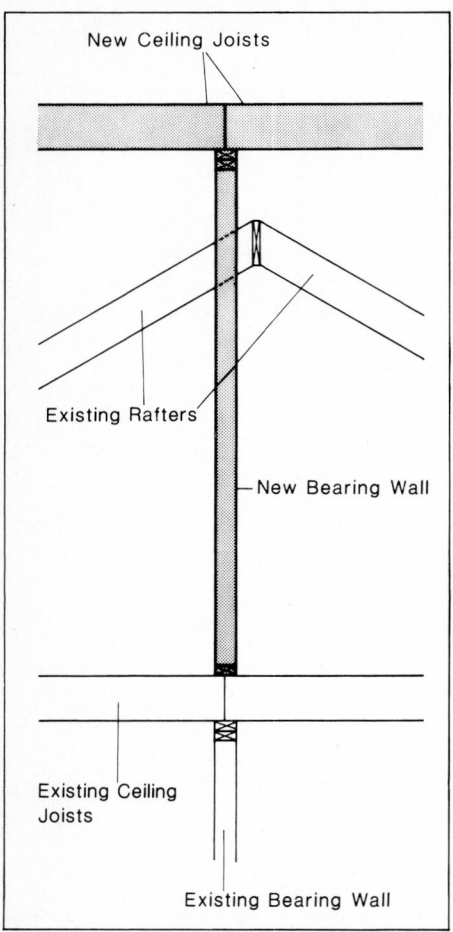

If the garage is so large that there is a load bearing wall in the garage, you may locate a second floor bearing wall directly above it.

as for the outside walls, toenailing into the top plates of the wall below. Construct "T"'s where the bearing wall meets the outside wall and existing second-floor wall. The second top plate of the bearing wall should extend completely across the walls it ties into. The upper top plates of these walls must be notched for the extension.

Step three: attaching the ceiling joists. Toenail the new ceiling joists into the top plates of the wall using 10d common nails. The end of the joist should be flush with the outside face of the wall and trimmed so that it will be flush with the run of the new rafters when they are in-

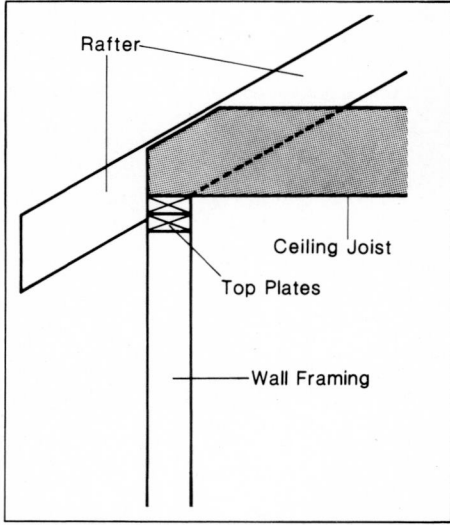

Ceiling joist extends to the outside of the wall framing and the upper corner of the joist is cut to match the line of the rafter.

stalled. Do not make this trim cut too deep, or it will weaken the joist. Cut the new joists identical to the joists above the first floor.

Step four: sheathing the walls. As soon as you have framed the walls, apply exterior sheathing. Use exterior-grade plywood or other exterior sheathing material such as asphalt-impregnated board. Sheathing is available in 4x8 foot sheets and may be installed horizontally or vertically. If it is installed horizontally, you will have to provide 2x4 blocking along the horizontal of the center joint as a nailer. Cover joints in sheathing with strips of 15 lb. asphalt-impregnated felt or polyethelene.

Cut out window openings after the sheathing is in place. Drill a hole in the approximate center and at each corner. Cut from the center toward one side with a keyhole or sabre saw. Cut around the inside of the frame to remove the sheathing.

Step five: installing the ridge and rafters. Place a ridge board, the same size as the ridge board that was removed for construction, at the same relative height above the joists. The ridge board must be level and in the exact center of the new space. Nail the ridge board into the existing home's second-story wall framing, after nailing blocking to the siding to support the ridge. Use 16d nails; if the house exterior is masonry, use masonry nails. At the new gable end, support the ridge board with a 2x4 toenailed to the top plates. Use

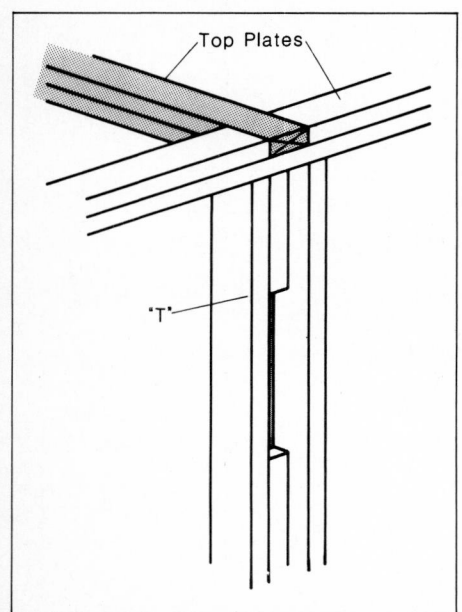

At a T intersection of the framing, the new upper top plate should extend into the upper top plate of the existing wall.

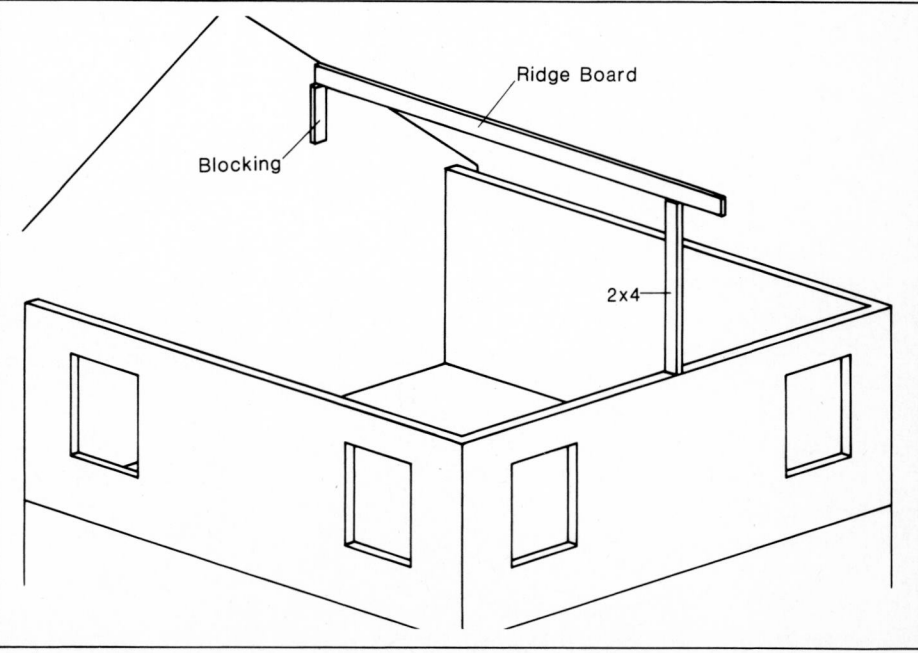

Find the position and desired height of the ridge board and support it with blocking nailed to the house wall and a stud brace attached firmly to the top plate of the new wall framing.

an existing rafter as a model and cut the new rafters in the same size and manner; they should be of equal stock lumber. Toe-nail rafters into the ridge board and the top plates with 10d common nails.

Step six: creating the overhang. The overhang at the gable can be constructed by using 2x4 blocking installed every 12 to 16 inches. Blocking is set into notches in the last two rafters, extending out from the rafters by the length of the overhang, less 2 inches. Nail blocking into the rafters with 10d or 12d common nails.

Nail a 2x4 nailer into the ends of the blocking with 16d common nails. Attach the fascia to the nailer with 8d galvanized finishing nails. Take care to match the fascia on the house. On the front and back, the fascia can be nailed directly into the rafter ends with 8d galvanized finishing nails.

Installing roofing materials. The installation of the roof deck, felt, flashing and shingles is the same as explained for dormers in Chapter 10. Galvanized steel flashing will be required everywhere the new roof meets the existing construction. Apply roof sheathing as soon as possible. Then cover with roofing felt. Apply flashing and drip edge before laying shingles.

Access to the Second Story

To provide access to the new area, you may need to rework the existing second floor. Extend a hall to the new space, through a closet if possible. If the new space is to be a workroom, you may provide access by building stairs at the back or on one side of the garage. If this area is to be part of a master bedroom suite or a teenager's retreat, direct access through a new door may be required. You may need professional assistance to cut the new opening and frame the door.

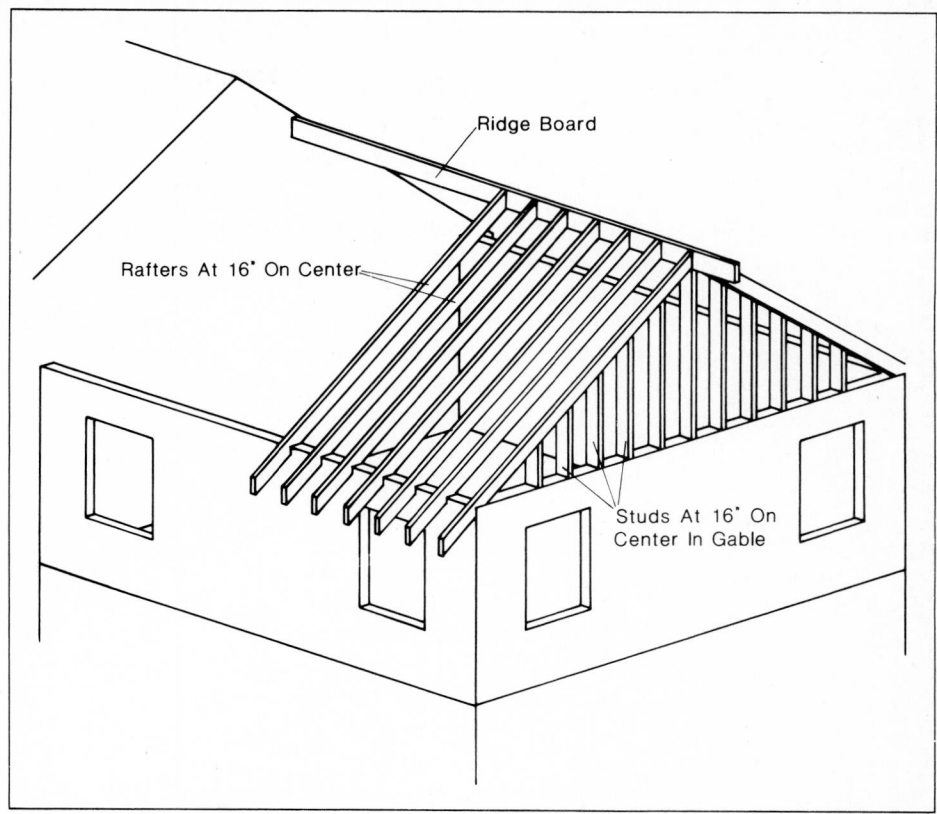

Rafters are cut to fit as described in Chapter 10. Place rafters on 16 inch centers. Gable studs are also on 16 inch center and should be in place as support before additional rafters are installed.

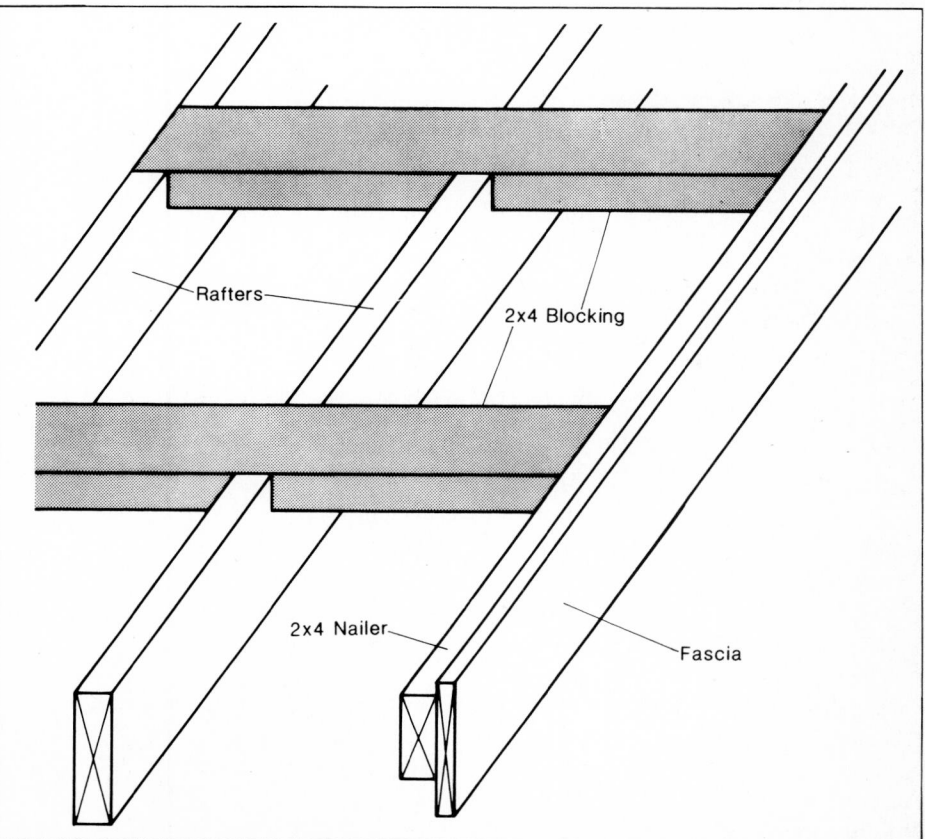

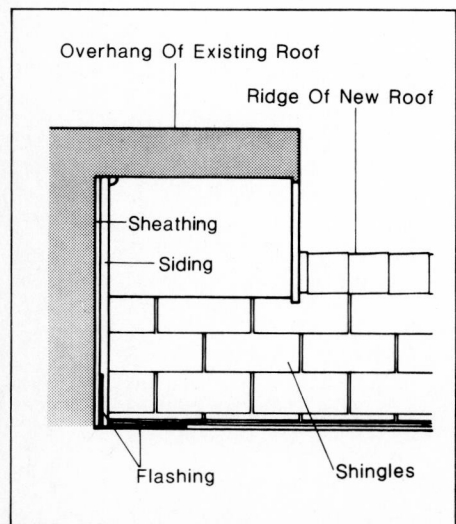

Install decking, flashing, roofing felt and shingles. Seal joints at roofs and walls.

Notch rafters to accept 2x4 blocking to bring the overhang beyond the gable wall line. Attach a nailer to the ends of the blocking and attach fascia board in position. Add roof decking.

INDEX

GLOSSARY

Backfill   The replacement of excavated earth into a trench around and against a basement or foundation wall.

Bridging   Cross pieces of wood or metal between joists or rafters to keep them in vertical alignment and braced against twisting or warping.

Butt joint   The junction where two framing members meet in a square cut joint.

Chalkline   A straight line made by "popping" a taut string covered with chalk dust.

Corner bead   A strip of formed sheet metal placed at corners to reinforce finish materials.

Cove molding   A molding with a concave face used as trim or finish interior corners.

Decking   Wood board or plywood surfacing to provide a nailing surface for roofing materials.

Door jamb   The surrounding case into which and out of which a door closes and opens. It consists of two upright pieces, called side jambs, and a horizontal head jamb.

Dressed and matched (tongued and grooved)   Boards or planks machined in such a manner that there is a groove on one edge and a corresponding tongue on the other so that two boards can be "locked" together by engaging the tongue of one into the groove of the other.

Fiberboard   A building board, made usually of wood or vegetable fibers, having some insulating quality. Most often used for exterior sheathing or siding.

Finish floor   The top layer of flooring material, that part of the floor that is seen when the work is complete such as carpet, cushioned vinyl, ceramic tile, etc.

Fly rafters   End rafters of the gable overhang supported by roof sheathing and lookouts.

Grain   The direction, size arrangement, appearance, or quality of the fibers in wood.

Gusset   A flatwood, plywood, metal plate, or similar type member used to provide a connection at the intersections of wood members. Most commonly used at the joints of wood trusses. Fastened by nails, screws, bolts, and/or adhesives. Also called truss plate.

Gypsum compound   A premixed gypsum based material with the consistency of mortar used to fill the seams in gypsumboard construction. Also called joint compound.

Insulation Board, rigid   A structural building board made of coarse wood or cane fiber in ½ or 25/32-inch thicknesses. It can be obtained in various size sheets, in various densities, and with several treatments.

Joint   The space between the adjacent surfaces of two members or components joined and held together by nails, glue, cement, mortar, or other means.

Lumber   Lumber is the product of the sawmill and planing mill not further manufactured other than by sawing, resawing, and passing lengthwise through a standard planing machine, crosscutting to length, and matching.

Masonry   Stone, brick, concrete, hollow-tile, concrete-block, gypsumblock, or other similar building units or materials or a combination of the same, bonded together with mortar to form a wall, pier, buttress, or similar mass.

Millwork   Generally all building materials made of finished wood and manufactured in millwork plants and planing mills are included under the term "millwork." It includes such items as inside and outside doors, window and door frames, blinds, porchwork, mantels, panelwork, stairways, moldings, and interior trim. It normally does not include flooring, ceiling, or siding.

Mullion   A vertical bar or divider in the frame between windows, doors, or other openings.

Muntin   A small member which divides the glass or openings of a window sash or door.

Overhang   That portion of the roof, including the cornice, which extends beyond the outside face of the exterior wall.

Paper, building   A general term for papers, felts, and similar sheet materials used in buildings without reference to their properties or uses.

Particleboard   A structural sheet material composed of compressed wood chips, flakes, or small wood particles such as sawdust, held together with special glues.

Pier   A column of masonry, usually rectangular in horizontal cross section, used to support other structural members.

Plasterboard   A sheet material consisting of a sheet of plaster covered with fibrous paper used for drywall construction or as a backing for plaster. Today the term is used more often to refer to gypsumboard.

Plywood   Pieces of wood made of three or more layers of veneer joined with glue, and usually laid with the grain of adjoining plies at right angles. Almost always an odd number of plies are used to provide balanced construction.

Polyethylene   Refers to the film material made from polyethylene, a thermoplastic resin, and used for waterproofing in home construction.

Prefabricated   A subassembly of a house whose components were assembled in a factory and shipped to the site to save on-site construction time.

Roof sheathing   The boards or sheet material fastened to the roof rafters on which the shingle or other roof covering is laid. See Decking.

Rout   The removal of material, by cutting, milling or gouging, to form a groove.

Scribing   Fitting woodwork to an irregular surface. In moldings, cutting the end of one piece to fit the molded face of the other at an interior angle to replace a miter joint.

Seaming tape   A special tape used to join carpet edges together with a hot-melt glue.

Seepage   The infiltration of water from outside to inside through cracks, seams, or pores.

Shed dormer   A dormer with a shed roof rather than a gable roof.

Sill   The member forming the lower side of an opening, as a door sill, window sill, etc.

Suspended ceiling   A ceiling system supported by hanging it from the overhead structural framing.

Acknowledgements

Few home remodeling books are written without the assistance of a great number of people. I owe a debt of gratitude to the individuals who allowed me to photograph their remodelings, to the professionals who offered various types of assistance, and to the manufacturers who provided graphic material and/or information.

This book is dedicated to Charlotte, Dana, and Louise.

Thanks To:

Barganier - McKee - Simms, Architects
Tommy and Patsy Butler
Barry and Laura Harmon
Joe and Anne Levin
Jack and Barbara Mazzanovich
Mackie and Denise Oliver
Frank Porter Construction Co.
Professional Engineering Consultants, Inc.
Ray and Sarah Roton
Turner Seale, Seale Construction Co.
Watson, Nichols, and Borden, Architects.

CONTRIBUTORS ADDRESSES PICTURE CREDITS

Allmilmo Corporation c/o Hayes-Williams, Incorporated 261 Madison Avenue, New York, New York, 10016 79 center and lower right

American Olean Tile 2583 Cannon Avenue, Lansdale, Pennsylvania 19446 26, 79, 93 lower center

American Plywood Association Box 1119A, Tacoma, Washington 98401

Armstrong Cork Co. Liberty Street, Lancaster, Pennsylvania 17604 77

Azrock Floor Products P.O. Box 34030, San Antonio, Texas 78233 79 lower left

Briggs, A Jim Walter Company 1500 North Dale Mabry Highway, Tampa, Florida 33607

California Redwood Association One Lombard Street, San Francisco, California 94111 98

Celotex Building Products Division of Jim Walters Company 1500 North Dale Mabry Highway, Tampa, Florida 33607

E.I. Dupont de Nemours Wilmington, Delaware 19898

EPCO The Engineered Products Company 601 Elso Street, Flint, Michigan 48501

Evans Products Company 1121 SW Salmon Street, Portland, Oregon 97208

Flexi-Wall Systems A Division of Wall & Floor Treatments, Inc. 207 Anderson Drive, Liberty, South Carolina 29657

Formica Corporation A Division of American Cyanamid Company, Wayne, New Jersey 07470

Richard J. Froze, designer, 2712 North Maryland, Milwaukee, Wisconsin 53211 14 upper, 43, 141

Georgia Pacific Corporation 900 SW 5th Street, Portland, Oregon 97204 38, 41, 66, 67, 118, 129

Glidden Coatings & Resins Division of SCM Corporation 900 Union Commerce Building, Cleveland, Ohio 44115

Gold Bond Building Products Division of National Gypsum Company 2001 Rexford Road, Charlotte, North Carolina 28211

Nancy Greenebaum artist, Racine, Wisconsin 25

Heatilator Fireplaces Mount Pleasant, Iowa 52641 20

Joseph Kaminsky designer, 250 West 99th Street, New York, New York 10025 117, 150

The Kohler Company Kohler, Wisconsin 53044 29

Kentucky Wood Floors, Inc. 7761 National Turnpike, Louisville, Kentucky 40214

Carl Landgren 1640 N. Jackson, Milwaukee, Wisconsin 53202 33, 83, 113

Elizabeth Levins Applied Imagination, Inc., 3005 East Hampshire, Milwaukee, Wisconsin 53211 12 upper right and center right, 15, 116

Law J. Litzaw architectural, interior and graphic designer, 225 East St. Paul, Milwaukee, Wisocnisn 53202 84, 140

William Manly Associates Interior Design, 6062 North Port Washington Road, Milwaukee, Wisconsin 53217 92, 122

Masonite Corporation 2601 Grant Avenue, Bellwood, Illinois 60104 89, 114

Maytag Corporation Newton, Iowa 50208 93 lower left

Memphis Hardwood Flooring Co. 1551 Thomas, Memphis, Tennessee 38107

Monsanto Company 800 North Lindbergh Blvd., St. Louis, Missouri 63166

David Morgan 129 West 75th Street, New York, New York 10023 cover, 117

National Oak Flooring Manufacturers Association Sterick Building 8 Third Street North, Memphis, Tennessee 38103

Nutone-Scovill Madison and Red Bank Streets, Cincinnati, Ohio 45227

Laura Odell Kitchen Design, 130 East 75th Street, New York, New York 10021 93 lower right

Potlach Corporation Wood Products Group W222 Mission, Spokane, Washington 99201

Quakermaid A Division of Tappan Rt. #61, Leesport, Pennsylvania 19533 89 upper center

Schlage Lock Company 2401 Bayshore Blvd., San Francisco, California 94134

James Seeman Studios Division of Masonite, c/o Harold Imber 60 Thorn Avenue, Mount Kisco, New York 10549 19, 63, 94

Everett Short 95 Christopher Street, New York, New York 10014 16 upper, 117, 119, 120, 121

Stark Ceramics, Inc. Church Street Extension, Canton, Ohio 44711

Thomas Strahan Company c/o Lis King Box 503, Mahwah, New Jersey 07430 19

Teco Products & Testing Corp. 5530 Wisconsin Avenue, Washington, D.C. 20015

Richard Thompson designer 21 Grove Street, New York, New York 10014 120,121

Thoro Systems Products Division of Standard Dry Wall Products 7800 NW 36th Street, Miami, Florida 33166 107, 108

The Tile Council c/o Lis King Box 503, Mahwah, New Jersey 07430 79 right center

Ventarama Skylight Corporation 75 Channel Drive, Port Washington, New York 11050

Wasco Products, Inc. Pioneer Avenue, Sanford, Maine 04073

James Eaton Weeks, Interior Designs, Inc., 223 East Silver Spring Drive, Milwaukee, Wisconsin 53217 119

Western Wood Products Association Yeon Building, Portland, Oregon 97204

Woodbridge Ornamental Iron Company 2715 North Clybourn, Chicago, Illinois 60614 82

Z-brick Division of VMC Corporation 13929 NE 190th Street Woodinville, Washington 98072 71, 86

LUMBER

Sizes: Metric cross-sections are so close to their nearest Imperial sizes, as noted below, that for most purposes they may be considered equivalents.
Lengths: Metric lengths are based on a 300mm module which is slightly shorter in length than an Imperial foot. It will therefore be important to check your requirements accurately to the nearest inch and consult the table below to find the metric length required.
Areas: The metric area is a square metre. Use the following conversion factors when converting from Imperial data: 100 sq. feet = 9.290 sq. metres.

METRIC SIZES SHOWN BESIDE NEAREST IMPERIAL EQUIVALENT

mm	Inches	mm	Inches
16 x 75	⅝ x 3	44 x 150	1¾ x 6
16 x 100	⅝ x 4	44 x 175	1¾ x 7
16 x 125	⅝ x 5	44 x 200	1¾ x 8
16 x 150	⅝ x 6	44 x 225	1¾ x 9
19 x 75	¾ x 3	44 x 250	1¾ x 10
19 x 100	¾ x 4	44 x 300	1¾ x 12
19 x 125	¾ x 5	50 x 75	2 x 3
19 x 150	¾ x 6	50 x 100	2 x 4
22 x 75	⅞ x 3	50 x 125	2 x 5
22 x 100	⅞ x 4	50 x 150	2 x 6
22 x 125	⅞ x 5	50 x 175	2 x 7
22 x 150	⅞ x 6	50 x 200	2 x 8
25 x 75	1 x 3	50 x 225	2 x 9
25 x 100	1 x 4	50 x 250	2 x 10
25 x 125	1 x 5	50 x 300	2 x 12
25 x 150	1 x 6	63 x 100	2½ x 4
25 x 175	1 x 7	63 x 125	2½ x 5
25 x 200	1 x 8	63 x 150	2½ x 6
25 x 225	1 x 9	63 x 175	2½ x 7
25 x 250	1 x 10	63 x 200	2½ x 8
25 x 300	1 x 12	63 x 225	2½ x 9
32 x 75	1¼ x 3	75 x 100	3 x 4
32 x 100	1¼ x 4	75 x 125	3 x 5
32 x 125	1¼ x 5	75 x 150	3 x 6
32 x 150	1¼ x 6	75 x 175	3 x 7
32 x 175	1¼ x 7	75 x 200	3 x 8
32 x 200	1¼ x 8	75 x 225	3 x 9
32 x 225	1¼ x 9	75 x 250	3 x 10
32 x 250	1¼ x 10	75 x 300	3 x 12
32 x 300	1¼ x 12	100 x 100	4 x 4
38 x 75	1½ x 3	100 x 150	4 x 6
38 x 100	1½ x 4	100 x 200	4 x 8
38 x 125	1½ x 5	100 x 250	4 x 10
38 x 150	1½ x 6	100 x 300	4 x 12
38 x 175	1½ x 7	150 x 150	6 x 6
38 x 200	1½ x 8	150 x 200	6 x 8
38 x 225	1½ x 9	150 x 300	6 x 12
44 x 75	1¾ x 3	200 x 200	8 x 8
44 x 100	1¾ x 4	250 x 250	10 x 10
44 x 125	1¾ x 5	300 x 300	12 x 12

METRIC LENGTHS

Lengths Metres	Equiv. Ft. & Inches
1.8m	5′ 10⅞″
2.1m	6′ 10⅝″
2.4m	7′ 10½″
2.7m	8′ 10¼″
3.0m	9′ 10⅛″
3.3m	10′ 9⅞″
3.6m	11′ 9¾″
3.9m	12′ 9½″
4.2m	13′ 9⅜″
4.5m	14′ 9⅓″
4.8m	15′ 9″
5.1m	16′ 8¾″
5.4m	17′ 8⅝″
5.7m	18′ 8⅜″
6.0m	19′ 8¼″
6.3m	20′ 8″
6.6m	21′ 7⅞″
6.9m	22′ 7⅝″
7.2m	23′ 7½″
7.5m	24′ 7¼″
7.8m	25′ 7⅛″

All the dimensions are based on 1 inch = 25 mm.

NOMINAL SIZE (This is what you order.)	ACTUAL SIZE (This is what you get.)
Inches	Inches
1 x 1	¾ x ¾
1 x 2	¾ x 1½
1 x 3	¾ x 2½
1 x 4	¾ x 3½
1 x 6	¾ x 5½
1 x 8	¾ x 7¼
1 x 10	¾ x 9¼
1 x 12	¾ x 11¼
2 x 2	1¾ x 1¾
2 x 3	1½ x 2½
2 x 4	1½ x 3½
2 x 6	1½ x 5½
2 x 8	1½ x 7¼
2 x 10	1½ x 9¼
2 x 12	1½ x 11¼

NAILS

NUMBER PER POUND OR KILO

Size	Weight Unit	Common	Casing	Box	Finishing
2d	Pound	876	1010	1010	1351
	Kilo	1927	2222	2222	2972
3d	Pound	586	635	635	807
	Kilo	1289	1397	1397	1775
4d	Pound	316	473	473	548
	Kilo	695	1041	1041	1206
5d	Pound	271	406	406	500
	Kilo	596	893	893	1100
6d	Pound	181	236	236	309
	Kilo	398	591	519	680
7d	Pound	161	210	210	238
	Kilo	354	462	462	524
8d	Pound	106	145	145	189
	Kilo	233	319	319	416
9d	Pound	96	132	132	172
	Kilo	211	290	290	398
10d	Pound	69	94	94	121
	Kilo	152	207	207	266
12d	Pound	64	88	88	113
	Kilo	141	194	194	249
16d	Pound	49	71	71	90
	Kilo	108	156	156	198
20d	Pound	31	52	52	62
	Kilo	68	114	114	136
30d	Pound	24	46	46	
	Kilo	53	101	101	
40d	Pound	18	35	35	
	Kilo	37	77	77	
50d	Pound	14			
	Kilo	31			
60d	Pound	11			
	Kilo	24			

LENGTH AND DIAMETER IN INCHES AND CENTIMETERS

Size	Length Inches	Length Centimeters	Diameter Inches	Diameter Centimeters*
2d	1	2.5	.068	.17
3d	1 2	3.2	.102	.26
4d	1 4	3.8	.102	.26
5d	1 6	4.4	.102	.26
6d	2	5.1	.115	.29
7d	2 2	5.7	.115	.29
8d	2 4	6.4	.131	.33
9d	2 6	7.0	.131	.33
10d	3	7.6	.148	.38
12d	3 2	8.3	.148	.38
16d	3 4	8.9	.148	.38
20d	4	10.2	.203	.51
30d	4 4	11.4	.220	.58
40d	5	12.7	.238	.60
50d	5 4	14.0	.257	.66
60d	6	15.2	.277	.70

*Exact conversion

WOOD SCREWS

SCREW GAUGE NO.	NOMINAL DIAMETER Inch	NOMINAL DIAMETER mm	LENGTH Inch	LENGTH mm
0	0.060	1.52	3/16	4.8
1	0.070	1.78	1/4	6.4
2	0.082	2.08	5/16	7.9
3	0.094	2.39	3/8	9.5
4	0.0108	2.74	7/16	11.1
5	0.122	3.10	1/2	12.7
6	0.136	3.45	5/8	15.9
7	0.150	3.81	3/4	19.1
8	0.164	4.17	7/8	22.2
9	0.178	4.52	1	25.4
10	0.192	4.88	1 1/4	31.8
12	0.220	5.59	1 1/2	38.1
14	0.248	6.30	1 3/4	44.5
16	0.276	7.01	2	50.8
18	0.304	7.72	2 1/4	57.2
20	0.332	8.43	2 1/2	63.5
24	0.388	9.86	2 3/4	69.9
28	0.444	11.28	3	76.2
32	0.5	12.7	3 1/4	82.6
			3 1/2	88.9
			4	101.6
			4 1/2	114.3
			5	127.0
			6	152.4

Dimensions taken from BS1210; metric conversions are approximate.

BRICKS AND BLOCKS

Bricks

Standard metric brick measures 215 mm x 65 mm x 112.5. Metric brick can be used with older, standard brick by increasing the mortaring in the joints. The sizes are substantially the same, the metric brick being slightly smaller (3.6 mm less in length, 1.8 mm in width, and 1.2 mm in depth).

Concrete Block

Standard sizes
390 x 90 mm
390 x 190 mm
440 x 190 mm
440 x 215 mm
440 x 290 mm

Repair block for replacement of block in old installations is available in these sizes:
448 x 219 (including mortar joints)
397 x 194 (including mortar joints)

PIPE FITTINGS

Only fittings for use with copper pipe are affected by metrication: metric compression fittings are interchangeable with Imperial in some sizes, but require adaptors in others.

INTERCHANGEABLE SIZES mm	INTERCHANGEABLE SIZES Inches	SIZES REQUIRING ADAPTORS mm	SIZES REQUIRING ADAPTORS Inches
12	⅜	22	¾
15	½	35	1¼
28	1	42	1½
54	2		

Metric capillary (soldered) fittings are not directly interchangeable with imperial sizes but adaptors are available. Pipe fittings which use screwed threads to make the joint remain unchanged. The British Standard Pipe (BSP) thread form has now been accepted internationally and its dimensions will not physically change. These screwed fittings are commonly used for joining iron or steel pipes, for connections on taps, basin and bath waste outlets and on boilers, radiators, pumps etc. Fittings for use with lead pipe are joined by soldering and for this purpose the metric and inch sizes are interchangeable.

(Information courtesy Metrication Board, Millbank Tower, Millbank, London SW1P 4QU)